Praise for
The Gangs of New York

"*The Gangs of New York* is one of the essential works of the city, as deserving of a permanent place on the shelf as Stephen Crane's *Maggie*, Walt Whitman's chapters on horse cars and theatres in *Specimen Days*, F. Scott Fitzgerald's "My Lost City," Chester Himes's *Blind Man with a Pistol*, and Martin Scorsese's *Mean Streets*."

—Luc Sante, author of *The Factory of Facts*
and *Low Life: Lures and Snares of Old New York*

"The suppressed history of American life . . . *Gangs* provided a New York romantic with something that wasn't otherwise in evidence—a richly feudal and ritualistic past. (And newcomers to New York are romantics, or they wouldn't have come.) In its raffish invocation of a lost subculture, it seemed heart-lifting, thrilling, even if the more sober parts of your mind knew that Asbury's violent criminals were no different from the violent criminals who were still around to make your life miserable. . . . an irresistible book."

—Adam Gopnik, *The New Yorker*

"A universal history of infamy . . . [that] contains all the confusion and cruelty of the barbarian cosmologies, and much of their gigantism and ineptitude."

—Jorge Luis Borges

SUCKER'S
PROGRESS

ALSO BY HERBERT ASBURY

The Gangs of New York:
An Informal History of the Underworld

The Gangs of Chicago:
An Informal History of the Chicago Underworld

The Barbary Coast:
An Informal History of the San Francisco Underworld

The French Quarter:
An Informal History of the New Orleans Underworld

SUCKER'S PROGRESS

An Informal History
of Gambling in America

HERBERT ASBURY

THUNDER'S MOUTH PRESS

NEW YORK

SUCKER'S PROGRESS: AN INFORMAL HISTORY OF GAMBLING IN AMERICA

Copyright © 1938 by Dodd, Mead and Company, Inc.

Published by
Thunder's Mouth Press
An Imprint of Avalon Publishing Group, Incorporated
161 William Street, 16th Floor
New York, NY 10038

Library of Congress Cataloging-in-Publication Data:

Asbury, Herbert, 1891–1963.
   Sucker's progress: an informal history of gambling in America / by Herbert Asbury
         p.cm.
   Originally published: New York : Dodd, Mead & Co., 1938.
   Includes bibliographical references and index.
   ISBN 1-56025-495-5
      1. Gambling—United States. I. Title.

HV6715.A75 2003
306.4'82'0973—dc21

                                                        2003040200

                     9 8 7 6 5 4 3 2 1

                 Printed in the United States of America
                 Distributed by Publishers Group West

TO

HELEN WOODWARD

WHO SUGGESTED IT

CONTENTS

PART ONE

PART TWO

ILLUSTRATIONS

ILLUSTRATIONS

PART ONE

CHAPTER I

FARO

DESPITE the proverbial ingenuity of the Yankee, he has never created a gambling game of the first rank; in this particular field his inventiveness has been confined to variation and adaptation. All of the famous short card, dice and banking games upon which the American gambler has relied for his big killings, even such traditionally American institutions as Faro, Poker, and Craps, are of foreign origin, and only a few were known in the United States before the beginning of the nineteenth century.

2

The genesis of Faro, for nearly three hundred years one of the most popular of all banking games, is uncertain, and is quite likely to remain so. It appears, however, to have been derived by French gamblers from the Venetian game of *Basetta* and the Italian *Hocca,* both of which, in turn, were adaptations of the German *Landsquenet,* played in the camps of the Teutonic foot-soldiers as early as 1400. Faro was a popular game in Paris before the middle of the seventeenth century, and under the name of *Pharao* or *Pharaon*—so called because the backs of the early French cards bore a picture of an Egyptian king—it was played extensively in France until 1691, when Louis XIV prohibited it by royal decree. The game was revived during the latter part of that monarch's reign, and was once more in full favor during the Regency of the Duke of Orléans, who gained control of the French throne upon the death of Louis XIV in 1715. The revival

3

was due principally to John Law, the celebrated Scottish adventurer, whose phenomenal success at the gaming tables of Brussels, Vienna and other European capitals had earned him the nickname of King of the Gamblers. Law arrived in Paris in 1708, set up a Faro bank at the home of the actress Duclos, and won 67,000 pounds sterling before the French police concluded that he was a suspicious character and ordered him to leave the country. He returned in 1715, and the Duke of Orléans, as Regent of France, adopted his famous financial and colonization schemes, with Louisiana as the bait, which threw all France into an orgy of gambling and speculation. French historians record that nothing went on in Paris "except eating, drinking and gambling with fearful stakes." Fortunate speculators in the shares of the Mississippi Company, believing their sources of income to be limitless, gambled at *Piquet* with bank notes of 100,000 livres "as if they were only ten-sou pieces"; and in one night the Duchess of Berry lost the incredible sum of 1,700,000 livres at Faro, and apparently thought nothing of it.

Faro was played in England soon after it had become popular in France, and was probably introduced by the roystering blades who had shared the French exile of Charles II.[1] The change in spelling, from the French *Pharaon* to the English corruption Faro, occurred soon afterward, when the game began to make headway among the common people. Throughout the reign of Charles II Faro was one of the favorite diversions of the ladies and gentlemen of his court, who gambled for huge stakes; it is recorded that Lady Castlemaine, one of Charles' mistresses, won 15,000 pounds in a single night, and on another occasion, in February, 1667, lost 25,000 pounds in a similar length of time. Faro retained its hold upon the affections of English gamesters until it was specifically prohibited by Act of Parliament in 1738.

[1] Another famous game, Whist, also appeared during the reign of Charles II. It was invented between 1664 and 1680, and was founded upon an old game called Ruff and Honors.

The game then declined rapidly, and Edmund Hoyle, in his famous book on games published a few years before his death in 1769, remarked that Faro was "played but little in England," and that it was purely a game for winning and losing money. A new period of popularity for Faro began about 1785, when the gambling houses of London installed the game, and a Faro bank became the principal attraction at the routs and other entertainments of the English nobility. For more than two decades around the turn of the nineteenth century advertisements such as this, from the London *Courier* of March 5, 1794, were not uncommon:

> "As Faro is now the most fashionable circular game in the *haut ton,* in exclusion of melancholy Whist, and to prevent a company being cantoned into separate parties, a gentleman, of unexceptionable character, will, on invitation, do himself the honor to attend the rout of any lady, nobleman, or gentleman, with a Faro Bank and Fund, adequate to the style of play, from 500 to 2,000 guineas.
>
> "Address G. A., by letter, to be left at Mr. Harding's, Piccadilly, nearly opposite Bond-Street.
>
> "N.B. This advertisement will not appear again." [2]

It seems certain, although no documentary proof exists, that Faro was brought to America by the French colonists—among them many professional and amateur gamblers—who settled Alabama and Louisiana early in the eighteenth century; and the first game in what is now the United States was probably played either in Mobile, or in New Orleans, which was destined to become the port of entry for many other famous card and dice games. From the French possessions in the South Faro was spread eastward and northward by sailors and travelers, and

[2] *The Gaming Calendar, to Which Are Added, Annals of Gaming,* by Seymour Harcourt, Esq.; London, 1820; page 84.

later by the peripatetic gamblers who worked the early flatboats and steamboats, and by the sharpers who traveled the wilderness trails on foot or horseback and found their suckers in the roadside taverns or the cabins of the lonely settlers. In New York, Boston, Philadelphia and other Eastern cities—with the exception of Charleston, where it was a favorite gambling game among the French Huguenots and the refugees from Acadia— Faro was little known, if at all, before the American Revolution. It is said to have been introduced into New York by camp followers of the British Army, but it is more probable that it was brought to the East by visitors from New Orleans or Charleston, or by the French soldiers of Lafayette and Rochambeau.

The dissemination of Faro was quickened by the Louisiana Purchase, and within a decade after that historic event it had become the most widely played game in the United States, and had gained a foothold from which it was not dislodged for more than a hundred years. Today Faro is seldom heard of, and it is doubtful if a dozen Faro banks are in regular operation between the Atlantic and the Pacific; but until the early years of the twentieth century, when it began to succumb to a changing public taste, Faro was the mainstay of every important gambling house north of the Rio Grande River, and the ruin of thousands who tried to beat it. No other card or dice game, not even Poker or Craps, has ever achieved the popularity in this country that Faro once enjoyed, and it is extremely doubtful if any has equaled Faro's influence upon American gambling or bred such a host of unprincipled sharpers. It was the medium of the first extensive cheating at cards ever seen in the United States, and the rock upon which were reared the elaborate gambling houses and the wolf-traps of the early and middle nineteenth century; while around it developed the system of cappers and ropers-in which is still used effectively by American gaming resorts.

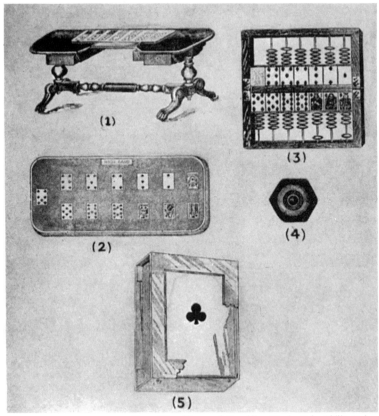

From "Gambling and Gambling Devices" by Philip Quinn

FARO APPARATUS: (1) TABLE WITH LAYOUT; (2) FOLDING BOARD WITH LAYOUT; (3) CASE-KEEPER; (4) COPPER; (5) DEALING BOX

3

Many changes and improvements have been made in dealing and betting at Faro since the first Frenchman "called the turn," but the basic structure of the game remains unchanged, and essentially it is the same as when Hoyle first collated the rules almost two hundred years ago. Briefly, the cards are drawn one at a time from a full pack, and alternately win and lose for the bank and the player, the denomination only being considered. In greater detail, this is the way Faro was played in the United States during the golden age of the game:

The dealer sat at a table, and at his right was an assistant who paid and collected the bets, and watched for trickery among the players. In front of the dealers was the dealing box, and the layout, the latter a suit of thirteen cards, usually spades, pasted or painted on a large square of enameled oilcloth. On the left of the dealer was another assistant who manipulated the case-keeper, a small box containing a miniature layout, with four buttons running along a steel rod opposite each card. The buttons were moved along, as on a billiard counter, as the cards were played, so that the players could tell at a glance what cards remained to be dealt. In some houses the progress of the game was also kept by the players on small printed sheets. The use of these sheets, however, was not general.

The cards in the layout were arranged in two parallel rows, with the ace on the dealer's left and the odd card, the seven, on his extreme right. Sufficient space was left between the rows for the players to place their bets. In the row nearest the players were the king, queen and jack, called the "big figure," and the ten, nine and eight. In the row nearest the dealer were the ace, deuce and trey, called the "little figure," and the four, five and six. The six, seven and eight were called the "pot." The king, queen, ace and deuce formed the "grand square"; the jack, three, four and ten were the "jack square," and the nine, eight, six and five were the "nine square."

All preliminaries having been arranged, the dealer shuffled and cut the cards, and then placed them face upward in the dealing box, the top of which was open. The card thus exposed was dead, as was the last card in the box, although as originally played, and in some sections of the country until comparatively recent times, both counted for the bank. When play began the cards were drawn through a slit in the box, a spring pushing the remainder of the pack into position. They were placed in two piles, one close to the box and the other about six inches away. The dead card began the farthest pile, on which all winning cards were placed.

The first card exposed in the box when the dead card had been withdrawn was a "loser" and counted for the bank. It began the pile nearest the box. The next card was a "winner," and counted for the players. Every two cards drawn in this manner were called a "turn," and the game thus proceeded until twenty-five turns had been made, in each of which there was a "winner" and a "loser." If two cards of the same denomination appeared on a single turn, it was called a "split," and the bank took half of all money which had been bet on the card. When the last turn was reached, with a "winner," a "loser," and a dead card remaining in the box, the players were invited to make bets on the order in which they would appear. To the correct guesser the bank paid four to one. If, however, two of the cards were of the same denomination, the odds were only two to one. On all turns before the last even money was paid.

To avoid the confusion of betting upon a dead card, wagers were not placed until the pack had been cut and placed in the dealing box. In the early days of Faro bets could be made only upon the figures, the squares, the pot and single cards, but as the game developed they were allowed on innumerable combinations; for example, by using systems called "heeling" and "stringing along," it was possible to bet on twenty-one different groups of cards, all playing a single card to win.

The limit of a Faro game was determined by the prosperity of the banker, who announced before bets were made the amount for which he would play. The top limit was allowed when two, three or four cards, commonly called doubles, triples and quadruples, of a particular denomination remained in the box. When only a single, or case, card remained, thus giving the bank no chance of a split, the limit was halved. The banker also announced whether the limit would be open or running. If the former, a player was permitted to bet only a stipulated amount, but he could bet it as often as he pleased. If the latter, a gambler was given the privilege of "going paroli," a phrase which, incidentally, has been corrupted into parlay and is in common usage on the race tracks. In other words, a Faro player could parlay his winnings, if any, to a sum previously agreed upon as the extreme running limit, and then, if he wished, bet the whole upon a single card or combination. The running game was popular for many years, especially in New York and the East, but it was so obviously advantageous to the bank that eventually it fell into disfavor. By the beginning of the Civil War it had been abandoned everywhere except in the skinning-houses, where the best luck the player could expect in any event was a split.

For a hundred years after Faro had been transplanted to America, the game was dealt from a pack held face downward in the dealer's left hand. Dealing boxes were an American innovation, and made their appearance about 1822, when a Virginia gambler named Bayley constructed the first one and put it into a game at Richmond. It was of brass, about half an inch wider than a pack of cards and a little longer, and was covered over the top except for an oblong hole in the center, just large enough to enable the dealer to insert a single finger and push the top card through a slit in the side of the box, in which the pack had been placed face downward. Bayley attempted to market his invention, but it was not generally well received because it concealed the pack. The gambling houses in New Orleans refused to install it, and Faro continued to be dealt from the left hand until 1825, when a Cincinnati watchmaker named Graves invented and introduced an open dealing box which quickly caught the public fancy. Within a few years it was in use throughout the country, and with minor alterations and improvements has remained the standard. With the adoption of Graves' box, a change in the method of dealing was made—the pack was placed in the box face upward, and the top card was always exposed.

4

In the hands of a square dealer, Faro as played in the United States sixty or seventy years ago was the fairest banking game ever devised. In no other was the percentage against the player so small; many experts of the period, indeed, declared that with the first and last cards dead the bank had no advantage at all except what might be found in the splits, and that this was so slight as to make the game almost pure chance. Others estimated the percentage in favor of the bank at from one and one-half to three, still others held that it could not be precisely calculated; and some contended that if "heeling" and "stringing along" were permitted the percentage was actually in favor of the player. Said an old-time gambler in 1873:

"Faro is the only banking game of chance known to us, whose percentage cannot be clearly defined. The best algebraists among the gambling community of this country have been unable to show us that Faro has one and three-fourths per cent in its favor. . . . Many mathematicians have set their brains to work to discover the exact percentage on Faro, but in every instance they have ignominiously failed. They have told us that on one thousand deals of the game, the splits on each deal will average one and one-half. Some of these astute calculators have told us that two splits per deal is a fair average, but it seems that none of them, as yet, have come to any definite conclusion on that or any of these points. They have also told us that a pack of cards in twenty-five turns, counting the 'soda' and 'hock' [3] as dead cards, can come six hundred and two different ways, counting among that number, twenty-five splits which may take place. They have calculated the chances of quadruple, triple and double cards splitting at any stage of a deal. Still these clear heads are unable to arrive at the exact percentage on the game. Some think it will reach two and one-half per cent, while a majority of the most intelligent gamblers in the country believe it will not exceed one and one-half." [4]

An almost conclusive argument for the theory that the percentage at honest Faro is virtually non-existent is the fact that the canny management of Monte Carlo has never permitted the game to be played at that celebrated resort. "At Monte Carlo," wrote R. F. Foster, the foremost American authority on games for many years before the World War, "everything is perfectly fair and straightforward, but no games are played except those in which the percentage in favor of the bank is evident, and is openly acknowledged. In Faro there is no such advantage, and

[3] The first and last cards.
[4] *Wanderings of a Vagabond, An Autobiography,* Edited by John Morris; New York, 1873; pages 64, 74–5. Morris was the pseudonym of John O'Connor, a novelist of the period. Much of this book is obviously fiction, but the greater part is a very circumstantial account of the adventures of a gambler from the late 1820's until after the Civil War. Whenever possible O'Connor's statements have been checked against other sources. In every such instance he has been correct.

no honest Faro bank can live. It is for that reason that the game is not played at Monte Carlo, in spite of the many thousands of Americans who have begged the management to introduce it. The so-called percentage of splits at Faro is a mere sham, and any candid dealer will admit that they do not pay for the gas." [5]

Foster estimated that in an honest game of Faro splits should occur about three times in two deals. But an honest game has always been a great rarity; Faro was a cheating business almost from the time of its invention. The earliest of the great Faro bankers of whom much is known, John Law and de Chalabre, were notorious cheats, and so, in the main, were their predecessors and successors. As early as 1731 the *Gentleman's Magazine,* of London, publishing a list of the employees of a first-class gambling house, referred to "a cheating game called Faro." Swindling at Faro on a large scale in the United States began soon after the introduction of the open dealing box, which also marked the beginning of the game's period of greatest popularity. Crooked boxes were in use within a few months after the invention of the watchmaker Graves had been placed on the market, and for years there was a steady stream of dishonest appliances bearing such impressive names as gaff, tongue-tell, sand-tell, top-sight tell, end squeeze, screw box, needle squeeze, lever movement, coffee-mill, and horse-box. They were all dealing boxes with the exception of the gaff, which was a small instrument shaped like a shoemaker's awl and worn attached to a finger ring. Occasionally one of the gadgets got out of order and caused considerable embarrassment to the unlucky sharper who owned it, but as a rule they worked perfectly in the hands of competent operators, although some of them were intricate contrivances of springs, levers, sliding plates, thumb screws, and needle-like steel rods. Many were devised and manufactured by

[5] *Foster's Complete Hoyle, an Encyclopedia of Games,* by R. F. Foster; New York, 1914; page 517.

Graves himself, and others were invented by Louis David of Natchez, also a watchmaker, who made a fortune in the 1840's selling German silver tongue-tell boxes at from $125 to $175 each.

These artifices were accompanied and followed by a flood of prepared cards. Some were strippers, which meant that the sides and ends of certain cards in each suit had been trimmed; others were readers, marked on the backs; while the backs of still others had been sanded or otherwise roughened—the best process was perfected by Graves—so that any two could be made to stick together. Strippers were cut in various ways, the most popular being hollows, rounds, rakes, wedges, and concave and convex, also known as "both ends against the middle." Any variety could be bought ready for use, but the careful gambler purchased shears, knives and trimming plates, and prepared his own stock. The portion shaved from each card was so slight—about one-thirty-second of an inch—as to be unnoticeable to the ordinary player, but it was large enough for the gambler to tell where the stripped cards lay in the pack. With the marked, stripped and sanded cards the sharper could stack the pack as he wished, and by using them in the crooked boxes he could make splits appear at his pleasure, deal two cards at a time, deal a card to lose when there was a heavy play on it to win, and arrange the last turn in a way that would mean most to the bank.

The advantages thus given the dealer were so widely used that cheating soon became as much a part of Faro in America as a pack of cards. The fundamental fairness of the game made such a situation well-nigh inevitable. A gambler who operated a Faro bank was put to considerable expense to provide quarters and the necessary apparatus, and he wasn't in the business for fun. "To justify this expenditure," wrote Foster, "he must have some permanent advantage, and if no such advantage or 'percentage' is inherent in the principles of the game, any person playing against such a banker is probably being cheated." Moreover, in the heyday of American gambling a first-class Faro dealer, variously called a "mechanic" and an "artist," was paid from $100 to $200 a week and a percentage of the profits, and as Foster pointed out, "it is hardly necessary to say that he was not paid that amount simply for pulling cards out of a box. . . . The proprietors of some fashionable clubs, especially at watering places, pretend to be above such things as cheating at Faro, and get indignant at the suggestion of the possibility of there being anything crooked in their establishments. The author has but one reply to such. If it is true that there is nothing unfair in your game, let me put a type-writer girl in the dealer's place to shuffle and pull out the cards, and let your men just see to paying and taking bets." [6]

5

Besides bringing about the development of new methods of cheating, Faro also made a very considerable philological contribution to American culture, for an extraordinary number of the terms, technical and otherwise, which were employed by Faro players in the palmy days of the game have passed into the language, and into the nomenclature of other games, and are commonly used by millions who never heard of Faro. Here are some of them:

Lookout—The dealer's principal assistant, the one who paid and collected bets and kept a watchful eye on the players.

Case card—The last card of each denomination.

Case-keeper—A device for keeping a record of the cards as they were drawn. Also, the man who operated the device.

Keeping cases—Manipulating the *case-keeper*.

Tabs—Printed sheets on which the players noted the cards as

[6] *Ibid.*, page 534.

they won or lost.

Keeping tabs—Making this record.

Brace game—A crooked Faro bank.

Tiger—Faro. During the early 1830's a first-rate professional gambler carried his Faro outfit in a fine mahogany box on which was painted a picture of the Royal Bengal Tiger. A representation of the animal was also carved on the ivory chips and painted on the oilcloth layout. The gamblers adopted the tiger as the presiding deity of the game, and Faro soon became known throughout the country simply as "the tiger." Many large gambling houses had oil paintings of tigers hung above their Faro tables.

Bucking the tiger—Playing Faro.

Break even—A system of betting by which each card was played to win and lose an even number of times.

Both ends against the middle—A method of trimming cards for dealing a brace game of Faro. A dealer who used such a pack was said to be *"playing both ends against the middle."*

Cat—When two cards of the same denomination were in the last turn, it was called a *cat*. Also *cat-hop* and *cat-harpen*.

Chips—The counters at Faro. At Poker they were properly called *Checks*.

Calling the turn—To guess correctly the order in which the last three cards in the box would appear.

Coppering a bet—Betting a card to lose. To do so the player placed upon his stake a small copper disk provided by the dealer.

Heeled bets—Wagers which played one card to win and another to lose.

Heeler or heel—A player who consistently made heeled bets.

In hock—The last card in the box was said to be *in hock*. Originally it was known as the *hockelty card,* and in the early days of Faro, when it counted for the bank, a player who had bet on it was said to have been caught *in hock*. Also, a gambler who had been trimmed by another sharper was said to be *in hock* to his conqueror; and as late as the middle 1880's, in the underworld, a man was *in hock* when he was in jail. The phrase is now principally used in reference to pawnshop pledges, but it seems to have acquired that meaning in recent years.

Last turn—The last three cards in the box.

Losing out—Betting on a card which loses four times in one deal.

Making a pass—Putting the two parts of a pack of cards back as they were before the cut.

Open bets—Wagers which played cards to win.

Piking—Making small bets all over the layout.

Piker—One who made piking bets.

Paroli—Parlay came from this word by way of *parolet, parlieu* and *parlee*. It meant exactly the same at Faro as it does in race track gambling.

Sleeper—A bet placed on a dead card. In many houses it belonged to the first man who grabbed it.

Soda—The first card, exposed face up before bets were made. Said to have been a corruption of zodiac. For many years a common expression was "from soda to hock," meaning the whole thing, from soup to nuts.

Deal—Twenty-five turns.

Square deal—Twenty-five turns in which the dealer used a pack with squared edges. With these cards the chances of a crooked deal were minimized.

Square game—Faro bank which used squared cards exclusively.

Hell—A gambling house.

Leg—A professional gambler. Probably a corruption of *blackleg*. In earlier times sharpers were also known as *Greeks*.

Pigeon—From about 1600 to recent times the victim of a professional gambler was called a *pigeon*.

Stool-pigeon—Originally this word meant a pigeon used to decoy others into a trap. A few years before the turn of the nineteenth century it came into general use among American gamblers to designate a capper or a hustler for a Faro bank, and was still so used as late as 1915. An early mention of the word in this connection may be found in the New York *Herald* of July 31, 1835. The *Herald* reprinted a letter from a citizen of Baltimore to the Chief Judge of the Baltimore County Court, and quoted the citizen as saying that the gamblers of the Maryland metropolis preyed upon "such strangers as they can decoy in, by means of what they call stool-pigeons." The use of *stool-pigeon* as a synonym for police spy is apparently of comparatively recent origin; as late as the middle 1880's such an informer was known in the underworld simply as a *pigeon*.

Stringing along—Betting all odd or even numbered cards to play one way.

Whipsawed—Losing two different bets on the same turn.

Winning out—Betting on a card which won four times in one deal.

Snap—A temporary Faro game. A *ten-dollar snap* was a temporary game with a ten-dollar capital.

Throwing the game—Permitting a player to win by crooked dealing.

Marker—An article, sometimes a small piece of ivory provided by the bank, used by a player whose credit was good. He announced the value of the *marker* as he made his bet, and was supposed to settle after each deal.

Velvet—The bank's money.

Playing on velvet—Betting money previously won from the bank.

Snaking a game—Stealing, marking and returning a dealer's cards, a trick often practiced in the days when the pack was dealt face downward from the dealer's hand.

Playing a shoe-string—Starting with a small sum and running it into a large amount by consistently lucky bets.

Stuck—A player who went broke trying to call the turn was *stuck*.

Passed in his checks—He cashed in. Originally this expression was "passed in his chips."

Various adaptations of Faro were introduced during the long period of the game's popularity, but none held the interest of the gambling public more than a few years. Perhaps the most important of these innovations were Short Faro, Rolling Faro, and Stuss, called also Jewish Faro. The last-named developed on the East Side of New York about 1885, and most of the games were crooked, controlled by Big Josh Hines, Johnny Spanish, Kid Twist, Monk Eastman and other celebrated gang leaders. Stuss was little more than a simplified Faro, very similar to the game as it was played in the early days of American gambling; bets were made only on single cards; the top card counted for the bank, and the bank took all money bet on splits. In Short Faro, which was played in the Middle West during the 1890's, the layout consisted of six cards, from the ace to the nine inclusive, and the dealer used two, and sometimes three packs of cards, which he dealt three at a time from his hand. The first three were for the house and were not shown. The second three were for the players and were dealt face upward. Throughout the game the bank's cards remained hidden and those of the players were exposed. The mode of play was thus described by a gambler in 1892:

> "Suppose a player wagers a dollar on the queen. If one of the three cards exposed happens to be a queen he wins one dollar; if two are queens he receives double the amount of his stake; if all three should prove to be queens the dealer returns him his original stake augmented by three times the

amount; if no queen is shown the house gathers in the stake. It does not require a particularly erudite mathematician to discover that the odds at this game are enormously in favor of the bank." [7]

Rolling Faro appeared in the South about 1840. It was played with an ordinary Faro layout and a wheel, somewhat similar to that used at Roulette, on which a suit of cards had been painted. Instead of drawing cards from a box the dealer spun the wheel, and winners and losers were determined by the position of a pointer. This game was never very popular, principally because most of the wheels were crooked, being worked by body pressure or by mechanical devices, and it vanished from the gambling scene long before the Civil War.

Another swindle called Rolling Faro was extensively played for a few years around 1890 in the gambling houses of Chicago and at mid-western fairs and carnivals, but it bore little or no resemblance to Faro. It was simply a Wheel of Fortune with four jacks, and as many colors, painted on its face, and prizes of cheap jewelry posted at various points. In the houses money prizes were offered instead of jewelry, and the players bet on the jacks and the colors.

[7] *Fools of Fortune, or, Gambling and Gamblers,* by John Philip Quinn; Chicago, 1892; page 210.

CHAPTER II

POKER

THE most widely played short card game ever dealt in the United States came into this country by way of New Orleans, but most of the features which were responsible for the popularity and extraordinary fascination of Poker were added during the process of Americanization, mainly by gamblers who had no knowledge of the original sources of their additions. As first played in Louisiana, with a deck of twenty cards, five cards to a player, and all of the modern hands except straights and flushes, Poker was simply the ancient Persian game of *As Nas,* also called *Dsands,* under a new name and in a new setting. As played today Poker is an assembled game, formed by superimposing upon *As Nas* two important American innovations— Jackpots and Stud—and various features found in many English, French and Italian games of the sixteenth, seventeenth and eighteenth centuries, among them Post and Pair, Brag, *Primero, Gilet, Brelan, Bouillotte, Poque* and *Ambigu.* Borrowings from these sources include the ante, the draw, the raise before the draw, the freeze-out, table stakes, bluffing, straights and flushes, wild cards, and the use of the joker, formerly called *Mistigris.* In all of the French and Italian games which contributed to Poker three cards were dealt to each player from a pack of thirty-two. In some a fourth card, common to all hands, was turned up on the remainder of the pack, whence came Spit-in-the-Ocean. In the English games of Brag and Post and Pair three cards were likewise dealt, but from a full pack of fifty-two. Only in Persia was a pack of twenty cards used, and only in *As Nas* was a playing hand composed of five.

Bluffing and wild cards were special features of Brag, which was played extensively in America during the long period in which Poker was developing. In the English version of this game the jack of clubs, the ace of diamonds, and the nine of diamonds were wild, and were called "turners" or "braggers." In American Brag there were eight "braggers"—the jacks and nines of each suit. Bluffing at Brag was described in Seymour's *Court Gamester,* published in 1719, as "the endeavor to impose on the judgment of the rest who play, and particularly on the person who chiefly offers to oppose you, by boasting or bragging of the cards in your hand. Those who by fashioning their looks and gestures, can give a proper air to their actions . . . shall out-brag a much greater hand and win the stakes." This could very well have been written of Poker today, although in the modern game it is advisable for the player to let his money do the bragging.

The influence of Brag upon Poker was so great that the latter was sometimes called a "brag game," but for the name by which it is now known throughout the world Poker is indebted to the French *Poque,* of which Poker is simply an American mispronunciation. The French game was popular in Paris as early as 1700, and was described for the first time in the 1718 edition of the *Académie Universelle des jeux,* one of the oldest known works on card games. "The peculiarity of *Poque,*" wrote the American authority R. F. Foster, "is that after the cards are dealt and each player has taken from the common pool the counter for the rank of the highest cards held, he is at liberty to bet upon the various combinations of cards he holds, triplets, pairs, etc. In the French description of the game we are told that a player opened the betting by saying '*Je poque d'un jeton,*' or two chips, or as many as he pleased, and that the others could see him, raise him, or drop out in their turn. . . . In all the English descriptions of the game of *Poque,* we find the player instructed to say in English, 'I poque for so much,' and the following players are to respond, 'I poque against you.' " [1]

The early settlers of Louisiana were familiar with *Poque*—since a majority of them were the scum of the Paris underworld it is reasonable to suppose that they were familiar with all French gambling games—and as New Orleans increased in population and economic importance it became a favorite game in the taverns and the coffee-houses. The Persian game, *As Nas,* is believed to have been brought to New Orleans about the time of the American occupation, when the city began to develop an extensive foreign commerce, and was probably introduced by sailors. Its similarity to *Poque* was at once recognized, as well as its superiority, which was due largely to the five-card hand that permitted more combinations than the simple pair and triplets of the three-card *Poque.* The latter was superseded by *As Nas* within a few years, but the French inhabitants of New Orleans discarded the unfamiliar terminology and retained that of their own game, and added to *As Nas* some of the most important features of *Poque.* Thus *As Nas* became *Poque.* Exactly where the transition from *Poque* to Poker occurred is unknown. It was, of course, a gradual process, and in all likelihood began when the American flatboatman came down the Mississippi, encountered the game in New Orleans, and attempted to wrestle with the French spelling and pronunciation. If he chanced to see the name of the game in French, he did what any unlettered English-speaking person would do—separated the word into two syllables and pronounced both. If he heard it properly pronounced, and had occasion to write it, he would spell it Poke. So the game became, among the Americans up and down the river, Poke and Po-que, and from these to Poker was a short and nat-

[1] New York *Sun,* May 22, 1904.

22

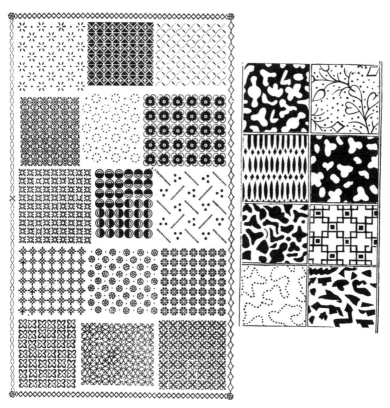

MARKED CARDS OF THE 1840'S

ural step.[2] "One correspondent," wrote R. F. Foster, "said that as he recollected the game in New Orleans it was first called Poke. This name appears in an early description of the game, but seems to have been generally regarded as a misprint." Sometimes, because of its dominant characteristic, and the general recklessness of play in the early days, the game was known as Bluff, and was so called occasionally until about the time of the Civil War. As late as the early 1850's the anonymous author of *New York by Gaslight,* a vivid account of the city's wickedness, informed his readers that Poker, "under the name of Bluff, has been and probably will be for all time the favorite game with the southerners, who never feel so happy as when they can succeed in 'bluffing' somebody off."

The Americanization of the word *Poque* was probably completed by 1825, although there was no printed reference to the game as Poker, so far as diligent research could discover, until 1836. In that year the author of a book published in New York described Poker as "a favorite game of cards at the south and west," [3] indicating that it must have been common in those sections for several years, though it was certainly but little known in the East. The reformed gambler Jonathan H. Green, in an exposé of gambling published in 1843, mentions Poker as having been a popular game on the Mississippi River for many years. "There was a time," he wrote, "when this game was not so dan-

---

[2] The word Dixie provides a case in point. A few years after the Louisiana Purchase one of the New Orleans banks issued ten dollar notes, on one side of which was the French word for ten, *dix.* To the flatboatmen one of the notes was a dix, and collectively they were dixies, while New Orleans was known as "the town of the dixies," and, later, simply as Dixie. The word does not appear to have been used to designate the entire South until after 1859, when D. D. Emmett wrote his famous song.

[3] *Dragoon Campaigns to the Rocky Mountains; being a History of the Enlistment, Organization, and first Campaigns of the Regiment of United States Dragoons; together with incidents of a soldier's life, and sketches of scenery and Indian character,* by a Dragoon (James Hildreth); New York, 1836; pages 128–30.

gerous as it has come to be of late years. It was then common to see men of almost all classes amuse themselves at this game; and landlords would join their guests in a game for social amusement. Captains and other officers of packets and steamboats, generally, would engage freely in a game with their passengers for recreation. And little, if anything, was wagered or lost at the game, and all got up pleased, and seldom had any cause for dissatisfaction." Green also described a famous set-to at Poker which occurred in New Orleans during the early years of the game, perhaps the first of the many endurance contests that Poker players have staged:

"Sometime in the year 1835, in the city of New Orleans, there happened at one of its haunts of gambling, several of that unfortunate class of men who are addicted to that vice; and having large amounts of money in their possession, there was a proposition that five of the most monied men among them should sit at play until their money was exhausted. The five began, and played on, under the influence of great excitement, for some thirty hours, when two of the party quit, either from the want of money or strength. The other three continued for some fifteen hours longer, when one of them had to quit also. The other two played on about ten hours more, when one of them dropped to sleep, and this broke up the game. But next came the dreadful consequences of this rash and wicked undertaking. One of this party lived, when at home, somewhere eastward; another lived in Alexandria, on Red River; a third lived in Cincinnati; a fourth, in or near, Covington, Ky., and the fifth near Lawrenceburg, Ia.; and this last is the only one that now survives of that unfortunate party. The eastern man was, from the time of this desperate act, afflicted, and died of disease of the lungs in '37 or '38. The one from Alexandria survived, I

24

think, until the year '39 or '40. The one from Covington became, from that time, the subject of sore affliction, and lingered along until the year '42, when he died, having suffered more than it is in the power of language to describe . . . he died a sincere convert to Christianity, and was buried in the Methodist grave-yard, near Covington. . . . The fourth one of these young men died in Cincinnati in the year 1842. . . . One other still survives, and is yet pursuing the odious practice of gambling, and most sincerely do I desire that, ere it is too late, he may take into serious consideration the many risks he is running of not being so fortunate as the last two mentioned in this narrative; (for as I have never learned the particulars of the death of the two first, I cannot give any information of their last days that would be definite or satisfactory). . . ."[4]

These unfortunate addicts probably held the record for Marathon Poker until four rich New Jerseyites—Silas Daniels of Philipsburg, James Howe of Ewing, John Strange of Titusville, and Hosea Brockway of Princeton—started a game at Andy McDonald's tavern in Atlantic County during the deer-hunting season of 1875. The opening bet was $1,000, and the smallest made at any time during the game was fifty dollars, but when the players finally fell asleep on the table after seventy hours of continuous play no man was out more than twenty-five dollars.

But even this terrific battle was a trivial affair in comparison with that great Poker session of Texas legend—the game played at Austin by Major Danielson and Old Man Morgan, wealthy planters and old friends, who for years had had a little session every night. At eight o'clock on the evening of June 15, 1853,

[4] *An Exposure of the Arts and Miseries of Gambling,* by J. H. Green; Cincinnati, 1843; pages 122–26.

they began to play as usual, and for two hours the luck shifted from one to the other. Then, with Major Danielson dealing, each drew a wonderful hand, and the betting became heavier. At dawn on the 16th of June they agreed to abolish the limit. Stopping only for meals, and to change their property into cash, they continued to bet. The game went on and on, day after day, week after week, and month after month. From all over Texas people came in such crowds to see the two old men hunched over their cards, that more railroads were built into the town, and hotels sprang up like toadstools. The Civil War was fought, the carpet-baggers came, and Reconstruction began, but Major Danielson and Old Man Morgan were not interested; they were still betting. In 1870, when they had been playing for seventeen years, the cards, faded and torn, were sealed and placed in a safe deposit box in the National Bank of Austin. And the game went on. In 1872 the players died at exactly the same moment, but in their wills they left orders for their eldest sons to carry on. This was done for five years, when one of the sons was killed by a railroad train and the other went crazy. But still the mighty game continues. Both families are very poor, but whenever a Morgan or a Danielson gets a few dollars together he hurries to Austin and makes a bet. As long as the W.P.A. holds out the identity of the cards drawn on that June evening eighty-five years ago will probably remain a secret.

The Poker played in the memorable contest described by Jonathan Green was the original game with twenty cards, everything below the tens being omitted from the pack. Early in the existence of the game the French *Piquet* pack of thirty-two cards was sometimes used, and the full pack of fifty-two cards seems to have been introduced during the middle 1830's. In another of his moral treatises on gambling, published in 1857, Jonathan H. Green mentioned fifty-two card Poker as having been played on the Mississippi in 1837, but spoke of it as an innovation not generally known. The twenty-card game, however, was not wholly displaced until the draw, which became a part of the game in the early or middle 1840's and was impracticable with a short pack, had come into general use.[5] Apparently this important addition made fairly rapid progress in the affections of Poker players—in 1860 a writer said that "at the present day, what is termed draw bluff is played more extensively, perhaps, than the old way of playing the game." But Poker was still being played with twenty cards in New York as late as 1857, for in that year the author of a warning guidebook to the metropolis specifically cautioned his readers against the game, which he described as one of the most dangerous pitfalls to be found in the city. He thus concluded his preachment:

> "And now don't, for Heaven's sake, any of you go and make insane jackasses of yourselves by running into the very snares that we have warned you about." [6]

In twenty-card Poker, and in the full pack game as well for many years, the players cut for first deal, and the winner of the opening pot thereafter dealt until he lost, when the privilege went to his conqueror. The practice of passing the deal to the left after each hand was inaugurated soon after the introduction of the draw, which gave the dealer at least a moral advantage, and led to the picturesque custom of using a buck, which originated on the Western frontier during the late 1860's or early 1870's. The buck could be any object, but was usually a knife, and most Western men in those days carried knives with buck-

---

[5] An early reference to Draw Poker is in the advertising section of *Gamblers' Tricks With Cards, Exposed and Explained,* by J. H. Green, copyrighted in 1850. There the publishers, Dick & Fitzgerald, announce "a new edition of *The American Card Player,* containing all the . . . modern methods of playing the games of . . . Draw Poker. . . ."

[6] *Tricks and Traps of New York City,* Anonymous; Boston, 1857.

horn handles, hence the name. As first used, the buck simply marked the deal; it was placed in front of the dealer, and passed along at the conclusion of each pot. In some sections a player who didn't wish to deal was permitted to ante and "pass the buck." In gambling-house Stud, where the deal never changed, the buck was used to indicate which player received the first card. Nowadays, when used at all, the buck is placed in the pot, and whoever wins it deals a jackpot.

Until the introduction of straights and flushes, the relative value of the hands was the same in thirty-two and fifty-two card Poker as when the game was played with only twenty cards. There were two unbeatable combinations—four aces and four kings with an ace, and when either hand appeared it was greeted with as much reverence as Poker players now accord to an ace high straight flush. Only occasionally, however, was even a set of big fours able to command the backing obtained by the hand which figured in this famous Poker story of the 1870's:

"One morning the janitor of a Denver bank opened the door and was surprised to observe three rather tired-looking citizens seated on the steps, the center one of whom held a sealed envelope carefully in sight of his companions.

" 'Want to make a deposit, gentlemen?' asked the cashier, who shortly arrived. 'Step inside.'

" 'No, I want to negotiate a loan,' said the man with the envelope, 'and there ain't a minute to lose. I want $5,000 quicker than hell can scorch a feather.'

" 'What collaterals have you—Government?' inquired the bank official.

" 'Government nothin'. I've got something that beats four per cents all hollow. You see I've been sitting in a poker game across the street, and there's over $4,000 in the pot. There are three or four pretty strong hands out, and as I've

28

every cent in the center the boys have given me thirty minutes to raise a stake on my hand. It's in this envelope. Just look at it, but don't give it away to these gentlemen. They're in the game, and came along to see I don't monkey with the cards.'

" 'But, my dear sir,' said the cashier, who had quietly opened the envelope and found it to contain four kings and an ace. 'This is certainly irregular—we don't lend money on cards.'

" 'But you ain't going to see me raised out on a hand like that?' whispered the pokerist. 'These fellows think I'm bluffing and I can just clean out the whole gang. I've got 'em right in the door.'

" 'Can't help it, sir. Never heard of such a thing,' said the cashier, and the disappointed applicant and friends drifted sadly out. On the corner they met the bank's president, who was himself just from a quiet little all-night game. They explained the case again, and the next moment the superior officer darted into the bank, seized a bag of twenties, and followed the trio. In about ten minutes he returned with the bag and an extra handful of twenties, which he flung on the counter.

" 'Here, credit five hundred to interest account,' he said to the cashier. 'Why, I thought you had more business snap. Ever play poker?'

" 'No, sir.'

" 'Ah, thought not—thought not. If you did you'd know what good collateral was. Remember that in future four kings and an ace are always good in this institution for our entire assets, sir—our entire assets.' " [7]

[7] *Poker Stories as Told by Statesmen, Soldiers, Lawyers, Commercial Travellers, Bankers, Actors, Editors, Millionaires, Members of the Ananias Club and the Talent, Embracing the Most Remarkable Games 1845-95,* Collected and Edited by John F. B. Lillard; New York, 1896; pages 88–90.

During the past fifty or sixty years a dozen or more so called "eccentric hands," such as the bob-tailed flush and an old-timer called Tiger, have gained a certain standing in Poker and are regularly played throughout the country by a great many people who should know better. The Tiger became popular about 1885, and was described in the 1887 edition of *Hoyle's Games* as "a dreadful innovation." It is the lowest hand which can be held, the deuce, trey, four, five and seven, and as originally played was better than a straight and not as good as a flush. The most famous of all eccentric hands, the Looloo, is said to have been invented in a saloon in Butte, Montana, during the 1870's in a game between a stranger and a Butte miner. John F. B. Lillard thus tells the tale in his *Poker Stories:*

"Luck favored the stranger from the start, and he won steadily. Finally, he drew four aces, and after the stakes had been run up to a comfortable figure he magnanimously refused to bet further.

" 'This is downright robbery,' he exclaimed, 'and I don't want to end the game here by bankrupting you. So here goes.' He threw down four aces and reached for the money.

" 'Hold on!' cried his antagonist. 'I'll take care of the dust, if you please.'

" 'But I held four aces—see?'

" 'Well, what of it? I've got a looloo.'

"The stranger was dazed. 'A looloo?' he repeated. 'What is a looloo, anyway?'

" 'Three clubs and two diamonds,' coolly replied the miner, raking in the stakes. 'I guess you ain't accustomed to our Poker rules out here. See there?'

"He jerked his thumb toward a pasteboard sign which ornamented the wall of the saloon. It read:

A LOOLOO
BEATS FOUR ACES

"The game proceeded, but it was plainly evident that the unsophisticated tiger hunter had something on his mind. Within five minutes he suddenly braced up, his face was wreathed in smiles, and he began betting once more with his former vigor and recklessness. Just at this juncture the bartender quietly hung up another card behind the bar.

"The stranger threw down his cards with an exultant whoop. 'It's my time to howl just about now!' he cried, as he reached for the money. 'There's a looloo for you—three clubs and two diamonds.'

" 'Tut! Tut!' exclaimed the miner. 'Really this is too bad. You evidently don't understand our rules at all. You certainly don't mean to tell me that you play Poker in such a fast-and-loose, slip-shod way down East, do you? Why, look at that rule over there.'

"He pointed directly over the head of the busy bartender. The bit of pasteboard bore this legend:

THE LOOLOO CAN BE PLAYED
BUT ONCE A NIGHT.

At the end of the Civil War the development of Poker had so far progressed that there remained only straights and flushes, the jackpot, and Stud to bring the game to its present form. These appear to have been added in the order named, although there is a possibility that Stud preceded the jackpot. By the late 1860's straights and flushes were being played all over the country. A bitter controversy raged among Poker addicts for some ten years regarding the relative value of a straight and three of a kind, but the former hand finally settled into its proper niche between threes and a flush. The jackpot is supposed to have been devised about 1870 by a group in Toledo, O., to protect liberal players against tightwads who wouldn't come in on less than a high pair. The first mention of jackpots in print that Foster was able to find was in *The Spirit of the Times,* a New York sporting paper, in 1874, when a correspondent asked if, when called, he was required to show his full hand or only his openers. The editor replied that he knew of no rules for jackpots. The Toledo innovation apparently made little headway for several years, but by the middle 188c's had been accepted everywhere as an established feature of the game. In 1887 *Hoyle's Games, the Standard Authority,* declared that as the jackpot "is universally played, stringent rules should be adopted for it," and noted that "this peculiar phase of Poker is not old enough to have crystallized into its concrete form." This volume gave the jackpot rules then in vogue in New York, which were almost precisely the same as those used today.

The origin of Stud Poker, and of its name as well, is uncertain, and so are the date and place of its invention and the processes of its development. One story is that it was devised by Union soldiers during the Civil War, and for that reason became known as "the old army game," but the present author could find no mention of it in the various accounts of gambling in that period, nor do any of the old-time gamblers refer to it in their reminiscences. More plausible is the theory that Stud was born in one of the Western frontier towns in the 1870's, and that it received its name because a stallion was at stake the first time a game was played with exposed cards. Partially supporting this story is the fact that Stud was popular in the West long before it became well known in the East. As early as 1880 Stud was the favorite game in San Francisco, except among the most high-toned of gamblers, and flourished to such an extent that in 1884 the California Legislature specifically prohibited it under penalty of fine and imprisonment. The latest version of the beginnings of Stud is provided by George Henry Fisher of Los Angeles, author of a recently-published volume called *Stud Poker Blue Book, the Only Standard Authority.*[8] According to Mr. Fisher Stud Poker originated "in a backwoods saloon" in "the region of the Ohio," during "that reckless period which followed the Civil War." On this occasion the game began as Draw, and there finally came a pot which one of the players opened with three kings. The dealer and one other man stayed, and there was much raising both before and after the Draw. At length, all his money having been staked, the opener flung his hand down and rushed excitedly outside to the hitching post. He reappeared in a moment leading a spirited stallion, which he tied to the back of his chair. Then he realized that during his absence the other players had probably seen his three kings. So he made a proposition:

"You fellows know damned well what I'm betting on," he said, "and I've got all my money up on it. Now I propose that to make it fair all around each man turns three of his cards face up —discards two—and draws two more faced down. I'll gamble this here thoroughbred studhorse on *my* chances."

So far as the present author could ascertain, Stud Poker is not mentioned in any standard work on card games prior to 1880. The 1887 edition of *Hoyle's Games, the Standard Authority,* gives this brief description of Stud, which is certainly not "the old army game" of today:

"In dealing, five cards are given as in Poker. The first card is placed face down, the others with their faces up. Then a card or cards are drawn, which are not exposed. The raising and all else as in usual Poker."

[8] Los Angeles, 1934; pages 16–17.

33

Of all the many varieties of Poker which have appeared since the game was first played in New Orleans, only Stud has achieved real importance as a gambling house attraction. It became popular in New York in the late 1880's, and since about 1890 a Stud table, with a house man dealing and taking a kitty from each pot, has been part of the equipment of almost every gaming resort in America. In private gambling Stud is now more popular than Draw. It is frequently played with seven cards, three down and four up, and with wild cards this can be a very wicked business.

2

Poker was briefly described in a few books on games before the Civil War, but the first serious attempt to collate and explain the rules was made by Robert C. Schenck, member of Congress from Ohio in the 1840's and 1860's, Minister to Brazil in the 1850's, Brigadier-General in the Union Army during the War, and American Ambassador to Great Britain from 1871 to 1876. His treatise on Poker, published about 1875—incidentally it mentioned neither Stud nor jackpots—was the recognized authority for a dozen years, although it was not written as much for the benefit of American players as for the instruction of Queen Victoria and the British Royal Family, whom General Schenck taught to play the game. The General was a famous Poker player in Washington in the days when the national capital was the greatest Poker town in the country. He engaged in many memorable sessions with Daniel Webster, Henry Clay and other noted statesmen during the early period of his career, and in his later years was accounted the best amateur in America. The most remarkable game in which he was concerned, one that really made Poker history, was played at the Blossom Club in New York, a favorite rendezvous of William M. Tweed and his gang of Tammany highbinders. General Schenck's opponents were three New York politicians, Isaac Oliver, Jacob Sharp, and Richard Flannigan. When the hands were finally shown, after a great deal of heavy betting, each man had a straight flush from the three to the seven. Oliver, who had dealt, was suspected of having stacked the cards, but he insisted that he had not, and since the other players had watched the shuffle and the cards had been properly cut, and as Oliver had no reputation as a card manipulator, they accepted his denial. Coincidence got the credit.

3

As Jonathan Green wrote in 1843, "the methods of cheating at Poker are so very numerous, that I do not think it requisite that I should give an account of the whole of them." The sharper who specialized in Poker and other short-card games used the marked and stripped cards which had proven such a boon to the dishonest Faro dealer, and in much the same way—to stack and milk the pack, to deal from the bottom, and to cold deck the sucker, or surreptitiously exchange his own pack for one actually in the game. He also employed a system called "itemsing," in which a confederate, known in the profession as "items" or "an itemer," signaled the hands held by the other players; and developed a variety of devices for holding out cards, and for seeing the pips as they appeared during the deal. Among them were miscroscopic spectacles, glass reflectors which were hidden among the chips or in the bowl of a pipe, and a great number of vest, leg, knee, belt and sleeve holdouts, some of which were complicated gadgets operated by wires, coil springs, and small clamps. Many of these have survived and are still in use.

Bottom dealing was one of the first ways in which the American gambler sought to supplement his natural skill at Poker; it is said to have been brought to perfection in this country by a

sharper named Wilson in the early 1830's. For some twenty years
it had a great vogue, finally falling into disrepute because of the
bungling of unskillful operators. When properly done, bottom
dealing was—and still is—an almost certain killer, but it is not
so easy as it sounds. "Almost any person, with a little practice,"
wrote John O'Connor in 1873, "can deal from the bottom, but to
perform the feat while several pairs of keen eyes are concentrat-
ing their gaze on your fingers and the pack held by them, without being detected, requires an amount of coolness and nerve,
which is possessed perhaps by not one man in a million." And
besides fumbling a bottom deal, the cold deck artist and the
marked-card sharp sometimes overreached themselves in other
ways. One such instance, which occurred in Seattle in the middle
1880's, was thus described by an old-time gambler:

"There were five men playing. Two of them were in together to do up another two, but they did not want to take
anything from the fifth fellow, who was a kind of a friend of
theirs, although he did not know there was anything wrong
about the game. One of the two who were doing the crooked
work rung in a cold deck, and he dealt great hands to the
two fellows that were to be skinned. One was four nines, I
think, and the other a jack full. He was careful to give no
pair to the man he wanted to befriend, and he dealt his
partner the winning hand. Well, to the surprise of the men
who had put up the cold deck, the fifth fellow with no pair
stayed right in and saw every raise. They didn't dare kick
him out or wink at him, so he piled his money in with the
rest. In the draw he took a card, and then he was raising
more than anyone else around the table. There was $3,600 in
that pot at the show-down, and the fellow that had no pair
won it all. The man that had fixed the deck paid no attention to suits; he was looking out only for pairs and threes or

fours. He dealt the fifth man a four straight of clubs, and the one card he drew made a straight flush." [9]

In the early days of Poker the marked cards used by sharpers were prepared beforehand by the gamblers themselves, and were known as "paper;" or were marked during the progress of the game with the finger nail or a needle point embedded in a ring. This process was called "blazing," and cards so marked were "scratch paper." But marking cards in a game was a tedious and dangerous business, and a man could lose his shirt before the job was completed; while those marked by hand were seldom good enough to escape detection in a game where every player handled and scrutinized the cards in turn. They were more suitable for Faro, where only the dealer manipulated the pack. By 1835 both "paper" and "scratch paper" had been largely supplanted by a variety known as "stamped cards," on which the markings were concealed in the design printed on the backs. These were first manufactured in New York about 1830, and later in New Orleans, Chicago and Cincinnati. As a rule the marked designs were stamped on blank cards procured from legitimate manufacturers, and with the exception of the secret markings were identical with the designs on the legitimate cards. Even in the early days some of the markings were very intricate, and it was never possible to read the best of them without a key.

Sometimes an unscrupulous dealer sold the cards to one gambler and a duplicate key to another, but such dishonesty was comparatively rare, and the stamped cards soon became very popular. They were bought in great quantities by sharpers who introduced them into their games in various ways. On the steamboats they bought all the packs in the bars and replaced them with their own stock; and did the same in towns where they de-

[9] *Poker Stories,* pages 153–54.

signed to make a killing, either letting dealers have the cards at low prices or promising them a percentage of the gains. Thus when new cards were called for in a game they came from apparently innocent sources.

The most ambitious project of this nature in the history of American gambling was undertaken in 1847, during the War with Mexico, by a syndicate of Southern gamblers headed by Bill Clemmens, who devoted some fifty years of his life to trimming the verdant sucker. In company with hundreds of other sharpers Clemmens and his associates had been working the American lines of communication for more than a year, and when the decisive battle of the War was fought in September, 1847, they entered Mexico City on the heels of the American Army. The principal gambling game in Mexico City at that time was *Monte,* and to the surprise of the Americans the dealers were using honest cards and giving the players as much fair play as any man has a right to expect at that deceitful game.

The Clemmens group saw at once that enormous sums could be made by introducing stamped cards. Accordingly Clemmens and two or three others went to New York and consulted with a manufacturer named Bartlett, with the result that by January 1, 1848, Mexico City and all of the other Mexican cities occupied by American troops were flooded with stamped *Monte* cards. But the gamblers had not taken into consideration the fact that the manufacture of cards in Mexico was a monopoly, and that the product of the company holding the monopoly was of very fine quality. Gamblers and players alike refused to use the inferior Bartlett cards. Clemmens and his partners then approached the Mexican manufacturers, who agreed, for $5,000 in advance, to make 100 gross, or 14,400 packs, of stamped cards, the plates to be furnished by the gamblers. Clemmens had the plates made in New York, and the manufacture of the cards was begun. But before the work could be completed peace was declared and the

Americans began to evacuate Mexico.

Clemmens and his fellow-tricksters were thus left holding a bag containing some 15,000 packs of marked *Monte* cards, in which they had invested several thousand dollars. They were unable to use or dispose of the cards in the United States, for *Monte* was but little played in this country, and the manufacturing company which held the monopoly would not permit them to be sold anywhere in Mexico. While the gamblers were considering their problem gold was discovered in California, and the rush to San Francisco began. Since the original town of Yerba Buena was Mexican, the game of *Monte* was already known, and as it offered quick action on large amounts, it grew steadily in popularity among the reckless miners and adventurers who soon made San Francisco the wildest and wickedest city on the continent. The syndicate of gamblers immediately took their stamped cards to the California settlement, and during the summer and winter of 1849 used them extensively and with great success there and in the gold fields. Several members of Clemmens' group retired from professional play with fortunes, but others returned to Mexico City in 1850, and ordered an additional two hundred gross of the stamped cards. These they took to San Francisco, but suspicion had been aroused, and the *Monte* dealers and players not only refused to use the syndicate's cards but for several years rejected all others that had been made in Mexico.

CHAPTER III

CRAPS

THE third of the gambling games which have achieved great popularity in the United States is Craps. Like Faro, it is of French origin, a Gallic simplification of the English Hazard, the oldest dice game of which any extensive knowledge remains. The *Oxford Dictionary* cites a mention of Hazard as early as 1300, and says that according to William of Tyre, who died in 1190, the game was invented during the Crusades by English soldiers at the siege of an Arabian castle called Hazart, or Asart. Various changes were made in Hazard in the course of centuries, but substantially it remained the same for some seven hundred years. Following is the method of play used in America in 1887, about the last year in which the game was included in any of the standard American *Hoyles*. It shows clearly the relationship of Hazard to Craps.

"The player, who takes the box and dice, throws a main— i. e., a chance for the company, which must exceed four, and not be more than nine, otherwise it is no main; he consequently must keep throwing till he produce five, six, seven, eight or nine; this done, he must throw his own chance, which may be any above three, and not exceeding ten; if he should throw two aces or trois ace (commonly termed crabs) he loses his stakes, let the company's chance, which we call the main, be what it may. If the main should be seven, and seven or eleven is thrown immediately after, it is called a nick, and the caster (the present player) wins out his stakes.

40

If eight be the main, and eight or twelve be thrown immediately after, it is also termed a nick, and the caster wins his
stakes. The caster throwing any other number for the main,
such as are admitted, and brings the same number immediately afterward, it is a nick, and he gains whatever stakes
he has made. Every three successive mains the caster wins
he pays to the box, or furnisher of the dice, the usual fee.

"The meaning of a stake or bet at this game differs from
any other. If anyone choose to lay some money with the
thrower or caster, he must place his cash upon the table,
within a circle destined for that purpose; when he has done
this, if the caster agrees to it, he knocks the box upon the table at the person's money with whom he intends to bet, or
mentions at whose money he throws, which is sufficient, and
he becomes responsible for whatever sum is down, unless the
staker calls to cover; in which case the caster is obliged to
stake also, else the bets are void. The person who bets with
the thrower may bar any throw which the caster may be going to cast, on condition neither of the dice is seen; but if one
die should be discovered, the caster must throw the other to
it, unless the throw is barred in proper time." [1]

Compared to modern Craps, Hazard, especially in its earlier
forms, was a complicated business, and for successful play the
caster required a thorough knowledge of the odds and proba-
bilities. "It is absolutely necessary," says *Hoyle's Games,* "to be a
perfect master of these odds, so as to have them quick as thought,
for the purpose of playing a prudent game, and to make use of
them by insuring bets, in what is termed hedging, in case the
chance happens to be not a likely one; for a good calculator se-

[1] *Hoyle's Games, the Standard Authority. A Complete Guide and Reliable
Authority upon All Games of Chance or Skill Now Played in the United
States, etc.;* New York, copyrighted 1887; page 434. For a slightly more com-
plicated method see the *Encyclopaedia Britannica.*

cures himself by taking the odds, and often stands part of his bet to a certainty." [2] Craps puts no such strain upon the mind, which is one of the reasons that it has always been primarily a game of the lower classes. Assuming that the dice are honest, an imbecile has as much chance to win at Craps as the most intelligent of men; he is required only to roll the dice away from him, grunt heavily, and utter one or more of the magic phrases, such as "Baby needs new shoes!" and "An eighter from Decatur!" which have been introduced into the game by the American Negro. Incidentally, it is interesting to note that in England before the beginning of the nineteenth century dice were commonly known as "the bones" and "the doctors," while casting them was "rolling the bones." Loaded dice were called "dispatches" and "dispatchers" then as now, and to prepare them thus for cheating was to "plumb the bones" or "load the doctors."

A great many of the technical terms used in Craps, including "nick" and "natural," are derived from Hazard, and so is the name of the game. A throw of two aces at Hazard has always been called a crab, and at various times in the long history of the game casts of three, seven, and twelve have likewise been known as crabs. To throw these numbers at Hazard was to crab, and to throw them at Craps, unless the seven is a natural, is to crap. Craps, originally spelled Creps, is simply a French corruption of the English Crabs, and is so defined in every French and English reference work, wherein the word is mentioned at all, to which the present author has had access. Webster's *New International Dictionary,* an American authority, says "(Cf. E. *crabs,* a throw of two aces at hazard, whence *F. crabs, craps,* a game of dice.)." The French *Dictionnaire Analogique de la Langue Française* says, *"de creps, on dit aussi Krabs";* [3] and the monumental *Dic-*

[2] *Ibid.,* page 435.
[3] Page 368.

tionnaire Général de la Langue Française lists both Creps and Craps, in each instance refers the reader to Crabs, and gives this explanation of the latter word:

> *"Crabs (Kraps) s.m. (Etym. Emprunté de l'angl.) Crabs, ambesas. S'écrit souvent craps et même creps. [1789 Kraps. Encycl. Méth.] Jeu de dés, d'origin anglaise on le point à amener, dit point de chance, est determiné pour la partie par celui qui sert."* [4]

The *Dictionnaire's* bracketed reference is to the famous *Encyclopédie Méthodique,* in 194 volumes, primarily the work of Denis Diderot and Jean le Rond d'Alembert, which was begun in 1782 and concluded in 1832. The first volume of the group headed *Mathématiques* is dated 1789. The third volume of this group, dated 1792, contains a long article, of four double-columned pages, about a dice game called *Krabs,* the method of play being virtually identical with that of Hazard. The source of *Krabs* is further indicated. The definition of the word at the beginning of the article is:

> *"C'est une sorte de jeu anglois, qu'on joue avec deux dés, qui produisent trente-cinq variations."* [5]

At the conclusion of the article is a *Vocabulaire explicatif des termes usités au Krabs,* which contains:

> *"Krabs. C'est tout à la fois le nom de jeu anglois dont il s'agit, & celui qu'on donne aux points de deux, de trois, de onze, & de douze, quand ils sont amener au premier jet."* [6]

It is thus certain that a variation of Hazard known as Krabs was played in France during the last quarter of the eighteenth

[4] Pages 581, 584, 589.
[5] Page 138.
[6] Page 142.

43

century, and in all probability it was so called for a long time before that. It is unlikely that a work such as the *Encyclopédie Méthodique* would have devoted four pages to a game unless it had been known in France for many years. Research in Paris would probably disclose the approximate time at which Krabs was simplified by the French commonalty and the word corrupted into Creps and Craps. Apparently this occurred a considerable time before the French Revolution; Taylor's history of playing cards, quoting indirectly from the memoirs of Barère and de Bachaumont, says that Creps was one of the chief games played at the gambling houses in the Palais Royal during the latter part of the eighteenth century, when Paris was in a fever of gambling comparable to that of the days of John Law.[7] In 1818, long before Craps was popular in the United States, the *Bibliothèque Historique* of Paris published an account of the profits and expenses of the nine gambling houses of Paris, listing the twenty tables in operation as follows: "7 tables of Trente et un, 9 ditto of Roulette, 1 ditto of Passe-dix, 1 ditto of Craps, 1 ditto of Hasard, 1 ditto of Biribi."[8] Curiously enough, there were no Faro banks, that game having become virtually obsolete in the country of its origin.

2

The year in which Craps made its appearance in the United States is unknown. Jonathan H. Green, writing in the spring of 1843, described Craps as "a game lately introduced into New Orleans,"[9] but it certainly was played in New Orleans long before that time. There is ample evidence that it was popular

---

[7] *The History of Playing Cards, with Anecdotes of Their Use in Conjuring, Fortune Telling, and Card-Sharping.* Edited by the late Rev. Ed. S. Taylor, B.A., and others; London, 1865; page 366.

[8] *The Gaming Calendar, to Which Are Added, Annals of Gaming,* by Seymour Harcourt, Esq.; London, 1820; page 160.

[9] *An Exposure of the Arts and Miseries of Gambling,* by J. H. Green; Cincinnati, 1843; page 88.

among the Creole aristocrats of New Orleans, and probably of Mobile as well, as early as the turn of the nineteenth century. The game might conceivably have been brought to this country by Louis Philippe and his brothers, the Duke de Montpensier and the Count de Beaujolais—they visited New Orleans in 1798 and were entertained at the mansion of Bernard de Marigny, head of a rich and powerful Louisiana family, whose great passion was gambling. De Marigny was the most distinguished votary of Craps during the period of the Louisiana Purchase, and is said to have lost enormous sums of money at the Crap-table. About 1804, after the Americans had begun to tear down the walls and fortifications of New Orleans, de Marigny laid out a portion of his princely estate, which lay outside the walls of the old city, in building lots. With a characteristic gesture he called one of the streets, an extension of the old Burgundy Street, *Rue de Craps,* in honor of the game at which he had been so unlucky. The street retained this name for a decade or so, when it was abandoned and the entire thoroughfare was called Burgundy Street.

A recently advanced theory of the origin of Craps [10] says that "the new dice game, Hazard," was introduced into New Orleans by de Marigny, and that the Americans, to whom a Creole or a Frenchman was Johnny Crapaud, called the game Crapauds, then Crapo, and finally Craps. In the opinion of the present author this theory is unsound for several reasons. In the first place, Hazard and Craps are not the same, and the former could scarcely have been a new game in 1800 when it had been played in Europe for some six hundred years. In the second place, Hazard was a common game throughout the English-speaking parts of the United States, and it is unlikely that the Americans, encountering it in New Orleans, would have given it a new name. Finally, de Marigny's hatred of the Americans was as

---

[10] By Edward Larocque Tinker, in *The Palingenesis of Craps,* 1933. Quoted in the New York *Herald Tribune,* July 26, 1937.

intense as his passion for gaming, and is commented upon by many New Orleans and Louisiana historians—Castellanos describes him as "the Saxon-hating Creole," [11] and Kendall says that "he was notoriously a hater of the Americans." [12] If the Americans had actually coined the word Craps, it is extremely unlikely that de Marigny would have bestowed it upon a street in his own subdivision.

Although Craps appears to have been widely played in New Orleans for some time before the Louisiana Purchase, the Americans who swarmed into the city after the Louisiana Purchase were more interested in Faro and Poker. Few, if any, of the early gambling houses provided Crap-tables, and interest in the game declined rapidly. It experienced a great revival in the late 1830's, as Green indicated when he said that it had been "lately introduced," and for a few years Craps was the most popular game in New Orleans, although the laws against gambling were strictly enforced during most of this period and the gambling houses were cheap joints in the river-front and underworld districts. Jonathan Green expressed the belief that Craps was "fully equal to Faro in its vile deception and ruinous effects," and predicted that "by the time this game is as old as Faro, as many persons will probably be ruined by it, unless some great and mighty check is given to its prevalence." He continued:

"All classes of people in New Orleans have abundant reason to cry, 'Down with the monster!' Ask many of the merchants, what has resulted to them in consequence of their clerks being decoyed to the Crap's table. Ask the wives of hundreds how their husbands have come home from such places of robbery. In short, numerous are the sufferings in

[11] *New Orleans As It Was*, by Henry C. Castellanos, A.M. LL.B.; New Orleans, 1895; pages 251–52.
[12] *History of New Orleans*, by John Smith Kendall, A.M.; Chicago and New York, 1922; Vol. I, page 125.

every class, from this source, except the keepers themselves, who revel and riot in the lowest depths of dissipation on their ill-gotten wealth." [13]

From New Orleans Craps spread gradually along the Gulf Coast and up the Mississippi River. Only occasionally was it played by the professional gamblers who worked the steamboats; they disliked the very feature which has made the game so popular in recent years—its quick action. Throughout the South Craps soon became a favorite with the Negroes, and the colored brethren contributed most of the picturesque jargon with which the earnest Crap-shooter accompanies each cast of the dice. But it was more than three-quarters of a century before the game was received in good gambling society in this country, and as late as 1887 it was not deemed worthy of inclusion in any of the standard *Hoyles*. Except among Negroes who had come up from the South, Craps was almost unknown in the East until the 1890's, although in the 1850's a game was played in Boston which was occasionally called by that name. More often, however, it was known as Props. This game was played with small oblong sea shells, the tops of which were sliced off. The hollows were then filled with red sealing-wax, and the player bet that he could throw the shells so that an odd or even number of red spots would show. A similar game is frequently played with two dice.

The great era of Crap-shooting in America began soon after the turn of the twentieth century; by 1914 the game had become so popular that R. F. Foster, in his *Complete Hoyle*, expressed the opinion that it was "rapidly replacing Faro as the gambling game of America." It was one of the principal games played by the soldiers of the American Expeditionary Force in France, and it had a great vogue in the 1920's at private parties, sup-

[13] *An Exposure of the Arts and Miseries of Gambling*, pages 88–90.

plementing bootleg liquor as an excitement-breeder. Since the World War a Crap-table has been standard equipment in virtually all American gambling houses.

Honestly played, Craps is one of the fairest of all games, since there is practically no percentage in favor either of the caster or the fader. But like all gambling games, Craps has been the medium of a great deal of cheating. Occasionally experts have appeared who, by the use of hard, soft and wheeling throws, and a bit of judicious palming, could make a pair of honest dice do everything but sit up and beg. But such skill is rarer than is commonly supposed. Since the earliest days of Hazard, and probably before, the sharper who was really out for blood has used loaded dice. And the art of "plumbing the bones" has kept pace with human progress in other fields. Today crooked dice can be, and are, so perfectly made as to defy detection by the most experienced Crap-shooter, yet the gambler who knows their peculiarities can beat the averages, which is enough to get the money.

CHAPTER IV

SMALL FRY

IN addition to Faro, Poker and Craps, a great many other games of chance, some of them downright swindles from start to finish, have enjoyed more or less lengthy periods of popularity in various sections of the United States, and have all contributed their parts in the development of American gambling. Perhaps the most important were Roulette, Loo, All-Fours, Seven-Up, Pitch, *Monte,* Keno, Three-Card Monte, Hearts, Thimble-Rig, Chuck-a-Luck, Banco, Euchre, *Ecarté,* Boston, Cassino, *Vingt et Un;* and Whist, called Whisk in earlier times, which survives in an altered and complicated form as modern Bridge. With the exception of Boston and Thimble-Rig, all of these games were either European importations or American variations of European games. Boston is said to have been invented by French Army officers during the Revolution, and was named in honor of the Massachusetts metropolis. For many years it was the favorite game of the gentry in New Orleans, and the medium of some very expensive gambling.

The French, of course, are responsible for Roulette, *Ecarté,* and *Vingt et Un,* and the first-named is today the best known and most popular gambling house game in the world. In all likelihood gaming places have won more money by means of the wheel than by any other method of play ever devised, for the percentage in favor of the bank is fixed and immutable, and it is virtually impossible for a Roulette wheel to lose in the long run. *Vingt et Un,* better known in England as Van John and in America as Twenty-one and Blackjack, is much older than either

Roulette or *Ecarté;* it was popular in Mobile and New Orleans early in the eighteenth century, and was not new even then. It is said to have been the favorite game of Napoleon. Only in recent years has it been called Blackjack. As late as 1915 that name was applied to a variation of Hearts. The latter game was first played in America, and is of fairly recent origin—the 1887 edition of *Hoyle's Games* says that it "has only been played in the United States during the past five years." This authority says that "Hearts is probably of German origin, although there is some slight resemblance between it and the Miseries,[1] played in Boston." Foster points out that the leading principle of Hearts, losing instead of winning tricks, is found in many old card games, among them Slobberhannes, Schwellen, Polignac and The Four Jacks.[2]

2

Loo and All-Fours, sometimes called All-Four, are English games of the seventeenth century, and are believed to have been the first card games ever played in the United States. They were popular in all of the English-speaking colonies long before the Revolution, and Loo was an especial favorite of the ladies for many years after the founding of the Republic. Sir Augustus Foster, Secretary of the British Legation during Jefferson's first administration, said in his description of Washington society that "Cards were a great resource of an evening. . . . Loo was the innocent diversion of the ladies, who, when they were looed,[3] pronounced the word in a very mincing manner." All-Fours, which got its name from the four points of high, low, jack and game, was one of the professional gambler's standbys until about

---

[1] The game of Boston, sometimes called the Miseries because of the frequent use of the French word *misère* in its technical terms.

[2] *Foster's Complete Hoyle,* page 349.

[3] A player was looed when he made a misdeal, and for various infractions of the rules of the game.

the time of the Civil War. There were a great many American variations of All-Fours, chief among them, from the viewpoint of the gambler, being Three-Up, Five-Up, Seven-Up or Old Sledge, and Pitch. All but the last-named are virtually obsolete now, but Pitch has retained its popularity and is still played all over the country. Cassino, or Casino, is a very old game, probably of Italian origin. It has always been surrounded, in the United States at least, by an aura of innocence and respectability, but before the Civil War it occupied an important place in the repertoire of the professional sharper; he frequently had recourse to it when a sucker shied away from the usual skull-duggery. Royal and Spade Cassino are American innovations, introduced since 1900.

3

Keno is the old English game of Lotto masquerading under a more explosive and exciting name. It was introduced into New Orleans about the time of the War with Mexico, and first appeared in New York about 1857. After the Civil War it spread to virtually every large city in the country, and became such a nuisance that many laws were passed against it. Except in a few under-cover dives, the game vanished during the anti-gambling crusades which swept over the United States during the late 1890's and the early 1900's. It was revived a few years ago in several Western states, and recently, under various names, has been introduced in many moving picture theaters, and even in churches, as a feature of pulling-in systems.

A purely percentage game with no betting, Keno was properly played with a large globe called a "Keno goose," ninety small ivory balls numbered from 1 to 90, and Lotto cards, which were sold to the players at whatever price might be fixed by the operator of the game, who was known as the "roller." In the cheaper houses the cards cost from ten to twenty-five cents each; in a

few of the higher-class resorts—notably a famous place run by
John Curry in New Orleans in 1888—they sold for as high as
a hundred dollars. When the Lotto cards had been distributed
the roller released the ivory balls one by one from the neck of the
goose. The number on each ball was called off as it appeared,
and any player finding such a number on his card covered it
with a button. The first thus to cover a row of five numbers called
"Keno!" and won all the money which had been paid for the
cards, minus the operator's take of from ten to fifteen per cent.
In most of the Keno houses the operator made certain that his
profit would be sufficient by cheating. This was a very simple
matter—the roller palmed the balls as they came from the goose
and substituted others which matched cards already handed out
to cappers.

4

Chuck-a-Luck is one of the oldest of dice games, and in England was originally called Sweat-Cloth. The derivation of the
latter name is uncertain, but it may have had some connection
with a system of play known in early times as "sweating." A
player was said to be "sweating" or "sweating out" if he proceeded cautiously, taking no risks and contenting himself with
whatever points might naturally fall to his share; in other words,
if he played them close to his vest. Sweat-cloth was known in the
United States at least as early as 1800, with the name generally
shortened to Sweat. About 1820 it began to be known in some
sections of the country as Chucker-Luck, and by the Civil War
this had begun to give way to Chuck-Luck and Chuck-a-Luck.
In recent years it has often been called Bird Cage. Originally, the
game was played with a layout containing spaces numbered
from 1 to 18, and a funnel, with horizontal bars across the center,
down which three dice were thrown to the table. In modern
Bird Cage a somewhat more complicated layout is used, and the

dice are whirled from one end to the other of a metal cage shaped like an hourglass and turning on an axle. The actual odds against the player range from 7 to 1 to 215 to 1, but few house games have ever paid better than from 6 to 1 to 180 to 1. Loaded dice have always been used by Chuck-a-Luck sharpers, and frequently the bars and bottom plates of the cage are magnetized. In the old days many operators were adept at sliding one die down the outside of the funnel while the others went tumbling between the bars.

<h2 style="text-align:center">5</h2>

Monte is an ancient Spanish game with a very large percentage against the player. It contains various elements also found in Faro, especially Short Faro, and may have sprung from or been influenced by the same source. In playing *Monte* a Spanish pack of forty cards, with no eights, nines or tens, was used, although sometimes only the nines and tens were discarded and a forty-four card pack put into the game. Before play began the money staked by the bank was piled upon the table, usually in silver dollars. This coin, incidentally, is still used extensively instead of chips in border gambling houses. After the shuffle and cut the *Monte* dealer held the pack face downward, drew off the two bottom cards and placed them on the table face upward. This was called the "bottom layout." Then from the top he drew two cards for the "top layout." The pack was now turned face upward, and the card exposed was the "gate." If it matched in denomination a card in either layout, the dealer paid all bets which had been made on that layout. In some establishments it was necessary only to match the suit, in which case bets were paid only on the matching card, and not on the whole layout. In some places, also, the pack was reversed after the first exposure of the "game," and new layouts were drawn off and a new "gate" shown, the old ones being discarded. In others, the pack remained face upward and the dealer continued to draw from it as in Faro.

This simple but effective means of enriching a gambling-house keeper was a favorite game in Cuba and Mexico for generations, and is still popular in many Spanish-speaking countries. It was introduced into the Southern and Southwestern states by Mexican gamblers at least a hundred years ago, and was carried into other parts of the United States by the American sharpers who had followed the Army into Mexico in 1846 and 1847. *Monte* was never played to any great extent in the North and East, however; it achieved its greatest popularity in El Paso and other Texas towns along the Rio Grande, and in San Francisco and the California and Colorado gold fields, where the Mexican influence was strong.

6

Three-Card Monte was a Mexican invention, and a misnomer if ever there was one, for it had no more actual relationship to *Monte* than to Old Maid. The operator of the game, commonly called a "thrower," took three playing cards, known in the vernacular as "the tickets," slightly bent them length-wise for easier handling, and showed one, usually an ace or a queen, to the players. He then made a few passes and threw the cards face downward upon a flat surface, inviting his victims to bet which was the one they had seen. Honestly thrown, the game would have been a fair guessing contest if the thrower had paid two to one, but since he never offered better than even, and had no intention of paying anything, the player was always betting against himself. Moreover, it is doubtful if any of the American sharpers who specialized in Three-Card Monte ever made an honest throw; in their hands the game was one of the most effective of all the swindles with which they preyed upon the

From an old print

THE BANCO SKIN

Great American Sucker. Most of the *Monte* tricksters were accompanied by from one to five confederates, who worked up interest in the game and brought the victims to the block. One of the cappers then started an argument with the thrower, and while the latter's attention was distracted another marked the chosen card by turning down a corner or making a tiny spot on the back. This was shown to the sucker, who was naturally eager to bet upon what appeared to be a sure thing. But in making his passes the thrower erased the mark and repeated it on one of the losing cards. Sounds a bit silly, but it worked nine times out of ten.

Three-Card Monte first appeared in the United States during the early 1830's, when it was introduced into New Orleans from Texas, then a part of Mexico. One of the early throwers was a Louisianian named Phillips, whose career was abruptly halted by the New Orleans police in 1837, when he was sent to prison for two years for fleecing a countryman out of $700. This summary action frightened the Monte throwers out of New Orleans, and that city was free of them for some ten years. But they soon appeared elsewhere. Although they never gained much of a foothold in the East, from about 1845 to the early 1880's a horde of these rascals, shrewd, slick, glib and dexterous, crowded the steamboats and the railroad trains and swarmed in the towns of the South and West. "In the early days of California," wrote John O'Connor, "the country was overrun with three-card Monte throwers and their confederates. . . . These light fingered gentry could be found plying their calling in every city and mining camp of any importance in the state. In the streets of San Francisco and Sacramento, numbers of them might be seen any day seated on the sidewalks throwing their cards, as well as in every vile den with which those cities then abounded." [4] A curious bit of Three-Card Monte history is the

---

[4] *Wanderings of a Vagabond,* page 437.

55

fact that in April, 1860, the Legislative Council of Denver legalized what a Colorado historian has described as "this nefarious business." But one member of the Council resigned in protest, and honest residents raised such an uproar that the ordinance was soon repealed.

7

Banco fell into the same category as Three-Card Monte; it was entirely in the hands of sharpers, and was never used for any other purpose than the despoliation of suckers. As Phil Farley, a famous New York detective, wrote in 1875, it was "the means by which a whole host of sharpers prey upon unsuspecting visitors to large cities." Banco was played with eight dice or specially prepared cards numbered 1 to 8, and a layout with from fourteen to fifty-four spaces, varying at different stages of the game's development. On each space was a number, but it was only pinned on or glued lightly, and could be removed at a second's notice. The dice were thrown, or the cards drawn from a shuffled pack, the total of the numbers shown determining whether the player won or lost. Some of the numbers on the layout called for money prizes, others were called "conditionals," and still others were embellished by stars, which signified that they lost. Two of the numbers were covered by metal cups or hoods, and were called "Banco." If a player hit a conditional he was required to put up an amount equal to that already owed him by the bank, and draw or throw again. At this stage of the game he could lose only by throwing "Banco," and curiously enough he always did so, for Banco was not uncovered until the last throw, and a little sleight-of-hand made the number under the hood the same as the total of the dice or cards. The usual *modus operandi* was to permit the sucker to win a few money prizes, then give him a conditional, and finally to demolish him with Banco.

Although this so called gambling game, under its original name of Eight-Dice Cloth, was played in England during the eighteenth century, it was unknown in the United States until about 1855, when it was introduced into San Francisco by a crooked gambler who made various changes in the method of play and christened it Banco. After a few years this was corrupted into Bunco, sometimes spelled Bunko, and in time Bunco came to be a general term applied to all swindling and confidence games, while the sharpers who practiced them were called Bunco men. These expressions are still in use, although the game from which they derived has not been heard of in America for almost half a century.

The original American Banco dealer was expelled from San Francisco in 1856 by the second Vigilance Committee, and for several years thereafter operated with more or less success in St. Louis, Cincinnati and other towns along the Ohio and Mississippi Rivers. Sometime in the late 1860's he opened his game in New York, and was so successful that Banco was at once adopted by a multitude of sharpers. By 1870 Banco games were being operated in virtually every large city in the country, and the swindle retained its popularity among the tricksters until the early 1890's, after which it seems to have declined rapidly. The game was in full growth in New York during the 1870's and the early 1880's, when scores of Banco Skins, as the police called the games, were scattered throughout the city. Some were housed in elaborate quarters. "These offices," wrote Detective Farley, "are furnished with all the appointments of first-class commercial houses, and have an air of substantial value about them, that immediately puts to flight any suspicion that may come into the minds of visitors. All the furniture, desks, maps, books, are of the very best material, and selected and disposed to the very best advantage. There is a private room, a consulting room, a waiting room, and a general office. In the 'best houses' glass partitions and glass doors abound, and an impression is made on the mind of the 'customer' that large wealth is certainly at the back of the institution." [5]

The Banco establishments employed large numbers of steerers and ropers-in—one Banco game on Fulton Street in 1879 had ten, all disguised as countrymen and small-town merchants—and on the success of the steering system depended the prosperity of the game. Usually the steerers worked in pairs, a Feeler and a Catcher. The Feeler scraped acquaintance with a likely-looking prospect, and learned where the victim was from and as much as possible about his financial condition. Then the Catcher appeared, and utilizing the information obtained by the Feeler, assiduously cultivated the lonely stranger. When the friendship had ripened sufficiently, the Catcher contrived an excuse to take the victim to the Banco office. Once there, the gull had little or no chance of escaping with his money.

To understand how anyone could succumb to such an obvious brace game it is necessary to remember that before the telephone, the radio, and widely circulated magazines and newspapers, the average American countryman and small-town resident was a real greenhorn, made to order for the city slicker. For that matter, many supposedly intelligent men were victimized by shrewd Banco operators. Charles Francis Adams, a famous American diplomat, lost $7,000 in 1882 playing Banco in Boston with Johnny Norton and Red Jimmy Fitzgerald; and in that same year the English author, Oscar Wilde, in the United States on a lecture tour, was caught for several thousand dollars by Hungry Joe Lewis, a cadaverous crook who always had a well-filled wallet but never, apparently, enough to eat. Adams complained to the Boston police, and although Norton escaped, Fitz-

[5] *Criminals of America; or, Tales of the Lives of Thieves, Enabling Every One to Be His Own Detective,* by Phil Farley, Detective; New York, 1876; page 274.

gerald was convicted of fraud and sentenced to five years in the state penitentiary at Charlestown. Wilde stopped payment on a check which he had given Lewis, but declined to prosecute, and Hungry Joe continued to fleece the unwary until 1888, when a Baltimore judge sent him to prison for eight years for swindling a Baltimorean out of $5,000. Before this setback occurred Hungry Joe was the foremost Banco sharper in America; according to Inspector Thomas Byrnes of the New York police he had trimmed more "flats" than any five of his contemporaries. Hungry Joe sometimes worked alone, but more often in partnership with Tom O'Brien, after Lewis' incarceration called King of the Bunco Men, and Peter Lake, better known as Grand Central Pete. O'Brien was the last of the really important Banco swindlers; he continued to operate with great success until 1895, when he murdered Reed Waddell, his associate and the originator of the gold-brick swindle. The crime was committed in Paris, and O'Brien ended his days in a French prison.

8

Thimble-Rig, which is none other than that venerable cheat the Shell-game, is one of the few games of chance which are still played exactly as when they originated. Today, as a hundred years ago, the Thimble-Rigger uses a dried pea or a little rubber ball, and three cup-shaped receptacles—in the early days of the game he favored three ordinary thimbles, but in recent years walnut shells or metal cups have been principally used. The object of the game, if there is anybody in the world who doesn't know it, is for the player to guess which of the shells or cups the elusive little pea is under after the Thimble-Rigger has moved them about a bit. Ten times out of ten, unless the bet was a come-on, it is between two of the Thimble-Rigger's fingers, or has been shifted by a confederate during the excitement of betting. The whole business is another of the swindles which sound a trifle implausible to modern ears, but it was the main reliance of thousands of sharpers for many years, and properly handled is still a good killer at country fairs and carnivals.

The Thimble-Rig is also the only gambling game of any consequence for which a purely American ancestry may be claimed, although as a matter of fact it is essentially the same as the Mexican Three-Card Monte. According to Jonathan H. Green, Thimble-Rig was invented by a certain Dr. Bennett of Shreveport, La., a famous professional gambler of the early days who was commonly believed to have made a fortune playing the game on the Red and Mississippi River steamboats, where he was known as King of the Thimbles and the Napoleon of the Thimble-Riggers. The Doctor and a group of his disciples, in the early 1840's, created such havoc among the bucolic sports of Georgia, Alabama, Tennessee and Mississippi that stringent laws were passed in those states specifically prohibiting the game.

Just when Dr. Bennett gave Thimble-Rig to a waiting world of sharpers and suckers is unknown, but it was probably a few years before 1800, for when he was seventy years old, about 1845, he said that the game had been his principal source of income since boyhood. At seventy the King of the Thimbles was a kindly-appearing old gentleman, with snow white hair and a disarming trick of peering over his spectacles and saying, "Sometimes, my boy, I am very severe, then again not quite so sly." But he was still the most expert Thimble-Rigger in the business, and unless there were heroes whose glories have remained unsung, his equal did not appear until the notorious Soapy Smith, of Denver and Klondike fame, came along in the 1890's. J. H. Johnson, author of an *exposé* of gambling published in 1927, believed that Soapy was the king-pin of them all. "Soapy Smith," he wrote, "was without a question the one and only con man who cleaned up with this. He took them as fast as they laid their money on the layout. His boosters dragged the sucker in and Soapy put the axe to them, where Nellie wore the beads. . . . Soapy Smith was beyond doubt the slipperiest of the slippery with his line of bull con and the simple little walnut shell game." [6]

9

The only form of solitaire ever played in an American gambling house was a game in which the bank sold a pack of cards for fifty-two dollars, and paid the player five dollars for each pip visible on the ace pile when the game had ended, kings being rated at thirteen, queens at twelve, and jacks at eleven. This game had a brief vogue in a few New York resorts around 1905 and 1906, and is still the most widely played of all solitaire games, though not for money. Its proper name is either Canfield or Klondike, or both; it was originally copyrighted as Canfield, and is called Canfield by almost everyone who plays it today, but it is described as Klondike in all of the *Hoyle's Games* and *Official Rules of Card Games* which have been published since 1912. It is popularly supposed to have been devised by Richard Canfield, but as a matter of fact that famous gambler never invented it, and there is no record that he ever played it or that it was ever used in any of his gambling houses.

The present author made a diligent effort to trace the origin of the game, but ran into a curious maze of confusion, complicated by the fact that there was also a dice game known as Klondike, which was played in virtually all of the second-class houses in New York around 1900. Apparently the first time the card game appeared in print as Canfield was in 1908, when it was published in *Dick's Games of Patience or Solitaire,* edited

[6] *The Open Book; Cards, Dice, Punch Boards, Hold Outs, Schemes and Devices, Secrets of the Gambler All Exposed in Words of Fire,* by J. H. Johnson; Kansas City, 1927; page 84.

by Harris B. Dick and issued in New York by Dick & Fitzgerald. Dick's description of the game carried the line, "Copyright 1908 by Dick & Fitzgerald," and this comment: "This game has attained a certain degree of notoriety as having been employed as a game of chance." In this book there is no mention of Klondike. But in *Hoyle's Games, Autograph Edition,* copyright 1907 by The McClure Company and in 1913 and 1914 by A. L. Burt Company, Canfield is not mentioned, and two versions of Klondike are given, with the significant notation: "There are several ways of playing this game." One version, called Seven-Card Klondike, is the game that Harris B. Dick described and copyrighted as Canfield. The other, called Klondike, is a different game, but with enough points of similarity to indicate that it sprang from the same source as Seven-Card Klondike.

In *Lady Cadogan's Illustrated Games of Solitaire or Patience,* copyright 1914 and published in Philadelphia by David McKay, the game which Dick called Canfield is described as Canfield *or* Klondike. In his *Complete Hoyle, an Encyclopedia of Games,* a monumental work copyright in 1914 and published in October of that year by Frederick A. Stokes Company of New York, R. F. Foster describes as Klondike the game which Harris B. Dick had copyrighted as Canfield, and says that "this game is sometimes mistakenly called Canfield." The game which *Hoyle's Games, Autograph Edition,* published as Klondike also appears in Foster's book, but is called Canfield, with the comment that "this form of solitaire is often confused with Klondike." The 1913 edition of the *Official Rules of Card Games,* which has been published every year or two since 1887 by the United States Playing Card Company of Cincinnati, described the Harris B. Dick game and called it Canfield *or* Klondike. Subsequent editions, however, including that of 1937, followed Foster. Of forty or fifty other books on card games which were consulted, some described the Harris Dick game as Canfield, some called it Klondike, and some gave two games, as Foster had done.

One conclusion which may be drawn from the Canfield-Klondike situation is that there were two versions of Klondike, and that Harris B. Dick took advantage of Richard Canfield's notoriety, chose the version which was being played in the gambling houses, and called it Canfield. Another conclusion, possibly more logical, is that the whole thing is a mess.

10

Until Anthony Comstock went on the rampage in the late 1870's and started a crusade which eventually resulted in the United States Postal Laws being fitted with a set of sharp teeth, the professional gambler bought his stamped and marked cards, crooked dealing boxes, loaded dice, and other apparatus for cheating, all known by the generic name of "Advantage Tools," from manufacturers and dealers who advertised openly in the newspapers and by circulars sent through the mails without concealment. Some maintained staffs of traveling salesmen, and with samples and order books these energetic drummers called on the trade in the larger cities and on the rivers. One of the Eastern dealers had a form letter which was sent to every person seeking information regarding prices and equipment:

"Dear Sir:—In reply to yours, there is only one sure way to win at cards, etc., and that is to get Tools to work with and then to use them with discretion, which is the secret of all Gambling and the way that all Gamblers make their money."

Most of the factories and salesrooms which supplied "Advantage Tools" were located in New York, New Orleans and

Chicago. One of the best known of these dealers was E. N. Grandine, who was in business for many years before and after the Civil War at No. 41 Liberty Street, New York. Grandine's circular was very elaborate. The first page was given over to a large picture of the American Eagle, Grandine's name and address, and the announcement that he was a "Manufacturer and Dealer in Advantage and Marked-Back Playing Cards, by which you can tell the size and suit, by the Back as well as the Face." Below the Eagle was a bit of verse:

> He either fears his fate too much,
>   Or his deserts are small,
> Who dare not put it to the touch,
>   And win or lose it all.

A few extracts from Grandine's circular follow:

EVERY STYLE OF BACK CONSTANTLY ON HAND

These cards are an exact imitation of the fair Playing Cards in use, and are adapted for Bluff or Poker, Seven-Up, Forty-five, Euchre, Cribbage, *Vingt et Un,* or Twenty-one, Loo, and all other games of cards, where knowing just what your opponent holds in his hand would enable you to win. Square and marked Cards cut to order for Stocking Hands, for every game. Also Faro-boxes, Lay-outs, and Tools. Roulette-wheels, Keno-sets, Ivory Goods, Eight and Ten Dice . . . and every variety of Sporting Implement. My cards are now issued on a quality of board, which, though in exact imitation of the Square Cards of the same pattern, is, in toughness and elasticity, but little inferior to a Faro Dealing Card, and unequaled by anything to be obtained in this country in the way of Marked Cards. I have the greatest variety of styles, and have them *perfect,* both in mark and finish.

SMALL FRY

Faro Boxes, Tools, and all other goods herein advertised, are of the very best quality, and parties wishing goods for practical use, will do well to favor me with their order. . . . Full and explicit directions for reading and using will be sent with All Cards and Tools. Should you wish for Cards, state the style of back as per sample-book accompanying, and they will be forwarded to *any* address.

PRICE LIST OF MARKED CARDS

Per pack, any style on sample sheet, postpaid by mail .. $ 1.25
One dozen by express for 10.00

DEALING, SQUARE AND ADVANTAGE CARDS

	Per pack	Per doz.
Hart's Linen Eagle Faro Cards, squared for dealing	$1.50	$15.00
The same cut in any form, either wedges, rounds, and straight, or end rounds	3.00	30.00
Spanish Monte cards	.75	6.00
Ordinary Cards, cut for strippers, brief, or any style	1.25	9.00
Three-Card Monte Tickets	1.00	8.00
Flag-backs, marked, per pack	1.50	12.00

Any of the above cut for strippers, 50 cents per pack extra, or $3 per dozen.

FARO BOXES AND TOOLS

Square Dealing Faro Box, German Silver, extra heavy silver plate	$25.00
Two-Card Faro Box, top sight tell, improved lever, best in use	60.00
Back up, second card box, for Red and Black	35.00
Trimming Shears, double edged cutter	35.00
Knife, small	20.00
Knife, large	50.00
Stripper Plates, to use with knife, set	5.00

65

DICE, ETC.

Set Loaded Dice, best Ivory, 9 Dice, 3 high, 3 low,
   3 Square; warranted sure, exact imitation of common
   Dice .... $ 5.00
Set 3 High or Low Dice 2.50
Three Square, to match 1.00
Eight-sided Top Dice, that you can spin high and low,
   and force your opponent to spin as you desire 2.50

SPECIALTIES

The Sleeve Machine, for holding out, or playing extra cards, the most perfect piece of mechanism ever invented for this purpose. This article works in the coat-sleeve noiselessly, admits of holding the hands in the most natural manner, requires no false movements, and weighs about four ounces. This article is manufactured by no other firm in this country, and is guaranteed to be all it is advertised. Price, with full directions for use, $35.00.

Right and Left Snap Roulette Wheel, small, for high or low numbers, 6 inch center. Price $20.00.

The Breastworks, or "vest hold-out," concealed in vest front, and worked by the foot with spiral coils and catgut. Price $25.00.

The "Bug," a contrivance for playing an extra card, utterly defying detection, price $1.00.

These bargains were offered by other dealers in New York and Chicago:

ADVANTAGE, OR MARKED PLAYING CARDS

By which you can tell the color, suit and size, as well by the backs as by the faces. They are an exact imitation of the fair playing cards in common use, and are adapted for any game, where it would be impossible for your opponent to

66

win, as you would know just what he had in his hand and could act accordingly. These cards can be learned in an hour with the instructions which are sent with each pack, so that you can tell every card the instant you see it, both size and suit. N.B. Be sure and ask for the Key or Directions, as without them the cards would be of no use to you unless you are a first-class professional gambler.

Cutter, for cutting round corners on cards .... $ 20.00
Trimming Plates, will cut any style cards 8.00
Dealing boxes, lever movement .... $35.00 to 60.00
    "   " End, or Needle Movement .... $60.00 to 100.00
    "   " Sand Tell .... $13.00, $15.00 to 18.00
Ivory dice, for top and bottom, three fair, with ringer .. .80
    "   " double, 3 high, 3 low, 3 fair, with box 2.00
    "   " LOADED, 3 high, 3 low, 3 fair, with box 5.00
Vest Hold Out, with late improvements 10.00
Table Hold Out, something new, works with knee 10.00
Sleeve Hold Out, arm pressure 25.00
Sleeve Hold Out, Keplinger's Patent 50.00
Nail Pricks, for finger nails .... .50
Shiner, for reading cards dealt opponents 1.00
Shiner, in half dollar 2.00

CRAP DICE

In reference to dice, loaded dice come in sets of 9,—3 High, 3 Low, and 3 Fair to match. But loaded dice, generally speaking, are not strong enough for craps, as it is impossible to load dice so as to make them come up any particular number every time; the best that can possibly be done is to make them come up about every other time in an average. They are generally used to beat Sweat or to throw High or Low, or to bet on averages, or in various other ways, too numerous to mention, to get the money. The best way to fix dice for craps is to have one dice with two aces, 2 fives and 2 sixes on, and one with 2 threes, 2 fours and 2 fives on. With this pair of dice it is impossible to throw 7, and there is only one possible chance to throw eleven. But, if you want dice to throw 7 or 11 sure, the only way we know of is to have one pair thus: one dice with all sixes and one with all fives to throw eleven; and one with all fours and one with all threes on to throw seven; or, one with all fives, one with all deuces on to throw seven.

STRIPPERS

The benefit of these cards can be estimated only in one way, and that is: How much money has your opponent got? For you are certain to get it, whether it is $10 or $10,000; the heavier the stakes the sooner you will break him, and he never knows what hurt him. . . . In sending for Strippers be sure and state what game you wish to play with them, so that I can send you cards especially adapted for that game.

THE SPY

This simple and valuable little Advantage Tool, with which you can read each card as it leaves the pack, has now reached *Perfection,* as far as we are concerned, as we have steadily improved upon it until we can improve no further. The *Reflector,* which is convex, is imported direct from France, and is made *specially* for this purpose. It can be used with perfect safety either on the table or on the knee, and should the suspicion of any of the players be aroused, it can be removed in an instant; your hand completely covers it, as it is only the size of a silver half dollar, and you can hold a half dozen of them without their being seen; you are at perfect liberty with your hands all the time, and if you wish you can be using the *Bug* or *Strippers,* or any other advantage implement with your hands at the same time, without

68

interfering with the *Spy* in the least, but everything else would be unnecessary, as the *Spy* is to the ordinary player advantage enough in itself.

THE POKER RING

An ingenious little contrivance for Marking the cards while playing, in a perfectly safe and systematic manner, so that in half an hour you can tell each card as well by the back as by the face. Although it is not as yet generally known, it is now in use by a few of the oldest and best professional players in the country. Anybody can use it at once. For second dealing they are invaluable, and no second dealer should be without one for a day. But comment is unnecessary, as anyone understanding second dealing will see in an instant its value, the moment the subject is brought to his mind.

THE BUG

This is an entirely new invention, for the purpose of "holding out" any number of cards, *and it will do it*. It is very simple in its construction, easy to operate, and any person who knows that two and two are four can use it. It can be carried in the vest pocket all the time, is always ready for use, and not liable to get out of order, but should it do so any watchmaker can put it in order for a trifle, as the whole expense of manufacture is only about fifty cents. "Then why ask $3.00 for it?" you may say. For this reason— That one is all you will ever want to buy, as they do not wear out like cards. Also, after seeing it you can get one made as well as I can, and make them for your friends and sell them to all the sporting men in your vicinity, thereby injuring my trade and I get nothing for my invention; and you will wonder that the thing was never thought of before. With it you can "hold out" one or twenty cards, shift and make up your hand to suit, and your hands and person are at perfect liberty all the time. Your opponent may look in your lap and up your sleeve, but there is nothing to be seen! After having used it once you would not be without it for *any* price. . . .

MARKED BACK BARCELONA MONTE CARDS

The want of this article has long been felt by the sporting men on the Pacific Coast and South and Western States and Territories. But of the thousands of gamblers who could win barrels of money with them, none have been willing to pay the price for them or the first cost of getting up plates, engraving, printing, etc. Therefore none have been made for the past fifteen years; and anyone that deals the game or plays it, or knows anything about the game, will see at once the value of a pack of cards with which they tap a game for all it is worth, in a minute, and anyone that will not pay for the privilege of a sure thing to break a Monte game had better go to work on the railroad, for he can make more money there than he can gambling. Or any *Great American Smart Dealer* that will not pay to protect his game from being broke, had better go with the other men on the railroad, as he is not qualified to deal his or any other man's money away, for with these cards the dealer can always tell exactly where three or four cards lay in the pack all the time, and act accordingly, and such a percentage with the dealer is worth half a dozen packs of cards each deal. Some gamblers seem to forget, or never to have known, that there is only one way to gamble successfully, and that is to *get Tools to gamble with.*

70

TO POKER AND SHORT CARD PLAYERS—VEST HOLD OUT

Gents: I am now prepared to furnish you with the latest improved Vest Holdout, which for simplicity, finish and durability is Par Excellence. It will not break or get out of order, anybody can use it, it works smooth and noiseless, and is as perfect as it can be made after many years of careful study. It does away entirely with the old-fashioned and clumsy Breast Plate, it is now an article of merit and Value received for the money 10 times over, anybody can use it successfully with very little practice without fear of Detection for months in any game where it has not been previously exposed. . . . The only Holdout I now make is the Vest Holdout which I occasionally use myself as opportunity offers, and I know it is practical and with an ordinary amount of caution it can be used in 8 out of 10 of all the Gambler's Games in the country, any old Poker player knows that if he can win 5 or 6 of the Big Pools during the night and play on his judgment or on the square during the remainder of the night and hold his own he is bound to get all the money in time. This is the proper way to use the Vest Holdout and if used on this principle any ordinary Poker player with a moderate amount of discretion can use it month after month in 9 out of every 10 Poker Games in the country, it is a fine Invention and anyone that plays cards for a living needs it more than they do snide Jewelry or Flashy Clothes with holes in their pockets instead of Dollars. There is but *one* way to gamble successfully, and that is to *get Tools to work with and have the best of every Game you get into.*

CHAPTER V

THE LOTTERY

GAMBLING with cards and dice, even in those parts of the United States where games of chance were occasionally legalized, has always been regarded with great disfavor by the respectable elements of the population, and the men who engaged in it, especially the professionals, have in general been looked upon as lost souls destined for the brimstone pit. The only method of gambling that ever won the approval of all classes in this country was the Lottery; from early colonial days throughout the first quarter of the nineteenth century it was as much an established feature of life in America as it was in Europe. During all this long period no stigma attached to any phase of the business. Everybody gambled in the Lottery, and prominent men ran the ticket offices and lent their names and influence to the schemes—Benjamin Franklin was one of the organizers of a Lottery in Philadelphia in 1746, and as late as 1820 the largest Lottery shop in New York was owned by Aaron Clark, who was later elected mayor of the city. Clergymen as well as the most besotted of bar flies bought tickets, and were equally grateful if they won. A few years before his death in 1764 the Rev. Samuel Seabury, father of the famous Bishop Seabury, wrote in his journal:

"The ticket No. 5866 in the Light House and Public Lottery of New York, drew in my favor, by the blessing of Almighty God, 500 pounds sterling, of which I received 425 pounds, there being a deduction of fifteen per cent; for

which I now record to my posterity my thanks and praise to
Almighty God, the giver of all good gifts." [1]

The first Lotteries drawn in America were private enterprises,
but although very popular and apparently honestly conducted,
they were suppressed everywhere before the middle of the eighteenth century, principally for reasons similar to those given by
the Rhode Island Legislature in 1733—that by these "unlawful
games, called Lotteries, many people have been led into a foolish
expense of money." A few years later, however, such consider-
ations seem no longer to have applied, for by 1760 Lotteries had
been revived in all of the colonies. Thenceforth they were operated by municipalities, churches, public utility and development
companies, and educational institutions. They became an inte-
gral part of public financing, and were taken into account when
budgets were considered. The actual management of the drawings, and the sale of tickets, remained for the most part in the
hands of private contractors, promoters and agents, a fact which
eventually had much to do with the collapse of the whole system.
In most of the colonies, and later the states, the sale of tickets
originating elsewhere was forbidden by statute, but these laws
were generally ignored. In New York, Boston, Philadelphia and
other large cities, it was always possible to purchase tickets for
any Lottery drawn in America.

From the proceeds of this wholesale gambling churches were
built, colleges founded and endowed; and roads, bridges, canals
and other public works constructed. Some of the finest of colonial
religious edifices, many of which are still standing, owe their
existence to Lotteries, among them the Market Square Presby-
terian Church of Harrisburg, Pa., and the First Baptist Church
of Providence, R.I., where the students of Brown University

---

[1] *Magazine of History with Notes & Queries,* February–June, 1907; Articles
by A. Franklin Ross on "The History of Lotteries in New York."

hold their commencement exercises. The latter church, first occupied in May, 1775, was erected with 2,000 pounds obtained through a Lottery granted in 1774 by the General Assembly of Rhode Island. Another of that state's historic landmarks benefited by a Lottery in 1762, when funds were thus raised to build a steeple on St. John's Episcopal Church, also in Providence. On December 6, 1746, the government of the colony of New York authorized a Lottery to raise 2,250 pounds "for the advancement of Learning and towards the Founding of a College," and that was the beginning of Columbia University. Many other famous schools now among the richest in the country, including Harvard, Yale, Dartmouth, and Williams, were likewise helped by Lotteries in the early years of their existence. Harvard appears to have been more interested in this method of financing than any of the others. In 1772 and 1774 the Massachusetts university conducted Lotteries which raised $18,400 for the building of Stoughton Hall, and the college itself bought 2,000 tickets and drew a $10,000 prize. Another Harvard Lottery in 1794 sold 25,000 tickets at $5 each, and a third, in 1805, realized $29,000, which was applied to the construction of Holworthy Hall.

Two of the most unusual Lotteries in American history were never drawn, although in each instance all arrangements were made and the tickets placed on sale. In 1776 the Continental Congress authorized a Lottery to raise $10,000,000, with four classes of tickets from $10 to $40, and $5,000,000 in prizes ranging from $20 to $50,000. The drawing was postponed several times because of the difficulties in selling so many tickets to a country torn by war, and finally the scheme was abandoned. In March, 1826, the Virginia Legislature authorized Thomas Jefferson, who was eighty-three years old, owed $80,000 and faced the prospect of leaving his family in poverty, to dispose of his real estate by Lottery. The condition was imposed that he should not realize from any piece of property an amount greater than its

Literature Lottery

BY AUTHORITY OF THE STATE OF KENTUCKY

Class No. **205** Com Nos **10 48 75**

This Ticket will entitle the holder to one QUARTER of such Prize as may be drawn to its Numbers, if demanded within twelve months after the Drawing: Subject to a deduction of Fifteen per cent.: Payable forty days after the Drawing.

For A. BASSFORD & CO, Managers.

Covington, 1841. QUARTER.

A KENTUCKY LOTTERY TICKET OF 1841

A LOTTERY WHEEL OF THE 1830's

fair value as determined by an official appraisal. A supervisory committee was appointed by the Legislature, but the actual management of the Lottery was entrusted to J. B. Yates and A. McIntyre, of New York, agents and promoters who handled many of the big drawings of the period.

Tickets for the Jefferson Lottery were ready for distribution a few weeks after the act of authorization had passed the Virginia Legislature, but the sale was postponed at the request of a group of Jefferson's friends, headed by Mayor Philip Hone of New York, who relieved the great man's immediate necessities with a gift of $16,500. Of this amount, $8,500 was raised in New York, $5,000 in Philadelphia, and $3,000 in Baltimore. Mayor Hone also attempted to start a movement for the purchase of the entire Lottery and the public destruction of the tickets in New York, but the plan fell through when Jefferson died on July 4, 1826. Arrangements for the Lottery were then completed by Yates & McIntyre, and the details were thus announced in *Niles' Weekly Register,* of Baltimore, on July 29, 1826:

"Messrs. Yates and McIntyre, the agents of the managers of this Lottery, have laid before the public the scheme, which consists of only three prizes, viz.: one prize, the Monticello estate, valued by appraisers, under oath, at $74,000; one do. the Shadwell mills, $30,000; one do. the Albemarle estate, $11,500—total $115,500. There are 11,480 tickets, at $10 each. It is contemplated to draw the Lottery the latter end of October next. . . . The following is the address of Messrs. Yates and McIntyre, on offering the scheme to the public:—

" 'The agents . . . feel a confidence that they [the tickets] will be immediately purchased up; and the only child of the late Mr. Jefferson, and her family, be relieved from the painful consequences which must inevitably and speedily follow, if the debts are not discharged. The agents have engaged to prepare the tickets and to conduct the Jefferson Lottery throughout, without compensation for services or expenses. . . . The funds for these tickets shall be kept sacred and distinct from all other funds, and the managers be advised from time to time to draw them, as they accumulate, to answer the objects of the grant. . . . It cannot for a moment be supposed that any will be found so heartless as to say, that since Mr. Jefferson is dead, they feel themselves under no obligations to his descendants.' "

The Lottery probably would have sold out quickly during Jefferson's lifetime, but as one of his biographers said, "the feelings which at first would have made it salable had now died away." It soon became evident that the Lottery would be a failure, and the scheme was abandoned. Jefferson's personal property was sold in 1827 and 1828, and the real estate in 1829. The proceeds of these sales, together with money contributed by Jefferson's son-in-law and executor, Thomas Mann Randolph, before the latter's death in 1828, satisfied the creditors, but Jefferson's daughter was penniless until the Legislatures of Virginia and South Carolina each voted her a gift of $10,000. In 1923, after having passed through the hands of various owners, Monticello was acquired by the Thomas Jefferson Memorial Foundation, and is now preserved as a national memorial.

2

Lotteries multiplied with great rapidity after the Revolution, when money for public works was scarce and systems of taxation had not been fully developed. By 1790 about two thousand legal Lotteries were in operation, and the list of drawings and prizes daily required a half column of fine print in the New York newspapers. A legislative session was seldom held anywhere in the country without one or more Lottery grants being authorized. New York and Philadelphia were the most important centers of ticket distribution, and in each of these cities sales approximated $2,000,000 a year, an impressive figure when it is considered that neither had yet reached the 100,000 mark in population. During the first thirty years of the nineteenth century the Lottery business in America reached enormous proportions, for while the actual number of schemes decreased, drawings were held more frequently, and the amount spent for tickets and offered in prize was many times greater than in the colonial period. There were sixty Lottery offices in New York in 1819, but by 1827 this number has increased to 190, and the *Evening Post* remarked that a stranger might suppose that "one-half of the citizens get their living by affording the opportunity of gambling to the rest." In 1832 Philadelphia, with about 180,000 inhabitants, supported 200 Lottery offices, and in Boston a year later a newspaper estimated that fifty ticket vendors did an annual business of $1,000,000, on which they made a profit of $250,000. And this was six months after the Massachusetts Legislature had passed a law abolishing Lotteries within the state.

In the latter part of 1830 the Grand Jury of New York County, in a presentment to the Common Council of the metropolis, declared that from August 12 to November 1, 1830, fourteen Lotteries were drawn in the city, with 500,000 tickets sold for a total of $2,124,000. "As Lotteries are drawn once in a week," said the presentment, "by this ratio there would be for the year fifty-two lotteries drawn, with about $9,270,000. The deduction of fifteen per cent on this sum is $1,390,000. The usual profit of the vendor over the scheme price is one dollar for each ticket, being $1,857,000." On August 3, 1833, *Niles' Weekly Register* published a recapitulation by the Boston *Mercantile Journal,* showing that in 1832, in the eight states of New York, Virginia, Connecticut, Rhode Island, Pennsylvania, Delaware, North Carolina and Maryland, 420 Lotteries were drawn, the tickets selling for a grand total of $53,136,930. The *Mercantile Journal's* list did not include drawings in Maine, Missouri, Kentucky, Alabama, Tennessee, Louisiana and other states, or some fifty county and local Lotteries in Virginia. "But independently of these," said the newspaper, "the sum above named, with the addition of 25 per cent brokerage, makes an amount of *sixty-six millions, four hundred and twenty thousand dollars!*—that is, of five times the sum of the annual expenses of the American government, and of nearly three times the whole yearly revenue!" Operation of Lotteries on a similar scale today would mean annual ticket sales of almost $40,000,000,000.

Public officials and thinking people generally began to realize about 1820 that the Lottery as an institution was rapidly becoming a monster which threatened to dwarf legitimate business and industry and transform America into a nation of petty gamblers. From about the end of the War of 1812 until Lotteries were legally abolished in most states the agents and promoters were, in the main, sharpers; and there began to be heard a rising volume of complaint about the unreasonable profits exacted by these gentry, the gross frauds which they perpetrated, and the questionable methods by which they disposed of the huge numbers of tickets necessary for successful drawings. *Niles' Weekly Register* said on February 12, 1831, that "the Lottery system is becoming exceedingly unpopular, perhaps, because of the deceptious manner in which it is now managed—which on an average, is about 43 per cent against an adventurer. . . . It is a vile tax on the needy and ignorant." A New York historian wrote in 1828 that "Within ten years the number of ticket venders has multiplied to a great extent, and they display great ingenuity in their puffs, advertisements and other expedients . . . in coaxing the ignorant and careless out of their hard-earned money, and to dupe the credulous purchaser . . . to the

From an old print

A FAKE LOTTERY OFFICE

great advantage of a few cunning individuals, but at a dreadful sacrifice of the morality and resources of the people." The Boston *Mercantile Journal* said in 1833 that "the business is so systematically arranged, that the city is divided into districts, and persons appointed in each, to board vessels just arrived, visit certain bar-rooms, cellars and other resorts, and contrive means generally for the good of *the trade."* Governor DeWitt Clinton of New York, in a message to the Legislature in 1827, remarked that the establishment of Lotteries was "dubious in the eye of morality and certain in the most pernicious results," while the New York Grand Jury which investigated the subject in 1830 reported that "Lotteries, as now managed, are an evil of the most alarming nature, both in a moral and pecuniary point of view." And in 1833 *Niles' Weekly Register* noted that "a 'dead set' is making at the Lottery system in several of the states," called it "a most wicked gambling for money," and predicted that "it will soon 'go by the board,' as it ought."

The profits which legally accrued to the promoters, managers and agents of Lotteries were enormous, but they were increased by every sort of fraud and chicanery that could be devised. As most Lotteries were conducted the official beneficiary received only the proceeds of a fifteen per cent deduction on all prizes. Frequently the payments were less than this percentage, and sometimes they were comparatively infinitesimal, as in the famous Plymouth Lottery of 1811, which was authorized by the Massachusetts Legislature to enable the town of Plymouth to raise $16,000 for improvements on Plymouth Beach. Drawings were held regularly in this Lottery for nine years, and during that period only $9,876.17 was expended on the Beach, although the promoters pocketed a fortune and paid prizes aggregating $886,439.75.

In many Lotteries neither the beneficiaries nor any of the prize winners were paid, for it was not at all unusual for a promoter or agent to sell all the tickets and then vanish with the money. Governor Clinton of New York called attention to this practice in his 1827 message to the Legislature when he said that "great losses had been sustained by the defaults of managers and contractors." A famous case of this sort occurred in 1823, in connection with the Grand National Lottery authorized by Congress for the benefit of the City of Washington. The drawings were made and the winning numbers announced, but before the prizes could be paid the contractor, one Gillespie, skipped out with several hundred thousand dollars. Most of the prize winners accepted their losses without protest, but a resident of Richmond named Clarke, whose ticket had drawn a grand prize of $100,000, was made of sterner stuff. He immediately brought suit, and after four years of litigation the Supreme Court of the United States held that the city was liable for the full amount.

Another lucrative custom often practiced by unscrupulous lottery men was the selling of counterfeit tickets in real lotteries, and of tickets in lotteries which never existed save in the imagination of a shrewd promoter. One of the most noted swindles of this character was the Great Louisiana Real Estate Lottery in the late 1830's. The promoters of this extraordinary fraud, which assumed gigantic proportions, offered as capital prizes some of New Orleans' finest buildings, including the Hotel Veranda, Bank's Arcade, and the St. Charles Hotel, which had just opened its doors and was regarded as one of the architectural wonders of the New World. Thousands of tickets in this scheme, priced at $20 for a whole ticket, $10 for a half, and $5 for a quarter, were sold to gullible gamblers all over the country, but when the time came for the drawing the promoters quietly decamped. Hundreds of sharpers of this stripe were operating successfully in New York as late as the 1870's and the 1880's, but most of them were eventually driven out of the city or put in jail by the redoubtable Anthony Comstock.

80

3

Of all the frauds practiced in the Lottery when the drawings were legal, however, the commonest was the sort of skull-duggery which the New York *Republican Chronicle* exposed on September 16, 1818:

"CITIZENS, LOOK OUT!

"It is a fact that in this present lottery now drawing in this city [the Medical Science Lottery] there is SWINDLING in the management. A certain gentleman in town received intimation that a number named would be drawn on Friday last! and it was drawn that day! This number was insured high in several different places. A similar thing had happened once before in *this same Lottery;* and on examination of the managers' files the number appeared soiled as if it had been in the pocket several days. . . ."

The editor of the *Republican Chronicle,* Charles N. Baldwin, was arrested and indicted for libel, but at his trial was triumphantly acquitted because he proved his charges up to the hilt. The high point of the testimony was the sworn statement of N. Judah, one of the managers of the Lottery, that he had dreamed the number would be drawn, and naturally had hastened to insure it heavily. After Baldwin's acquittal the New York Legislature appointed a Select Committee on Lotteries to investigate the Medical Science drawing. In its report of April 6, 1819, the Committee disclosed that John H. Sickles, one of the complainants against Baldwin, was a secret contractor for tickets, and frequently gave advance information on numbers. The recipients of Sickles' generosity were principally politicians, whose slimy trail, as was to be expected, wound in and out of the jungle of corruption in which the Lottery business was entangled. The report also said that Sickles, as manager of another Lottery, the Milford & Oswego, had drawn a prize of $35,000 for a legislative agent, or lobbyist, at Albany.

The immediate result of Baldwin's *exposé* and the Committee's investigations was a law, passed early in 1819, which licensed all sellers of Lottery tickets at $250 a year. Actually, the incident marked the beginning of a campaign which culminated in the inclusion of an anti-Lottery article in the State Constitution of 1821, declaring that "no Lottery shall hereafter be authorized in this state, and the Legislature shall pass laws to prevent the sale of all lottery tickets within this state, except in Lotteries already authorized by law." The final clause kept the lottery alive in New York until January 1, 1834, when the last authorized Lottery was reported fulfilled. The article then went into effect, and since that date Lotteries have been illegal in New York.

The movement against Lotteries had been gaining ground in other states as well as in New York, and by the time the Empire State's constitutional ban became effective they had already been abolished by law in Pennsylvania, Ohio, Vermont, Maine, Massachusetts, New Jersey, New Hampshire and Illinois. Louisiana and Virginia fell into line a few years later, the former in 1838 and the latter in 1840. In most of these states, as in New York, provision was made for the continuance, for specified periods, of Lotteries which had previously been authorized. But no new grants were made, and at the beginning of the Civil War the Lottery was legally extinct almost everywhere in America, and the only remaining regular drawings were comparatively small ones in Alabama, South Carolina and other Southern states.

During the 1840's and the 1850's one of the principal Lottery centers of the United States was Charleston, S.C., where the newspapers were filled with advertisements and lists of prizes, and weekly drawings of $30,000 were made in one Lottery alone. From early colonial times Charleston had been a veritable hotbed of Lottery gambling; the habit of buying tickets was as widespread in proportion to the population as in New York and Philadelphia. Indirectly, one of the best organized slave rebellions in the old South was due to a Charleston Lottery. The insurrection was planned and led by Denmark Vesey, a Negro of great physical strength and unusual intelligence—he spoke fluently half a dozen languages which he had learned in twenty years of attendance upon his master, a Charleston sea captain. Vesey was an inveterate Lottery player, and in 1800 won a $1,500 prize in the East Bay drawing. With $600 of his winnings he purchased his freedom, and is said never to have bought another Lottery ticket. Thereafter he worked in Charleston as a carpenter, and exercised great influence among the Negroes. For twenty years he worked to secure their allegiance and convince them they should attempt to gain their liberty by force. Early in 1822, with the assistance of a Negro named Peter Poyas, he made definite arrangements for a general insurrection of all the slaves in and around Charleston. Large numbers of Negroes from neighboring islands were to arrive in the city by boat and canoe on a Sunday, and take possession of the fort and the shipping in the harbor. But a slave whom the conspirators had approached divulged the plans, and Vesey and several others were arrested. They were released when they denied all knowledge of the plot, and on June 15, 1822, made an attempt to carry out their design. But the rebellion, lacking to a large extent the element of surprise, was quickly suppressed, and thirty-four of the plotters were hanged, Vesey and five of his principal lieutenants on July 2, 1822, and the others at later dates.

4

Lotteries were revived in some of the Southern states after the Civil War as offering a possible way out of the financial chaos resulting from that conflict, and many of them were still in existence as late as the early 1880's. One of the largest and best known, except for the Louisiana Lottery, which was the most celebrated of all American drawings, was the Literature Lottery of Kentucky, drawn twice daily at Covington, which had been in more or less successful operation since the early days of the state. This was a seventy-eight number lottery; that is, the numbers from 1 to 78 were placed in the wheel, and from eleven to fifteen abstracted at each drawing. A careful record was kept of the order in which they appeared, as it had a great deal to do with determining the winners. For example, the grand prize of $30,000 went to the ticket bearing the first, second and third numbers drawn, in that order. A New York journalist who witnessed a drawing of the Literature Lottery about 1870 reported that he found it "to all appearances a marvelously proper proceeding, but painfully tedious." He continued:

"The wheel was of glass, and stood where all the spectators could see that at the commencement of the operation it was absolutely empty. As the first step, one of the commissioners picked up the numbers from one to seventy-eight successively, and having held them up to the view of the audience, which on that occasion was composed of a small negro boy and myself, rolled up the pasteboards on which the numbers were printed, and, putting each one in a small brass tube open at both ends, dropped it into the wheel. When all the numbers had been thus disposed of, the aperture in the wheel was closed and locked, after which another commissioner turned the wheel rapidly several times in both directions so as to mix the numbers thoroughly. A blind boy whose arms were bare to the shoulder was then led up to the wheel, and, the aperture having been opened, thrust in his hand, took out one of the brass tubes, and handed it to

84

one of the three commissioners. This official took out the pasteboard, and having displayed the number upon it, called it out to a clerk, who wrote it down and bellowed it in his turn to a telegraph operator sitting at his instrument in a remote corner of the room. All this having been done, the wheel was again closed and turned twice around. This operation, with the one before described, was repeated until all of the thirteen numbers of the scheme had been drawn, and the proceedings were then concluded by the commissioners signing a certificate, stating the time and place of the drawing, the numbers placed in the wheel, what ones were drawn, and the order in which they were drawn. The certificate is a printed form, and copies of it can be found in every office in New York where the tickets of the lottery are sold. . . . As to the risk of the three-number prize, the managers have nearly a hundred thousand chances to one against each of their customers, and hold almost equally tremendous odds against them for the two-number prizes." [2]

The Louisiana Lottery was authorized by the Louisiana Legislature in 1868 and granted to a company which agreed to pay $40,000 a year toward the upkeep of the Charity Hospital in New Orleans. The first scheme issued by the company was a very modest proposition—it called for monthly drawings, the issuance of 100,000 tickets at twenty-five cents each, and a grand prize of only $3,750. As the business developed the size of the schemes increased, first to a $7,500 prize and a fifty-cent ticket; and in time to such proportions that a capital grand prize of $600,000 was awarded twice a year on a $40 ticket, while the monthly and semi-annual schemes reached a total of $28,000,000. No one person ever won the capital prize of $600,000, but a New

[2] *The Nether Side of New York, or the Vice, Crime and Poverty of the Great Metropolis*, by Edward Crapsey; New York, 1872; pages 105–6.

Orleans barber once held a $20 ticket, and was paid $300,000 without question. To inspire the public with confidence the company employed Generals P. G. T. Beauregard and Jubal A. Early, among the most famous of Southern military leaders, as Commissioners to supervise the drawings. During their regime a winning ticket was accepted everywhere in the country as the equivalent of a certified check.

The original charter of the Louisiana Lottery Company was for twenty-five years, but it was canceled by the Legislature in 1879. A year later, however, the new State Constitution provided for another, with even greater privileges, to expire in 1895. When the question of a renewal came up in the early 1890's, the company was prosperous enough to offer the state $1,250,000 a year. Throughout its existence, the Lottery aroused great opposition in Louisiana, partly because of its pernicious effects upon the poor, and partly because of the flagrant misuse of the great political power which it possessed. It was almost the sole issue in the bitterly contested gubernatorial campaign of 1892, the result of which blasted the hopes of the company for a new charter. Before this blow, however, the Lottery business had been seriously interfered with by a law, passed by Congress in 1890, which closed the mails to tickets and all printed matter relating to Lotteries. In 1895 another Federal statute prohibited the interstate transportation of Lottery tickets, and the company removed its headquarters to Honduras. There it maintained a precarious existence until 1907, when it was driven out of business by vigorous Federal prosecution of its American agents.

When the anti-Lottery article in the New York State Constitution went into effect on January 1, 1834, Philip Hone wrote in his diary, "If the laws are enforced prohibiting the sale of tickets in the Lotteries of other states, we shall be relieved from the most ruinous and disgraceful system of gambling to which our citizens have been exposed." But the enforcement of these laws in New

DRAWING OF THE LOTTERY.

The following are the numbers which were this day drawn from the 78 placed in the wheel, viz.

1	2	3	4	5	6	7	8	9	10	11	12
20	51	61	24	74	77	46	36	69	29	26	3

And that the said tickets were drawn in the order in which they stand: that is to say—No. 20 was the first that was drawn; No. 51 was the 2nd, No. 61 was the 3rd; No. 24 was the 4th; No. 74 was the 5th; No. 77 was the 6th; No. 46 was the 7th; No. 36 was the 8th; No. 69 was the 9th; No. 29 was the 10th; No. 26 was the 11th; No. 3 was the 12th, and last.

Those tickets entitled the 110 highest prizes were drawn in the following order:

| 1 2 3------ **$30,000** | 7 8 9---------- **$5,000** |
| 4 5 6------ **10,000** | 10 11 12-------- **2,367**20 |

Those 6 tickets having on them the

2 3 4|3 4 5|5 6 7|6 7 8|8 9 10|9 10 11 }each---**1,500**

Those 100 tickets having on them the

1	2	4	1	4	7	1	7	9	2	3	11	2	6	10
1	2	5	1	4	8	1	7	10	2	3	12	2	6	11
1	2	6	1	4	9	1	7	11	2	4	5	2	6	12
1	2	7	1	4	10	1	7	12	2	4	6	2	7	8
1	2	8	1	4	11	1	8	9	2	4	7	2	7	9
1	2	9	1	4	12	1	8	10	2	4	8	2	7	10
1	2	10	1	5	6	1	8	11	2	4	9	2	7	11
1	2	11	1	5	7	1	8	12	2	4	10	2	7	12
1	2	12	1	5	8	1	9	10	2	4	11	2	8	9
1	3	4	1	5	9	1	9	11	2	4	12	2	8	10
1	3	5	1	5	10	1	9	12	2	5	6	2	8	11
1	3	6	1	5	11	1	10	11	2	5	7	2	8	12
1	3	7	1	5	12	1	10	12	2	5	8	2	9	10
1	3	8	1	6	7	1	11	12	2	5	9	2	9	11
1	3	9	1	6	8	2	3	5	2	5	10	2	9	12
1	3	10	1	6	9	2	3	6	2	5	11	2	10	11
1	3	11	1	6	10	2	3	7	2	5	12	2	10	12
1	3	12	1	6	11	2	3	8	2	6	7	2	11	12
1	4	5	1	6	12	2	3	9	2	6	8	3	4	6
1	4	6	1	7	8	2	3	10	2	6	9	3	4	7

each--**1,000**

REPORT OF A DRAWING OF A 78-NUMBER LOTTERY ABOUT 1840. IN ADDITION TO THOSE LISTED THERE WERE APPROXIMATELY 30,000 SMALLER PRIZES RANGING FROM $10.00 TO $100.00

York, and of similar statutes in other states, has never been seriously attempted by the authorities. An investigation made in 1851 by Jonathan H. Green for the New York Association for the Suppression of Gambling disclosed that the lottery offices in the metropolis "do not pretend to conceal the true character of their business. . . . They are well known to the police as places for the sale of lottery tickets, and yet they are suffered to continue their mischievous operations. . . ." Twenty years later, in 1872, a New York journalist, Edward Crapsey, found that "there is scarcely a street in the whole city, from the Battery to Harlem Bridge, where the shops of the lottery dealers cannot be found." Similar conditions prevailed in the 1890's, and not until after the beginning of the twentieth century did the Lottery sellers really begin to operate under cover. In recent years the business has been largely in the hands of peripatetic vendors, and at least two-thirds of the millions of lottery and sweepstakes tickets sold in this country every year are counterfeits.

CHAPTER VI

POLICY

ONLY the Lottery's illegitimate offspring, Policy, has surpassed Faro and the Lottery itself in popularity, or obtained as firm a hold on the gambling public of America. For more than a hundred years Policy was the favorite game of the masses, and is still the most widespread method of gambling in the United States, although it is better known nowadays as Numbers. Thousands play the Numbers game every day in virtually every large city and town in the country, and at least $300,000,000 a year flows from this source into the pockets of the racketeers who, in the main, control the business. Numbers is popularly supposed to be a fairly recent invention; even such a careful investigator as the magazine *Time,* in an article on January 4, 1937, in which Numbers was described as "the biggest, richest racket in the U.S. today," failed to identify it with Policy, and noted the current belief that the game was devised in the offices of the New York *Sun.* As a matter of fact, Numbers is simply Policy reduced to the simplified form in which it was played in England almost two hundred years ago. The only real difference, aside from changes in terminology, is in the source of the figures upon which the play is based. Originally they were taken from the Lottery drawings; nowadays the Numbers backers use bank clearings, pari-mutuel totals, baseball scores, cattle and custom-house receipts, and other combinations of figures which appear regularly in the newspapers. When Horace Walpole thus wrote to the Countess of Ossory on December 17, 1789, he might have been describing the game which now does its part toward making the poor poorer and the racketeer richer:

> "As folks in the country love to hear of *London fashions,* know, Madam, that the reigning one among the quality, is to go, after the opera, to the lottery offices, where their Ladyships bet with the keepers. You choose any number you please; if it does not come up next day, you pay five guineas; if it does, receive forty. . . . The Duchess of Devonshire, in one day, won nine hundred pounds. . . ." [1]

Policy appears to have originated in the London Lottery shops in the first half of the eighteenth century, and was developed by the ticket dealers as a sideline to their regular business. As Horace Walpole suggested, it was at various periods a diversion of those titled rakehells known as the "quality;" but its main purpose, which it certainly fulfilled after being transplanted to America, was to bring gambling within the reach of those who couldn't afford to buy even a share of a Lottery ticket. For a trifling sum—in many places as little as a farthing—a player could "insure a number;" that is, he could bet that any number of his own selection would appear in the drawing of a designated Lottery. The clerks who recorded these bets, and the runners who drummed up trade on the outside, were called "insurance solicitors," and the receipts or memoranda slips given the players were "insurance policies" or "Lottery policies."

This curious form of "insurance" was well known during the early days of the Lottery in this country, but apparently it attracted no particular attention until after the Revolution. But by 1800, although it had not yet begun to reach down into the lowest stratum of American society and snatch the pennies of the poor, it was a part of every Lottery, and was generally recog-

---

[1] *The History of Gambling in England,* by John Ashton; New York and London, 1899; page 234.

nized as the most pernicious feature of the system. As the Select Committee on Lotteries of the New York Legislature pointed out in 1819, it was the medium of most of the fraud and dishonesty in the drawings. Moreover, it produced an enormous revenue in which neither the state nor the official beneficiary of the Lottery shared. The report of the Committee emphasized this point by citing the fact that in 1818, in three days' time, one Lottery office in New York had made a profit of $31,000 on Policy alone. There were about sixty such establishments in the metropolis at the time, and if all were equally prosperous Policy was a tidy racket a hundred and twenty years ago, when New York could boast of no more than a hundred thousand inhabitants.

A great many of the Policy frauds perpetrated in the days when the game was still a sideline of the Lottery were of the type exposed by the New York *Republican Chronicle* in 1818, and required advance knowledge of the numbers. Not all, of course, were successful. Frequently an alert editor laid the swindlers by the heels, and sometimes Fate stepped in and made them victims of their own smartness, as in the late 1820's, when a group of New York sharpers embarked upon a little adventure with the number 44. When this coup was attempted most of the Policy dealers paid off on the results of a Lottery drawn in Jersey City, across the Hudson from New York, which was well known to be carelessly conducted. The conspirators bribed the boy who drew the numbers, and the lad agreed to steal the brass tube containing 44. He was to hide the tube in his sleeve, and when the drawing began slide it down into his hand and produce it as the first to be taken from the wheel. The schemers insured the number heavily in the Lottery shops, and stood to win about $30,000. But the day before the drawing the boy reported that he had been unable to steal the tube. In desperation the swindlers prepared a duplicate and ordered the boy to proceed as planned, knowing that there was but a very slight chance that the legitimate number would appear. Nevertheless, the improbable happened, and the real 44 was the sixth number drawn. The managers of the Lottery discharged the boy, the Policy shops canceled all "policies" on the number, and a new drawing was announced. And this time the first number that appeared was 44!

2

For almost seventy-five years after it had been introduced into this country Policy remained a comparatively minor part of the Lottery business despite its steadily increasing popularity. But the death agonies of the Lottery proved to be the growing pains of Policy, and as the former was gradually legislated out of existence in America the latter took its place as the one system of gambling in which everybody could participate. While the Lottery was trembling on the brink of legal extinction, Policy was being established on a firm foundation throughout the United States, and it continued to expand as new areas were settled and the country increased in population. Until Policy thus crawled from under the sheltering rock of the Lottery, it retained the simple form of its early days, and was still known as "Lottery insurance." By the middle 1830's, however, this dignified but clumsy nomenclature had been abandoned, and the game was known everywhere simply as Policy. At about the same time various changes in the method of play were introduced, and Policy began to acquire the picturesque terminology which became one of its most interesting features. During the first decade of this transition the Policy shops of New York, and of the country generally, continued to quote their bets on the result of the New Jersey drawings; but about 1840 that Lottery was abolished, and the Policy men transferred their operations to the Kentucky Literature Lottery at Covington. This in turn was replaced during the early 1870's by the Kentucky State Lottery and the

Frankfort Lottery of Kentucky, both of which were likewise drawn at Covington. Drawings in Georgia and Missouri, both illegal, were also used occasionally, and the Policy shops in many Southern cities, after 1868, paid off on the figures of the Louisiana Lottery.

As soon as a drawing had been certified by the Lottery Commissioners, the winning numbers were telegraphed to New York and other cities, where copies were made and carried by runners to the Policy shops, which were usually filled with eager gamblers waiting to hear the results. Even in the days of the horse-car and hansom cab this distribution had been completed within an hour after the last number had been drawn from the wheel. The combinations upon which the players could lay their bets were numerous, but these were the most important:

Day Number—Any number from 1 to 78, played to be one of the eleven to fifteen drawn, and to appear anywhere on the winning list. On this the Policy shops paid 5 to 1.

Station Number—A number played to appear in a specified position on the list. The odds were 60 to 1.

Saddle—Two numbers to appear anywhere on the list. Odds, 32 to 1.

Station Saddle—Two numbers to appear at specified positions on the list. Odds, 800 to 1.

Capital Saddle—Two of the first three numbers drawn. Odds, 500 to 1.

Gig—Three numbers, to appear anywhere on the list. Odds, 200 to 1. The gig was always the favorite bet of the Negroes, and the most popular of all was 4-11-44, known as the "magic gig" and the "Washwoman's gig."

Flat Gig—Three numbers to appear at specified positions. Odds, 1,000 to 1. This play was so called because it was seldom used by anyone but "flats," suckers who were fascinated by the

92

enormous odds. The chances of winning were only slightly better than none at all.

Horse—Four numbers to appear anywhere on the list. Odds, 680 to 1.

Cross Play—A bet on any of the combinations, the numbers to appear in either of two drawings. The same odds prevailed as on straight plays, but twenty per cent was deducted from all winnings.

If a player was successful, he was said to have *hit,* a term which was a part of the jargon of Policy as early as 1840. It is now commonly used in the Numbers game.

The odds here given, which were current in New York for more than half a century, varied somewhat in other cities, and were also subject to a slight change according to whether eleven, twelve, thirteen, fourteen or fifteen numbers were drawn from the Lottery wheel. In general, however, they were standard throughout the country. Apparently they gave the Policy player plenty of chances to win a great deal of money, but they don't seem so terrific when it is considered that in the seventy-eight numbers from which eleven to fifteen were drawn there were more than 3,000 possible *saddles,* about 75,000 *gigs,* and almost a million and a half *horses.* Since on these three plays the generous Policy man paid respectively 32, 200 and 680 to 1, a comfortable margin of chance remained for the house. Even on the players' best prospect, the day number, the actual odds were about twenty-five times as large as those offered.

It was clearly impossible to devise a mathematical system for playing Policy, hence the Policy addict was debarred from using the methods by which gamblers of another type have lost huge sums to Faro and *Monte* banks and Roulette. Instead, he depended upon hunches, kept a watchful eye open for signs and portents, and, especially in the South where Policy was even more popular among the Negroes than Craps, consulted fortune tellers, dream books, and used magic formulae to gain winning information from the spirit world. One of these time-tried bits of necromancy is popular today among Numbers players, and is regarded as almost sure-fire. Before going to bed the player moistens the index finger of his right hand with spittle and outlines an X on his forehead, and when he is sound asleep "they" will appear and give him a number which is bound to win if played immediately.

The most prolific source of numbers for playing Policy, however, was the dream books, which have always been the real bestsellers of American literature. Millions of copies have been sold in the United States during the past hundred years, and the presses are still turning them out almost as rapidly as ever. So far as Policy was concerned, however, they were probably at the height of their popularity and influence from about 1860 to 1880, when a huge compendium called *The Wheel of Fortune,* was kept chained to the wall in every Policy shop. Some dealers even charged a client two cents for consulting it. Here are some typical extracts from a volume called *Old Aunt Dinah's Policy Dream Book,* which had a great vogue in the 1830's and 1840's:

"To dream of seeing a person's corpse, lying on a bed, is a good dream for the dreamer. If the scene is viewed with surprise and awe, it is good to play fifty-sixth fourth, or your age and the person's age in a gig. If you interest yourself in describing the scene to some other person, it is a sure sign of its being drawn soon, which will be *safer to play heavy*.

"To dream of seeing a negro man, or one of a very dark complexion, is a favorable token for the dreamer for fourteen first. If the person be very dark, inclining to a jet black, is more favorable. If the viewing of the person is very exciting to you, the number may with safety be anticipated very

94

A POLICY SHOP OF THE 1890's

soon, and would advise the player to play heavy, as it is a *sure thing.*

"To dream that your sweetheart is very anxious to see you, because he or she has got something to tell you of great importance, and appears as though she or he wished to tell, is good for the day of the month, her age and yours in a gig. If near the moon's change, the sooner it will be out; but if the moon has changed, her age or his is very good to play first, for it will *surely be out soon.*

"If you dream of a friend running to you in great haste, and telling you that some particular number is sure to be drawn, or is drawn, is good to play as speedy as you can, if he appeared candid in telling you; but if he appeared trifling it will not come so soon; but to play is middling safe.

"If you dream of seeing a number of large boots standing amidst a number of small ones, is very sure in playing seven for each large boot in a station corresponding with the number of small ones. If the seeing of these boots creates an intense interest it is a very safe play. The greater the interest the sooner will the numbers be drawn.

"To dream that you hear a clock strike, if it strikes loud and plain, is a good dream to play the number of times you hear it strike first, more especially in the night lottery. If it appears to strike very fast, the sooner will the number be drawn first." [2]

3

The first attempt to control Policy by legislative action in this country was made in 1805, when Pennsylvania passed a law forbidding Lottery offices to "insure for or against" the drawing of tickets. A somewhat similar measure, designed to "restrain"

[2] Quoted from *Report on Gambling in New York,* by J. H. Green; New York, 1851; page 45.

Lottery insurance, was enacted in New York in 1807, but no really stringent anti-Policy statutes were adopted anywhere in the United States until 1819, when the New York Select Committee on Lotteries made its report. Soon after the publication of this revealing document, the New York Legislature passed a law positively prohibiting Policy under penalty of a year in jail or a fine of $2,000. In 1835 legislation against Policy was enacted in Tennessee, and during the next thirteen years laws prohibiting the game were adopted in seven other states—Mississippi and Indiana in 1838, Arkansas and Missouri in 1840, Illinois in 1845, Ohio in 1846, and Kentucky in 1848, although Covington was at the time, and continued to be for years, the fountain-head of the business. The ball thus started was kept rolling, and after the Civil War scores of statutes were adopted in the unsuccessful attempt to subdue the most formidable antagonist that the anti-gambling element has ever encountered. Unlike many other gambling games, Policy was never given the protection of law anywhere in the United States except in Louisiana, which alone enjoys the dubious distinction of having legalized the game which has taken more money from the pockets of the poor than any other gambling scheme ever devised. In that state the new charter granted to the Louisiana Lottery Company in 1880 gave the Company a monopoly of the business, and almost immediately New Orleans and other large cities of Louisiana were transformed into vast Policy shops. Said a New Orleans historian:

"Before long the city was Policy mad. Visitors to New Orleans in the 80's, remember well the open policy booths in the main business streets of the city, and the lines and crowds of negroes and whites that thronged the 'book,' seeking to bet their nickels and dimes on the innumerable combinations of figures which superstition or fancy dictated. There were policy booths in front of laundries, bar-rooms, groceries and markets. There were instances where as much as $5,000 was paid for a stand if the location were favorable enough, which might not be more than four feet square of space, with a small table and a chair. More than a hundred policy shops existed in New Orleans. The profits from the policy game, in which there were two drawings daily, were large enough to pay all the expenses of the Lottery proper in which the drawing was monthly, leaving the profits from the national business, over the payment of prizes, clear gain." [3]

The game might just as well have been legalized everywhere in the United States, for it is doubtful if any laws have ever been so consistently ignored as were those relating to Policy. They interfered scarcely at all with its progress about the country. From 1840 to the World War thousands of Policy shops were in more or less successful operation. New York alone supported from 200 to 700, and Chicago, after about 1875, almost as many —and during most of that long period Policy completely overshadowed, in popularity, receipts and number of addicts, all other forms of gambling in America. The profits of the ordinary gambling houses were trifling compared to those of the Policy shops—in New York in 1851, when the Policy craze was just getting under way, the gains of the Policy men were conservatively estimated at from $6,000 to $8,000 a day. And they were proportionately as large in other cities. For all this there were several important reasons. In the first place, the men who controlled Policy always maintained very cordial relations with the politicians, and freely disbursed huge corruption funds whenever danger threatened. In the second place, it was difficult to obtain convicting evidence when all a Policy dealer required to carry on his business was a notebook, a pencil and a handful of

[3] *History of New Orleans,* by John Smith Kendall, A.M.; Chicago, 1922; Volume II; page 487.

slips. And in the third place, there was seldom any glory to be gained by attacking gambling establishments whose clients were of the lower orders of society, and possessed no publicity value whatever.

4

New York was always the heart of the Policy octopus, and it was there that the most powerful of the so called Policy kings arose who dominated the game, not only in the metropolis but in other cities as well, and drew tribute from a wide area. John Frink was perhaps the first of these gambling monarchs, but he was actually little more than a front for Reuben Parsons, one of the most celebrated of early American gamblers, whose chief personal interest lay in banking Faro. With Parsons in the background pulling the strings, Frink occupied the throne for some fifteen years after 1840, and owned or controlled from 300 to 350 Policy shops which were scattered up and down Manhattan Island. These places operated virtually wide open, displaying on their counters and in their windows piles of gold and silver coin and, after 1848, nuggets from the newly opened gold fields of California. "They are located in every part of the city," said a memorial of the New York Association for the Suppression of Gambling in 1850, "and in addition to the stationary venders, there are a large number of male and female traveling Agents, who penetrate our workshops, counting-houses, and even the family circle. . . ."

Parsons and Frink, however, appear to have confined their operations to New York. The first Policy king to extend his power beyond the Hudson River was Zachariah Simmons, a New Englander who came to New York with his three brothers soon after the Civil War and opened half a dozen Policy shops and Lottery offices. At that time the metropolis was about as Policy mad as New Orleans was some fifteen years later; it was estimated that one-fourth of the city's 900,000 inhabitants played the game with more or less regularity. There were between 600 and 700 Policy shops, thinly disguised as "Exchange" offices—"Go where you will," wrote a journalist in 1867, "their signs will meet your eye" —and most of them were prosperous enough to employ from five to ten clerks, or writers, who received twelve and one-half per cent of the money that came over the counters. Besides the writers, there was a veritable horde of runners, or "Traveling Agents," who made their rounds twice daily and had begun to devote most of their attention to the tenement districts. The standard rate of pay for the runners was fifteen per cent of whatever business they brought in.

The situation was a setup for a man with Simmons' energies and ambitions, for Frink had vanished from the scene and Parsons, with a fortune gained from Policy and Faro, had retired to the rarefied financial air of Wall Street, from which he was soon to descend stripped of his riches. Simmons' first care was to form an alliance with Tammany Hall, and arrange with the greedy statesmen of that organization for a proper division of the spoils in return for protection. The Policy dealers were not receptive to his plans, however, until mid-summer of 1870, when every Policy shop in New York was suddenly raided by the police under the direction of the District Attorney. They were closed just one day, and the incident proved to be only a gesture, but the Policy men accepted it as an indication that Simmons meant business. Most of them hastened to join forces with him, and with the backing of the Tweed Ring, which was then systematically looting the metropolis, Simmons formed the Central Organization, which divided the city into districts, allotted the Policy privileges therein, and absorbed most of the profits. Within a year Simmons and his brothers controlled about three-fourths of the Policy shops in New York, and had established or taken over the game as far west as Milwaukee and as far south as Richmond. From

99

the managers in this territory the Central Organization received huge sums every week—from 1872 to 1875 the net profits from twenty cities, among them Chicago, Baltimore, Philadelphia, Richmond and Washington, exceeded one million dollars.

Until Zachariah Simmons became the Policy king of New York and its gambling dependencies, a nickel was the smallest amount for which a bet could be made. To reach those who couldn't produce even this trifling sum Simmons and his henchmen, sometime in the middle 1870's, devised a simplified version of Policy which they called "the envelope game," and opened places for playing it in the poorer sections of various cities. Bets of from one to five cents were accepted in the envelope game, and drawings were supposed to be held every ten or fifteen minutes in the presence of the players. What actually happened was that at regular intervals the manager of an envelope dive simply posted a list of numbers and announced that they were the winners in the drawing. For many years this game was extensively played, especially among Negroes and school-boys, and as late as 1900, according to the New York *Times* of March 9, its operators were able to pay $30,000 a year to the politicians for protection in the metropolis alone. At the same time Policy was assessed $125,000 annually.

To make assurance doubly sure in the regular Policy game, Simmons is said to have tampered with the drawings in Kentucky and to have changed the numbers after they arrived in New York. This iniquity was exposed when Anthony Comstock, after one of his headlong dives into the cesspool of metropolitan sin, sputtered to the surface with two notes signed with Simmons' initials—"Dear Bill; Make it 32, 35, 47"; and "Please change 21 and 70 to something else." Such manipulation was easy enough at any time, but it was an especially simple matter after 1875, when Simmons became one of the managers of the Kentucky State Lottery and the Frankfort Lottery of Kentucky.

Some very curious things occurred in connection with the drawings of these Lotteries, not the least of which was an extraordinary coincidence, described by an indignant rival as "simply an impossibility" and doubtless unique in the history of Lotteries. On August 25, 1879, the Commissioners of the Kentucky State Lottery certified that a drawing had been held, and that these numbers had been drawn in this order—45, 30, 59, 42, 37, 34, 3, 18, 27, 31, 19, 61, 44. On the same day the same Commissioners certified a drawing of the Frankfort Lottery, and said that exactly the same numbers had been drawn in exactly the same order!

5

The practice of increasing the actual odds against the Policy player to astronomical proportions was carried to its logical conclusion by Albert J. Adams, better known as Al, who was boss of the Policy business from the early 1880's to 1901. Adams didn't even bother with real drawings, although he pretended that two were held each day. The New York *Herald* of March 4, 1900, thus described how Adams ran the Policy game in the days of his prosperity, when there were 800 Policy shops in the city and a million people regularly played their favorite gigs and saddles:

"At this office, in West Thirtieth Street, near Broadway, which he shares with a real estate firm, he is said to map out his plans for the carrying on of the games. There he also receives reports from his lieutenants, it is said, to whom, in turn, the 'backers' of the game in the thirty policy districts into which the city is divided make their reports. 'Protection' is arranged for, and if any employes of the policy shops get into trouble, lawyers, who are constantly retained by the policy chiefs, are ready to do whatever may be necessary to extricate them from the clutches of the law.

"It is alleged by the policy men that the actual drawing of the winning numbers takes place twice each weekday in Frankfort and Louisville, Ky. This story, as well as the added statement that the winning numbers are taken from a wheel by a child who has previously been blindfolded, is circulated and implicitly believed by the policy dupes. As a matter of fact, the winning numbers are selected each day by the policy kings in New York city. The combinations played daily are recorded sufficiently in advance of the alleged drawings to enable those in charge of the swindle to select as winning numbers only those on which the least money has been placed, thus reducing the amount to be expended in the payment of winnings and increasing the amount of losses to be suffered by the players.

"The policy managers having selected the combinations that are to win at each alleged drawing, these numbers are telegraphed in cipher to Frankfort and Louisville. From there they are sent to Cincinnati, Ohio, the Western head-quarters of the policy king's combination. By use of a different cipher the same numbers are telegraphed without delay to Jersey City and from there again telegraphed to New York. Here they are sent to certain printing offices in the employ of the policy men, and the printed slips bearing the winning numbers are later distributed by rapid messengers to the hundreds of policy shops throughout the city. . . .

"There are two 'drawings,' as they are called, each day. One is known as the morning drawing, which takes place ostensibly in Frankfort, Ky., and for which no money or selection of combinations of figures is accepted after twelve o'clock, noon. Then there is the afternoon drawing, which is said to be made in Louisville, where the entry of combinations closes at five o'clock. The winning combinations for the morning drawings are posted in the different policy

102

From the New York World. Courtesy the Press Publishing Co.

AL ADAMS, THE POLICY KING, LEAVING THE TOMBS FOR SING SING

shops shortly after two o'clock in the afternoon and the afternoon drawings at seven o'clock in the evening. . . . The policy kings realize that money must be paid out to keep the public interested, but the winning numbers are purposely arranged so that the amount to be paid out shall be as small as possible. . . ."

Adams was a native of Rhode Island who first appeared in New York in 1871 as a brakeman on the New Haven railway. The metropolis offered greater opportunities than railroading, and after a year or so Adams quit his job to become a Policy runner for Zachariah Simmons. Later, with Simmons' consent and backing, he opened his own Policy shops, and as he prospered began to invade other fields. Before 1880 he was the backer of a five-cent Roulette house and several crooked Chuck-a-Luck games, and was associated in various other gambling enterprises with the notorious Shang Draper, a Tammany heeler, bank robber, sneak thief, and panel-game operator who employed thirty prostitutes to lure men into a house where they were robbed. At one time Adams and Draper owned three-fifths of all the cheap Faro banks in New York. Despite these activities Adams continued to expand his Policy operations, and when Simmons withdrew from the business Adams was the logical man to succeed him. As Simmons had done, Adams kept his political fences intact, and during most of his reign as king of Policy he was something of a power in Tammany Hall, the most consistently crooked political organization in American history.

Adams seems to have been cordially disliked even by men of his own stamp. One of the exceptions to this rule, and one of Adams' few intimate friends, was Big Bill Devery, who was Chief of the New York Police from 1898 until the office was abolished by the Legislature in 1901. For years Adams was widely known as "the meanest gambler in New York," and was a notorious tightwad, the direct antithesis of the big-hearted, open-handed gambler of legend. He paid his henchmen the lowest salaries in the history of the Policy business, and never offered anyone a cigar or a drink, nor gave anything away except his umbrella, which he always carried tightly rolled and disposed of as soon as it got wet. But this was not through generosity; he considered it bad luck to use an umbrella on which rain had fallen. In common with many other successful gamblers, Adams had social ambitions, and cherished the idea that he was a great business man. At one time he employed a press agent to exploit the glories of his mansion in East Sixty-ninth Street and relay his wisdom to a waiting world. A circular issued from his office early in 1906, when he was attempting to establish a chain of 300 bucket shops, contained this gem:

> "Al Adams is like unto Andrew Carnegie in that, being a marvelously successful business man himself, he has drawn around him a corps of men almost equally brilliant as himself, not the least of whom are his four sons."

Two of Adams' sons were lawyers, educated at Harvard and Heidelberg universities. Another was sentenced to six months in jail in 1904 for assaulting his father.

Despite his peculiarities and obsessions, Adams amassed a very considerable fortune, all of which, of course, was built upon the nickels and dimes of the victims of his Policy cheating; it is doubtful if he ever earned an honest penny after quitting his job as brakeman. The exact extent of his wealth was never known, but the New York *World* on December 10, 1901, said that he was many times a millionaire. Besides his Policy interests, from which he received an enormous income, Adams owned two breweries, $2,000,000 worth of real estate, was the backer of a hundred saloons, and had an interest in every gambling house west of Broadway from the Battery to 110th Street. But whatever he owned when the *World* published this summary was all he ever possessed for he had been marked for the slaughter by an organization which had been a source of great annoyance to the New York underworld for more than a decade—the Society for the Prevention of Crime, better known as the Parkhurst Society.

Agents of the Society made a raid upon Adams' main offices about the time that the *World* was speculating upon his riches, and found evidence directly connecting him with eighty-two Policy shops. The Policy king was arrested and released on bail, and that he never thought he would be tried is indicated by the fact that he and Shang Draper immediately began remodeling and connecting two adjoining houses in West Forty-fourth Street, intending to open a gambling house and move the paraphernalia back and forth between the two buildings as raids threatened. But in spite of the efforts of the politicians, Adams was brought to trial in June of 1902, and was promptly convicted. For several months after his conviction he was permitted to live at the Hotel Waldorf-Astoria with two Deputy Sheriffs, a privilege accorded to no other prisoner since the days of William M. Tweed.

In April, 1903, however, Adams was finally sentenced to pay a fine of $1,000 and serve not less than twelve nor more than eighteen months in Sing Sing. On April 27th he was booked at the Prison, where he gave his age as sixty-two and his occupation as "gentleman." Adams returned to New York when his sentence expired on October 11, 1904, and was described by the newspapers as "broken in health and bent with disgrace." Apparently he made no attempt to re-enter the Policy business, but turned his attention to bucket shops. He made little headway with a scheme to form a bucket shop chain, however, and became increasingly discouraged. On October 1, 1906, he went to his suite in the Hotel Ansonia, where he had been living apart from his family, and blew out his brains.

The Policy kingdom established by John Frink and Reuben Parsons and enlarged to such huge proportions by Zachariah Simmons and Al Adams, began to disintegrate as soon as Adams went to jail, and never wholly recovered from the thumping it had received at the hands of the Parkhurst Society. The Policy men who attempted to fill Adams' shoes were kept on the jump by the reform administration which had been elected in New York a few weeks before the raid on Adams' offices, and cities began to drift away from the metropolitan combine and run their own games. The business showed the lack of a firm directing head, and in some places the operators became so demoralized that they even attempted to hold honest drawings. Bob Mott, the Policy boss of Chicago, attempted to usurp the throne, but he was unable to gather up the loose ends, and never gained the power that had been wielded by Simmons and Adams. By 1905 Policy playing was definitely declining, and within another ten years it was no longer an important phase of American gambling. After the World War little was heard of it until it was simplified and revived some fifteen years ago as Numbers.

A POLICY PLAYER OF THE 70's

PART TWO

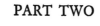

CHAPTER VII

PIONEERS

GAMBLING in America experienced its greatest growth
and expansion during the half-century which followed
the Louisiana Purchase. In addition to the evolution of Faro and
Poker, the introduction of Craps, Thimble-Rig and *Monte,* and
the Phoenix-like rise of Policy from the ashes of the Lottery, this
period saw the spread of public gaming throughout the country,
the first organized anti-gambling crusades, the rise and fall of
the picturesque sharper of the Western rivers, the citizens' war
against the gamblers of the Mississippi, and the development of
the gambling house and its transformation from a tolerated rarity into a political and social menace.

2

The fountain-head of gambling in this country was New Orleans. Virtually all of the famous gamblers of the flush times
before the Civil War learned their trade in that celebrated hatch-
ery of sin and gayety; it was the gateway through which entered
the most important of the games that the American sharper has
used for more than a hundred years to trim the eager sucker;
and it was the focal point of the gambling fever which began to
spread over the United States like a pestilence soon after the
American flag had been raised in the Place d'Armes and the
American politician had moved bag and baggage into Louisiana. New Orleans was a gambling town almost from its earliest
beginnings in 1718, when the French colonists under Jean Bap-
tiste LeMoyne, Sieur d'Bienville, chased away the frogs and

109

alligators, cleared and drained the swamps, and began to erect huts, warehouses and barracks. Most of the early taverns, coffee-houses and grog-shops, which were the social and amusement centers of the town, provided rooms and tables for private and public gaming. As New Orleans increased in wealth and pop-ulation these facilities for play became correspondingly greater, and the prevalence of gambling was a source of constant concern to the provincial governors, who tried unsuccessfully to check the evil with a long series of official scoldings and reprimands, and laws which prescribed such punishments as branding, whip-ping, expulsion from the colony, and exposure in the stocks and the pillory. One of these statutes attempts to tackle the problem at both ends, imposing twenty-five lashes not only upon the convicted professional gambler but upon his victim as well.

No record remains of the actual number of gambling houses in New Orleans during the French and Spanish occupations, but it probably wasn't very large, for before the arrival of the Amer-icans the town was small—it had a population of not more than 4,000 when Louisiana was retroceded to France in prep-aration for the transfer to the United States—and was virtually isolated from the remainder of the continent. But public resorts of every description increased enormously in numbers when the Louisiana Purchase and the opening of the Mississippi to com-merce brought traders, river bullies and adventurers swarming into New Orleans by land and water. Half a dozen years after Louisiana had become American territory, when the city could boast of approximately 25,000 inhabitants and as much disorder as any town ten times its size, it probably harbored as many gam-bling places as New York, Boston, Philadelphia and Baltimore combined, although each of these cities surpassed New Orleans in population.

In the confusion of establishing the American form of govern-ment and attempting to reconcile the embittered and disappointed Creoles to their fate, the authorities of New Orleans found neither time nor inclination to make any gestures against such a minor sin as gambling. In consequence the resorts flourished with little or no restraint until 1811, when the Legislature passed a law prohibiting gambling anywhere in the state. Three years later, at the behest of a well-organized gamblers' lobby, the legislators amended the law to permit gambling in New Orleans under strict municipal regulation. Ordinances designed to control the vice were enacted by the Municipal Council, but the city was without an efficient police force to enforce its edicts, and as the preamble to one of the ordinances said, the attempt at regulation only "encouraged this alarming vice under the sanction of the law." Moreover, the Creoles were still numerically stronger and politically more powerful than the Americans, and public sentiment was decidedly in favor of gambling.

Despite these handicaps the city government continued its efforts at regulation until 1820, when the Legislature re-enacted the statewide prohibitory law. To some extent this drove the gamblers under cover, but they continued to operate, and there was little decrease in the number of gaming places, or of men engaged in the business. In 1823, at the request of the municipal authorities, and to provide much-needed revenue, the Legislature passed a law which permitted New Orleans to license six gambling houses at $5,000 a year each. Of the money thus raised, four-fifths was to be applied to the support of Charity Hospital, and one-fifth to the College of Orleans. Only three licenses were issued the first year the law was in effect, but thereafter until the statute was repealed New Orleans had its full quota of legal gambling houses. A writer in the *Louisiana Advertiser,* in the summer of 1826, made a detailed estimate of the necessary expenses of the six places, and fixed upon $80,475 as the amount they were required to pay out before entries could be made on the profit side of their ledgers. This total he itemized as follows:

Six licenses at $5,000 each $30,000
Twenty-four journeymen, that is, 4 to each bank,
    each $100 per month 28,800
Boarding of the same at $25 per month each 7,200
Servants' hire, one to each bank at $25 per month,
    including board 1,800
House rent for each bank, not less than $100 per
    month 7,200
Liquors to induce customers to play freely, for light
    and fuel, say $2.50 per day for each bank 5,475
                                                       $80,475 [1]

At the request of the keepers of the licensed houses, who advanced the reasonable argument that since they paid taxes they were entitled to protection, the city made a real effort to suppress gambling elsewhere than in the resorts operated by the chosen half-dozen. This campaign, carried on energetically for more than a year, succeeded to such an extent that by 1826 public gaming was virtually non-existent in New Orleans except in the legal houses and the districts wherein the river men congregated for their frolics, into which the police were afraid to venture. Although six gambling establishments were thus given a practical monopoly of the business, they do not appear to have taken full advantage of their opportunities. During the first few years of the license system the houses were comparatively small and crudely furnished; they offered no entertainment and no refreshment save liquor, and none operated more than a single Faro bank or Roulette wheel. Scant provision was made for the private games at which the really big money changed hands, and in consequence the resorts were not supported by the Creole aristocrats and other men of means. However, they were heavily patronized by *hoi polloi,* and occasionally hooked a fat sucker

[1] Quoted from *Niles' Weekly Register,* August 12, 1826.

from the upper classes. One of these, tardily overtaken by re-morse, scribbled this endorsement upon the back of a $20 bank note which was in circulation in New Orleans in 1826:

"This is the last note of $10,000 lost at gambling in the city of New Orleans. May he or they into whose hands it next falls turn it to better account than did

D. A. M." [2]

Notwithstanding faulty management and inadequate equip-ment, the gaming resorts licensed in New Orleans occupy posi-tions of considerable importance in the history of American gambling. They were the first recognized houses in the country, the first to acquire the status of semi-permanency necessary to successful operation, and the forerunners of the gaudy "palaces of fortune," as the gamblers loved to call them, which within another twenty-five years were running more or less wide-open in almost every large city of the Union. The first of these ornate houses was opened in New Orleans in 1827 by John Davis, father of big-time gambling in the United States and a unique figure in the history of the city. A wealthy *émigré* from San Domingo, with a fine classical and musical education acquired in French colleges, Davis achieved considerable political power and great social prestige. He built the famous Theatre d'Orleans and or-ganized a musical stock company which sang light opera in French, and otherwise assisted in the development of whatever culture the city possessed. In New Orleans tradition, however, he is chiefly remembered as the owner of the Orleans Ballroom, scene of the celebrated Quadroon Balls of fragrant memory.[3]

Davis' new gambling house adjoined the Ballroom at Orleans and Bourbon Streets. It was kept open day and night, with deal-

---

[2] *Ibid.*, October 7, 1826.
[3] A full account of the Quadroon Balls may be found in the present author's *The French Quarter, an Informal History of the New Orleans Underworld;* New York, 1936.

113

ers and croupiers working four-hour shifts. To accommodate the
week-end trade, Davis opened a branch house on Bayou St. John,
about a mile from the city, which was in operation only from
Saturday noon to early Monday morning. Both the main establishment and the branch were high-class houses in every respect;
worthy of comparison with such famous New York resorts of
later years as Pat Herne's, John Morrissey's, Richard Canfield's,
and the House with the Bronze Doors. The furnishings and appointments were nothing short of magnificent; the finest wines
and liquors, and bountiful helpings from a well-stocked buffet,
were served without cost to the players; and on Sunday evening
an elaborate dinner of many courses was provided at the house
on Bayou St. John. At both places there were luxurious chairs,
couches and divans for those who became wearied and over-
wrought, and while they relaxed in comfort obsequious servants
ministered to their wants. In such an atmosphere of elegance and
refinement it must have been a real pleasure to lose money, and
there were plenty of ways to do it. In the public casinos were
Faro layouts, Roulette wheels, and tables of *Vingt et Un,* all presided over by experts versed in the best methods of protecting the
interests of the house. For officials and aristocrats who wished
to avoid the contaminating touch of the mob, Davis provided
private rooms, where the principal games were Brag, *Ecarté* and
Boston,[4] and occasionally the new game of Twenty-Card Poker.
From these the house took a percentage of the money staked, and
furnished a player if one was required to round out a session.

Davis had this lucrative field to himself for a year or two, for
the shoe-string sharpers who ran the other licensed houses offered little real competition. His extraordinary success, however,
soon attracted a swarm of imitators, and within half a dozen
years a score of high-class places were in operation, although

---

[4] New Orleans' oldest and most famous club, the Boston, was founded in
1845 by a group of business and professional men who named it after their
favorite game.

none equaled Davis' magnificence. Most of them came into existence after 1832, when the Louisiana Legislature removed the restriction upon the number of licenses that might be issued and increased the annual tax to $7,500. Perhaps the best known of these houses were those of Elkin, Pradat and Charton on Canal Street; Duval, St. Cyr and Touissant on Chartres Street; and James Hewlett, one of the early managers of the old St. Louis Hotel, at St. Louis and Chartres Streets. Hewlett's place, which was second in importance and popularity only to John Davis', was on the second floor of his saloon and coffee-house, formerly Maspero's Exchange, where Andrew Jackson had held several meetings with his officers to discuss the strategy of the Battle of New Orleans.

Only a few of the licensed resorts of the John Davis era placed a limit on their games, and it is doubtful if any American city witnessed consistently higher and more reckless gambling until some thirty years after the Civil War, when John W. Gates and the Chicago wheat kings began throwing their financial weight about in the gambling houses of New York, and Saratoga. Losses of $25,000 and more at a single sitting were not uncommon at the card and dice tables of early New Orleans, and many wealthy men squandered as much as $100,000 in a single year. The New Orleans of this period, besides giving to the gambling annals of America such men as Davis and Hewlett, also produced the Perfect Sucker, whose very entrance into the game was as good as a certified check. This answer to a gambler's prayer was Colonel John Randolph Grymes, one of Louisiana's most noted lawyers, who was District Attorney of New Orleans, Attorney-General of the state, member of the Legislature, and "engaged during his practice in almost every case of importance in the courts of New Orleans and the surrounding counties." One of his clients was the pirate Jean Lafitte, who paid him a fee of $20,000 for legal services when Governor W. C. C. Clairborne attempted to

jail Lafitte in New Orleans. When Colonel Grymes went to Lafitte's headquarters in the Bay of Barataria to collect his money,
to earn which he had resigned as District Attorney, the pirate
entertained him lavishly and then suggested a game of cards. At
the conclusion of the last hand Grymes had lost his $20,000, as
well as a similar amount which he had collected for Edward
Livingston, his associate in the defense of Lafitte.

Colonel Grymes earned a very large income by his law practice, but practically all of it went to enrich the gambling house
keepers and the friends with whom he played privately. Although he lived frugally, he was nearly always in debt, and was
a poor man when he died in 1854. He gambled at every opportunity and tried all sorts of games, but if local tradition is to be
credited his bad luck was phenomenal. Not once in years of
play did he hold a winning hand at cards or make a winning
cast of the dice; never did his choice of cards or numbers come
up at Faro or Roulette. Over a period of more than a decade his
losses are said to have averaged at least $50,000 a year. Several
men amassed small fortunes simply by coppering his bets at
Faro.

Gambling of this character continued in New Orleans until
late in 1835, when the licensing acts of 1823 and 1832 were repealed by a Legislature alarmed by the growing power of Davis
and his colleagues, the war against the sharpers at Vicksburg
and other towns along the Mississippi, and the revelations of
John A. Murrel's great conspiracy, in which many gamblers
were involved. A new law, making the operation of a gambling
house a felony punishable by a fine of from $5,000 to $10,000 or
imprisonment from one to five years, became effective early in
1836, and Davis immediately closed his house and thereafter devoted himself to his theatrical enterprises. Many of the other
places were operated clandestinely, with indifferent success, for
another year or so, but all succumbed to the depression and

money panic of 1837. Except for a few brace games in the underworld and river-front districts, and an occasional under-cover skinning house near the new St. Charles Hotel, gambling was rigidly suppressed in New Orleans for almost ten years; and not until the middle 1850's did the type of resort introduced by John Davis reappear.

3

As a mobilization center and supply base for the American armies operating in Mexico, and as one of the principal points of departure for the California gold fields, New Orleans from 1846 to the middle 1850's was thronged with soldiers and camp-followers, and with thousands of adventurers and fortune-hunters en route to and from San Francisco by way of Nicaragua and the Isthmus of Panama. The bulk of this immense transient population was composed of reckless fellows ready to stake everything they possessed on the turn of a card or the cast of a die, and hundreds of river sharpers temporarily deserted the steamboats and rushed ashore to reap the harvest, and to restore New Orleans to its rightful position as one of the great centers of gambling in America. With the connivance of city officials and the police—New Orleans was then in the midst of a period of political corruption which eventually brought about the Vigilante movement of 1858 [5]—Faro artists and short card sharks operated openly in the hotels, Monte throwers and Thimble-Riggers infested the saloons and coffee houses, and gambling resorts were opened "in all directions, all over the city . . . wherever returning soldiers or emigrants quartered or congregated." By 1850 at least five hundred houses were going full blast, a considerable number of places having been licensed by the city in 1848 to play Rondo and Keno. These games were enormously popular

[5] An account of the Vigilantes, and of political conditions in New Orleans during this period, may be found in the present author's *The French Quarter*.

in New Orleans, but so many dives were opened that after a few years it became necessary to suppress them as nuisances, and they were officially prohibited by an ordinance enacted in 1852. Rondo soon became obsolete as far as New Orleans was concerned, but Keno was widely played there as late as 1900.

None of the gambling houses which were hastily opened at the outbreak of the War with Mexico and the discovery of gold in California "assumed any pretensions to luxury or elegance," and most of them went out of existence when the war ended and the stream of gold-seekers dwindled to a trickle. But they had succeeded in re-establishing gambling in New Orleans, and had paved the way for the return of richly-appointed houses in the tradition of John Davis. The first of these places was opened by Allen Jones, ex-saddler and one-time partner of Colonel J. J. Bryant, a famous river gambler. The Colonel left him to hunt the gold-bearing sucker in California, and Jones tried short card sharping on the Mississippi steamboats, dealing Faro in Mobile and St. Louis, and capping for a Three-Card Monte gang on the Red River. He did well enough at Poker and Seven-up, but fared poorly as a Faro artist and a capper at Monte because of his attempts to double-cross his employers. He landed in New Orleans in 1852, and before he had made his peace with the politicians was twice arrested and fined for dealing Faro snaps. During the winter of 1852 Jones roped for a second-class skinning-house, and in so doing discovered his true vocation—he proved to be a roper-in of exceptional skill. He spent the summer of 1853 on the Mississippi, and in the fall of that year, in partnership with two other sharpers, opened a gambling house on Royal Street, a first-class place where everything was of the best, including the cheating.

Jones soon swindled his partners out of their interest in the establishment, and with himself roping and hired Faro artists performing the actual dirty work with the dealing boxes, the

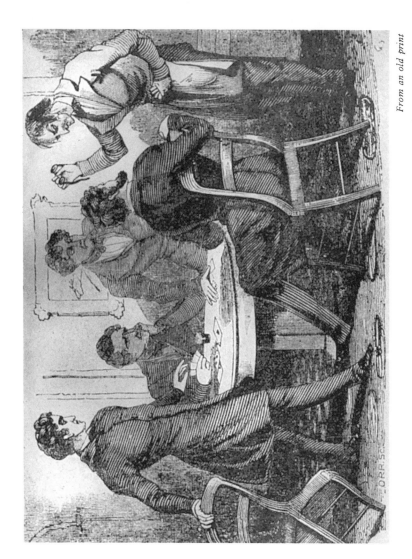

From an old print

TROUBLE IN A NEW YORK GAMBLING HOUSE IN THE 1860's

house was operated with great success until the beginning of the Civil War, at which time Jones had amassed a fortune of approximately $400,000—he owned a fine plantation near Vicksburg, about 250 slaves, and several houses and lots in New Orleans. During this period of prosperity the law annoyed him only once. That was in 1854, when the reform element of New Orleans joined forces with the Whigs and succeeded in partially wresting control of the city from the Democrats. The reformers procured the arrest of several gamblers, and Allen Jones and others were indicted by the Grand Jury. Only Jones, however, was brought to trial. A conviction automatically meant imprisonment, since he had already been twice found guilty of gambling, and the reformers hoped to make an example of him. But Jones bestirred himself to good effect among the politicians. He was tried, convicted despite an elaborate defense, and sentenced to two years in the penitentiary. But the Judge had scarcely finished speaking when Jones produced a pardon signed by the Governor of Louisiana, and walked out of the courtroom a free man. He said afterward that the pardon had been in his pocket throughout the trial. Jones gave financial support to the Native American or Know Nothing movement, and when the Know Nothings became the dominant factor in New Orleans politics in 1856 his was an important voice in their councils. The effrontery with which he carried on his skin games after he had thus become immune to prosecution earned for him, as one of his contemporaries said, "the unenviable reputation of being the meanest and most sordid wretch that ever disgraced the fraternity of sharpers."

Within a year or two after the opening of Allen Jones' house a dozen other first-class houses were in operation, practically all of them owned or controlled by sharpers who had won their gambling spurs on the Mississippi. Among them were Price McGrath, James Sherwood and Henry Perritt, forming the firm

of McGrath & Company; Augustus Lauraine and his partner
Charley Cassidy, who had journalistic ambitions and wrote racing news for a New York newspaper under the name of "Lar-
kin"; Montiro, still recalled in New Orleans as the man who
fought and wounded a famous burglar named Charles Alexander Gordon; Sam Levy, and Lorenzo Lewis, better known as
Count Lorenzo. About the only gambling house keeper of the
period without experience on the river was a courtly old Frenchman named Curtius, who had come to New Orleans from
Charleston. At Chartres and Toulouse Streets Curtius presided
over the most high-toned gambling resort in the city, and almost
the only one which didn't depend on crooked dealing boxes
and a staff of cappers and ropers-in. Faro was unknown at Curtius' place; only Boston, Chess and Poker were permitted, and
not more than $100 could be wagered on a single hand at Poker.
The revenues of the house were derived from small kitties on
each game, and fifty cents an hour paid by each visitor. Dinner
and wine were free. One of the habitués of Curtius' house, although he appears to have been a kibitzer rather than a gambler,
was an eccentric individual known in New Orleans as the Golden
Man, because of the extraordinary quantity of the precious metal
with which he adorned his person. For half a dozen years it was
his custom to promenade for several hours each Sunday morning
in the vicinity of the City and Veranda Hotels, laden with some
fifty pounds of gold chains, rings, bracelets, pins, buckles, buttons, and medallions. He acquired a new piece of jewelry in
1852, and one of the newspapers thus commented on the event:

"One would think that he had already ornaments enough
to satisfy any mortal; but he, it appears, is not of the stuff
every-day people are made of, and he could not be satisfied
until his fingers boasted another ring. The new prodigy is,
like its predecessors, of pure solid gold. It is worth 500 dol-

lars, and weighs nearly, if not quite, a pound. This small treasure is intended for the owner's 'little' finger . . . and is adorned with small carved figures, standing out in bold relief, and of very diminutive size, yet distinct and expressive. The right outer surface represents the flight of Joseph, the Virgin, and the infant Jesus into Egypt. Joseph, bearing a palm-branch, leads the way, the Virgin follows, seated on a donkey, and holding the Saviour on her lap. On the left outer edge of the ring is seen the prophet Daniel, standing between two lions. The prophet has not got a blue umbrella under his arm to distinguish him from the lions. The face of the ring exhibits an excellent design of the crucifixion, with the three crosses and the Saviour and the two thieves suspended thereto. The ring is certainly a curiosity." [6]

The principal member of McGrath & Company—and one of America's most successful gamblers—was Price McGrath, a native of the little Kentucky town of Versailles, near Lexington. As a youth he was taught the trade of a tailor, and at this period was religiously inclined, a shining light of the church and of the Sunday School. But he abandoned both the tailoring business and the godly life when he was about twenty-two years old, and went to Lexington, where he inaugurated his life work by capping for Chuck-a-Luck games and Thimble-Riggers during the racing season. Within a few years he had become a Faro artist, an expert at short cards, and a roper-in who always got his sucker. As a contemporary gambler remarked, "he now began to make some headway in life." From about 1847 to the middle 1850's McGrath played short cards on the steamboats, and roped for and dealt Faro in gambling houses in Lexington, Frankfort, Louisville and Cincinnati. In 1855 he arrived in New Orleans,

[6] Quoted from *Lands of the Slave and the Free, or, Cuba, the United States and Canada*, by Captain the Hon. Henry A. Murray, R.N.; London, 1857; pages 147–8.

where he met James Sherwood, a North Carolinian who had successfully operated a house in Richmond; and Henry Perritt, a veteran of the steamboats and for several years a well-known figure in the sporting world of St. Louis. At a cost of more than $75,000 the trio fitted up a gambling house at No. 4 Carondelet Street which was the most luxurious "palace of chance" that New Orleans had seen since the palmy days of John Davis. And as that pioneer had done, they invested their establishment with an atmosphere of extreme elegance and refinement. Only high-class suckers were admitted, the dealers and croupiers wore frock coats in the afternoon and full evening dress after dinner, and the service used for the nightly buffet suppers was of solid silver. Comparatively, the house was honest; no cappers or ropers-in were employed, and the partners boasted that they permitted no one to gamble who could not afford to lose. But a resort of this character needed no cappers, and Price McGrath was himself probably the most proficient roper-in of his time, while from the viewpoint of the professional gambler any sucker could afford to lose. Canada Bill Jones, a noted Monte thrower, once summed up the sharper's attitude when he said that suckers had no business with money, anyway.

McGrath & Company's palatial house was in operation, without interference from the police, for more than six years, and during that time the annual profits ranged from $80,000 to $100,000. McGrath received half as his share, so that his takings from this source alone amounted to approximately $250,000. In common with other important New Orleans gambling houses, the resort was closed when the Civil War began. Sherwood and Perritt remained in the city and contributed liberally to the Confederate war chest—Perritt equipped and sent to the front a military company called the Perritt Guards—but McGrath went to St. Louis. He returned to New Orleans late in 1862 and attempted to reopen the house in Carondelet Street, but was thrown into prison by the Federal military authorities.

4

From every viewpoint the prohibitory laws passed by the Louisiana Legislature in 1811, 1820 and 1836, and the license acts of 1823 and 1832, were momentous measures with far-reaching consequences. They made it possible for the gambling house to evolve into the form which was destined to exert a considerable influence upon American social and political life, and gave impetus to a great exodus of sharpers which had begun as soon as the Louisiana Purchase had made possible unrestricted travel to and from New Orleans. These pioneer tricksters carried the gospel of the Faro layout throughout the United States, spreading eastward and northward from New Orleans in two streams as clearly defined as population movements of a more reputable character. One went to New York by way of Mobile, Washington, Baltimore, Richmond, Philadelphia, Boston and other Eastern cities; the other followed the Mississippi and Ohio Rivers, penetrating the interior and planting troublesome colonies at Natchez, Vicksburg, Memphis, St. Louis, Cincinnati, and elsewhere on the road to Chicago.

During the progress of this hegira the United States was in the midst of the great boom which began about the turn of the nineteenth century and was intensified by the opening of the Western territories to settlement and their rivers to navigation. The entire country was in a ferment of restlessness; thousands were continually on the move to and from the Ohio and Mississippi Valleys; towns and cities were rising in the wilderness; the first wave of European immigration was washing upon American shores; and fortunes were being made overnight by men who, with no background or tradition of wealth, promptly squandered their riches in riotous dissipation. Most of the large cities were experiencing an extraordinary expansion in population and industry—Baltimore, with 80,000 inhabitants in 1827, was five times as large as in 1822, while New York grew from about 60,000 in 1800 to almost 175,000 in 1825, and Boston and Philadelphia doubled in size during the same period. Everywhere the underworld was flourishing, and burglars, footpads and other criminals, commonly called "crossmen," stalked the streets and went about their affairs with only occasional setbacks from inefficient and demoralized police departments. In many cities the rowdy element—the plug-uglies of Baltimore and the bullies and shoulder-hitters of New York and Philadelphia— had already begun to acquire the power and influence which were destined to prove so useful to the politicians in perpetuating the rule of their corrupt machines. Riots were of common occurrence, and lawlessness and disorder, fighting and drunkenness, prevailed to an extent that brought wondering comment from visiting foreigners and itinerant journalists.

Such conditions bred gamblers as naturally as a swamp breeds mosquitoes. A dozen years after the Louisiana Purchase there was scarcely a city of importance in the country that didn't harbor at least one gaming house and a group of industrious and prosperous gamblers, formed by the local talent, apt and eager pupils, around a nucleus of sharpers from New Orleans. These garrisons were heavily reinforced during the 1820's and the 1830's by fresh drafts from the South and by tricksters who had been driven from the towns along the Ohio and Mississippi Rivers. Throughout this period the Eastern newspapers published with increasing frequency accounts of the depredations of the gamblers and the efforts of the authorities to suppress them. Occasionally they were successful, as these few extracts from *Niles' Weekly Register* indicate:

"Baltimore. . . . Some nests of gamblers have been sorely disturbed since the new Mayor [Edward Johnson] came into office . . . they were punished to the very extent of the law, and have decamped for new quarters, after having ruined some promising young men."—*November 9, 1832.* On July 30, 1835, the New York *Sun* declared that there were five hundred gamblers in Baltimore, and ended its account with the admonition, "Drive them out, Baltimore! Drive them out!"

"Gamblers. A lot of about sixty were lately disturbed by the police in Philadelphia—but all escaped by jumping out of the windows, &c., except nine, who were conducted to prison. The regular establishment has thus been broken up —it was snugly fitted for deeds of darkness."—*December 3, 1831.*

"The Mayor of Philadelphia is winning for himself 'golden opinions.' He has lately broken up several nests of gamblers."—*March 14, 1835.*

"Large nests of gamblers in Richmond and Norfolk were completely routed a short time ago, by summary processes —numerous bodies of young men having taken the matter in charge. They broke into the gambling houses, destroyed all the apparatus and furniture—but farther than this, committed no acts of violence. Some curious disclosures of the great profits made by the knaves have been brought to light by these proceedings."—*October 4, 1834.*

Twenty-eight years before the godly young men of Norfolk dealt this knockout blow to the sharpers, the town was the scene of a famous gambling tragedy. In 1806 two brothers from Charleston, named Davis, opened a Faro bank in a back room on the third floor of an old building in Little Water Street, and for several weeks did a large business with the local sports. But they either ran an honest game, or, more probably, were clumsy and inexpert dealers, for one night an Italian commonly called Coalminer, whose name was Colmini, had an extraordinary run of luck and broke the bank. Wrote a Norfolk historian:

"The Davises and another of their fraternity charged him with cheating; he protested his innocence, but it was to no purpose. They attempted to seize him, but he broke from them and fled down the narrow stairway, all three in close pursuit. On the second landing he stepped aside, unperceived, and as each passed him on the right, he gave him a fatal stab with a stiletto in the left side, and a push down the next flight. The two Davises were mortally wounded and died within twenty-four hours; their companion lingered several weeks and died also. The Italian escaped." [7]

The gamblers who operated in the Eastern part of the United States during the first twenty-five or thirty years of the nineteenth century were numerous enough to worry and bedevil the authorities, and to arouse the antagonism of the respectable elements of the population. But the quarters in which they conducted their games were anything but impressive; compared to the palatial houses which flourished in New Orleans at the same time they were shabby and dismal dens, about as comfortable and attractive as the cheap speakeasies of the Prohibition era. They were generally located in the back rooms of grogshops, in alleys, in cellars, or, as in the early days at Norfolk, in old buildings which had been abandoned by legitimate business. The floors were strewn with sand or sawdust to absorb the tobacco

[7] *Historical and Descriptive Sketches of Norfolk and Vicinity, Including Portsmouth and the Adjacent Counties, During a Period of Two Hundred Years,* etc., by William S. Forrest; Philadelphia, 1853; page 113.

juice with which they were deluged by the gamblers and their customers, and there was no furniture except a few battered tables, benches, and hard-bottomed chairs; carpets, curtains and drapes, sideboards and divans, were unknown. Usually the house provided a bucket of water and a tin cup, but otherwise no refreshments were served, although liquor could be ordered from nearby gin-mills. No effort was made to keep out undesirable characters, and in consequence there was so much fighting and disorder that the keeper of every such resort was obliged to employ bruisers to battle for the house and eject refractory and obstreperous suckers.

Such hideaways, in numbers according to the needs of the population and the degree of corruption among the police and the politicians, were common enough in every large town on the Atlantic seaboard. Only Washington and New York could boast anything better before the middle 1830's, when first-class, well-ordered houses made their appearance in Philadelphia, Boston, Baltimore, and Richmond. None of these last four cities, however, despite their size and economic importance, ever became of any real consequence in the gambling history of the United States. In Baltimore and Richmond the sharpers were interfered with by the police and an indignant citizenry often enough to keep them in check; while in Boston and Philadelphia the first gamblers to open decently-equipped resorts were driven away by the rowdies, to whom they had refused to pay tribute. Except for an occasional unsuccessful venture, there were no first-class gambling facilities in Philadelphia until the early 1850's, when houses were opened by Doc Boyden and Billy Cheatham, from New Orleans, and Joe Hall, from New York. The first top-notch place to remain open in Boston any length of time was established about 1844 by Lyman Brittain, who had once dealt Faro for John Davis in New Orleans. Brittain ran his house successfully for some fifteen years, when he sold out and went to New

York. He died in the metropolis about 1862. Other gamblers who followed Brittain into Boston were less fortunate; most of them closed their doors within a few months, and as John O'Connor said, "those who failed did so more from want of patronage than any hostility shown towards them by the authorities." Gambling houses were not notably prosperous in Boston until after the Civil War, when for a few years around 1867 there were eleven resorts, four of them run by John Stuart, within gunshot range of the City Hall.

5

Only New York and Washington, among Eastern cities, and Mobile, in the South, achieved fame as gambling centers comparable to that enjoyed by New Orleans. The first of the trio to reach this eminence was Mobile, next to New Orleans the largest and busiest town on the Gulf Coast; and, in proportion to population, probably the most lawless and disorderly. As late as 1861 William Howard Russell, a famous English war correspondent, noted in his journal, during a visit to Mobile, that "the city . . . abounds in oyster-saloons, drinking-houses, lager-beer and wine shops, and gambling and dancing places." An old-time gambler thus described Mobile in the early 1830's, when it was the metropolis of Alabama and an important cotton-shipping port:

"I doubt if there could have been found on the face of the globe, a place with even five times its population, where crime, debauchery, and lawlessness reigned rampant to such a fearful extent. . . . The stranger could see without difficulty, even on his first visit to the place, that the godless were there greatly in the ascendancy. In nearly every single building along the street facing the river, could be found a liquor shop of one kind or another. . . . In the suburbs of

128

the city were several dance houses of the lowest order, where lawlessness, indecency and debauchery reigned supreme. . . . No police force dared intrude their unwelcome presence on the orgies carried on in those vile dens; and the peaceable and timid avoided their vicinity as they would have done that of a pest-house.

"From dark to dawn, lawlessness stalked abroad rampant in Mobile. Gangs of drunken boatmen, sailors and reckless adventurers, staggered through the streets, making night hideous with obscene songs and loud oaths, hunting for the next dram-shop or a fight, both of which were conveniently on hand. The imbecile police were utterly powerless, and could not in the least prevent the full-deck fights which were constantly going forward. . . . Every person, nearly, secretly carried weapons upon their persons, which they used upon the smallest provocation, and sometimes with none at all. . . . Nor did the lower class monopolize the vices and crimes afflicting the place. Duels, street fights, and cowardly assassinations, were ordinary pastimes among the rich and influential. The seduction of a wife, followed by the cold-blooded assassination of the seducer at the hands of the husband, or shooting a man immediately down for disputing the veracity of the slayer, were trivial matters which scarcely called for a passing notice, while forgeries and embezzlements were but venial offenses which were quickly whitewashed over. It was well for Mobile in those days that a divine Providence had ceased to destroy cities for the crimes and vices of its inhabitants, or it would certainly have shared the fate of ancient Sodom and Gomorrah." [8]

Founded in 1702 by Bienville's brother, Sieur d'Iberville, and settled by the same breed of riff-raff colonists who were sent out

[8] *Wanderings of a Vagabond*, pages 459–62.

from France to transform the site of New Orleans into a paradise, Mobile was occupied in turn by the French, English, Spanish and Americans, who took possession in 1813. The town thus had virtually the same racial backgrounds and traditions as New Orleans, and these factors, together with a lawless population and nearness to the Louisiana city, made it the natural stopping place for many of the gamblers who had been driven from New Orleans by harsh laws and force of circumstance. On a somewhat smaller scale, gambling was about as prevalent in Mobile during the colonial period as in New Orleans, and in much the same form—Faro, Roulette and *Vingt et Un* in the taverns and coffee-houses, and Brag and *Ecarté* among the gentry. It increased enormously as sharpers from New Orleans filtered into Mobile, and especially after the Americanization of the town had begun with a tide of immigration from the back country of Alabama and Georgia. By the middle 1820's the gamblers were in the saddle and riding high, virtually secure from molestation in a disorderly town fairly swarming with suckers yearning to be trimmed. Open games, principally Rondo, Chuck-a-Luck and others in which the naturally high percentage in favor of the bank was increased by trickery, flourished in almost every grogshop, especially those along the water front and in the underworld districts. Even the bordellos and dance-houses operated percentage games as adjuncts to their other amusements.

Most of the higher-class gambling resorts, none of them in any way comparable to the gilded dens of New Orleans, were housed in a block of red brick buildings, called the Shakespere Row, in the business part of the town. This block was built in the Spanish fashion around a large patio or courtyard, which was entered from two streets through arched gate-ways. Twenty-eight rooms, opening on an enclosed verandah, faced the courtyard, and all but a few were devoted to gambling. They offered principally Faro, with limits ranging from $10 and paroli of

$50, to $100 and paroli to $800; and Roulette, with limits of from $25 to $700. At one time there were forty-four Faro banks and thirty-seven Roulette wheels operating in the Shakespere Row. O'Connor described the courtyard as "one vast gambling-hell, the resort, of evenings, of persons moving in the different upper walks of life; and from early candle-light till the break of day, the rattling of Faro checks and the spinning of Roulette wheels could be heard without cessation."

During the sessions of the Alabama Legislature many of the gamblers of Shakespere Row closed their resorts in Mobile and went to Tuscaloosa, capital of the state from 1826 to 1847. There they opened Faro snaps and set up Roulette wheels for the convenience of the lawmakers, who were noted for the reckless manner in which they gambled and the ease with which they could be victimized by crooked dealing boxes, strippers and magnetized Roulette wheels. The proprietor of one of the Tuscaloosa houses, fearing the results of attempted trickery on experienced players, posted this notice in his Faro room:

"Members of the Legislature please take the table to the right; gamblers take the table to the left—it's hard to tell you apart."

Perhaps the best known gambler in early Mobile, and certainly the most picturesque, was an old man named Silas Greene, part owner of a gambling resort above the Sans Souci Coffee-House, across the street from the old Waverly Hotel. Greene's partner, George Kent, devoted most of his time to the lucrative business of dealing in slaves for the Mobile and New Orleans markets, and Greene ran the gambling place, which was housed in two large, well-furnished rooms. In one were several Faro banks and a Roulette wheel, while the other was fitted with chairs and tables for short card and dice games. Greene was well-liked despite his many peculiarities, his dealers were skillful and courteous, and for many years the house, patronized principally by business and professional men, did a flourishing business. The games appear to have been square except when a player had such an extraordinary run of luck that one of Greene's artists found it necessary to "protect the house." During the height of his success in Mobile Greene was a fairly rich man; he always had a bountiful supply of cash, and owned several parcels of real estate in the city, besides fifty slaves and a cotton plantation on the Tombigbee River.

O'Connor said that Greene had "risen to the surface somewhere among the red lands of Georgia, and had groped his way along until he reached Mobile." There he pursued the gambler's trade for some thirty-five years, except for a brief period when he attempted unsuccessfully to set up a game in New Orleans. He was a generous, kind-hearted old man, but he offset these excellent traits by being ignorant, stubborn and credulous; he could barely read and write, and believed everything he was told, so that he was the butt of innumerable practical jokes. Moreover, he was superstitious to a degree that was remarkable even for a gambler; he conducted his business and his whole life by means of signs and omens, and consulted every fortune teller he could find. When his Faro bank, the apple of his eye, began experiencing a run of bad luck he would convince himself that his own presence in the room was the cause. He would then go downstairs to the street, and for hours at a time pace back and forth in front of the building, hands clasped behind his back, and chewing tobacco as fast as he could move his jaws. When anyone came down from the gambling rooms the old man asked:

"How's the old mill grinding now?"

If the bank had started to win he would buy a drink at the bar of the Sans Souci; if the bank was still losing he would resume his pacing, shaking his head and muttering:

132

"There's a Jonah in that room, sure!"

When it finally became clear that he was not himself the Jonah, Green would return to the gambling rooms, pick out a player whom he suspected of bringing bad luck to the house, and pay him to leave and stay away for a week. Since none of the bank's losing streaks lasted that long, the old man would be certain that he had thus broken the spell.

During one of these unhappy periods, when the bank was almost $30,000 in the hole, some of Greene's friends connived with a fortune teller to sell him an extraordinary horoscope. This document informed him that if he would go to the race track, about three miles out of town, for nine successive days at nine o'clock in the morning, and walk once around the track, his Faro dealers would not only regain what they had lost but would win $49,000 for the bank besides. The old man dutifully performed this task for eight days, while those privy to the hoax, who soon included almost everyone in Mobile except Greene, went along to watch what they called "old Greene's morning workout." On the night of the eighth day Greene, at the urging of his friends, opened a bottle of champagne to celebrate the imminent coming of prosperity. Then he opened another, and another, and so on through the night, the upshot being that at nine o'clock on the morning of the ninth day he was too drunk to get to the track. He hurried to the fortune teller and begged for another chance, but she told him coldly that the stars were no longer interested in him, and that he could expect nothing but bad luck. The old man gloomed around for several days before he learned how he had been victimized; but when he did he went looking for the jokers with a shotgun. Fortunately for them the Sheriff haled him into court and had him placed under a bond of $5,000 to keep the peace.

6

The development of gambling in Washington followed much the same pattern as in New Orleans and Mobile. A few gamblers, probably from Charleston,[9] were on hand when Congress held its first session in the new capital in 1800, and more drifted in as the city filled with office holders, job hunters, lobbyists and politicians, the American equivalent of the French rabble which had colonized Alabama and Louisiana. These pioneer sharpers set up their games in the grogshops, and prospered for several years. Houses exclusively for gambling appeared sometime between 1815 and 1820, when Washington had begun to outgrow its early nicknames of "The Capital of Miserable Huts" and "The Great American Mudhole." By 1825, despite stringent anti-gambling laws passed by Congress, there were at least a dozen such resorts in operation, and about 1828 many of them began to follow the example of John Davis in New Orleans and serve free liquor and more or less elaborate suppers. All of these places were on the north side of Pennsylvania Avenue near the Capitol gate, and all depended for existence upon the patronage of government officials, employes, and hangers-on.

Faro was the principal banking game, but the best of the early Washington gambling houses also provided rooms for Brag, *Ecarté,* All-Fours, and later, Poker. One of these rooms, said to have been in the house operated by Samuel Shirley, was the scene of a famous game of Brag between Montjoy Bailey, Sergeant-at-Arms of the Senate, and Montford Stokes, United States Senator

[9] Charleston was important as a gambling center for several years around the turn of the nineteenth century, when the French population was considerably increased by refugees from San Domingo. The Duke de la Rochefoucauld-Liancourt, a distinguished French publicist and politician, who visited Charleston during this period, reported that he found gaming houses "very numerous." He wrote that in them "aristocracy and *sans culottes* mix in friendly intercourse and indiscriminately surround the tables. It is asserted that they play very high."

PENDLETON'S "LADY LOBBYISTS" PRACTICING THEIR ARTS

from North Carolina from 1816 to 1823. The two men began to play on a Thursday afternoon, the Senate having adjourned to Monday, as was the custom in those days, and there was nothing to stop them except weariness or bankruptcy. "The game was continued Friday night and Saturday," wrote Perley Poore, a noted Washington journalist, "through Saturday night and all day Sunday and Sunday night, the players resting for a snatch of sleep as nature became exhausted. Monday morning the game was in full blast, but at ten o'clock Bailey moved an adjournment, alleging that his official duties required his presence in the Senate chamber. Stokes remonstrated, but the Sergeant-at-Arms persisted, and rose from the table, the Senator grumbling and declaring that had he supposed that Bailey would have thus prematurely broken up the game he would not have sat down to play with him." [10]

Another version of this Gargantuan joust says that it was played in a sitting room of the old Indian Queen Tavern, which in common with many other hotels of the period, provided facilities for private gambling. In its time the Indian Queen was Washington's most celebrated inn, and the residence of many noted statesmen. The landlord, Jesse Brown, was an interesting figure. When guests arrived he met them at the curbstone, standing under the big sign—a portrait of Pocahontas painted in glaring colors—which swung in the breeze of Pennsylvania Avenue for almost half a century. "A glance at the travelers as they alighted and were ushered by him into the house," wrote Perley Poore, "would enable him mentally to assign each one to a room, the advantages of which he would describe ere sending its destined occupant there under the pilotage of a colored servant. When the next meal was ready, the newly arrived guest was met at the door of the dining-room by Mr. Brown, wearing a

[10] *Perley's Reminiscences, or, Sixty Years in the National Metropolis,* by Ben: Perley Poore; Philadelphia, 1886; Vol. I, page 61.

large white apron, who escorted him to a seat and then went to the head of the table, where he carved and helped the principal dish. The excellences of this—fish, flesh or fowl—he would announce as he would invite those seated at the table to send up their plates for what he knew to be their favorite portions; and he would also invite attention to the dishes on other parts of the table, which were carved and helped by the guests who sat nearest them. . . . Brandy and whisky were placed on the dinner-table in decanters, to be drunk by the guests without additional charge therefor. . . ." [11]

The custom of ballyhooing the bill of fare was continued in many American hotels long after the advent of the printed menu card. One of the last and most famous landlords of this type was General McMackin, whose Washington Hotel at Vicksburg was a favorite resort of the river gamblers for many years; it was famous up and down the river for the quality of its meals. William Howard Russell, who visited Vicksburg in the summer of 1861, said that when he went in to dinner he "found the tables closely packed with a numerous company of every condition in life, from generals and planters down to soldiers in the uniform of privates. At the end of the room was a long table on which the joints and dishes were brought hot from the kitchen . . . and as each was brought in the proprietor, standing in the center of the room, shouted out in a loud voice, 'Now, then, here is a splendid goose! ladies and gentlemen, don't neglect the goose and apple-sauce! Here's a piece of beef that *I* can recommend! Upon my honor you will never regret taking a slice of the beef. Oyster-pie! oyster-pie! never was better oyster-pie seen in Vicksburg! . . . Ladies and gentlemen, just look at that turkey! who's for turkey?'—and so on, wiping the perspiration from his forehead and combating with the flies." Another traveler, Bishop George F. Pierce, said of General McMackin that "all his various

[11] *Ibid.,* page 43.

directions worked into a sort of song. . . . He says, I understand, that the reason he adopted this unique method was that some years ago he kept a public house in Jackson, and many of his boarders were members of the Legislature, and could not read, so he had to *call out* for their information." In his Jackson establishment General McMackin always began his harangue with the sonorous announcement, "Gentlemen, we are a great people!"

Samuel Shirley, who was probably the most important gambling-house keeper in Washington during the pre-Pendleton era, made his debut in the capital about 1820, when he opened a resort next door to the Indian Queen Tavern. Other gamblers disliked Shirley because of his supercilious manner and haughty, overbearing disposition, but he was popular enough among the politicians and statesmen, and his house prospered until Pendleton came along in 1832 and lured away most of his best customers. For more than a decade Shirley's Faro bank offered the same limit that prevailed in other first-class houses—$25 and paroli to $100—but after a run of bad luck in 1833 he became very timid, refusing to accept any bet higher than $10, and tightening his game to such an extent that it was attractive only to low-salaried clerks and other persons of small means. His takings were thus very meager despite the best efforts of his dealers, and late in 1834, to retrieve his fortunes, he took into partnership two itinerant gamblers, new-comers to Washington, named John Cotton and George Simpson.

Cotton was in his early twenties, while Simpson was about fifty, a big man with sandy hair and whiskers, and white eyebrows and lashes. He had been a slave trader and had toured the South with a band of sharpers and a stable of quarter-horses, and in Washington gambling circles was believed to have been a member of John A. Murrel's gang of bandits, horsethieves, gamblers, and Negro-stealers. In dress, both Simp-

son and Cotton outshone any gambler of the period, at least
in Washington, and their gaudy raiment set new standards of
sartorial display, to say nothing of bad taste. Simpson appears
to have been the first gambler in the East to wear a big diamond in his ruffled shirt-bosom, while Cotton, besides a similar
stone, sported a long gold chain, looped several times around
his neck and attached to a gold watch. Except for the chain and
a few other minor details, Simpson and Cotton dressed iden-
tically, and O'Connor's account of the former's favorite outfit
also describes Cotton's.

". . . a green 'shad-bellied' coat, with long flaps hanging
over its many pockets, and ornamented with rows of bright
brass buttons embossed with rampant steeds in the last
stage of prancing. His vest, of green velvet, was adorned
with round, gold-varnished buttons, on each of which a
dog's head shone conspicuous, and which also possessed
wide pockets covered by deep flaps. His nether limbs were
encased in a pair of drab inexpressibles, the bottoms of
which had modestly retired from public view, into the legs
of a pair of red-top hunting boots. A broad-brimmed hat
covered his head, and in the voluminous ruffle which
sprang from his shirt bosom, sparkled a large and valuable
diamond. He wore a high shirt collar, and around his neck,
below it, the ample folds of a large red handkerchief. A
heavy embossed chain, from which dangled a few seals and
a miniature jockey's cap, saddle, spurs, horse-shoes, whip,
etc., hung from his watch-fob. . . ." [12]

Physically Cotton was the direct antithesis of Simpson; he
was short and inclined to stoutness, with tow-colored hair and
eye-brows; a fat, stupid-looking face; and pop eyes of pale

[12] *Wanderings of a Vagabond*, page 142.

blue, dull and lusterless. His appearance, however, concealed unusual gifts; actually he was a smart gambler, and a master of all the devices and tricks for cheating at Faro that had been invented up to that time. He did most of the dealing after he and Simpson had bought an interest in Shirley's house, while Shirley acted as a sort of general manager. Simpson was the roper-in; he was very affable and free with his money, and spent most of his time in the bar-rooms and hotel lobbies, angling for prospective suckers. Under the new setup the limit was removed from the Faro game, and Simpson industriously spread the news that the firm of Shirley, Simpson & Cotton would accept bets of any amount. Since no limit games were scarce in Washington, this policy brought into the house a great many big-money players, including professional gamblers whose hankering for action overcame their judgment. They plunged heavily against Cotton's dealing with disastrous results to themselves, and for several months the house played in what seemed to be phenomenal luck. But the good fortune of this precious trio came to an end early in 1835, when Cotton was caught dealing sanded cards and strippers. The day after the exposure half a dozen of Cotton's victims went to the resort to demand reparation and exact revenge, but found the place closed and the partners gone. What became of Shirley and Simpson was never known in Washington, but Cotton is said to have gone west to try his luck on the Mississippi, arriving in Natchez just in time to be chased off the river in the uprising that followed the lynching of several gamblers by a mob at Vicksburg. He remained in that part of the country, however, long enough to set a fashion, and among the steamboat sharpers a gold chain soon became almost a standard article of adornment. The size and length of the chain depended upon the gambler's prosperity and the strength of his neck muscles.

7

In all the long history of gambling in the capital, no other figure ever arose comparable to that of Edward Pendleton, who for some twenty-five years before the Civil War operated the most famous of all Washington gaming resorts in Pennsylvania Avenue near Fourteenth Street—a luxurious "hell" known to Faro players as the Hall of the Bleeding Heart, although Pendleton himself preferred to call it the Palace of Fortune. Pendleton was the prototype of the legendary gambler of fiction and the movies—handsome, suave, highly educated, elegant in dress and manner and, like all good gamblers of song and story, on occasion spectacularly generous to his victims; he was often warmly commended for making partial restitution, in the form of a loan, to a sucker whom he had despoiled.

In addition to these qualifications for immortality, Pendleton was the black sheep of an illustrious Virginia family and well-connected by marriage—his wife was Jacqueline Smith Mills, most beautiful of the four daughters of Robert Mills, a noted architect who designed the Pennsylvania State Capitol at Harrisburg, made the original plans of the Washington Monument, and supervised the construction of the Post Office, Treasury, and Patent Office Buildings. Besides being one of the reigning beauties of the capital, Mrs. Pendleton was in great favor at the White House during the administration of James G. Buchanan, and at one time was appointed by the President to act as confidential emissary between the governments of France and the United States. According to Robert Mills' biographer, President Buchanan was said to have been "devotedly attached" to Mrs. Pendleton, and wrote the "rarely beautiful obituary address" which was delivered at her funeral.[13] The Washington *Star*

[13] *Robert Mills, Architect of the Washington Monument, 1781–1855,* by H. M. Pierce Gallagher; New York, 1935; page 185.

said that the President was one of those present when she died on April 17, 1859, at the age of forty-five, and a clipping from another newspaper, found among the Mills family documents, said that as she expired "President Buchanan stood, hat in hand, at the foot of her bed." Long and extremely laudatory obituaries of Mrs. Pendleton were published by the Washington newspapers, but none mentioned her husband except to say briefly that he had died a year or so before.

Pendleton opened his gambling house in 1832 in partnership with a Kentuckian named Marshall, who had learned his trade in the Faro dens of Natchez and Vicksburg. Marshall was a roughneck in every respect, utterly unlike the courtly Pendleton, but in handling a crooked dealing box and manipulating a stripped and sanded deck of cards he was one of the foremost experts of his time. During the first year or two the house was in operation Pendleton and Marshall took turns at the Faro table, but as the resort became popular Pendleton devoted his energies to running the establishment and ministering to the comfort and convenience of the suckers, while Marshall attended to the technical details of the business and trained the artists who relieved and eventually succeeded him. Marshall was Pendleton's partner and principal artist for eight or ten years, but the latter finally dissolved the association because of Marshall's dissolute habits and inordinate love of gambling; when he was not dealing Faro at Pendleton's he was in other gambling houses being victimized by the same tricks which he employed so successfully at the Hall of the Bleeding Heart. "He made ten fortunes while with Pendleton," wrote O'Connor, "of all of which he got rid, either by the most reckless extravagance, or bucking at Faro, and finally died a miserable drunkard in his native state."

The Hall of the Bleeding Heart prospered almost from the day the first customer attempted to cope with Marshall's crooked dealing, but its palmy days were from about 1845 to the late 1850's, when it was the favorite resort of high government officials, and of the Abolitionist and Secessionist agitators and politicians, who forgot animosities and cares of state in the excitement of attempting to tame the tiger. Throughout this period Pendleton's was one of the most magnificently furnished gambling houses in America, and the company which frequented it was by far the most select. The journalist Perley Poore thus described Pendleton's as he saw it in the early 1850's:

"His rooms were hung with meretricious pictures, and the art of wood-carving was carried to great perfection in the side-boards, secretaries, and tables, which served the various purposes of the establishment. The dining and supper tables were loaded with plate of the pure metal. The cooking would not have shamed the genius of Soyer, and it was universally admitted that the wines were such as could have been selected only by a connoisseur. This incomparable provider had ten thousand dollars invested in his cellar and his closet.

"The people who nightly assembled to see and to take part in the entertainments of the house consisted of candidates for the Presidency, Senators and Representatives, members of the Cabinet, editors and journalists. . . . In the outer parlors, as midnight approached, might have been seen leading members of Congress, quietly discussing the day's proceedings, the prospects of parties, and the character of public men. A few officers of the Army added to the number and variety of the groups which occupied this apartment. Here all were drinking, smoking and talking, generally in a bright and jocose vein. Servants were gliding about with cigars, toddies, cocktails, and 'whiskey-

THREE OF A KIND BEAT A STATESMAN

From an old print

"BEAU" HICKMAN

straights' on little silver trays. Among them were two 'old Virginny' darkies, very obliging and popular, who picked up many quarters and halves, and not a few 'white fish,' representing one dollar each." [14]

Washington fairly swarmed with lobbyists during the troublous times which preceded the Civil War, and Pendleton's was their special rendezvous; it offered almost ideal conditions for the practice of their profession. These "master workmen of the third house" gambled infrequently, but they were always on hand to lend money to or assume the gambling debts of Congressmen and government officials who had been clawed by the tiger. These loans were repaid with votes and influence, and the necessary support for many a Treasury steal was obtained by lobbyists who thus came to the financial rescue of distressed Senators and Representatives. Pendleton himself was one of the most successful lobbyists of the period, for as Perley Poore pointed out, "his professional position gave him great facilities," and "he assisted in the passage of many useful bills of a private nature, involving considerable sums of money." It was understood among venal Congressmen and officials that successful advocacy of one of Pendleton's measures would be followed by a happy evening at the Faro table.

To influence Congressmen who were immune to the fascinations of Faro Pendleton utilized the services of women who were politely referred to by journalists as "lady lobbyists," a tèrm which by no means fully describes their activities. "The parlors of some of these dames," wrote Perley Poore, "were exquisitely furnished with works of art and bric-a-brac, donated by admirers. Every evening they received, and in the winter their blazing wood fires were surrounded by a distinguished circle. Some would treat favored guests to a game of Euchre, and as

[14] *Perley's Reminiscences*, Vol. II, pages 43–5.

midnight approached there was always an adjournment to the dining-room, where a choice supper was served. A cold duck, a venison pie, broiled oysters, or some other exquisitely cooked dish with salads and cheese, generally constituted the repast, with iced champagne or Burgundy at blood-heat. Who could blame the Congressmen for leaving the bad cooking of his hotel or boarding-house, with an absence of all home comforts, to walk into the parlor web which the adroit spider lobbyist had cunningly woven for him?"

In addition to lobbying for the bills in which Pendleton was interested, many of these ladies also lobbied for the gambling house, receiving a fixed percentage of the losses of any sucker whom they might induce to visit the place. They supplemented the regular staff of ropers-in who hung about the hotels, bar-rooms and railroad stations, scraping acquaintance with likely prospects from out of town. Curiously enough, one of the smartest of Pendleton's ropers was an eccentric character known as Beau Hickman, a Virginian, who appeared in Washington in the early 1840's and was on Pendleton's payroll for some fifteen years. Shabbily but fashionably dressed, with white cravat, plug hat and soiled white gloves, Hickman became a familiar figure around the hotel lobbies and bar-rooms. When strangers were introduced to him he always demanded, and quite often received, an "initiation fee." Besides roping for Pendleton he also acted as guide to more questionable resorts, and from all of his various activities managed to eke out a very respectable living.

The Hall of the Bleeding Heart was exclusively a Faro house, and there is no record that Pendleton ever permitted any other banking game to be played on the premises. A few private rooms were available for Brag, Whist, Poker and other short card games, but only to high government officials; as far as he could Pendleton discouraged this sort of gambling, in which there is comparatively little money for the house. In the Faro room white chips were a dollar each and reds five dollars, and the bank set no limit, either on straight bets or on parolis. Sometimes the play was very high, but there is a wide variation of opinion as to the height it actually reached. According to Richard Canfield's biographer two of Pendleton's customers, about 1855, "won close to $50,000 each at a sitting," [15] but Perley Poore, who was in Washington when the Hall of the Bleeding Heart was at the peak of its popularity, says that the largest amount ever won from the bank was $1,200, on successive parolis of an original stake of $100.

It is extremely doubtful if anyone ever won as much as $50,000 from Pendleton, either at one or fifty sittings, for his dealers were experts who always had command of the game, and were greatly aided by the fact that Pendleton never introduced tabs or a case-keeper. The honesty of the deal depended upon the importance of the player, politically or to Pendleton's lobbying schemes. Cabinet members and candidates for the Presidency were treated with deference befitting their stations; they had no obstacles to surmount other than the natural percentage of the game unless they got started on a phenomenal run of luck. But when ordinary Congressmen, politicians and officials bucked the tiger the dealers "protected the house" at all times; in other words, these smaller fry got the works. "Scores of Senators and Representatives," wrote a Washington historian, "particularly from the South and West, squandered their salaries . . . and some impaired their private fortunes by the same indulgence." [16] It was not uncommon for Pendleton's customers to be placed in positions similar to that in which Humphrey Marshall, a relative of John Marshall and during the Civil War

[15] *Canfield, the True Story of the Greatest Gambler,* by Alexander Gardiner; New York, 1930; page 25.

[16] *Washington, the Capital City, and Its Part in the History of the Nation,* by Rufus Rockwell Wilson; Philadelphia, 1901; Vol. I, page 392.

a Brigadier-General of the Confederate Army, found himself in 1852, when he was appointed Minister to China by President Franklin Pierce. To celebrate the appointment Marshall bucked the tiger at Pendleton's, where he lost his savings, the expense money advanced by the government, and six months' pay, for which he gave his note. Pendleton saved his job and reputation, and incidentally made certain of the six months' pay, by lending him sufficient money for the voyage to China.

Pendleton was a spendthrift and a high liver, but money poured into his pockets in such a stream that despite his extravagance he left a comfortable fortune. Moreover, his prestige and influence increased with the years, and when he died in 1858 he had become such an important personage in Washington that President Buchanan attended his funeral, while several prominent Democratic Congressmen were among his pallbearers. The furnishings and equipment of the Hall of the Bleeding Heart were sold at auction, and before the sale the house was thrown open for inspection. It was visited by large crowds of Washington's most fashionable folk, "and," wrote Perley Poore, "probably for the first time since the descent of Proserpine, the gates of Hades were passed by troops of the fair sex."

8

In the smaller communities and country districts before the Civil War gambling was dominated by a new type of sharper who appeared soon after the Louisiana Purchase and quickly became a pest throughout the South and South-West—the peripatetic gambler who toured the country with a fast quarter-horse [17] and a band of cappers, ropers-in, Faro artists, Thimble-Riggers, and dice and card experts equipped with loaded dice, readers, strippers and cold decks. They were ready for any sort

[17] That is, a horse trained to run very fast for a quarter of a mile.

of game that might be proposed, and at all of them, even such an old-maidish business as cribbage, they were accomplished cheats. Some of these bands numbered as many as twenty men, and they worked the small towns with a thoroughness worthy of a better cause—matching the quarter-horses against racers owned by farmers and local sports eager to back their own animals, and then fleecing the same farmers and sports after they had been inveigled into the gambling rooms by the ropers-in and prepared for the slaughter by the cappers.

The biggest killings were made during the fairs, and the frequent frolics which were attended by everyone from miles around and were the great social and sporting events of the period. At these gatherings the afternoons were devoted to horse racing and fighting—free-for-alls, and single combats in which the victor was the man who could gouge out an eye or bite off a nose in the most workmanlike manner—and the evenings to dancing, fighting, and gambling. All of these activities were accompanied by an amazing consumption of Monongahela whisky, the favorite tipple of the times. *Niles' Weekly Register* of April 18, 1812, described a great and bloody frolic at Wheeling, in those days one of the really tough towns of the country, "which 'would have rivaled Pittsburg long since' had it not been unfortunately placed in Virginia,[18] a state whose inhabitants are too much addicted to drunkenness, horse racing, cock fighting, gambling, and plundering the Indians, to attend to commercial dealings or industrious pursuits." The *Register* continued:

"This part of the state, especially, seems to have been to the United States, what Botany Bay colony was to England, the asylum of thieves and swindlers, and outlawed vagabonds of every description. Here 'they formed a species of

[18] Now in the state of West Virginia, formed by partition from Virginia in 1861.

nefarious republic, where equality of crime constituted a
social band.' . . . The price of a saddle was offered to be
run for, and in an instant, as if by magic, the town became
a desert; the stores and warehouses were shut, 'blacksmiths,
shipwrights, all left work' and 'six poor devils were started
for the saddle.' The race was disputed, but as every spectator
had something depending on the issue, no proper umpire
could be found to decide, and *'a general battle ensued.'*
This continued some time, when two individuals—a David,
and a Goliah! like Paris and Atrides of old, stepped forth,
from the contending powers, and offered to decide the fate
of the day, by single combat. [An account of the bloody
fight follows.]

"The day's *sports* ended in a ball at the principal inn
where our traveler lodged; to a participation in the pleas-
ures of which, he was politely told by his landlord . . .
that his quality of stranger and a gentleman, would gain
him free admission. Profiting by this invitation, he entered
the ball-room. Here new scenes, such as are never exhibited
at Carlton House, met his astonished view. Would that
Hogarth had lived to see that room! One corner was occupied by a portion of the assembly, engaged in the fascinating games of *all-fours, three-up* and *cribbag*e; in another stood a table of refreshments, *whiskey and biscuit,*
surrounded by a crowd of drinkers and smokers; a group
of noisy politicians held possession in the third; and in the
fourth was stationed the *music* which consisted of two
bangies played by negroes nearly in a state of *nudity,* and a
lute through which a Chickasaw breathed delightful har-
mony." [19]

---

[19] This was the second of four articles in which the *Register* reported on a
travel book by the English author, Thomas Ashe.

As Faro increased in popularity, and crooked dealing boxes and other devices for cheating were invented, the touring trickster gradually began to concentrate on the tiger, and to dispense with the quarter-horse and the motley crew which frequently got him into trouble, and cheated him almost as often as he cheated the sucker. By 1830 most of the itinerant sharpers were accomplished artists who went about the country opening Faro snaps, sometimes in the larger cities but more often, as the pioneers in their business had done, confining their attentions to the small towns and the country districts. If trouble impended after a cleanup, they skipped out immediately; but if the local suckers took their trimming in good part, they remained long enough to teach crooked dealing and manipulation of the deck to whoever would pay well for the knowledge. And thus thousands of comparatively honest amateur players were transformed into professional cheats, and in their turn took to the road and the rivers, or swarmed into the big cities.

A great many of the gamblers who prowled the American hinterland during the thirty years which preceded the Civil War operated under the patronage and direction of an extraordinarily astute and far-seeing gambler who introduced nepotism into gambling and performed the remarkable feat of putting Faro and *Monte* on a sort of chain-store basis. His name was Elijah Skaggs, but he was better known as "Brother Skaggs, the preaching Faro dealer," because of his costume, which never varied throughout his professional life regardless of climate or weather—frock-coat and trousers of black broadcloth, black silk vest, white shirt with high standing collar, white cravat of the choker type wound several times around his scrawny neck, black stove-pipe hat, and black patent-leather gaiters. These somber garments covered a long, gaunt and awkward frame and emphasized a sour and saturnine physiognomy. And Brother Skaggs' private life appears to have been as austere as his appearance—he neither smoked nor drank, women meant nothing to him, and he was never known to laugh, or even smile. He so closely resembled the traveling parson so common in early America that even among people who knew him he evoked surprise when he opened a Faro snap instead of a prayer meeting. But he was an amazingly successful gambler, and one of the cleverest tricksters that the United States has yet produced. Also, he probably had more to do with the spread of gambling in this country than any other one man.

Brother Skaggs was a Kentuckian, born in the back country near the Tennessee border, and reared with numerous brothers, sisters and cousins on a small farm from which, as O'Connor says, "they extracted sufficient hog and hominy to keep them from starvation." But Elijah had visions of greater things; he craved wealth and luxury, and as a youngster decided that the easiest and quickest way to get them was by gambling. He obtained a pack of cards, and while less ambitious Skaggses grubbed in the cotton patch young Elijah sat on a stump and practiced dealing, stacking, and otherwise manipulating the cards. At sixteen he began his career by trimming his cousins and brothers, and with the family cash for a bank roll began making trips to the Kentucky settlements, playing principally Brag, All-Fours, and Twenty-Card Poker, at none of which did he deal honestly. He even ventured as far north as Lexington, which an English traveler in 1812 [20] had described as "a flourishing town," where "the prevailing amusements are drinking and gambling." By the time he was twenty years old Brother Skaggs had accumulated $2,000, a considerable sum in those days, and the ease with which he had acquired the money convinced him that he was ready to set upon his travels and

[20] Thomas Ashe.

FARO ROOM IN THE HALL OF "THE BLEEDING HEART"

AN EARLY WASHINGTON GAMBLING HOUSE

enlarge his knowledge. So he crossed the state line into Tennessee and went to Nashville, a lively town at the junction of the Natchez Trace and the Wilderness Road, and one of the resorts of the bandits and cutthroats who prowled those lonesome trails.

In Nashville Brother Skaggs adopted the costume by which he became known throughout the South, and employed an itinerant school-master to teach him to read and write—he could already count the pips on a playing card. More important, however, he learned about Faro, which had lately been introduced into Nashville by a band of sharpers from New Orleans. Skaggs was too shrewd to play a game with which he was not familiar, but he was greatly impressed by the popularity of Faro, by the opportunities it offered for chicanery, by the fact that the deal remained always in the hands of the man who ran the game, and by the expedition with which the artists emptied the pockets of the local sports. He promptly settled upon Faro as his life work, and abandoned the short games, to master which he had devoted so much time and effort. For the next few years, accompanied by his private tutor, Brother Skaggs traveled about the country, gambling occasionally, but most of the time watching Faro dealers at work in such gambling centers as New Orleans, Mobile, the Pinch Gut district of Memphis, and those twin hell holes of the Mississippi, Natchez and Vicksburg. Whenever he saw a Faro dealer display a new bit of skullduggery, he compelled the sharper to divulge the trick under threat of exposure, or, if necessary, bought the knowledge—he is said to have paid $1,800 for the secret of manipulating tie-ups, with which he afterward made thousands.[21] Once he knew how a trick was done, he went into se-

[21] Tie-ups were cards, sometimes as many as nine, stacked to make the last four cases in a deal lose. Each card was pierced with a fine needle, and the lot tied together with a horse hair. After the shuffle the dealer cut the deck above the tie-ups, thus placing them at the bottom of the pack. "While plac-

clusion and practiced until he could perform it to his own satisfaction, so expertly that detection was unlikely.

By 1830 Brother Skaggs unquestionably knew as much about dealing Faro dishonestly as any gambler in the country. Also he had, as he considered, completed his secular education. So he dismissed his school-teacher and embarked upon a gambling tour of the South, returning to New Orleans about 1832 with $50,000. Then he began to put into effect one of the most extraordinary schemes in the annals of American gambling. On his tour he had bespoken the services of a large number of pleasant, personable young men whom he met in various gambling houses, and as they arrived in New Orleans he put them through an intensive course of instruction in cheating at Faro. When they had become proficient he sent them out in pairs, one to deal and the other to keep cases. Each team was under the supervision of one of Skaggs' brothers, cousins or nephews, of whom he seems to have had a great store. They acted as cappers and ropers-in and looked after the finances, and the dealers and case-keepers did the rest. Brother Skaggs paid all expenses, furnished money for the bank, and gave each team twenty-five per cent of its profits. One of these bright young men was the brother of John A. Murrel, who joined Brother Skaggs' forces after the famous bandit had been sent to prison for ten years in 1834. Murrel attempted to deal Faro in various Tennessee and Arkansas towns, and although there was a great deal of sentiment against him because he was supposed to have been concerned in his brother's schemes, he succeeded in avoiding trouble until he reached the little town of Columbia, Arkansas, late in 1835. He "was one night playing as usual," wrote

---

ing the cards in the dealing box," said O'Connor, "he cut the hair on the sharp edge of the plate inside the box, which was sharpened for that purpose. He now had four case cards to lose on the last four turns of the deal, and it is upon these turns that gamblers generally play their heaviest bets during a deal.

Jonathan H. Green, "when suddenly the lights were put out by someone in the room, and he was then literally cut up; one of his hands was cut entirely off, and he was most horribly mangled. Several stabs penetrated the region of the heart. He, however, escaped out of the house, and ran a short distance and fell dead. Several persons were arrested but no convictions ensued. The citizens generally approved the act, and thought it a good thing for the community that they were rid of such a man, even by such means. . . . There was no doubt of his being a very desperate man." [22]

At one time Brother Skaggs had no fewer than a hundred of these chain-store gamblers scattered about the country. Among other professionals they were known as "Skaggs' Patent-Dealers," and their names were synonymous with "all sorts of fraud and dishonesty at the gaming table." For almost twenty years Skaggs' patent-dealers prospered exceedingly, and the money rolled like an avalanche into the pockets of the Master in New Orleans, for strangely enough most of the traveling teams seem to have rendered an honest account of their labors. Meanwhile Brother Skaggs had invaded other fields—he speculated successfully in mules, cotton, and bank-stocks, financed gambling houses in New Orleans, and, in the middle eighteen-forties, bought two hundred slaves and a cotton plantation in Louisiana. He also turned a receptive ear to anyone with an idea for increasing the chances of the bank at Faro, and advanced money for experiments, the inventor agreeing to give him the exclusive use of the device or trick for one year before putting it on the market. Skaggs thus assisted in the development of many of the crooked dealing boxes which appeared during the 1830's and the 1840's. Brother Skaggs seldom gambled in New Orleans, but occasionally went on brief trips to make certain that he had not lost his dexterity. He added *Monte* to his repertoire during

[22] *An Exposure of the Arts and Miseries of Gambling,* pages 213–14.

the War with Mexico, and led a band of his patent-dealers into Texas and the border towns along the Rio Grande. He also spent a prosperous year in the mining camps of California, and for several months operated a Faro game in San Francisco.

During the late 1850's Brother Skaggs reached his goal—he was worth a million dollars. In 1858 or 1859 he liquidated his chain-store business, discharged his patent-dealers, and left gambling to its fate—never again did he turn a card or enter a gambling house. He also abandoned his distinctive dress, and outfitted himself with gaudy raiment made by one of New Orleans' fashionable tailors. Surrounded by his favorite relatives he settled down to enjoy the life of a gentleman on his cotton plantation. When the Civil War began, however, he lost his slaves, and his real estate depreciated in value to such an extent that he was again a very poor man. He made another fortune running the Federal blockade and speculating in sugar and cotton, but was ruined by an abiding faith in the future of the Confederacy. All of his resources went into Confederate money and bonds, and when the War ended he is said to have had about $3,000,000 tied up in this worthless paper. He sought relief from his disappointment in the whisky bottle, and died a drunkard in Texas in 1870, penniless except for a few acres of prairie land.

CHAPTER VIII

"VERY SPLENDID HELLS"

WITH the exception of the Lottery and its unholy off-spring, Policy, then known as Lottery Insurance, gambling in New York in colonial times was unorganized and more or less casual, while the money involved was trivial in comparison with the huge sums which passed over the gaming tables in later years. The gentry amused themselves in their homes and clubs with Loo, Hazard, Backgammon, Brag, All-Fours and Whist; but there was little or no "indulgence in the fashionable vice of extravagant gaming," and in no sense was the gambling table as important in the life of the town as in the French settlements of Mobile and New Orleans. Public gambling was confined to an occasional bank of *Landsquenet,* and a few tables of Hazard and Backgammon, in the taverns and coffee-houses, although gaming was forbidden by law in these premises. Backgammon was most popular, and the old records frequently mention the avidity with which this ancient game was played. Apparently it remained a favorite for many years. As early as 1660 several sailors were arrested for gambling at Backgammon in Jan Backus' tavern—incidentally, that same year a law was passed prohibiting the playing of golf in the streets—and more than a hundred years later, on June 13, 1768, an English visitor, Alexander Mackraby, wrote to a friend in London:

"They have a vile practice here, which is peculiar to the city. I mean that of playing at back-gammon (a noise I de-

155

test), which is going forward at the public coffee-houses from morning till night, frequently a dozen tables at a time."

The first attempt to operate a house exclusively for gambling in New York appears to have been made in 1732 by a group of adventurous Yankees from New England. But this resort, as well as others which subsequently made their appearance, was unsuccessful for various reasons, chiefly lack of support and the vigilance of the colonial authorities. Not until several years after the Revolution did New York have as many as 25,000 inhabitants, and even then the so-called sporting element formed a very small proportion of the population; while stringent laws and certainty of punishment made professional gambling a hazardous occupation. Moreover, throughout most of the colonial period the Lottery and Policy possessed great prestige and were extremely popular; they provided a sufficient outlet for the natural gambling instincts of the people, and the man who played them regularly had little inclination and less money for other forms of gaming. It is an interesting and perhaps a significant fact that the gambling house keeper, although he thrived in the French settlements from the earliest days, was unable to gain a foothold in New York and other English speaking towns until the Lottery began to decline in power and public favor.

2

The first great influx of sharpers into New York began soon after the Louisiana Purchase, and increased in volume as the exodus from New Orleans gathered momentum. None of these pioneers appear to have established gaming houses, but they fared well enough with games which were set up in saloons and in hotels, at the race tracks and the Long Island vacation resorts, and at other places of public concourse in the vicinity of the metropolis. By 1819, about the time of the scandal in connection with the Medical Science Lottery, professional gamblers had become so numerous and so brazen in and around New York that the management of the Bath Race Course, which was opened in that year on Long Island, barred them from the track and announced that Faro and Sweat-Cloth (Chuck-a-Luck) would not be allowed. In 1825 a gambling house, said to have been the first really successful resort of the kind in New York, was opened near the old Tontine Coffee-House at Wall and Water Streets. It was a modest establishment, with no banking games and only a few tables for dice, cards and checkers, but it soon became a popular rendezvous for sporty clerks, small tradesmen, and volunteer firemen. During the next four or five years a dozen other houses appeared, in most of which the sucker could lose his money at Faro, Roulette, Chuck-a-Luck and *Vingt et Un,* as well as at the current dice and short card games. The most popular of these places were operated by Charley Moon; George Rice, who was also a notorious rioter and bully and a leader of the Bowery B'hoys; Slab Baker, who was finally jailed in 1835 when he attempted to open a place at Hempstead Harbor, L.I.; and Shell Burrell, a round-shouldered giant with pleasing manners and a great capacity for making friends, who accumulated a fortune banking Faro games and running a Roulette house on the Bowery. As a Faro banker Burrell was cautious and conservative, but at Roulette, with an absolute percentage in his favor at every turn of the wheel, he would accept any bet a player wanted to make. Once when asked what the limit was he replied:

"Bet all you've got, and if that isn't enough, get on the table and I'll turn for you; but I must be allowed to put my own value on you."

Gamblers of a higher type than the Bakers and the Rices, or at any rate possessed of a more genteel address, began to operate in New York about 1830—an early mention of their activities is found in *Niles' Weekly Register* for January 8, 1831, which said that "New York is infested by an extensive gang of *accomplished* gamblers, and their depredations are to an enormous amount. They generally pass for gentlemen." And on July 30, 1835, a year and a half after the Lottery had been legally abolished throughout the state, the New York *Herald* noted the fact that gambling in the style of Pendleton and John Davis had at last been firmly established in the metropolis:

"There is a small and select number of very splendid hells in this city where young men with property are sent to perdition in no time. Some of them are elegantly fitted up —brilliant, fascinating and profitable. The small gambling houses are generally overhauled every now and then by the police, but the higher order of gamblers—the *haut ton* who can afford to furnish a splendid house, keep dexterous cooks, ready waiters and cunning porters—are never brought within view of the City Hall. . . . We would like to know the yearly profits of some of the New York hells that we could name. Will nobody make out an estimate and send us? Do, some of you, oblige us."

The quarter of a century which followed the appearance of "accomplished" gamblers in New York and the opening of the "very splendid hells" mentioned by the *Herald,* was one of the most important and spectacular periods in the history of the city. Croton water was introduced, gas superseded whale oil as the principal means of illumination, and travel on steamships and railroad trains became a commonplace. The population increased from about 200,000 to more than 800,000, while thousands of the millions of immigrants who landed at New York —in the 1840's alone 1,500,000—remained there, to add to the city's crime, vice and pauperism, and to create a social problem which has yet to be solved. Twice the metropolis was devastated by great fires, and three cholera epidemics took an enormous toll of lives. Tammany Hall completed its transformation from a patriotic society to the most predatory political organization that ever plundered an American city: the hoodlum and the saloon-keeper became dominant factors in practical politics and government, and the latter embarked upon the course of arrogant interference which eventually brought Prohibition upon the land. The police descended to the nadir of corruption and inefficiency; New York became the asylum and the rendezvous of criminals from all parts of the country; and the great brawling gangs of the Bowery and the Five Points rose to the height of their power and renown, and engaged in a score of riots which were suppressed only when the National Guard was called out with bayonets and loaded muskets. In one of these disturbances, in 1857, a thousand men fought for two days with guns, knives, clubs and stones. When they were finally dispersed by three regiments of troops, eight men had been killed and more than one hundred wounded.

Gambling more than kept pace with other phases of life in the metropolis. During the early years of this period there was a second great influx of gamblers into New York as a result of the citizens' uprising in Vicksburg and Natchez, the passage of anti-gambling laws in Louisiana, Kentucky and Ohio, and the consequent closing of most of the gaming resorts in New Orleans, Louisville, Cincinnati, and other cities. The general demoralization of society, and the venality of the politicians and the police, combined to form a perfect setup for the professional sharper, and from about 1835 to the Civil War he prospered in New York as never before or since. Thimble-Riggers, Three-Card Monte throwers and other sure-thing tricksters worked openly in the streets—they were so numerous in the vicinity of the City Hall during the 1850's as to occasion much complaint; and the hotels, the bar-rooms, and even business establishments were boldly invaded by ropers-in who received commissions on whatever their suckers lost, and who seem to have been fully as efficient as their brethren of Washington and New Orleans. Said a contemporary journalist:

"In order to decoy victims into their snares, the gamblers have a regular system of police established upon all newcomers to the city, whose business it is to watch the arrivals at the hotels, and ascertain who among them are likely subjects to be operated upon. The spies employed in this business are often men of considerable address, and make a flashy-genteel appearance, very impressive and taking with greenhorns. The principal means of leading strangers into the trap are an introduction to the innumerable houses of ill-fame, the inmates of all of which are connected with one or the other of the gambling houses. The decoy knows how to make himself agreeable to the stranger . . . and makes himself useful in a variety of ways. At evening they adjourn to the bar, fortify themselves with a julep, and by the time it is scientifically imbibed, Mr. Greenhorn is ripe for anything. . . . Once fairly in the harlot's den, and his fate is sealed. Bewildered with the strangeness of all he sees and hears, overcome by flattery and attentions, he does not refuse a glass of champagne, which is drugged with a small quantity of morphine, just enough to inspire self-confidence and audacity; and the spy finds no difficulty in leading a willing victim to the gambling house, where he is scientifically plucked, and left to make his way to his hotel, a ruined, miserable man." [1]

To accommodate the multitude of suckers upon whom the ropers-in worked their enchantments, and those who sought the perils and excitements of gaming of their own accord, gambling resorts of every description operated without concealment throughout the city. Early in 1850 it was estimated by the New York Association for the Suppression of Gambling that there were 6,000 places in the metropolis, or approximately one to every eighty-five inhabitants, where gambling in one form or another was permitted.[2] At least 25,000 men, or about one-twentieth of the population, depended upon them for a livelihood. In about two-thirds of these resorts gambling was the sole or principal business of the establishment, and no fewer than fifty were first-class houses, superior in many respects to Pendleton's gaudy mansion in Washington and the ornate casinos of an earlier day in New Orleans, and especially renowned for the quality of the suppers which were served free every evening. "You . . . saunter carelessly in," wrote the author of *New York in Slices,* "probably meeting one of the proprietors, who asks you, in a tone of perfect and unobtrusive hospitality, if you will take supper. You . . . sit down at a luxuriously furnished table, and mention to the waiter, who is instantly at your side, what you would like. You need not hesitate to consult your finest tastes. Game, according to the season, of every variety, and exquisitely cooked; the rarest French *entremets*—anything, in short, you have a fancy for, will be instantly forthcoming. A bottle of iced champagne—

[1] *New York in Slices,* by An Experienced Carver; New York, 1849; pages 28–9.

[2] In those days, of course, New York consisted only of Manhattan Island. A similar proportion today would mean about 85,000 gambling places. And counting slot machines, pin games, handbooks, private clubs, and Bingo, there probably are that many.

the genuine Heidsic—is at your elbow; and if you have a fancy for a glass of rare Burgundy, or old South-side Madeira, you have only to make it known, and you will be supplied directly." [3]

All of the regularly established houses paid tribute to the police and the politicians—an early historian of the old Volunteer Fire Department said that many policemen were employed by gamblers as steerers and guides; and commented upon "the many presentations of watches, tea-urns and diamond pins to deserving officers by the proprietors of these gambling places." [4] If a victim of position and influence made a complaint the sharpers, through a police or political intermediary, usually compromised by returning a portion of their winnings; but an ordinary sucker who squawked only succeeded in getting himself into deeper trouble. The experience of an upstate greenhorn named Gerald Spalding, in January, 1849, was typical. Spalding went before a Police Magistrate and said that he had been robbed and cheated in a Park Place skinning-house, and that the gamblers had thrown him out when he requested a loan of two dollars. The Magistrate told Spalding that his motives in demanding the prosecution of the sharpers were far from honest, and clapped him into jail as a material witness, meanwhile refusing to issue warrants or order the arrest of the gamblers. Spalding was released only when he agreed to withdraw his charges.

3

The New York *Herald* was on solid ground when it declared editorially in 1850 that the city had become "the great head quarters of the gamblers in this country," and that "there is,

---

[3] Page 27.
[4] *Reminiscences of the Old Fire Laddies and Volunteer Fire Departments of New York and Brooklyn,* by J. Frank Kernan, A.M.; New York, 1885; page 101.

probably, a larger business done in this line here, than in London." The *Herald* continued:

"The miserable inefficiency of our local authorities, and the greater abuse of wholesome restraints in our society, give peculiar facilities to the gamblers. By the remissness of the police, or rather the want of all police, these meanest of all thieves are enabled to plunder with impunity, and without fear of molestation, whilst the delightful freedom of society, which tolerates blackguards, provided they be well-dressed, gives abundant facilities for the discovery and apprehension of victims. Indeed, many of these common gamblers, these blacklegs, compared with whom the skulking pickpocket is respectable, mingle with the leaders of fashion in this city. They saunter along Broadway in the morning, drive out on the avenue in the afternoon, lounge at the opera in the evening, and cheat in Park Row and Barclay Street till five o'clock in the morning. They are the most *distingué* at the springs and watering places. Now and then they commit some *faux pas,* run off with a respectable lady, or filch a pocketbook, but after rusticating in the south or west for a season, they return to the city, and, like the Wall street financier who has taken the benefit of the act, shine as brilliantly as ever . . . public feeling begins to be properly aroused to a conviction of the prevalence and enormity of the vice of gambling, and . . . we shall see these sharpers who infest our cities, marked and hunted down as pests and curses of society."

In an article written by Horace Greeley about the same time the New York *Tribune* declared that throughout the metropolis gamblers were "numerous, daring and most pernicious. We believe," said Greeley, "that not less than five millions of dol-

lars are annually won from fools and shallow knaves, by blacklegs in this city alone; and that not less than one thousand
young men are annually ruined by them. The money is mainly
wasted on harlots, strong drink, and extravagant living. Gamblers are all libertines. . . . There is no other vice so devastat-
ing in its consequences in proportion to the number addicted to
it . . . our present laws are very defective, and our police either
bribed or powerless. We have no doubt that our Chief of Police
knows at this moment, where at least five hundred 'hells' are
in nightly operation; the captains of police know where they are
perfectly well; the policemen know; yet nothing effectual is
done."

Only in the lowest of these dives, in the private clubrooms,
and at the sessions organized in the hotels and saloons by free-
lance sharpers with no gambling house connections, were short
card games played to any great extent. In the resorts of a
higher type, except on rare occasions when a sucker insisted
upon his inherent right to be fleeced in a game of his own
choosing, nothing was permitted but the old banking standbys,
in which the percentages were definite and certain, and the
"tools" were handled exclusively by house artists. Faro, dealt
almost entirely with rounds and strippers from two-card boxes,
was an overwhelming favorite in New York as it was everywhere else in the United States—Jonathan H. Green declared
it to be "so peculiarly adapted to the taste of the American
people that it may almost be styled the national game." [5] In
some houses Faro was the only game available, but in most of
the better resorts a sucker could be accommodated at Roulette,
Rouge et Noir, and *Vingt et Un.* During the late 1840's *Monte*
enjoyed a brief season of popularity among Army officers and
sharpers who had followed the American troops into Mexico,

[5] All statements in this chapter credited to Jonathan Green are from *A Report on Gambling in New York,* made by J. H. Green; New York, 1851.

but it was never adopted by the rank and file of New York gamblers. Dice games, except Chuck-a-Luck, appear to have been almost unknown in the metropolis, as far as the public houses were concerned. Once in a while a newspaper commented upon the plight of a sucker who had been swindled at Hazard, but otherwise there is scant mention of dice in the gambling records of the period.

4

A large majority of the first-class houses were owned or controlled by fewer than a score of men, each of whom was interested in several establishments. The best known and most powerful of these gambling princes were Reuben Parsons, Pat Herne, Joe Hall, Sam Suydam, Henry Colton, Orlando Moore, and Sherlock Hillman. In all of their resorts the games were played fairly as long as that course was profitable, but the heat was turned on and the artists called into action whenever necessary to despoil a particularly opulent sucker or check a runaway winning streak. As far as available records disclose, Jack Harrison was the only gambling house keeper in the New York of this period who dealt every game honestly at all times and never took advantage of his customers—and in consequence was seldom more than two jumps away from bankruptcy. Harrison, described by a contemporary as "superior to most of his class" and as a man who "deserved a better fate," ran a popular house in Park Place for almost ten years. He died there on Sunday, March 10, 1850, "a few hours after the closing of his Faro bank, and the dispersion of the players, who had made the night hideous by their blasphemies over the gaming table."

Harrison's gambling house fell into other and less worthy hands, but his name was carried to new heights of renown by his son, whose career was calculated to make the anti-gambling reformers shake their heads in gloomy satisfaction. Young Harrison had been trained by his father to be an honest gambler, but he soon abandoned the family standards and became a sure-thing sharper. He dealt Faro in a few of the cheap gambling houses in New York for two or three years, but went to California about 1854, when he inherited considerable property from a woman known as Julia Brown, whose relations with the elder Harrison had occasioned much scandal. Harrison killed several men in the mining camps and in San Francisco, and was one of the ruffians and desperadoes driven from San Francisco by the second Vigilance Committee in 1856. He found refuge in Kansas, then torn by border strife and the rows between the abolition and pro-slavery elements, and soon acquired an unsavory reputation as a killer and the leader of a band of highwaymen and swindlers. One day while walking with a friend in Leavenworth he counted on his fingers eleven men whom he had killed.

"By God!" he cried. "I'll have a jury of my own to try me in Hell!"

And for no better reason than that he drew his pistol and shot an old German shoemaker sitting peacefully at work in an open window across the street. A mob formed to lynch him, but he fled with his gang to southern Kansas, where he continued his depredations. In 1861 Harrison and a score of his ruffians applied for enlistment in the United States Army, and were finally mustered into the Second Kansas Cavalry, but only after Harrison had promised to behave himself and control his men. But this he apparently had no intention of doing; after a few months in camp he led a band of his followers into Missouri and burned and looted a small town, killing most of the inhabitants. Harrison was tried by a court martial, but escaped and made his way into Indian Territory, now the state of Oklahoma. There he organized a band of half-breed Indians,

A RAID ON A NEW YORK GAMBLING HOUSE IN THE 1860's

and for a year or more terrorized the small towns and country districts of northern Arkansas. He was finally captured by a posse of citizens, who hanged him and then cut off his head and stuck it on a pole in the public square of a town which he had previously raided. The gruesome trophy was still there when the Second Kansas Cavalry occupied the town, and was recognized by Colonel A. C. Davis and other officers of the regiment. Several years later, Colonel Davis, then a lawyer in New York, was called as a witness in a suit over some of the property which had been left to Harrison by Julia Brown. His testimony established the fact of Harrison's death.

Reuben Parsons, known as the Great American Faro Banker, was the most industrious and business-like of early New York gamblers and, for a few years at least, the most successful and the richest. With John Frink as a figure-head he elevated Policy into the ranks of big business, and was also interested in eight or ten regular gambling houses, in some of which his partners were men whom he had ruined and then given a stake. Parsons was always something of an enigma to his fellow-gamblers. They knew virtually nothing about him except that he had come to New York from New England in the early 1830's, although rumor had it that he had been a silent partner in some of the New Orleans gambling resorts. For a year or two he played carefully but in general unsuccessfully in a few of the New York houses, and then suddenly announced his intention of banking Faro instead of bucking it. He is said never to have been on the wrong side of a Faro layout after making that decision. Unlike most sporting men of his time, Parsons dressed plainly, and his manner was quiet and unassuming. He refused to associate with gamblers, and seldom appeared in any of the houses in which he was a partner, although he maintained an efficient spy system and required frequent and comprehensive reports of all operations. Occasionally he did a bit of expert roping, and delivered to one or another of his resorts a fat sucker with his neck stretched out for the ax. As the money rolled in Parsons invested in real estate, and when he retired from active business, soon after the beginning of the Civil War, he was a rich man, worth at the very least a million dollars. But at the close of the War he went into Wall Street, and that proved his undoing, for in the Stock Market he was the most verdant of suckers. He died about 1875, almost penniless.

The principal gambling houses of which Parsons was the main backer were Sherlock Hillman's, Henry Colton's, and the swank place operated by Sam Suydam and Joe Hall. For a few years Parsons was also a partner of Pat Herne and Orlando Moore, and is said to have been a member of a gamblers' syndicate which in 1853 fitted up a most magnificent resort which was called the Crystal Palace in an attempt to capitalize upon the publicity accorded the famous exhibition building of the same name, likewise opened in 1853 in Reservoir Square, now Bryant Park. Pendleton of Washington was interested in the enterprise, and assumed the active management of the resort when Congress was in recess and his presence was not required in the capital. Despite Pendleton's drawing power and the luxuriousness of the house, however, the Crystal Palace was not a success, and would have been a flat failure if the roping staff hadn't brought in a defaulting bank cashier who was cheated out of $70,000 in a few weeks. The cashier was arrested when the gamblers began to boast of their *coup,* and the bank brought suit against the Crystal Palace. But Pendleton had taken the money to Washington at the first sign of trouble, and it could not be proved that he or anyone else had any connection with the gambling house. The bank exerted so much pressure at City Hall that early in 1854 Mayor Jacob A. Westervelt ordered the Crystal Palace closed. Meanwhile the gamblers had divided the loot and were very happy about the whole business.

Sherlock Hillman ran a house in Broadway for four or five years during the middle 1840's, but the really prosperous period of his career began about 1848, when Reuben Parsons bought an interest in the place and moved the gambling paraphernalia farther downtown, to Liberty Street. There Hillman operated from eleven A. M. to six or seven P. M., six days a week, omitting the dinners and the free cigars and liquors which had been served in his uptown establishment, and catering exclusively to the business and professional men of the financial district. The resort was very successful, but its importance in New York gambling is due mainly to the fact that it was the first of the so-called "Day Gambling Houses," which flourished in large numbers from about 1865 to the late 1880's. Parsons' principal partner was Henry Colton, with whom he was associated for some twenty-five years. They operated some of the "very splendid hells" mentioned by the New York *Herald* in 1835, and about 1840 opened several others in partnership with Pat Herne, the most important being in Broadway near Prince Street. Herne withdrew from the partnership in 1849, and in May of that year Parsons and Colton acquired control of a house in Barclay Street, which had been run by John Frink as an independent venture. They completely remodeled and refurnished the resort, and for almost two decades it was one of the most popular and successful gambling houses in New York, rivaled only by Orlando Moore's, Joe Hall's, and the new place opened by Pat Herne. Jonathan H. Green thus commented upon the Parsons-Colton establishment:

"The sporting saloons are most gorgeously furnished, exhibiting abundance of wealth and an exquisite refinement of taste. A most luxurious supper is announced at half past ten o'clock, of which the players and others are invited to partake, and those who desire intoxicating drinks, are furnished with costly wines or other alcoholic liquors of the most expensive kind. The expense of this entertainment, as it continues until the bank closes, cannot be less than from three to five hundred dollars a week. After the theatre, and other places of amusement or dissipation have closed, the gentlemen who visit this house, gradually drop in, and the supper being over, the game becomes quite brisk. Faro, of course, is the favorite, but players may be accommodated with *Rouge et Noir, Monte,* or almost any desirable game. The play is generally very heavy, thousands of dollars changing hands before the game closes, which is usually after day-light. At the tables may be seen merchants, bank, insurance and mercantile clerks, together with lawyers, editors, authors, officers of the Army and Navy, politicians, office-holders, gamblers, &c.; and as fast as they get broke retire from the table as though nothing had happened (if they are old players), and form themselves into groups, for the discussion of business, politics and wine."

Colton appears to have been much the same type of man as Jack Harrison—Jonathan Green declared that "for integrity of character, for fair, upright, honorable dealing, he has no superior in any profession, and if he pursued a respectable business, no man would be more highly esteemed." Green was also greatly impressed by the fact that Colton was always very polite and gentlemanly, and able to converse intelligently upon almost any subject. He was very popular among his customers, and even more so among professional gamblers. His knowledge of games was so extensive and accurate that he was regarded as a sort of supreme tribunal of gaming; questions of play and procedure were submitted to him for judgment, and in gambling circles throughout the United States his decisions were binding. Colton accumulated a great deal of money during his long career as a gambler, and kept it longer than did most of the men of his profession. Financial troubles, however, began to beset him in the middle 1870's, and he lost heavily in several enterprises. In 1877 he transferred the remainder of his property to his wife, to avoid lawsuits and to protect the interests of their children.

Both Sam Suydam and Joe Hall were protégés of Reuben Parsons; he found them, so to speak, in the gutter of respectability, and raised them to high rank in the kingdom of the professional sharper. Hall, indeed, achieved such eminence that he became known as the Gambling King of New York, and was a more important figure than his patron. As a youth Suydam was apprenticed to a baker, but spent most of his time running with the fire engines and following the chieftains of the Bowery B'hoys in their forays against the Dead Rabbits and other gangsters of the Five Points. He soon became a small-time sport and gambler, but had no particular standing until he attracted the attention of Reuben Parsons, who was impressed by Suydam's great personal beauty, his natural charm of manner, and his happy and lively disposition. Parsons took the young Bowery B'hoy under his wing, taught him to deal Faro for the benefit of the house, and installed him behind a Faro table. Meanwhile Parsons had met Joe Hall, a house painter who had been enjoying a notable run of luck against two or three of the honest Faro banks, and in particular had won heavily at Jack Harrison's. Hall was eager to open a gambling house, and at Parsons' suggestion took Sam Suydam in as partner. With some financial aid from Parsons, the two handsome young men—Hall, incidentally, was just as personable as Suydam—opened a house in Barclay Street which Jonathan H. Green described as "quite an exclusive and aristocratic establishment, as great care is taken not to admit any but approved cash customers. The house is gorgeously furnished," wrote Green, "and everything about it is conducted on a scale of liberality and magnificence. . . . Supper is served at

11 o'clock, at which costly wines and segars are bountifully dispensed by polite and respectful colored servants. . . . Most of the players at this house are professional or business men, lottery or policy dealers, and a few of the better sort of *sporting* men . . . as the play is usually heavy, the Bank is enabled to declare heavy dividends at the end of each month."

Hall was a partner in the Barclay Street resort until the early 1850's, when he withdrew, and thereafter played a lone hand. He opened a new house at No. 537 Broadway, near Prince Street, which became famous immediately for high play and the quality of the suppers served each evening upon "a long table . . . radiant with snowy damask and glittering plate . . . game of all kinds, fruits, flowers, sturdy cold joints, delicate pâté, delicious confectionery spread over the hospitable board. Sparkling wines," continued this enraptured historian, "flowed into silver goblets. The champagne creamed whitely, and the Rudesheimer gurgled in guttural German as it poured. There was brandy for those who found no consolation in the grape, and cigars to soothe the perturbed spirit of losers . . . this delightful banquet, free to all comers. . . ." [6] The New York *Tribune* said that Hall "knew how to cater to his guests better than any other gambler-host in New York."

Encouraged by the great success of his venture, Hall fitted up a similar house in Philadelphia, and in 1853 invaded the lucrative Washington field with a palatial resort which gave the elegant Pendleton the first real competition he had ever encountered and cut deeply into the profits of the Hall of the Bleeding Heart. In 1859 Hall opened his fourth establishment at No. 818 Broadway in New York, a four-story brownstone house near Twelfth Street and only a few doors from Grace Protestant Episcopal Church. This building was used exclusively for gambling purposes for some thirty years, and during most of that

[6] *Reminiscences of the Old Fire Laddies,* by J. Frank Kernan; page 104.

time was one of the best known gaming establishments in the metropolis. In Hall's day it was far uptown, but it attracted an extensive carriage trade, and more than paid its way. Hall received an enormous income from his four gambling resorts, but success went to his head, and he became a pompous, overbearing and presumptuous ass. He gambled heavily against other games and drank to excess, while his recklessness and extravagance were notorious even among his fellow sharpers, who ordinarily looked upon these vices as sterling virtues. About the time the Civil War began Hall became interested in racing, and soon squandered a fortune upon a large stable of trotting horses. When one of them, the celebrated stallion *Lantern,* won an important race, Hall bought the animal a solid silver drinking bucket. The gambler finally reaped the whirlwind in the late 1860's, when business fell off at his gambling houses and his creditors began to press for payment. Within a year or two he had lost everything he possessed; other sharpers moved into his gaming establishments, and all of his horses were sold. Many of them, including *Lantern,* were bought by Robert Bonner, publisher of the New York *Ledger* and owner of the famous trotters *Peerless, Dexter,* and *Maud S.* Hall dropped out of sight, and appears to have been unheard of until 1877, when the New York *Tribune* said that "a few years ago, worn out and crippled, Hall was soliciting alms to keep him from starving."

Pat Herne was an Irishman, a member of a respectable and moderately wealthy family, who came to the United States about 1830 to make a sight-seeing tour of the country. In New Orleans he succumbed to the fascinations of the tiger and lost all of his money. When his family refused to help him unless he promised to come home, Herne got a job in a notary's office, and thus earned an honest living for almost a year. He continued to hang around the gambling houses, however, and eventually realized his ambition—he was employed by John Davis, to rope and to deal Faro. He proved to be a very superior roper-in, and a better-than-average Faro artist. When Davis closed his establishment in 1836, Herne had no difficulty in making a connection with an undercover skinning house. "Having received a good education," said John O'Connor, "and being a man of polished manners, with a social and genial disposition, and having, withal, a large stock of rollicking Irish humor, he commended himself to all with whom he came in contact, and those fond of play and fast living found in Pat Hearn [Herne] a congenial companion . . . he soon recruited his fortunes, and lived in the most extravagant style until he came to New York, where he was allowed, almost without interruption, to carry on a skinning-den for about twenty years." [7]

Herne arrived in the metropolis early in 1840, and at once became associated with Reuben Parsons and Henry Colton. When he withdrew from the partnership, in 1849, he opened his own house at No. 587 Broadway, opposite Niblo's Garden and the Metropolitan Hotel, which Jonathan Green said was "one of the most elegant establishments of the kind in the United States." Herne's great personal charm, and the sumptuous entertainment which he provided, attracted a host of high-class suckers; for years his establishment was especially popular with the dissipated scions of wealthy and influential families. The New York *Tribune* once estimated that from these young greenhorns alone Herne won not less than half a million dollars, while suckers with more modest social backgrounds contributed several times that amount. The cheating at Herne's place appears to have been particularly flagrant, but complaints were remarkably infrequent, and the resentment and indignation of the players who did protest were seldom proof against the blarney that came so handily to Herne's Irish tongue. "We have known men," said Green, "almost ready to commit suicide in consequence of the

[7] *Wanderings of a Vagabond*, page 232.

losses sustained at his tables, whose feelings were so far subdued by Pat's kindness and civility that they almost forgot their misfortunes, and left the room fascinated with its gentlemanly proprietor." Herne's income was comparable to that of Joe Hall, but like that worthy he was a reckless and dissipated spendthrift, and a heavy player against Faro banks in other houses. As a result, he was frequently in financial difficulties, even during the years when his resort was experiencing its greatest prosperity. In one of these periods, in the early 1850's, he sold a share of the gambling house to a young sharper named Schuyler Halsey, who appears never to have been connected with any other New York establishment. Instead of acting as a brake, however, Halsey joined in Herne's extravagances, and during the next six or eight years the two men threw away several fortunes. Herne left his widow about $30,000 when he died in 1860, and Halsey was worth less than $50,000 at the time of his death in 1875.

Orlando Moore, a New Orleans gambler who opened a "very splendid hell" at No. 256 Broadway about 1836 in partnership with Henry Watson, was Herne's chief rival for the play of the aristocrats. Moore's house was almost painfully exclusive—professional gamblers were excluded, and no one was admitted unless he was acquainted with Moore or someone else connected with the establishment. "The players at this house," said Green, "are generally business men, and are all of the better order of society. Officers of the Army and Navy, members of Congress and State Legislatures, Professors and Tutors in Institutions of learning, Police officers and other officials, may all occasionally be found gambling in this house. A large front and back parlor on the second floor are used for sporting purposes, the Faro table being in the back parlor. An ordinary supper is served up every night at half past ten o'clock, of which the whole company may freely and gratuitously partake." Henry Watson sold his share of the Broadway house to Moore about 1845, and opened a place of his own at No. 2 Murray Street, where he died a few months later while seated at his Faro table. Moore prospered for many years, and finally retired with a comfortable fortune, most of which he spent in a vain attempt to improve the social position of his family.

5

The gambling houses of less prestige and magnificence which flourished in New York before the Civil War fell roughly into three classifications—second-class skinning houses (such resorts as Hall's, Herne's and Moore's were known to the profession as *first-class* skinning houses), Wolf-Traps; and the penny Poker dens of the Five Points and other slum districts. These latter places, lighted only by a tallow candle stuck in a bottle and unfurnished except for a battered pine table or a plank laid across a couple of empty whiskey barrels, were shudderingly described by the author of *New York in Slices* as "indescribably filthy and abominable holes, into which a man with healthy lungs might penetrate with about as much safety as he would go down a well with an air-damp at the bottom. Here," he wrote, "the various grades of small thieves and pickpockets may be seen, huddled together over a dark table, shuffling a pack of greasy and worn-out cards, drinking villainous brandy and fire-new whiskey— swearing, quarreling, fighting, and making the reeking air thick with blasphemy. In these dens men and women are indiscriminately mingled: and such men! but more especially, such women! The Enemy of Mankind could not possibly desire more fitting and accomplished instruments to perform all his dirtiest jobs upon earth."

The second-class skinning houses were of various types, differing considerably in methods of operation, but all, of course, working to the same end—the financial ruin of every player rash and silly enough to buck their games. Some were open to all comers, and imitated the first-class houses in every particular, but they were less luxuriously furnished and attracted a lower class of customers. Their suppers and entertainment were ordinary —in many only cigars and liquor were provided—and honest games were dealt even less frequently. There were probably a hundred of these resorts in New York, and like the first-class establishments, the most successful ones were controlled by a handful of sharpers, among them such noted cheats as Jim Bartolf, Jack Wallis; Frank Stuart and his partners, Hamar and Billy Eldredge; and Bob Willis and Jim Southall, who likewise were partners. The principal houses operated by Bartolf, Stuart and Wallis were in Park Place, while that of Willis and Southall was at Broadway and Warren Street. Bartolf did most of the dealing at his Park Place house, "and," said Green, "so nicely does he execute, that old Faro players are frequently deceived." Willis' place was the scene of an unusual raid in 1850. L. Gardinier, a lawyer, went before Police Judge Mountfort on behalf of a client who had been badly clawed by the tiger, and swore that "Willis not only kept a gambling house, but a house where the players could not win—that it was a house expressly for cheating." Judge Mountfort issued a warrant for Willis' arrest, but refused to authorize the seizure of the gamblers' equipment. So the lawyer procured a horse and a cart, broke into the gaming house, and hauled away a cart load of paraphernalia, which he presented to Judge Mountfort in open court. "The contents of the gaming table," said the New York *Tribune,* "its numerous secret drawers, silver boxes made to draw two cards as the occasion might require, the cards with rounded edges, the plates between which they are pressed for the purpose of shaving the edges; together with the loaded dice (of which there are several sets); are all secured, and will afford a rich display to the uninitiated." But if the uninitiated ever saw them it was in Willis' resort from the wrong side of the table, for a few hours after the lawyer's spectacular gesture the gambler was released in nominal bail and the seized property restored to him. Without evidence Gardinier's case collapsed.

Jack Wallis' house in Park Place was opened in the late 1830's by Jim Berry of Cincinnati and a New Orleans' sharper known as French Jose, who had left the Louisiana city when the authorities there began to enforce the anti-gambling law of 1836. Wallis, a Chinese who had renounced a respectable mercantile career to become a gambler, was one of their dealers, and was accounted one of the most expert Faro artists in New York. With Reuben Parsons' backing, Wallis acquired control of the house about 1846 or 1847, and operated it with great success for more than a decade. According to Jonathan H. Green, the place was frequented by "men of almost every profession, including gamblers, thimble-riggers, thieves, pickpockets, watch-stuffers, pocketbook droppers, &c. . . . nightly playing at the same table with merchants, clerks, lawyers, railroad-conductors, mechanics, and other men who pursue an honest livelihood, and maintain a respectable character."

Wallis' house was also a meeting-place of the professional pugilists, whose sudden accession of popularity in New York about 1840 brought great distress and mortification to the respectable citizens. "The amusement of prize fighting," wrote Philip Hone in his diary in 1842, "the disgrace of which was formerly confined to England . . . has become one of the fashionable abominations of our loafer-ridden city. Several matches have been made lately. The parties, their backers, betters, and abettors, with thousands and tens of thousands of degraded amateurs of this noble science, have been following the champions to Staten Island, Westchester, and up the North River . . . and the horrid details, with all their disgusting technicalities and vulgar slang, have been regularly presented in the New York *Herald* to gratify the vitiated palates of its readers, whilst the orderly citizens have wept for the shame which they could not prevent." Many of the pugilists owned small interests in skinning-houses, while others were employed by the gamblers, between bouts, to act as cappers and ropers-in. Among the several who worked for Jack Wallis was a notorious bruiser named Chris Lilly, or Lillie, who was also a henchman of Captain Isaiah Rynders, saloon-keeper and celebrated Tammany Hall politician. Lilly's most noted fight was with Tom McCoy at Hastings, N.Y., on September 13, 1842. The two men battered each other with bare fists for 119 rounds, when McCoy fell dead in the ring. The fight had lasted two hours and forty-three minutes, during which time McCoy received one hundred square blows and was knocked down eighty-one times. Lilly fled to Liverpool on the sailing ship *George Washington,* but returned to the United States a few years later under the protection of Captain Rynders, and was not molested by the police. In 1848 Lilly went to New Orleans, and for the benefit of the Democratic machine there organized gangs of bullies and repeaters, with which he introduced Tammany methods and put New Orleans politics on a practical basis.

When Jack Harrison died in 1850 his celebrated gambling house in Park Place was taken over by one of his Faro dealers, Frank Stuart, who immediately sold shares in the enterprise to another of Harrison's dealers, Hamar; and to Billy Eldredge, who had won a fortune playing Thimble-Rig in the California mining camps. These gifted sharpers completely changed the character of Harrison's house, eliminating the costly suppers with which Harrison had regaled his customers, admitting disreputable characters who had previously been barred, and operating the resort strictly as a skinning house. Under their management the place quickly superseded Jack Wallis' place as the headquarters of the pugilists, and was nightly filled with "crowds of fighting men, Bowery Boys, and other kindred spirits." As

Green said, "at times the scenes enacted here are truly *hellish.*" One of the peculiar customs of the house, and the cause of frequent rows, was that all silver money which appeared on the Faro tables became at once the property of the dealers.

Stuart's popularity with the so-called "fighting crowd" was due to the fact that he was himself a member in good standing—he had been one of the most ferocious battlers in the ranks of the Washington Market Boys, a gang of thugs and roughs captained by the redoubtable Butcher Bill Poole, the only man who ever whipped John Morrissey in a rough-and-tumble fight. Also, Stuart was the particular friend and backer of Yankee Sullivan, an Irishman whose real name was James Ambrose, and who is said to have been an escaped convict from Australia. Stuart promoted Sullivan's fight with Tom Hyer for the American heavyweight championship, which took place at Roach's Point, Maryland, on February 7, 1849, and was won by Hyer in seventeen minutes and eighteen seconds. Sullivan was so terribly beaten that his friends hurried him to Mount Hope Hospital at Baltimore, where for several days his life was said to be in danger. "He has a slight fracture of the skull behind the left ear," said the New York *Herald,* "one of his arms is broken, and his face is cut awfully; the scalp from his forehead, with the eyelid, has fallen on his cheek."

Tom Hyer went to California after the fight, but returned to New York late in 1850, announced his retirement from the prize ring, and bought an interest in Frank Stuart's gambling house, Stuart meanwhile having broken with Sullivan. Hyer roped and dealt Faro at Stuart's for several years, and the suckers esteemed it a great privilege to be trimmed by such a great man. Calling himself the American champion, Sullivan opened a saloon, the Sawdust House, in Walker Street. In October, 1853, he fought John Morrissey for the title, and was declared the loser when he left the ring in the fifty-third round. Business at the Sawdust

House declined after Sullivan's defeat, and early in 1854 he sold the saloon and went to San Francisco, where he soon became a leader of the band of plug-uglies and sluggers who helped maintain the political supremacy of David C. Broderick, a New York saloon-keeper who became United States Senator from California. Sullivan was arrested by the San Francisco Vigilance Committee in 1856, and on May 31 of that year, fearing that he would be hanged or sent back to Australia, committed suicide while confined in the Committee's headquarters.

6

Another type of second-class skinning house which met with great success in New York was not, strictly speaking, a public gaming resort at all. The stranger and the casual player were never admitted, and the place was operated only when a sucker was on hand to be trimmed. Then a staff of cappers made a great show of activity about the Faro table, betting heavily and ostentatiously counting their huge piles of chips. Always, until the victim actually began to play, the bank appeared to be losing. Establishments of this sort were usually well-furnished, and in most of them a table was prepared, complete with napery and silverware. But this appetizing layout was as phony as everything else about the place. If a sucker inquired about supper, he was told that it would be served in an hour or two, by which time he had been fleeced and thrown into the street. No entertainment was ever provided in a house of this description unless the gamblers desired to impress a particularly fat gull, in which case supper, or cigars and liquor, were sent in from the nearest restaurant or saloon. Under no circumstances was a game ever dealt honestly.

There is no record of the number of such dives, but they were all over the city. Many were in the back rooms of saloons and billiard halls and in the cheaper hotels, and almost invariably there was one or more on the premises of the fake auctioneers, located principally in Broadway, the Bowery, and Chatham Street. These latter gentry, commonly called Peter Funks, were themselves a source of great annoyance to the municipal authorities during the 1840's and 1850's, and many unsuccessful attempts were made to stop the sales of shoddy and worthless merchandise by which they robbed thousands of countrymen every year. Once, in 1854, Mayor Westervelt hired a large number of men to parade Broadway bearing signs inscribed, "Beware of Mock Auctions," but the Peter Funks met this attack by placing similar signs in their own windows.

The personnel of a skinning house which played roped games exclusively consisted of the proprietor and banker; from three to half a dozen cappers; as many ropers, or steerers, as the banker could form alliances with; an expert Faro artist, and a trusted man to keep cases, without whose connivance crooked dealing at Faro was difficult and dangerous—he was signaled when the artist drew two cards, and ran up the proper buttons on the case-keeper while the attention of the sucker was distracted. The roper did the outside work, frequenting the hotels, the saloons, the railroad stations, and wherever there might be a chance of flushing game. Acquaintance was scraped with a prospect, and when friendship had ripened over a few drinks, the sucker was invited to visit "my club house," which was usually described as "a place where a few gentlemen and board of trade men meet evenings to have a little game." In the majority of instances the victim assented and went eagerly to his doom. Wrote John O'Connor:

"Let us now take a peep into the brace room, while the steerer and his victim are on their way to it. The room is

From an old print

A LOW CLASS GAMBLING DEN OF THE 1850's

brilliantly lighted up. The 'artist' sits behind the table, mechanically shuffling, cutting, and butting in, a pack of cards. Scattered about the room, in various attitudes, are some half-dozen or more men—one or two of whom are asleep on the sofas—and several others playing casino, cribbage, or some game of the sort. The principal subjects under discussion are the merits of this or that prostitute, or perhaps one relates, in choice slang, garnished with an occasional oath, his exploits of the evening previous, and informs the company how much *I win,* never in any case using the word in a past tense. . . . Presently there is a ring at the door bell. . . . After a moment or two the bell is again rung twice in rapid succession. Presto! In an instant everything is changed. The 'artist' slides his cards into the box. The cappers gather round the table. Stacks of chips are passed to each of them, bets are put on the cards, the deal has begun; when enter the 'steerer' and his gull. The 'gentlemen and board of trade men' are deeply engaged in playing." [8]

The sucker is introduced around the table. He meets Mr. So-and-So the banker, Mr. What's-His-Name the merchant, and Mr. Whozis the lawyer. The steerer buys a stack of chips and begins to play, inviting the gull to sit beside him and bring him luck. He wins steadily, the dealer grumbles that everybody is beating the bank, and a capper tells of a man who ran a $5 bill up to $1,000, or $2,000, or $5,000. The sucker's cupidity is aroused; this looks like easy money, and he would be a fool not to get some of it. He buys some checks, and loses. He buys another stack and loses that also, and so on until the dealer has raked his last cent from the table. Then the cappers gradually quit playing, and the game is broken up. The steerer, full of sympa-

[8] *Wanderings of a Vagabond,* page 210.

thy, leads the victim outside, gets rid of him as soon as possible, and hurries back to the skinning house for his share of the loot. The usual division was forty-five per cent to the steerer or roper, ten per cent to the case-keeper, and forty-five per cent to the banker. Out of his share the banker paid the rent and other expenses of the house, and gave the Faro artist from twenty to twenty-five per cent of the balance. Each of the cappers received from one to four dollars, according to the time they worked and the size of the killing.

Such brace games were in their heyday before the Civil War, but they remained an important and well-organized feature of American gambling for many years. Nor were they confined to New York—as late as the early 1870's it was estimated that there were at least a hundred still in operation about the country, and only about fifteen of them were in the metropolis. "Philadelphia supports from four to six of these delectable institutions," wrote John O'Connor in 1873; "Baltimore one or two, Boston two or three; Washington City, during a session of Congress, from four to five; Richmond, two or three; Charleston, during the winter season, one; Savannah, two or three; Augusta, two; Atlanta, two; Montgomery, one; Mobile, four; New Orleans, from three to five; Memphis, two or three; Nashville, one or two; Louisville, four or five; Cincinnati, two or three; Indianapolis, generally two; St. Louis, from three to four; Chicago, about the same; Kansas City, two or more; Leavenworth, one; Omaha, one; St. Joseph, one; Denver, one or two; St. Paul, the same; Pittsburgh, Toledo, Columbus, Cleveland, Buffalo, Rochester, Syracuse, Saratoga, Albany, Providence, and other cities of the same size, have at least one 'brace-house' each, and sometimes more . . . nearly every capital seat in the country can boast of at least one brace-house, during the session of the Legislature." [9]

[9] *Ibid.,* page 212.

184

7

Those extraordinary gambling dens generally known as Wolf-Traps, but sometimes as Snap Houses, Deadfalls and Ten Per Cent Houses, are said to have originated in Cincinnati about 1835, when that town was filled with refugee sharpers from Natchez and Vicksburg. They soon spread to other parts of the country, and by the middle 1840's were running full blast in Philadelphia, Boston, Baltimore, St. Louis, Pittsburgh, and other sizeable towns. And, of course, in New York, where they attained their greatest development and popularity. In most of them Faro was the only game played, but in a few there were also tables for *Vingt et Un* and Chuck-a-Luck. The actual equipment of a Wolf-Trap was about the same as that of a second-class skinning house, but there the resemblance ended—in a Wolf-Trap a decoy table was never set out, no refreshments were ever served, ropers were seldom employed and cappers never, and there was no regular game banked by the house.

In every respect a Wolf-Trap was a public gambling house—not only was the casual player welcomed, but the casual and itinerant professional as well. Any man could walk into a Wolf-Trap and, if a table was available, open a Faro snap, or a game of *Vingt et Un* or Chuck-a-Luck, for any amount he pleased; sometimes, in the slack hours of the morning, a game was begun with a total capital of one dollar, the chips being issued at one cent each. Occasionally a plutocratic sharper started a $500 snap, but usually they ranged from $20 to $50. If a Faro dealer wanted to try his luck with, say, a fifty dollar snap, he bought chips for that amount from the owner or manager of the Trap, and sold them to his players at from five to twenty-five cents each. In no case, except once in a while in a $500 snap, was a chip ever worth more than a quarter. The house provided the requisite paraphernalia, as well as a lookout, who watched the players for the dealer and the dealer for the house, to make sure that no phony chips were introduced. When the bank had been broken, or the dealer wished to quit, the owner of the Wolf-Trap settled up the game, redeeming checks to the amount which had been deposited with him as the bank's capital. If the bank had won, the house retained ten per cent of the profits; if the bank had lost, no charge was made for the use of the tools. The house had no other source of revenue, except on rare occasions when a special game was arranged to trim a particular sucker. The house then took twenty-five per cent.

Cases were not kept in a Wolf-Trap, and unless a player could memorize them he had no way of keeping track of the cards as they were drawn from the dealing box. It would seem that this lack of a record opened the way for all sorts of skullduggery on the part of the dealer; actually, however, nine-tenths of the Faro games dealt in a Wolf-Trap were square, and strippers and two-card boxes were virtually unknown. For one reason, a dealer was not permitted to use his own paraphernalia. For another, cheating of this sort was too dangerous; the Wolf-Traps were frequented almost exclusively by rowdies, gangsters, thieves, and small-time sharpers, and they were naturally suspicious and exceedingly keen of eye. The operator of a two-card box, if detected, was fortunate if he escaped with his life. For a third reason, a Faro artist clever enough to fool such tough customers was never found wasting his time in a Wolf-Trap; he was making big money in a first or second-class skinning house. Nevertheless, a game was seldom played in a Trap in which trickery of some description was not in evidence. Square dealing was insisted upon, but it was considered legitimate practice for the dealer to steal the players' chips, short-change them, and otherwise to take what advantage he could. On their part, the players bedeviled the dealer in every way their imaginations could devise, and resorted to every sort of trickery of which they had knowledge. Sometimes, espcially in New York and Philadelphia, a dealer was robbed by a method known as "bonneting"—that is, a group of rowdies would fling a blanket over his head, and while he was struggling to extricate himself, make off with his chips and whatever money happened to be in the card box. The gambler had no recourse; he was supposed to take care of himself, and the owner of a Wolf-Trap cashed chips for whoever presented them, regardless of how they had been acquired.

The tricks most often practiced upon Faro dealers in the Wolf-Traps were the "horse-hair game" and "dropping a bet." The latter was frequently practiced in the days of John Law, and was simply dropping one or more checks on a winning card as it came from the box, while the attention of the artist was concentrated on making the deal. A dropper had to be quick, but properly done the cheat could be worked against the shrewdest of dealers. The "horse-hair game" was invented in Cincinnati soon after the opening of the first Wolf-Trap, and was used there and in other cities for many years. It was thus described in *Wanderings of a Vagabond:*

"To play the 'horse-hair game' scientifically, required two persons, a full board of players, and many bets on the layout. The manipulator took a position in front of the table and played small, until one of the cards near him became 'dead.' This card he made his base for operating. His 'pal,' immediately upon its becoming 'dead,' placed upon it a couple of stacks of white checks, of about twenty each. The operator places behind these, ten or fifteen red ones, to the bottom one of which is attached the end of a horse-hair, the other end being fastened to one of his vest-buttons. For example, we will say that the 'dead,' or base card, is the Jack, next to it on the lay-out are the ten and Queen, and four or five of these cards are still in the dealing box. Should he see one of these cards come winning, while the dealer is making his turn, and all eyes are concentrated on the cards as they fall from the box, he leans gently back in his chair, and as he does so the movement drags the stack of red checks from off the Jack, taking in the winning card behind it. This trick could be played two or three times during a deal, and on a verdant dealer twice as often. It was finally first detected one day, by a 'sucker,' who was playing in one of the 'traps.' He was petrified by the extraordinary spectacle of a stack of red checks creeping slowly from off a card, without any visible means of locomotion. After watching them for a moment in dazed silence, he gave vent to his amazement by bawling out, 'Look! Look!' pointing at the same time to the traveling checks, 'darned if them there checks aint alive!' " [10]

In New York most of the Wolf-Traps were on Barclay Street —the most disreputable of all was at No. 98, where eight Faro dealers were once bonneted in a single day—the Bowery; and Ann Street, where a dozen flourished in the short block between Broadway and Nassau Street. During the late 1840's and throughout the 1850's this short stretch was one of the most turbulent sections of New York—lined on both sides by gambling joints and low-class restaurants, and jammed almost from curb to curb with roistering groups of volunteer firemen, brawling over the merits of this or that fire engine; political rowdies and shoulder-hitters from Tammany Hall around the corner; truculent gangsters and ruffians from the Bowery and the Five Points; and hordes of sneak thieves, pickpockets, watch-stuffers, pocket-book droppers, confidence men and the lower order of gamblers, all quarreling over and subsisting upon the suckers

[10] *Ibid.*, page 379.

and countrymen who swarmed in and out of Barnum's American Museum and lunched and dined at Daniel Sweeney's House of Refreshment. Sweeney was a pioneer of the "fill-'em-up-quick-and-get-'em-out" school of restaurant keeping, and his House of Refreshment was by far the best known eating place of the period—a long, low-ceilinged room crowded with tables and benches, and three times daily a madhouse of bawling customers, shrieking waiters, and clattering crockery. No dish at Sweeney's cost more than about twenty-five cents, and most of them could be had for less than fifteen. A slice of roast beef sold for six cents, and acquired such renown for size and flavor that it was known everywhere in the East as the "Sweeney Cut." Sweeney went a trifle highfalutin about 1850 and introduced a printed menu, but before that he followed the example of Landlord Brown of Washington and had his offerings announced by a leather-lunged crier who stood just outside the doorway. A journalist attempted to transcribe the speech of Sweeney's gifted barker in 1849, with this cryptic result:

> Biledlamancapersors.
> Rosebeefrosegoosemuttonantaters—
> Biledamancabbage, vegetables—
> Walkinsirtakaseatsir.[11]

The House of Refreshment was at No. 11 Ann Street, and across the way, at No. 10, was the largest and most celebrated of all Wolf-Traps, the Tapis Franc. In earlier times the house in which this establishment was conducted had been occupied by the first large billiard hall in the United States, opened in 1832 by a prominent manufacturer of billiard supplies, Bassford. It had about eighteen tables, on which Pin Pool and Fifteen-Ball Pool were played for the first time in this country. The property was used for gambling purposes for some fifteen

[11] *New York in Slices*, page 68.

years after about 1840, and in 1865 was purchased by James Gordon Bennett, founder of the New York *Herald,* who erected on the site "an immense and massive structure" of six stories, which was the first large office building to be constructed of iron, and was considered a wonder of architecture and engineering.

The Tapis Franc was on the ground floor of the original building, with an ale house in front, entered from the street, and gambling in the rear, in a long, narrow room plainly furnished with a few chairs and a score of tables for Faro, *Vingt et Un,* and Chuck-a-Luck. For a few years there was also a Roulette wheel, said to have been the only one ever operated in a Wolf-Trap. The tiger was the most popular game; the Faro tables were in use twenty-four hours a day, for the Tapis Franc never closed, and usually there was a waiting list of dealers. In general, the resort was operated precisely the same as other Wolf-Traps—the house provided the tools, settled up the games, and took ten per cent of the winnings. But because of the great popularity of the place, the comparatively heavy play, and the unceasing demand for tables, there was a minimum on Faro snaps. None could be set up for less than $25 during the day, and at night, when the place was pack-jammed with a jostling mob, a capital of $50 was required. Snaps of $500 were not uncommon in the Tapis Franc, and once in a while there was one with a stake of $1,000. The largest game ever opened there was for $5,000, and was dealt by Ben Colvin, a famous Faro artist of the 1850's, who was better known as Toothpick Ben because he was six feet, seven or eight inches tall and thin as a bean-pole. Faro was an obsession with Toothpick Ben; nothing else interested him. He spent all of his waking hours in the gambling house, and his leisure time in calculating the chances and percentages of the game. Although he always had at least $5,000 in his pocket, he dressed shabbily, lived in a mean room, and never spent more than fifteen cents for a meal—he was saving his roll for the game. Toothpick Ben appears to have been an extremely competent Faro artist, and was frequently approached by big-time gamblers and urged to exhibit his skill in a first-class house. But he preferred the excitement and uncertainties of the Tapis Franc, and ran his game there with considerable success for several years.

Fighting, chip-stealing, pocket-picking, thievery, and cheating by means of dropping and the horse-hair game, went on in the Tapis Franc to an even greater extent that in other Wolf-Traps, because there were larger crowds and more games. But the dealers were protected from the roughs and their enveloping blanket, for the management of the Tapis Franc employed a staff of very efficient strong-arm men who violently discouraged "bonneting" and similar methods of robbery. Moreover, the house maintained very cordial relations with the police and the politicians. The police usually protested, when complaints were made, that they couldn't find any gambling houses, but a squad of reserves was always ready to lend a hand whenever the bouncers of the Tapis Franc were getting the worst of it.

8

The only fly in the gamblers' ointment in New York before the Civil War was Jonathan H. Green, widely known as the Reformed Gambler, whose revelatory buzzing annoyed the sharpers for several years around 1850. Green was born in 1813 near Lawrenceburg, Ind. His mother died when he was an infant, and his father, a dissipated and ungodly man, apprenticed him to an unkind master, from whom he ran away in 1829. He went to Cincinnati, where he soon got into trouble and was put in jail. There he learned to play cards, and for the next twelve years was a professional gambler, playing short cards up and down the Ohio and Mississippi Rivers, and swindling countrymen at Chuck-a-Luck and Thimble-Rig at the fairs and race meetings in Virginia, Kentucky and Ohio. In those days it was customary to sell the gambling privileges at the Southern race tracks, and in 1840, or 1841, the concession at Richmond was purchased by a gambler named John Campbell, who set up games of various kinds in a booth adjoining the grandstand. Meanwhile Jonathan Green and a score of other small-time sharpers had opened for business outside the gates, with Thimble-Rig and Chuck-a-Luck, and trimmed many suckers before they could reach Campbell's games inside the grounds.

Campbell sent a gang of bullies to drive the interlopers away, and in the fight that followed Green was terribly beaten. He now began to reflect seriously upon the evils of gambling, and a year or so later, in August, 1842, forsook the way of a sharper and entered upon a new life of writing, lecturing, and crusading against gaming in all its forms. His first book was published in 1843, and during the next twenty years several others flowed from his pen.[12] The most unusual of these volumes was called *The Secret Band of Brothers,* and was published at Philadelphia in 1847. According to Green, the *Brothers* were a great organization of gamblers, robbers and counterfeiters, formed in 1798 at Hanging Rock, in the western part of Virginia, with one Goodrich at the head of the band. Green further declared that in 1847 the gang had a thousand members, that its great headquarters was in New Orleans, and that the outlaws had been after him since 1830, when he divulged their counterfeiting plans to the police at Louisville. However, they never caught him; the Reformed Gambler lived to a ripe old age.[13]

John O'Connor declared that Green was a "low and debased

[12] See Bibliography.
[13] The present author has been unable to find any other reference to the *Brothers.*

192

fraud" and "the associate of thieves, desperadoes and counterfeiters," but there is nothing in the Reformed Gambler's writings, or in the record of his activities, that might indicate a lack of sincerity. Certainly he could have sold out to the New York sharpers a hundred times; nevertheless, he went after them hammer and tongs. His books sold well, his lectures drew large audiences, and for many years he aroused considerable interest throughout the country. He first appeared in the East about 1847, when he lectured in Philadelphia, arranged for the publication of his book, and engaged in a newspaper controversy with a gambler named Freeman. In the winter of 1849–50 Green went to Albany, where the New York Legislature was in session, and apparently on his own initiative lobbied vigorously on behalf of an anti-gambling bill, which he had written and had persuaded Senator Samuel Miller of Rochester to introduce. An unusual feature of the measure was a section which provided for the punishment of cappers and ropers-in.

Green's early efforts in Albany were so successful that a delegation of New York gamblers hurried upstate to stop the nonsense. At a meeting in an Albany hotel they decided that the only way to cope with Green was to expose him as a crook and a hypocrite, and thus discredit him. Accordingly, the Reformed Gambler was arrested by a New York detective and taken to the metropolis, where he was held in the Tombs for twelve days before being given a hearing on a trumped-up charge of obtaining money on false pretenses. He was released a few minutes after he had appeared in court, for no evidence whatever was produced against him, but was immediately rearrested. This time he was accused of possessing forged Treasury Notes with intent to pass them, two canceled notes having been found in his wallet. The charge collapsed with a thud when Green proved that the Notes were genuine, that they bore the cancellation stamp of the Treasury Department, that they had been given to him by a government official, and that he was an undercover member of the Secret Service.

Green thus emerged triumphant from his ordeal, but the attempted frameup had accomplished its purpose—the Reformed Gambler was unable to return to Albany because of illness which he had contracted in the Tombs, and the sharpers prevented the anti-gambling bill from reaching a vote. A few weeks later Horace Greeley wrote in the New York *Tribune:*

> "Where Green now is we know not, having lost sight of him since his release; but he ought to be located and supported in this city. We greatly need his services here, to watch the operations, and defeat the snares, of the gamblers . . . we would like to bear our part with a number in enabling Mr. Green to devote his time entirely to the extirpation of gambling from our city. . . ."

As a result of this editorial, a group of prominent men held a meeting on June 21, 1850, and another on July 1, at which they organized the New York Association for the Suppression of Gambling, with the avowed object of collecting and publishing information and statistics about gambling, procuring the passage of anti-gambling laws, preventing "the unwary from falling into the snare of gamblers," and attempting the suppression of Lotteries in other states. Rensselaer N. Havens was elected President of the society, and the other officers included such well-known New Yorkers of the period as Horace Greeley, Dr. John D. Russ, Joseph McKeen, George B. Butler, Joseph B. Collins, and W. Main Drinker. Jonathan Green was employed as Corresponding Secretary and Executive Agent in charge of the Intelligence Office. This last was the particular phase of the Association's threatened activities which enraged and frightened the gamblers—a system of private police which purposed to make an accurate list not only of all gaming houses, Lottery offices and Policy shops in New York, but also, as far as possible, of the men who visited them. The by-laws of the Association, however, provided that no man's name could be put on the list until he had been admonished by an officer of the Association and given a chance to mend his ways. Said Sections V and VI of the "Rules and Regulations of the Intelligence Office":

V. Persons desiring the benefit of the Intelligence Office may subscribe specially for this purpose. Such subscribers . . . shall be entitled to all the information in possession of the office relative to the gambling habits of individuals in their employ or confidence. . . .

VI. The following contributions shall entitle the contributors to the benefits of the Intelligence Office:

```
Banking associations  ......................  $100 per annum
Insurance companies  ......................  100  "    "
Railroad companies  ......................  100  "    "
Manufacturing associations  ......from $25 to 100  "    "
Other associations, employing a number of
    clerks and officers  .............from $25 to 100  "    "
Merchants, jobbers, etc., employing ten hands
    or less  .................................  10  "    "
Do . . . do . . . from 10 to 20 hands  .......  15  "    "
Do . . . do . . . from 20 to 50 hands  .......  25  "    "
Do . . . do . . . over 50 hands  ...........  100  "    "
```

At the Broadway Tabernacle on February 20, 1851, the Association heard and approved a comprehensive report prepared by Green, and decided to make an energetic campaign for the passage of the bill which had been defeated by the gamblers. With the support of the Association and most of the newspapers, Green returned to the fray at Albany, and on July 10, 1851, the Legislature enacted a law which prohibited gambling in New York State under penalty of imprisonment of from ten days to two years, and a fine not exceeding $1,000. Roping and capping were made misdemeanors, punishable by fines. At another meeting of the Association on May 14, 1852, the report of the Secretary said that since the law had gone into effect eighty-seven Policy shops, and several gambling houses in Park Place, Broadway, and Murray and Barclay Streets, had closed their doors. For some reason not divulged, this report discussed gaming in San Francisco and Cincinnati, and commented on the fact that in 1851 there had been a great deal of gambling in the far-off territory of Oregon. It also noted that at Oregon City on July 8, 1851, eight men were killed by lightning while playing cards.

The satisfaction of the Association over the closing of the Policy shops and gambling houses was a trifle premature, for all of them reopened after a few months, when it became apparent that the New York Police had not heard of the new law. In later years the statute was occasionally used to discipline obstreperous gamblers, but the only important sharper ever prosecuted under it was the celebrated Pat Herne, who was convicted and heavily fined. Jonathan Green left New York sometime in 1852, and with his departure the anti-gambling Association became moribund. No real check was given to gambling in New York for another fifty years.

CHAPTER IX

GAMBLING ON THE WESTERN RIVERS

WHILE one wing of the gamblers' migration was leading the tiger up the Atlantic coast and into the sparsely-settled interior, another, recruited principally among the dregs of the New Orleans gambling houses and the sharpers of the underworld, was moving up the Mississippi and Ohio Rivers, colonizing the river towns and gradually establishing the professional cheat as one of the major hazards of river travel. The invasion of this field, perhaps the most lucrative that the American gambler has ever enjoyed, began before the turn of the nineteenth century, when a few pioneer sharpers operated in a small way on the occasional flatboat and keelboat that carried passengers in cramped and uncomfortable quarters. It gained in momentum after the Louisiana Purchase had increased transportation facilities and removed the restrictions imposed by the Spaniards upon navigation of the Mississippi, and reached full tide when the steamboat, with its greater speed, superior accommodations, and crowded passenger lists, came into general use.

The first of these "swimming volcanoes" appeared on the Ohio and the Mississippi late in 1811, when the *New Orleans,* designed and built by Robert Fulton, was launched at Pittsburg and chugged noisily downstream to the Louisiana metropolis, arriving there early in 1812. The *New Orleans* sank near Baton Rouge within a year, but by the end of 1814 three other steamboats, the *Comet,* the *Vesuvius,* and the *Enterprise,* were in successful operation. The first to ascend the Mississippi above Natchez was the *Enterprise,* commanded by Captain Henry

197

Miller Shreve, a famous river man of the period and an important figure in the early history of the steamboat.[1] In May, 1815, carrying a cargo of ordnance stores, the *Enterprise* steamed from New Orleans to the Falls of the Ohio at Louisville in twenty-five days, two hours and four minutes, about one-fifth of the time required by the fastest of the keelboats under ideal conditions. Said Thomas Bangs Thorpe in *Harper's New Monthly Magazine* for December, 1855:

"The excitement occasioned by this event can not now be imagined. Captain Shreve was greeted by a public demonstration. Triumphal arches were thrown across the streets, and his appearance everywhere called forth bursts of enthusiasm. At the public demonstration given in his honor patriotic speeches were made, and it was formally announced that the *Enterprise* had accomplished all that was possible in inland navigation. Nothing tended to dampen the hilarity of the hour but a suggestion of the gallant captain, 'that, under more favorable circumstances, he could make the same trip in twenty days!' This was deemed an impossibility, and his boast was looked upon as the pardonable weakness of a man already intoxicated by unprecedented success."

The steamboats of this period were primarily freight carriers, and the few adventurers who traveled in them were stowed in rude bunks among the bales and boxes. One of the first to provide decent passenger accommodations was the second *New Orleans,* built by Fulton at Pittsburg in 1815 at a cost of $65,000. She was 140 feet long by 28 feet wide and, burning four-foot

[1] Shreveport, La., was named in his honor. From 1826 to 1841 he was Superintendent of Western River Improvements, and during that time had charge of the removal of the great Red River Raft, thus opening the river to navigation for a distance of 1,200 miles.

THE NEW ORLEANS LEVEE IN THE LATE 1850's

logs in a furnace capable of consuming six cords in twenty-four hours, could make four miles an hour upstream and ten miles downstream. She carried two hundred tons of freight and about fifty passengers. The ladies were isolated in a thirty-foot cabin below deck, "it being," as a traveler pointed out, "the most retired place," which no gentleman might enter except by permission of all the ladies. The men had the exclusive use of "an elegant roundhouse" above deck, forty-two feet long and fitted with twenty-six berths in thirteen staterooms. Above the roundhouse was "an elegantly decorated walk with iron railings and nettings," where the lordly males could "sit comfortably and have a commanding view over the boat, river and land, and enjoy the cool breeze," while the ladies sweltered below deck with their knitting and tatting. During the summer months a steamboat of this type was completely covered with bright-colored awning, so that she presented an arresting and eye-filling spectacle as she thundered down the river at the unprecedented speed of ten miles an hour. And after dark, with her glowing furnace, splashing paddle-wheels, clanking machinery, and sparks whirling in every direction, her resemblance to a "swimming volcano" was probably very striking. A German traveler who watched the passing of a steamer from a flatboat at night in 1817 wrote in his journal that it was "a most delightful sight. The dark night and the bright sparks which were flying out of the cylinder rendered to the eye only an instantaneous but a magnificent view. The vessel passed only about fifty feet from us. The water foamed, and one could perceive even the wind caused by the swiftness of the boat."

Two years after Robert Fulton's passenger boat had been put in commission, in March, 1817, Captain Shreve made the trip from New Orleans to Louisville in twenty-five days flat in the *Washington,* built by himself and incorporating several new features of his own invention, among them a cam cut-off which reduced fuel consumption by three-fifths. The *Washington* was clearly superior to Fulton's boats, and the latter and his associates promptly brought suit in an attempt to drive Captain Shreve from the river, claiming the exclusive right to navigate "all vessels propelled by fire and steam" on the rivers of the Western territories. They seized the *Washington* and other boats belonging to Captain Shreve, but were compelled to relinquish them when the litigation was decided in the Captain's favor. With Fulton's monopoly thus broken, an era of great building activity began, and the log-burners slid from the ways in ever-increasing numbers. By 1820 sixty were churning the muddy waters of the Mississippi with their cumbersome paddle-wheels, and in 1835 this number had been increased to about 250, with an average tonnage of 170. During the great days of steamboating, from about 1845 to 1860, when the whole Western country was booming and the one-time frontier towns of St. Louis, Memphis, Cincinnati and Louisville were being transformed into great cities, at least five hundred first-class vessels were in operation on the Mississippi and the Ohio. And the hulls of scores of others lay rotting on the river beds, for navigation of the Western waters before the Civil War was attended by an appalling loss of life and property. In 1846 a Congressional Committee estimated that the annual loss of boats and cargoes approximated $2,500,000; and in 1852, one of the few years in which accurate records were kept, seventy-eight steamboats and eighty-four vessels of other types met disaster. In that year alone four hundred persons were killed in river accidents, including one hundred who perished in the explosion of the steamer *Saluda*.

Great improvements in steamboat construction were made in the thirty years that followed the epochal voyages of the first *New Orleans* and the *Enterprise,* and the boats of the 1840's and the 1850's were superior in every respect to the vessels built by Fulton and Captain Shreve. To the ordinary passenger this superiority was manifest principally in increased size —they varied in breadth from thirty-five to fifty feet, and in length from 150 to the 365 feet of the gigantic *Eclipse;* in greater speed—few required more than six days to make the run from New Orleans to Louisville; [2] and in more luxurious appointments. Enormous sums were expended upon the fittings and furnishings of such famous steamboats as the *Eclipse,* the *Natchez,* the *Sultana,* the *Belle Key,* the *Reindeer,* the *A. L. Shotwell,* and the *Robert E. Lee,* and they richly deserved their world-wide renown as the last word in sybaritic travel. Even English voyagers, those energetic belittlers of all things American, were impressed by the lavish use of gilt and plush, and grudgingly admitted that the "floating palaces" and "palace-steamers," as they were commonly called, were "grand and imposing," both outside and inside.

Deck passengers on even the finest steamboats were herded like cattle among the freight, were required on many vessels to furnish their own food and bedding, and were otherwise accorded the treatment which their poverty and lowly estate deserved. But nothing was too good for the cabin passengers, especially those of wealth and position. The pilots, mates and engineers mingled freely with them on terms of equality, and even the Captain sometimes condescended to pass the time of day with a particularly important traveler. As a rule, however, the Captain remained aloof, fully aware of his position and responsibilities, for in those days Federal and state supervision of steamboat navigation was sketchy, to say the least, and the Captain was a veritable autocrat. His will was the law of the boat, and a passenger who violated one of his regulations or failed to show proper deference was apt to find himself ma-

[2] The record of four days, nine hours and nineteen minutes was made by the *A. L. Shotwell* in 1858.

rooned on the edge of a lonely canebrake, miles from a settlement. But unless a cabin passenger annoyed the Captain, he was permitted to go where he pleased and amuse himself in his own way. "This latitude," wrote an early traveler, "sometimes led to some rather strong contrasts; for instance, there might frequently be seen in the ladies' cabin a group of the godly praying and singing psalms, while in the dining-saloon, from which the tables had been removed, another party was dancing to the music of a fiddle, while farther along, in the social hall, might be heard the loud laughter of jolly carousers around the drinking bar, and occasionally chiming in with the sound of the revelry, the rattling of money and checks, and the sound of voices at the card-tables."

The Social Hall or Main Saloon, with the bar at one end and the floor dotted with brass spittoons, was the principal lounging place of the gentlemen passengers, and there each evening gathered the convivial travelers of every description. "The crowd of passengers ordinarily witnessed on our Mississippi steamers," wrote Thomas Bangs Thorpe, "present more than is anywhere else observable in a small space, the cosmopolitanism of our extraordinary population. Upon their decks are to be seen immigrants from every nationality in Europe; in the cabin are strangely mingled every phase of social life—the aristocratic English lord . . . the ultra-socialist . . . the conservative bishop . . . the graceless gambler . . . the wealthy planter . . . the 'northern fanatic' . . . the farmer from about the arctic regions of Lake Superior . . . the frank, open-handed men of the West . . . a party from 'down East' . . . politicians of every stripe, and religionists of all creeds, for the time drop their wranglings. . . ." [3]

These cosmopolites, with their wallets and money-belts choked with gold and their souls overflowing with good humor

[3] *Harper's New Monthly Magazine,* December, 1855, page 34.

and a yearning for high adventure, were made to order for the professional gambler, and the brethren of the nimble finger and the quick wit came aboard the steamboats in droves to pluck them. At first the sharper's presence was tolerated only so long as no outcry was made against him; if he was accused or even suspected of cheating, the boat was nosed in to shore and he was unceremoniously dumped off. Socially, in the early days at least, he was an outcast, and remained so even in death; when eleven persons were scalded to death by an explosion aboard the *Constitution* on May 4, 1817, a German traveler who saw the accident noted that "among them was a gambler, who was buried separately." [4] But within a decade after the sad end of this unfortunate wretch the status of the river-going sharper had changed; he had become almost as much a member of a steamboat's personnel as the pilot, and many captains considered it bad luck to leave port without at least one gambler among the passengers. Only occasionally was he interfered with when he set up his game in the Social Hall, and a steamboat's officers, who frequently shared in his takings, paid scant attention to the wails of a stricken sucker. In many instances the gambler silenced a squawking loser with a knife or a pistol and flung the body overboard, and unless the victim was a prominent man or had influential relatives such a crime was seldom reported to the authorities on shore. Said *Niles' Weekly Register* of August 18, 1838:

> "*Gambling on the western waters.* This is a most important as well as a most alarming subject; and we trust the authorities of Illinois and other Western states will enact such laws as shall suppress a demoralizing vice, which, as

[4] The accident occurred near Bayou Sara, about 175 miles from New Orleans, while the *Constitution* was racing against the *Washington*. Some months earlier, in 1816, the boiler of the *Washington* had exploded near Marietta, O., killing seven men.

will be seen, too often leads to assassination and murder. The Grafton (Ill.) *Backwoodsman,* has an article on the prevalence of gambling on board the steamers in the Western rivers. It records the death of several individuals in an unaccountable manner, and the following extract shows a state of morals almost too depraved for belief!

"'Numbers have come to the west, taken passage on board of a boat, and never been heard of again. In repeated instances within the last few years, letters have been addressed to us from a distance, with anxious inquiries for a friend, from whom no tidings had come since he was on the point of embarking on board of a boat. It was feared that he had fallen overboard, or died on the passage, and we were implored in the most affecting terms to seek intelligence of his fate. Our earnest endeavors in most instances have proved unavailing. Could the deep and turbid waters of our rivers reveal their secrets, they would tell but too often the long silence of those absent friends. The midnight gambling, the fierce quarrel, the dirk, the sullen plunge of the ghastly corpse, with heavy weights attached, all follow in quick succession, and with the unerring certainty that effect follows cause.'"

By the early 1830's between 1,000 and 1,500 professional gamblers more or less regularly worked the steamboats between New Orleans and Louisville, with the majority concentrated on the Mississippi below St. Louis, where their favorite prey, the rich planter and slave owner and the foolish young scion of a wealthy family, was found in greatest abundance. The river sharpers of this period were practically one hundred per cent crooked; it is doubtful if any of them ever dealt an honest card or made an honest throw of the dice. They were experts in the use of cold decks, marked cards, strippers, holdouts, reflectors, loaded dice, and innumerable other devices for cheating, and played only games which were well adapted to trickery. At short cards they favored Brag, Euchre, Poker, Whist, Boston, All-Fours, and Seven-up or Old Sledge; while the principal banking games were Faro, *Vingt et Un,* and Chuck-a-Luck. Roulette was played infrequently because of the bulky apparatus required. Thimble-Riggers displayed their shenanigans on the steamboats from the earliest days, and Three Card Monte throwers, also called "Broad pitchers" because a playing card was known as a "Broad," began to appear about the time of the war with Mexico. Apparently Craps never became very popular on the rivers except among the Negro deck hands and the lower class of deck passengers; almost no references to it are found in the reminiscences of old-time gamblers or other accounts of life among the suckers.

River gamblers seldom operated alone; usually they traveled in groups of from three to six, adopting various disguises and pretending never to have met until they boarded the steamboat. They capped and roped for one another's banking games, and when one succeeded in enticing a sucker or two into a short card session, the others were always on hand to help make up a table. If a sharper obtained a seat in an honest game of experienced players, where the usual methods of trickery were dangerous, "his confederates would seat themselves in such a position that they could see the cards held by his adversaries, and 'item' the strength of their hands to him by signs." These were made by hand, by twirling the head of a cane in a certain manner, by puffs of cigar smoke, by shifting a quid of tobacco in the cheeks, and in almost every other conceivable fashion.

One of the celebrated "itemers" of the early Mississippi was a lame gambler named James Ashby, who exercised his talents in a field wherein there was comparatively little competition— he preyed almost entirely upon his fellow sharpers. He usually worked with a partner who was disguised as a gawky young backwoodsman, en route home after selling a drove of hogs. Ashby impersonated the young man's fiddle-playing old Pappy who didn't have all his buttons, and was forever playing snatches of tunes on his fiddle, especially after the young backwoodsman had been inveigled into a card game. Not for a long time did the gamblers learn that the tunes were signals, or realize that the pseudo-backwoodsman always had a streak of "Nigger-luck" when Pappy started to fiddle. Ashby was eventually exposed in a dive at Natchez-under-the-Hill, and dropped out of sight until the early 1840's, when he appeared in St. Louis and for several years operated the town's principal Faro bank. During this period of his career the lame gambler clad himself in fine raiment of velvet and broadcloth, perhaps to enable him to forget the nondescript garments he had worn while "iteming" on the Mississippi. In addition to the elegant clothing, Ashby decorated his person with a great profusion of diamonds false and real, gold chains, rings and bracelets; and when he went abroad carried a gold-headed cane in each hand and a huge gold pencil, set with diamonds, in his mouth. He died in the early 1850's, and envious gamblers insisted that his death had been "greatly hastened by the enormous weight of jewelry with which he was accustomed to burden himself during his life."

2

The river sharpers often went to great trouble and expense in setting the stage of their operations, and usually their elaborate and well-planned schemes were successful. Sometimes, however, the gamblers came to grief at the last moment, either by the quarry becoming suspicious or through interference on the part of chivalrous passengers. One of the busiest of these knights-errant of the steamboats was no less a personage than the redoubtable James Bowie, inventor of the bowie-knife, once an associate of the pirate Jean Lafitte, and the most noted duelist of his time. This noble-minded killer, who died with Davy Crockett in the defense of the Alamo in 1836, was a menace to the river gamblers for several years; he spent considerable time on the lower Mississippi, and seems to have made a practice of ferreting out crooked gamblers, beating them at their own game, and restoring to suckers the money of which they had been fleeced. But he always required the sucker to swear a solemn oath that he would gamble no more.

Bowie's most celebrated exploit of this character was performed on the steamer *New Orleans* in the fall of 1832, when he saved a young gentleman of Natchez from dishonor and a suicide's grave. In the summer of that year this young gentleman, who fancied himself as a card player and a man of the world, went to New York on his honeymoon, and while there collected about $50,000 on behalf of various merchants and planters of Natchez. A syndicate of gamblers was formed to despoil him, and one of the sharpers was sent to New York, where he made the young gentleman's acquaintance and learned that the latter intended to go home by way of Pittsburg and Louisville, with a stop-over of several days in Louisville to visit relatives. When the young gentleman took a boat at Pittsburg the sharper was on board, and so were two "Louisiana planters," who made themselves very agreeable. Twenty-card poker was introduced, and the young man from Natchez was permitted to win several hundred dollars. By the time the boat reached Louisville the four men had become such friends that the "planters" and the sharper, who posed as a New Orleans merchant, agreed to wait and go down the river on the *New Orleans,* on which the young gentleman had booked passage for himself and his bride.

The gamblers went after the young gentleman in earnest when the *New Orleans* left the wharf at Louisville. In a few sessions they had cheated him out of $45,000, and he was betting frantically in a desperate effort to retrieve his losses. Bowie, wearing a black, broad-brimmed slouch hat and black broadcloth clothing of clerical cut, boarded the boat at Vicksburg and became an interested spectator of the game, which he saw immediately was crooked. After a few more hours' play the young man's last dollar vanished into the capacious pockets of the gamblers, and crazed by remorse he rushed to the rail and attempted to throw himself into the river. He was restrained by Bowie and his wife and taken to his cabin, where Bowie instructed that he be closely watched.

Bowie then went to the bar, casually displayed a bulging wallet, and asked for change for a hundred dollar bill. One of the gamblers, who were opening wine to celebrate the success of their *coup,* obliged, and after a few moments of conversation suggested a card game, to which Bowie agreed. On the first few hands Bowie won, and then the sharpers began to forge ahead. At length one of the "planters" dealt Bowie a hand which any Poker player would bet as long as he could see, and which Bowie recognized as being intended for the big cleanup. The "planters" dropped out after a few bets, but Bowie and the "merchant" continued to raise each other until $70,000 was piled on the table between them. Finally Bowie saw what he had been watching for—the gambler's hand flicking quickly into his sleeve. Like lightning Bowie seized the sharper's wrist, at the same time drawing from his shirt-bosom a wicked-looking knife.

"Show your hand!" he commanded. "If it contains more than five cards I shall kill you!"

The gambler attempted to break loose, but Bowie twisted his

wrist and his cards fell to the table—four aces, a queen and a jack.

"I shall take the pot," said Bowie, "with a legitimate Poker hand, four kings and a ten."

"Who the devil are you, anyway?" cried the discomfited gambler.

"I," said the famous duelist, "am James Bowie!"

"The voice was like velvet," says an account of the affair, "but it cut like steel into the hearts of the chief gambler's confederates and deterred them from any purpose or impulse they might have had to interfere. They, with the crowd, shrank back from the table, smitten with terror by the name. Bowie softly swept the banknotes into his large slouch hat and lightly clapped it on his head."

There are two versions of what happened next. One is that Bowie let the gambler go with a lecture, but kept the pot. The other is that the sharper insisted on a duel, and that Bowie borrowed a pistol and shot him off the wheelhouse "just as the great round face of the sun, like a golden cannon ball," appeared over a neighboring cliff. This trifling matter disposed of, Bowie gave the young gentleman of Natchez two-thirds of the contents of the hat, and kept the remainder as spoils of war. With tears in his eyes the young gentleman swore never to touch another card, and both he and his bride prayed that Heaven might bless their benefactor.

Occasionally when no chivalrous bystander was at hand to save him from the consequences of his folly, a desperate sucker would attempt to outsmart the gamblers. But almost always he was so nervous and clumsy that his cheating was soon discovered. And when it was, the indignation of the sharpers knew no bounds, and the punishment inflicted upon the luckless wight for his ungentlemanly conduct was swift and condign. What happened to one young planter who attempted to trick sharpers was thus told by an old-time river man:

"I was on one of the smaller boats one night on which were some gamblers going down the river to meet a large steamer coming up. I suppose the partners on the big boat had most of their gambling machinery. At any rate, when they saw two or three young plantation men on the boat they could only find one greasy pack of cards and no chips. The boat had a cargo of corn, so one of the party shelled some and it was used as chips.

"About the time this decision was made one of the planters disappeared. He had managed to slip down into the hold where the corn was, and in the dark he took the first ear he found, and, shelling it, put the corn in his pocket. He afterward joined the game, buying some chips, which he placed in another pocket. . . .

"Luck was against him, and he lost his last honest chip. It was his turn to ante. He plunged his hand down into his pocket, got some grains of corn, and slapped them down on the table. When he raised his hand, lo and behold, the grains were red. In an instant every man was on his feet. One held a pistol at his head, while the rest went through his pockets. Of course they brought up a whole lot of red corn. The corn that the dealers had shelled and given out was white. They bound him hand and foot, and were holding a council to determine what to do with him when we heard the whistle of the big steamer.

"They took him on board with them, and I never could learn what they did with him, but I was on the river for many years after that and I never saw him again." [5]

[5] *Poker Stories,* collected and edited by John F. B. Lillard; New York, 1896; pages 44–45.

When the enterprising gambler was not a-gambling on the Mississippi, when his flagrant cheating made the steamboats temporarily too hot for him, and when there was a dearth of traveling suckers, he was taking his ease or practicing his profession in the underworld districts of the larger river towns—the Swamp at New Orleans, a dozen blocks on Girod Street a half-mile or so from the wharves; Natchez-under-the-Hill, squatting in the miasmal mud flats below the town which early travelers described as, next to Charleston, the most beautiful in America; the Pinch Gut at Memphis, sprawling from the base of Chickasaw Bluff to the yellow waters of the Mississippi, and so called because of the terrible effect produced by the whisky sold there; and the Landing at Vicksburg, a tangle of vice and debauchery which was not included in the plans of the Rev. Newit Vick when he founded a city among the Walnut Hills.

The Swamp was the largest of these areas, but it differed from the others only in size and minor physical details; all were literally and figuratively stink-holes of creation—mazes of narrow streets and alleys teeming with gamblers, murderers, footpads, burglars, arsonists, pickpockets, prostitutes and pimps, and ruffians who would gouge out a man's eye or chew off his nose for the price of a drink. Every flimsy cabin, clap-board shanty, and abandoned flatboat with its bottom stuck in the mud, was a groggery, a brothel, a dance house, a gambling den or a low tavern which combined under one roof the worst features of the other establishments. All of them ran wide open twenty-four hours a day, brawling and debauchery of every description were virtually continuous, and murder was so common as to attract only passing attention; the body of a man stabbed or shot to death was simply rolled into the river and the incident forgotten.

Originally these cesspools of crime and corruption were built up principally to cater to the savage lusts of the flatboatmen, as a class probably the roughest, toughest and most quarrelsome of all the pioneers who penetrated the Western wilderness in the vanguard of civilization. When they came ashore they demanded women and whisky, and the river towns provided both in great abundance. And what time the flatboatmen were not guzzling the fiery liquor or enjoying the delights of the flesh, they were brawling and fighting—engaging in single combats which usually resulted in the mutilation of one or both antagonists; or embarking upon mass forays under the leadership of such celebrated river heroes as Bill Sedley, who was king of the flatboatmen until he killed two gamblers in New Orleans and fled from the river to escape the vengeance of their friends; Aleck Masters, a five-foot Kentuckian with prodigious strength and the disposition of a panther; Bill McCoy, who once paddled a home-made canoe 1,300 miles to keep his promise to appear in court at Natchez; and Big Jim Girty, nephew of the notorious renegade Simon Girty and a rough-and-tumble fighter of almost superhuman prowess. For several years Girty was regarded as invincible, the reason being, according to river legend, that he was "provided with a solid body casing on both sides, without interstices through which a knife, dirk or bullet could penetrate." Despite this miraculous protection, however, he was cut to pieces by a gang of gamblers in a saloon and brothel owned by his mistress, Marie Dufour, at Natchez-under-the-Hill. Madame Dufour shot two of Big Jim's assailants after he went down, and fired a bullet into her own head when she saw that he was dead.

Nowhere on the Mississippi were the police strong enough to discipline the brawling bullies of the flatboats or to interfere with the schemes and amusements of the underworld. Of necessity, the authorities of New Orleans, Natchez, Vicksburg and Memphis, as well as those of the smaller river towns, adopted the dangerous policy of ignoring these municipal festers and letting their denizens strictly alone unless they invaded the respectable business and residential sections. When this happened, as it frequently did, the decent citizens turned out *en masse* to drive them back to their holes, where they simmered and stewed until the next outbreak. And busily stirring the unholy mess were the gamblers; they financed the saloons, the brothels, and the taverns, had a finger in every unsavory pie cooked up in these dives, and ran gambling joints wherein they impartially fleeced the river men, stray suckers, and one another. For more than thirty years they dominated every underworld district on the Ohio and Mississippi Rivers from Pittsburg to New Orleans, and their arrogance and excesses, both afloat and ashore, aroused increasing fear and resentment throughout the valleys of the Western rivers. By the early 1830's the most startling rumors were current everywhere in that vast territory—the gamblers were rioting in New Orleans, stealing children and forcing them into the brothels; they were agents of the Northern abolitionists; they had burned Mobile, pillaged Natchez, driven all but their own kind out of Vicksburg, and massacred the passengers of a dozen steamboats. The ignorant attributed to the power of the gamblers such acts of God as floods, tornadoes, cyclones, and even the great earthquake which had rocked the Mississippi Valley in 1811;[6] while among the intelligent classes the belief prevailed,

---

[6] This was one of the major earthquakes of history, although the loss of life was comparatively small because the country was thinly settled. It changed the topography of a large part of the Mississippi Valley, creating the great swamps of Southeast Missouri, raising new islands in the Mississippi, and forming scores of lakes on either side of the river. One of these, Reelfoot, is twenty miles long and seven miles wide, and so deep that in places it is supposed to be bottomless. The ground around New Madrid, Mo., center of the disturbance, was so tormented that for a time the current of the Mississippi ran backward, carrying several flatboats to destruction upstream. The shocks began on December 16, 1811, and in the New Madrid country continued almost without intermission for more than three months. They were felt as far east as South Carolina, as far north as the mouth of the Ohio, and as far south as the mouth of the St. Francis River, in Arkansas.

and with some reason, that gamblers were involved in every crime that was committed, and that every criminal was a gambler. For as *Niles' Weekly Register* said on August 8, 1835:

"Under this name are classed a host of desperadoes who belong to the newly settled parts of the country, who are not only cheats at games of chance, but robbers, murderers, and felons in all crimes. They have their squads at all the principal points on the western rivers, and carry on crimes of all sorts by system. They have shown themselves too strong for the civil authorities, and have not hesitated to challenge anyone who dared to call them to an account. No one's life was safe who interfered with them."

In the summer of 1834 the people of the Mississippi country first became aware of the fantastic scheme concocted by John A. Murrel, most notorious of the bandits and slave-stealers who operated on the Natchez Trace, and a murderer whose killings, in number and sheer ferocity, have never been equaled in America. Murrel's plans were exposed by Virgil A. Stewart, a young Georgian who had wormed his way into the bandit's confidence, and had obtained the names of many of the leading conspirators, together with full details of the organization of the Clan of the Mystic Confederacy, with which Murrel proposed to foment a slave uprising and then, during the excitement of the insurrection, burn and pillage New Orleans, Mobile, Memphis, Vicksburg, Natchez and other Southern cities.

Murrel began to organize the Clan in 1832, and within a year had recruited, from among the most vicious elements of the underworld, almost 1,500 men, of whom some 400 were Councillors, or officers, and the remainder Strikers, or common soldiers. In addition to these there were about a hundred members of the Grand Council, the supreme governing body of the Clan, while

A WICKED GAME ON ONE OF THE OLD MISSISSIPPI STEAMBOATS

in every Southern state agents of the Clan were working among the Negroes, arousing them against their masters and organizing them into companies in preparation for the great day. Murrel told Stewart that on the date set for the rebellion—Christmas Day, 1835—he would have under his command at least 300 Grand Councillors, 600 Councillors, and 5,000 Strikers; and that the entire population of the underworld would rally around his standard once the killing and looting had begun.

Stewart fell in with Murrel in the spring of 1834 while searching for two slaves which had been stolen from a preacher near Jackson, Tenn. He accompanied the bandit chieftain to the headquarters of the Clan, a log house in an Arkansas swamp opposite the town of Randolph, Tenn., and procured the conspirator's arrest when they returned to Tennessee. In July, 1834, Murrel was convicted of stealing slaves and sentenced to ten years in the Penitentiary at Nashville, and whatever chance of success his scheme might have had vanished when he entered the prison gates. On the witness stand, and later in a pamphlet called *The Western Land Pirate,* Stewart described in detail the organization and aims of the Clan, and gave the names of the conspirators which he had obtained from Murrel. Many of them were well-known gamblers, and others were supposedly respectable planters, merchants, and tavern-keepers. There was also, of course, a considerable number of those slimy slugs the politicians, perennial allies of the American criminal.

Stewart's testimony, the additional revelations contained in his pamphlet, and the fact that Murrel's gangsters made several attempts to kill him, caused a tremendous sensation throughout the South, and intensified the feeling of uneasiness with which the activities of the gamblers were regarded. The pamphlet was purchased in large quantities and eagerly read and discussed, and it was everywhere agreed that something should be done to curb the growing power of the underworld and, in particular, of the gamblers. There was a great deal of talk, and considerable resolution-passing, but actually very little was accomplished. The Tennessee Legislature enacted a law "making the exhibition of the game of Faro punishable by fine and imprisonment," [7] and in some of the smaller towns a few gamblers were caught up and used according to "Lynch's Law" [8]—that is, they were given from 40 to 300 lashes, tarred and feathered, and ordered to leave town within twenty-four hours—but in the larger cities the signs of impending trouble were ignored, though visible on every hand.

With Murrel in prison, the Clan of the Mystic Confederacy was looked upon as a snake without a head, and almost a year passed before the people of the Mississippi Valley learned that it was still writhing in the dark places of the underworld. They finally awakened to a full realization of the danger in June, 1835, when two slaves were overheard discussing the insurrection on a plantation in Madison County, Mississippi. The Negroes confessed all they knew of the conspiracy, and an investigation begun by local authorities revealed that the Clan not only

[7] The gamblers attempted to evade the law by removing the sevens from the deck and calling the game "Forty-eight," but the Tennessee courts held that it was the same game within the meaning of the statute. One gambler was sent to prison for two years.

[8] This was the form in which the expression was generally used in those days. It didn't become synonymous with hanging until after the Civil War. The New York *Sun* of August 4, 1835, and *Niles' Weekly Register* of August 8, 1835, gave this version of the origin of "Lynch's Law": "In Washington county, Pa., many years ago, there lived a poaching vagabond who, it was believed, maintained himself and his family by pilfering from the farmers around him. . . . At length a Mr. Van Swearingen laid [a] trap for him, in which he was caught. . . . Van Swearingen told him he would give him twenty-four hours to leave the neighborhood, adding that if he remained longer he would prosecute him. The poacher only laughed at his threats, while the latter went to consult his neighbors as to what was to be done . . . five or six of them repaired to the poachers . . . proceeded to try him in due form, choosing one of their number, a farmer named Lynch, to be judge. . . . The case was submitted to the judge, who decided that the poacher should be tied up and receive three hundred lashes, 'well laid on,' and then be given twenty-four hours to leave the place, under penalty of receiving three hundred more if found after that time. . . ."

had not abandoned Murrel's scheme, but had advanced the date of the uprising to July 4, 1835. Unwilling to wait upon the slow and cumbersome processes of the law, the planters of Madison County held a meeting at Livingston and formed a Committee of Safety, of which Colonel H. G. Runnels, elected Governor of Mississippi that same year, was made Chairman. Similar organizations were formed elsewhere in Mississippi and in Tennessee, and under the authority of these Committees bands of Rangers and Regulators swept through both states, arresting all who were suspected of being implicated in the conspiracy.

One of the first brought to Madison County for trial was Joshua Cotton, a Steam Doctor, who was said also to be interested in several gambling houses in Natchez and Vicksburg. Cotton confessed that he was one of Murrel's principal lieutenants and a Grand Councillor of the Clan of the Mystic Confederacy. "Our object in undertaking to excite the Negroes to rebellion," he said, "was not for the purpose of liberating them, but for plunder . . . but from the exposure of our plans in Stewart's pamphlet, we expected the citizens would be on their guard at the time mentioned, that being the 25th of December next; and we determined to take them by surprise and try it on the night of July 4th. . . . There are arms and ammunition deposited in Hinds County, near Raymond." Cotton was hanged as soon as he had signed his confession, and within ten days a dozen other white men and twice as many Negroes, almost all of whom admitted participation in the conspiracy, had likewise been strung up to the nearest trees. Messengers on swift horses carried the news of the executions, and warning of the intended uprising, as rapidly as they could cover the country, and when the fateful day came the slaves had been so cowed by the loss of their white leaders, and the fact that the planters were ready for them, that they caused no trouble anywhere.

But the rank and file of the criminal armies with which the

Clan had expected to conquer the cities were not as easily convinced that their cause was hopeless. On the Fourth of July every underworld·colony on the Ohio and Mississippi Rivers from Cincinnati to New Orleans was in a ferment of disorder; mobs of drunken gamblers, ruffians and prostitutes raged through the narrow streets and alleys, cursing and fighting among themselves. Everywhere they made menacing gestures against the respectable elements of the population, but the captains who were to lead them to victory and loot were for the most part in flight, and only in Memphis and Vicksburg did the demonstrations reach alarming proportions. In Memphis a mob of several hundred men and women swarmed up the Bluff from the Pinch Gut, brandishing knives, clubs and pistols. They milled for an hour in the Public Square, yelling "Burn the Court House!" but lacking courage to apply the torch. All afternoon they roared through the town, looting a few stores and beating an occasional pedestrian, but scrambling away in fright whenever they encountered the groups of armed citizens who patrolled the residential section. At dusk the mob vanished into the Pinch Gut as suddenly as it had appeared, and during the night of brawling and carousing that followed the demonstration it succeeded in doing more damage in its own district than it had done on the Bluff. Half a dozen buildings were burned, among them the Pedraza Hotel, the Pinch Gut's most notorious resort and a veritable nest of gamblers and prostitutes.

Until the abortive revolt engineered by the Clan of the Mystic Confederacy, Vicksburg was the capital of the gamblers' empire. There they not only controlled the colony of ruffians and prostitutes at the Landing, but by the late 1820's had invaded the pleasant city in the hills with crooked gambling games and their concomitant crime and disorder. John O'Connor described Vicksburg as "the liveliest gambling place in the whole Southwest," and said that "gambling banks existed, of various kinds, both on the hill and under the hill; in log-cabins, board houses, canvas tents and in flatboats. Vicksburg was a great place in those days. . . ." [9] Jonathan H. Green wrote that he had "no doubt but that as many as three-fourths of all the citizens of Vicksburg were more or less addicted to gambling," and that "gambling so prevailed in Vicksburg that those citizens who did not encourage the gamblers, were continually exposed to the insults of those desperadoes; and those who did encourage them by playing with them, were constantly exposed to their villainous frauds and cheats. This class of men had become so entirely regardless of all order and decency, that they cared nothing for law, nor had they any respect for any person; and would, for the slightest offense, as soon spit in the face of the most respected citizen as they would kick at a snarling dog." [10] A letter from Vicksburg published in *Niles' Weekly Register* on August 1, 1835, further described the situation there:

"For years past, professional gamblers, destitute of all sense of moral obligations—unconnected with society by any of its ordinary ties, and intent only on the gratification of their avarice—have made Vicksburg their place of rendezvous—, and, in the very bosom of our society, boldly plotted their vile and lawless machinations. Here, as everywhere else, the laws of the country were found wholly ineffectual for the punishment of these individuals, and emboldened by impunity, their numbers and their crimes have daily continued to multiply. Every species of transgression followed in their train. They supported a large number of tippling houses, to which they would decoy the youthful and unsuspecting, and, after stripping them of their possessions, send them forth into the world the ready and desperate

[9] *Wanderings of a Vagabond,* page 248.
[10] *An Exposure of the Arts and Miseries of Gambling,* pages 211-12.

instruments of vice. Our streets everywhere resounded with the echoes of their drunken and obscene mirth, and no citizen was secure from their villainy. Frequently in armed bodies, they have disturbed the good order of public assemblages, insulted our citizens, and defied our civil authorities. Thus had they continued to grow bolder in their wickedness, and more formidable in their numbers. . . ."

On July 4, 1835, the Vicksburg Volunteers, the local military company, celebrated Independence Day with a barbecue and speech-making in a grove in the eastern part of the town. While the oratory was in progress half a dozen well-known gamblers, all of whom had obviously been drinking, appeared on the outskirts of the crowd, where they began talking and laughing in a loud and boisterous manner. One of them, Francis Cabler, a former blacksmith who had acquired a considerable reputation as a pugilist in Natchez before joining the gamblers' colony at Vicksburg, attempted to make his way to the speakers' stand, jostling ladies and overturning two or three tables in his blundering progress. An officer of the Volunteers, named Fisher, assisted by several citizens, tried to quiet him, and he "insulted the officer and struck one of the citizens." [11] Cabler was immediately seized by Fisher's comrades, but Captain Baumgard, commander of the Volunteers, intervened, and the gambler was released upon his promise to leave the grove.

At the close of the day's festivities the Volunteers, parading through the town before disbanding, were met in the public Square with the information that Cabler was coming up the hill to kill Fisher and anyone else who dared interfere with him. In a few minutes the gambler appeared in the Square, cursing and yelling and flourishing a pistol and a knife, while the hilt of a

[11] In the account of the disturbances at Vicksburg and elsewhere on the river this and other quotations not otherwise credited are from various issues of *Niles' Weekly Register*, July and August, 1835.

dirk peeped from his pocket. He staggered toward the waiting Volunteers, but was disarmed and placed under arrest before he could use his weapons. Then arose the question of what to do with him. "To liberate him, would have been to devote several of the most respectable members of the company to his vengeance, and to proceed against him at law would have been mere mockery, inasmuch, as, not having had the opportunity of consummating his designs, no adequate punishment could have been inflicted on him. Consequently it was determined to take him into the woods and *Lynch* him—which is a mode of punishment provided for such as become obnoxious in a manner which the law cannot reach." Followed by a large number of approving citizens, the Volunteers marched Cabler to the grove where the original trouble had occurred. There the gambler was tied to a tree, given thirty-two lashes with a whip, tarred and feathered, and ordered to leave Vicksburg within forty-eight hours.

The underworld forces of the Clan of the Mystic Confederacy at Vicksburg, larger in numbers and more efficiently organized than elsewhere on the Mississippi, were under the command of James Hoard, keeper of a gambling house and "the Lucifer of the gang," and Henry Wyatt, a Faro dealer and bartender who when he was hanged ten years later had committed seven murders. It is very doubtful if Hoard and Wyatt had anything to do with Cabler's crazy outbreak, but they quickly attempted to take advantage of the fury which the seizure of the gambler had aroused among the denizens of the Landing. They sent word to Captain Baumgard that if Cabler was whipped they would burn Vicksburg, and when the Volunteers ignored the ultimatum and proceeded with the lynching, Hoard and Wyatt summoned their followers and started up the hill to carry out the threat. The column set out from the Landing with much cursing and boasting, but men began to drop out before it had gone a hundred feet, and when Hoard and Wyatt reached the top of the hill not more than a dozen men straggled after them. So they perforce marched down again.

The sortie had failed to rescue Cabler, but it had implanted in the minds of the people of Vicksburg the conviction that they would not be safe until the colony of gamblers was destroyed. That night a great mass meeting, attended by virtually every respectable adult male in the town, was held at the Court House, and these resolutions were unanimously adopted:

"Resolved, That a notice be given all professional gamblers, that the citizens of Vicksburg are resolved to exclude them from this place and its vicinity; and that twenty-four hours' notice be given them to leave the place.

"Resolved, That all persons permitting Faro dealing in their houses, be also notified that they will be prosecuted therefor.

"Resolved, That one hundred copies of the foregoing resolutions be printed and stuck up at the corners of the streets —and that this publication be deemed notice."

By eight o'clock in the morning of Sunday, July 5th, copies of the notice had been posted at every street corner in Vicksburg. During the day many gamblers, and a large number of prostitutes and other inhabitants of the Landing, "terrified by the threats of the citizens," fled the town in boats, wagons and on horseback. But some of the principal gamblers, convinced that the storm would blow over, elected to remain and await developments, and if necessary defend themselves against attack. Among them were Hoard, Wyatt, Dutch Bill, McCall, Sam Smith; Hullum, the son of the Rev. Duke W. Hullum of Cincinnati; and John North, "one of the most profligate of the gang," who ran a hotel and gambling place which was the rendezvous of ruffians and thieves. Hoard and Wyatt concealed themselves

"CANADA BILL" DISGUISED AS A RUSTIC

HENRY WYATT

in Hoard's house, behind drawn blinds and locked doors; and the others garrisoned North's tavern, where they barricaded the doors and windows and laid in a store of arms and ammunition.

The defiant gamblers were not molested on July 5th, although great excitement prevailed throughout Vicksburg. But at 9 A. M. on July 6th the members of the Volunteers, fully armed, assembled in the Public Square under the command of Captain Baumgard. Preceded by a Negro fife and drum corps playing *Yankee Doodle* under the direction of the cashier of the Planters' Bank, the Volunteers "marched to each suspected house, and, sending in an examining committee, dragged out every Faro table and other gambling apparatus that could be found." At length they reached North's tavern, surrounded the building, and with axes smashed the back door. Captain Baumgard called upon the gamblers to surrender, "when four or five shots were fired from the interior, one of which instantly killed Dr. Hugh S. Bodley, a citizen universally beloved and respected." The Volunteers returned the fire, wounding Hullum, and "a crowd of citizens, their indignation overcoming all other feelings," burst open every door of the building. They overwhelmed the gamblers and dragged into the street McCall, Smith, Dutch Bill, and Hullum, who had not been seriously hurt. North escaped, but was caught by a pursuing posse a mile down the river and brought back to Vicksburg. With their hands tied behind them and ropes about their necks, the five gamblers were marched to the barbecue grove, presenting, the *Louisiana Advertiser* of New Orleans said, "such a horrible appearance that the passersby were moved even to tears." But as another account says, "all sympathy for the wretches was completely merged in detestation and horror of their crime," and so they were hanged in the presence of virtually the entire respectable population of Vicksburg.[12]

[12] Governor H. G. Runnels received a letter from the Rev. Mr. Hullum, father of one of the gamblers, on November 21, 1835. He demanded that the lynchers be punished, but the state took no action.

At 11 A. M., after the bodies of the gamblers had been dangling for about an hour, they were cut down, stacked like cord wood in a big box, and dumped into a hole which had been dug near the gallows. Then the Volunteers and the mob of citizens returned to the Public Square, where the gambling apparatus which had been seized was piled up and burned. All of the money found in the gambling houses was spread out upon a table and paid out to citizens who could prove that they had been fleeced by the sharpers. During these ceremonies word was brought to Captain Baumgard that Hoard and Wyatt were still in town and threatening reprisals. A posse was dispatched to search them out, but both men had escaped, Wyatt by boat and Hoard on a horse. Hoard "the next morning crossed the Big Black, at Baldwin's Ferry, in a state of indescribable consternation;" he had been so badly frightened that his hair had turned white. The townspeople of Vicksburg particularly regretted that Hoard had slipped out of their clutches, "as his whole course of life . . . had exhibited the most shameless profligacy, and been a continual series of transgressions against the laws of God and man." Hoard reached New Orleans in safety, and is said to have changed his name, and renounced gambling and conspiracy in favor of less dangerous pursuits.

Jonathan H. Green says that Wyatt was captured by the Volunteers, bound hand and foot, and set adrift on the Mississippi in a canoe; but this is probably untrue, for if he had been caught he certainly would have been hanged. In any event Wyatt made his way to Cincinnati, and lived there and in other Ohio towns for several years, committing two murders and serving a term in the Ohio State Penitentiary. About 1843 he and another gambler named Gordon appeared in upstate New York, and both were convicted of robbery and sent to the State Prison at Auburn. Wyatt made an unsuccessful attempt to escape during the fall of 1844, and on March 16, 1845, believing that Gordon

224

had given information to the prison guards, he stabbed his comrade to death as the convicts were returning to their cells from chapel. Wyatt was found guilty of murder and hanged, despite the then unique plea of moral insanity advanced by his lawyer, who was no less a personage than William H. Seward, a former Governor of New York, and later United States Senator and Secretary of State in Abraham Lincoln's cabinet.

While the flames from the burning gambling apparatus were still crackling in the Public Square, the leading citizens of Vicksburg held another meeting in the Court House and organized an anti-gambling society, "the members of which have pledged their lives, fortunes and sacred honor for the suppression of gambling and the punishment and expulsion of gamblers." Throughout the night of July 6th the streets of Vicksburg and the narrow by-ways of the Landing were patrolled by armed members of the Society and detachments of Volunteers, while the exodus of the gamblers and their underworld satellites continued by every available means of transportation. By dawn of July 7th every gambler had left the town, and the few prostitutes and ruffians who remained in the Landing huddled silently in their dens. Forty or fifty gamblers had rowed and paddled out to Palmyra Island in skiffs and canoes, and remained there for several days, although there was much talk in Vicksburg of chartering a steamboat to bring them back to the town for punishment. Finally a passing vessel took them off.

On the evening of July 10th several hundred residents of Natchez held a meeting at which a memorial from the citizens of Vicksburg was read, "asking the assistance of the people of Natchez in the suppression of gambling, and their co-operation in the expulsion of professional gamblers from the country." A committee was appointed to organize a "society for the suppression of gambling and other vices," and the meeting unanimously offered to "support with our services and lives such measures as the civil authorities of Natchez may direct for the suppression of gambling." Officially it was the sense of the meeting that the authorities should handle the situation; unofficially groups of citizens visited Natchez-under-the-Hill and told the gamblers and other undesirable characters that they must leave or be hanged. They left in droves, so salutary had been the warning of the five dead men at Vicksburg. The steamer *Mogul,* upon her arrival at New Orleans on July 13th, reported "that she saw at Natchez, as she passed down, several boats crowded with persons who had been ordered from that place, in consequence of their abandoned character, and also saw, at Ellis' Cliffs, 18 miles below Natchez, one or two flatboats freighted with the same description of person, but principally females—all bound down the Mississippi."

Resolutions deploring "any violent measures against the individual lately expelled from Natchez," and offering to co-operate with the Mayor in "the preservation of the public peace and good order," were adopted at a meeting of a thousand men in New Orleans, but nothing was done about gambling or conditions in the Swamp. Later in the year, however, the law prohibiting gambling anywhere in Louisiana was enacted by the Legislature, and it was well enforced in New Orleans for some ten years. In Mobile, on July 21, 1835, a meeting resolved that "the citizens of Mobile disapprove of gaming, and gamesters, and . . . will render their prompt and cheerful aid and assistance to the city authorities in suppressing gambling in this city, in preventing the introduction among us of gamesters and vagrants of any description, and in expelling them from the city whenever they may be identified." In Lexington, Ky., on Sunday, July 26th, a mass meeting ordered all persons without an honest means of livelihood to leave within twenty-four hours. Fifty men, most of them gamblers, left immediately. On the same day in Covington, Ky., a mob razed a gambling house, "well known as a rendezvous for infamous characters," a few hours after one gambler had killed another in a dispute over a bet of twelve and one-half cents. A Negro was concerned in the game, and the Cincinnati *Whig* said next day, "So much for gambling on Sunday with a Negro." The same paper on July 23rd published a letter from Madison County, Miss., saying that eighteen gamblers had been captured after killing several of their pursuers, and would be hanged.[13] At Cincinnati on July 23rd a mob formed to burn the gambling houses and hang the gamblers, but Mayor Samuel W. Davies prevented trouble by closing the saloons, swearing in a special police force of five hundred men, and issuing a proclamation:

". . . great excitement prevails among the citizens, produced by the presence of a number of persons called gamblers, whose offensive pursuits, it is said, have caused their expulsion from other places . . . it is known to me, that strong and violent measures are contemplated . . . for the purpose of compelling these persons immediately to leave the city . . . the police are fully competent to effect the object in view, and a resort to violence . . . may lead to consequences hereafter greatly to be deprecated."

A score of fugitives from Vicksburg reached the small town of Clinton, in Hinds County, Miss., on the evening of July 8th, but resumed their travels when they found this notice posted on the street corners:

"All gamblers found in Clinton after 12 o'clock, will be used according to Lynch's Law.

CAPT. SLICK.

"N.B. The importations from Vicksburg will look out."

[13] I can find no record that such a wholesale execution of gamblers occurred.

"Where will the exiled blacklegs turn their steps next?" asked the Louisville *Journal*. "Towards Louisville? We solemnly warn them against it . . . there are unequivocal indications, just at this time, that the gamblers already here cannot make their escape too precipitately."

So it went throughout the South and as far east as Baltimore, where a mob burned a gambling house about a month after the uprising at Vicksburg. Action of one form or another was undertaken against the gamblers everywhere along the Ohio and Mississippi Rivers south of Cincinnati; some communities maintained patrols for several months, and every stranger was required to give an account of himself and prove the legitimacy of his visit. The hanging of John North and his fellows had marked the end of the gamblers' supremacy, and the beginning of a widespread Vigilante movement which cleansed the underworld districts of most of the river towns and drove the worst of the sharpers from the steamboats. Many of the exiles found refuge in the Swamp at New Orleans, which had escaped the cleansing process and remained the most vicious underworld area west of the Atlantic seaboard. Others went up the rivers to St. Louis, Cincinnati, Pittsburg, and across country to the thriving little settlement of Chicago; and after a few years some returned to Natchez and other towns on the river and resumed their trade, though not in the brazen manner to which they had been accustomed, and not at all in Vicksburg. According to local historians there was no more public gambling in Vicksburg until the Civil War. Still others fled to New York, Washington, Baltimore, Philadelphia, and other Eastern cities. On August 25, 1835, the New York *Sun* noted that several Vicksburg gamblers were in the metropolis, and remarked that "they are safe enough here, in all conscience;" while the Philadelphia *Enquirer* reported that a sharper recently arrived from the West carried in his sleeve "a curious kind of butcher knife, the blade of which shoots in and out of the handle by a spring, and is known by the name of 'Bodie's Knife,' or 'The Arkansaw Toothpick.'"[14]

4

Gambling on the Western rivers languished for a year or so after the Vigilante outbreak at Vicksburg and the expulsion of the gamblers from Natchez and other towns, but by the beginning of 1837 the sharpers had begun to leave their hiding places and creep back aboard the steamboats. During the fifteen or twenty years which preceded the Civil War, when river travel was in its heyday, gambling was at least as prevalent as ever on both the Ohio and the Mississippi; no fewer than two thousand professional gamblers were actively and prosperously engaged in trimming the traveling sucker from Louisville to the Gulf of Mexico. More than five hundred operated between Vicksburg and New Orleans alone, for the lower Mississippi remained the sharper's favorite hunting ground and the scene of his greatest triumphs. The period in which this host of tricksters dominated life on the steamboats is celebrated in song and story as the "romantic" age of river gambling, the era of the chivalrous gambler who scorned to take advantage of an adversary, who righted wrongs, who won the beautiful octoroon slave girl from the besotted planter and then gave the dusky maiden her freedom. In the main, the rose-colored accounts of the good old days, of the noble gambler and the cruel planter, are just so much bosh. Cole Martin, a famous river gambler who afterward ran Faro banks in Chicago, St. Louis and St. Paul, said in 1896:

---

[14] This probably referred to a bowie-knife, but a real bowie-knife has no spring. It has a blade from ten to fifteen inches long, with a single cutting edge, and a straight back throughout most of its length. Near the tip the back curves concavely, while the edge curves convexly. The first of these knives was made by James Bowie from a blacksmith's rasp. Commercially they were first manufactured in Philadelphia.

"It's very pretty to read about, but the real thing was not so nice. The black-eyed, black-mustached hero gambler that you read about was anything but a hero. There was no chivalry in his nature, and he was ready for any dark deed that would profit him. Of course I am speaking of the professional gambler, for everyone gambled; if they had not done so the professional's occupation would have been gone. The chivalrous ones were the young Southern planters, reckless, but not mean, who would play the full limit and get fleeced.

"We read now, too, of beautiful octoroon girls, white as their masters, who were put up as stakes representing so much money, and who have been won and carried off by strange men, away from mother, father, husband or sweetheart. In the whole course of my experience I never saw an octoroon disposed of in this way. These light-colored Negresses, who have been the stakes in stories, are the creation entirely of the writers. The fact is that the octoroon and other light-colored Negroes are a great deal more common today than they were then. But I have seen Negro women disposed of in this fashion, but there was no romance to it. They were generally plantation Negroes, rough and hard, and fit for the severest work, and were sold at the first market where the winners happened to land." [15]

Probably ninety-five per cent of the gamblers who worked the steamboats during the so-called "romantic age" were just as crooked as their brethren of an earlier day—more so, in fact, for new schemes and devices for cheating were constantly being invented, and for all of them the Mississippi was the great proving ground. Except that Poker and Euchre were more common, and Brag, All-Fours and Boston less so, the sharpers who oper-

[15] *Poker Stories*, collected and edited by John F. B. Lillard; pages 42-3.

ated on the "floating palaces" played the same games and used much the same methods which had been so successful before the hanging of the gamblers at Vicksburg. And as an old-time river gambler, Tom Ellison, said in an interview at Vicksburg in 1896, "there's no telling how much money they did pull off the travelers." Ellison continued:

"It was dead easy money, too, all the time. Everyone who traveled had lots of stuff, and everyone was willing to bet, and bet high; so when a fellow did win he won right out of the hole at once. Those Southern planters used to lose money just like fun, and were skinned right and left. Occasionally they caught on and there was a shooting match, but the boys didn't take much chance on being plugged.

"I've seen forty gamblers on one boat, the *John Dickey.* That was in '57, when the officers at Natchez cleaned all the gamblers out of town. The whole gang met the boat at the wharf and started to come aboard, but the Captain wouldn't let them on unless they promised not to play a card aboard. They promised, and he took them on, and the boat came on up the river. You never saw a tireder-looking lot of gamblers in your life than them. They hadn't anything to do, and some of them looked as if they'd just as soon jump overboard as not. They kept their promise not to play a card, but how they did skin the passengers on other games.

"Well, sir, those gamblers all got on that boat, and though they didn't touch a card they cleaned out pretty near everybody that had stuff. We landed at a woodpile to take on wood, and the passengers all got out on the bank, and the gamblers all got to betting about running jumps, and of course the passengers dropped in. So they'd run off the gangplank and up to a tree to jump, when the first gambler would say, 'Hello, what's here?' and stop. Behind the tree one of the gang had begun throwing Three-Card Monte, while the other got up the jumping scheme. The gamblers won just to make the game good, and the way those fellows skinned the passengers was horrible. The Captain got on to the scheme, and when the boat started off upstream the whole gang—forty of them—were just marooned there in the woods on a cold night. But they took the next boat up or down, and worked their way up this way or down to New Orleans.

"That wasn't gambling—it was robbing; but that's what went as gambling in those times. The fellows had to be pretty slick, I can tell you. . . . I've seen fellows pick every card in a pack, and call it without missing once. I've seen them shuffle them one for one all through from top to bottom, so that they were in the same position after a dozen shuffles that they were in at first. They'd just flutter them up like a flock of quail and get the aces, kings, queens, jacks and tens all together as easy as pie. A sucker had no more chance against those fellows than a snow-ball has in a red-hot oven. They were good fellows, free with their money as water, after scheming to bust their heads to get it. A hundred didn't bother them any more than a chew of tobacco would you.

"There used to be some big games on every boat. Poker was mostly the game. They played Bluff and Brag a great deal, and the betting was high. I saw a man from Hopkinsville, Ky., lose his whole tobacco crop in one night and get up and never mind it particularly. Many a time I've seen a game player just skin off his watch and ring and studs and play them in. Men often lost their goods playing in their way bills. I've seen them betting a bale of cotton at a crack, and it wasn't at all uncommon to hear an old planter betting off his Negroes on a good hand. Every man who ever ran on the river knows that these old planters used to play in their lady servants, valuing them all the way from $300 to $1,500. I saw a little colored boy stand up at $300 to back his master's faith in a little flush that wasn't any good on earth. The niggers didn't seem to care particularly about it, and it was so common that nobody noticed it particularly. Gambling was commoner then.

"Why, it was nothing but gamble from the time the boat left St. Louis till it reached New Orleans. I've seen a Faro game, three Poker games, and *Monte* running in the cabin, and the deckhands playing at Chuck-a-Luck. Sometimes there'd be a kick and the captain would get hot. When a passenger would squeal the captain would ask him to pick out the man who robbed him, and the gambler, if nabbed, would have to give up the stuff and get off the boat anywhere the captain chose to run her in. The boys used to have false whiskers and wigs for these occasions, so that when the kick was made they couldn't be picked out under their disguises. Many a time I have known them to jump off the boat to get away before the kick was made and the victim could look at the passengers to pick out his man. I've swam ashore myself many a time. There wasn't much prosecuting then if a fellow was caught. The captain was boss, and he made the man give up, put him off the boat, and that settled it. They didn't jug a man right away." [16]

A sizable portion of the "stuff" that these slickers of the steamboats squeezed from the pockets of gullible travelers went for fancy clothing, for the river gambler of the 1840's and the 1850's, except of course when he was in disguise, was perhaps the gaudiest and most picturesque dresser of his day; compared to him the New York dude, who flourished about the same time, was a veritable scarecrow. Almost invariably, the sharper of the

[16] *Poker Stories,* pages 50–60.

Mississippi wore a black slouch hat, black broadcloth coat and trousers, black flowing tie, black high-heeled boots, and a white shirt with a low neck and a loose collar, granddaddy of the modern sport shirt. But all this was only the beginning. The white shirt was unbelievably frilled, ruffled and frizzled, and amidst its billowing folds gleamed a diamond, as large as he could afford and popularly known as "the headlight." Framing the shirt was a gaudy vest hand-painted with flowers or scenes of the chase, and further ornamented by rows of pearl, gold, diamond, silver or brass buttons. Gold and diamond rings encircled the smooth fingers which had never been roughened by honest toil, and in a pocket of his vest the gambler carried his watch. Usually this was a Jeurgunsen, which retailed in those days at from $600 to $1,000, a massive gold repeater set with gems and with a one-carat diamond in the stem. Attached to the watch and looped several times around his neck was the gambler's crowning glory —the golden chain introduced on the Mississippi by John Cotton of Washington, and without which no sharper's wardrobe was complete. In keeping with this dazzling ensemble was a cultivated appetite which forbade the gambler to drink anything but wine, and a fastidiousness which made him ride across the street in a hack rather than get mud on his glistening boots. "They were fine fellows," said old Tom Ellison, "educated men who could talk to anyone about anything, and as polite as anything you ever saw. What drunks they used to get on after they came in off a trip!"

The great dandies of the river were Jimmy Fitzgerald and Colonel Charles Starr, who obtained his military title by self-appointment. Fitzgerald is said to have been the most richly-dressed gambler on the Mississippi—his boots, gloves and underwear came from Paris, he owned four fine overcoats and a score of expensive suits made by the best tailors in New Orleans, and a dozen hand-painted vests; while diamonds gleamed from every finger and his gold chain was almost twenty feet long. Three slaves accompanied Fitzgerald on his travels, bearing the cases and boxes containing his garments. He was an expert at all short card games, but he had a weakness for Faro, and the fortune he won on the steamboats was dissipated in the gambling houses ashore. He dropped out of sight a year or so before the Civil War.

Colonel Starr, a man of distinguished appearance with the assurance and pomposity of a matinee idol, was famous among the river gamblers for his ability as a liar as well as for the elegance and extent of his wardrobe. He dearly loved to "talk big" —he had killed a dozen men in duels, rescued maidens in distress, invented appliances for steamboats, and he owned half the land and slaves on either side of the river, to say nothing of huge parcels of real estate in New Orleans and St. Louis. To make his stories more convincing, he would hire Negroes to meet his boat at various landings, posing as messengers from the managers and overseers of his vast estates. Colonel Starr made a great deal of money by his skill at Poker and Seven-up, but like Fitzgerald he was a Faro addict, and squandered huge sums bucking the tiger. During his latter years Colonel Starr abandoned the river and hung around the gambling houses in New Orleans, cadging food and drink from whoever would give him a handout, and panhandling money with which to play Faro. One night a year or so before the Civil War he went into a restaurant where he had once been welcome, and was requested by the manager to pay in advance. Colonel Starr left the place, but returned in an hour with five dollars for which he had pawned his overcoat. He ordered dinner, and when it was served he deliberately turned every dish upside down on the table. Then he walked out, and next morning was found dead in his bed.

Besides Fitzgerald and Colonel Starr, perhaps the best-dressed, and best-known, sharpers on the Western rivers during the "romantic age" of gambling were these:

Starr Davis, for whom a celebrated race horse was named. A heavy drinker throughout his career on the river, Davis finally fell down a flight of stairs in a St. Louis hotel while on a spree and broke his neck. Tom Ellison described him as "a great old boy."

Big Alexander, one of the few professional gamblers who never played Faro. He was widely known as a high liver, often spending two hundred dollars in one night for wine, yet in four years he sent $44,000 back to his relatives in Dover, Ky.

Jim McLane, whose wealthy mother gave him an allowance of $10,000 a year to keep away from her; and his partners Gib Cohern, Tom Mackey and Dock Hill, all of whom sent to Paris for their boots and underwear.

Jim McDonald, a crack shot with a pistol, who used to amuse himself shooting the heels off Negro roustabouts.

Charley Ashlock, who Tom Ellison said "could do more funny work with a deck of cards than I have ever saw before or since."

John Brogan, a great specialist in the use of marked cards at Poker. He was extraordinarily successful until he ran afoul of George Devol and another sharper named Neice, who was an extremely shrewd hand with a reflector. The three men played in a famous old hotel at Alexandria, La., called the Ice House, and within a few hours Devol and Neice had trimmed Brogan for $4,500 and all of his diamonds. The latter never knew why his marked cards had failed. "Both John Brogan and Neice have been dead many years," wrote Devol in 1886, "and, I trust, are happy in the spirit land—perhaps playing Chuck-a-Luck, marked cards and concave reflectors with St. Peter and the Apostles."

Jim Baisley, who met a dramatic end at the hands of a planter whose son the gambler had fleeced of almost $10,000. The planter won back the money the boy had lost, and when Baisley attacked him with a bowie-knife he seized the sharper by the throat and flung him overboard. No effort was made to rescue Baisley and nothing was done to the planter. "It was a fair fight," said an old-timer who described the incident, "and they didn't bother a gentleman for anything like that in those days."

Edward Ryan, a Poker shark and Monte thrower better known as Dad Ryan. He left the river at the beginning of the Civil War, and early in 1865 turned up in Fort Wayne, Ind., as the leader of a gang of pickpockets, Monte artists, Thimble-Riggers and confidence men, and was very powerful in Fort Wayne for several years. There were about thirty members of the gang, and their headquarters were in a saloon and gambling house, complete with trap doors and secret rooms and passages. During the Indiana State Fair in 1865 Ryan's pickpockets stole a bushel of pocketbooks. Ryan was finally sent to prison for two years, and never regained his old-time standing as a gambler. He died in Chicago about 1883.

5

The most brazen tricksters on the Western rivers were the Three-Card Monte throwers, who were especially active during the 1850's. They were all confidence men as well as gamblers, using any sort of swindle that might arouse the cupidity of the sucker and make him an easy victim; and a few were also proficient cheats at Faro, short cards and dice. Monte, however, was always their stand-by, and with this game as their basic fraud they probably took more "stuff" from the steamboat passengers than any other gamblers of their time. Fortunes were made on the river—and promptly lost in the gambling houses ashore—by such celebrated Monte throwers as George Devol, Charley Bush,

Jew Mose, Tom Brown, Holly Chappell, High Miller, Canada Bill Jones; Ephraim Holland, who later achieved considerable prominence as a politician in Cincinnati and ended his career in Hot Springs; Bill Rollins, one of the first Monte men to operate on the Mississippi; Posey Jeffers, who once won $10,000 in counterfeit money and never lived it down; and Rattlesnake Jack McGee, so called because in his youth he had earned a living catching rattlesnakes in the mountains of West Virginia. Four of these sharpers—Canada Bill, Devol, Brown, and Holly Chappell—traveled together on the Red, Ohio and Mississippi Rivers for some three years in the early 1850's, and when the association was dissolved each man's share of the spoil amounted to $240,000. But within a year every member of the syndicate had gambled away his fortune and was broke.

Accompanying these sure-thing swindlers, as body servant, was a young Negro boy named Pinckney Benton Stewart Pinchback, known in those days as Pinch, who afterward became an important figure in the carpet-bag government of Louisiana—he was a member of the State Legislature, Lieutenant Governor, and Governor from December 9, 1872, to January 13, 1873. In 1873 he was elected to the United States Senate, but after three years of debate that body refused to seat him, though allowing him the pay and mileage of a Senator. Devol and Canada Bill taught young Pinchback to throw Monte, play Seven-Up and Poker, and run a Chuck-a-Luck game, and while the white sharpers were trimming the cabin passengers Pinch was ripping the financial hide off the Negro roustabouts and deck hands, from which source came much of the money with which he financed his political adventures after the Civil War. Pinchback's only superior at trimming the deck hands and roustabouts was Sam Johnson, a Negro gambler from Memphis who was a familiar figure on the steamboats for many years. Johnson is said to have been a really remarkable Poker player, but his takings

238

were small because the black sucker's financial resources were limited. But he neglected no opportunity. Once when he boarded a steamboat to take advantage of a deck hands' pay day, he found that he had been forestalled by a dandified "high yaller" gambler, a stranger to Sam, who had organized a Poker game and was raking in the money at an almost indecent rate. Sam climbed up on a hogshead of sugar and watched the game closely. He soon discovered that the "high yaller" was brazenly palming cards, using "scratch paper," and "laying the bottom stock." Determined to have a share of the winnings, Sam began to sing:

> Gimme some o' dat or I'll break up de game;
> Gimme some o' dat or I'll break up de game;
> Gimme some o' dat or I'll break up de game,
> For Sam Johnson is my name!

Without turning his head or changing countenance, the "high yaller" replied:

> Dar's no use tryin' to break up de game;
> Dar's no use tryin' to break up de game;
> Dar's no use tryin' to break up de game,
> For I'se wid you from now on!

The greatest Monte thrower on the Mississippi was Canada Bill Jones, probably the cleverest operator who ever "pitched a Broad," and one of the few men who could display the Monte tickets and, in the very act of tossing them on a table, palm the queen and ring in a third ace, thus reducing the sucker's chances to minus nothing. And curiously enough, this monarch of the Monte men was the worst-dressed gambler on the river, and looked less like a sharper than the most verdant hayseed that ever stumbled aboard a steamboat. His clothing was always two sizes too large, his boots were scuffed and run down at the heel, and his linen was invariably rumpled as if he had slept in his shirt, which, as a matter of fact, he often did. The only thing needed to make him look thoroughly disreputable was a few days' growth of beard. But this Nature denied him. According to George Devol, who was his partner for many years, "his face was as smooth as a woman's, and never had a particle of hair on it." Devol continued:

"Canada Bill was a character one might travel the length and breadth of the land and never find his match, or run across his equal. Imagine a medium-sized, chicken-headed, tow-haired sort of man with mild blue eyes, and a mouth nearly from ear to ear, who walked with a shuffling, half-apologetic sort of gait, and who, when his countenance was in repose, resembled an idiot. For hours he would sit in his chair, twisting his hair in little ringlets. Then I used to say, 'Bill is studying up some new devilment.' . . . Canada was a slick one. He had a squeaking, boyish voice, and awkward, gawky manners, and a way of asking fool questions and putting on a good-natured sort of grin, that led everybody to believe that he was the rankest kind of a sucker—the greatest sort of a country jake. Woe to the man who picked him up, though. Canada was, under all his hypocritical appearance, a regular card shark, and could turn Monte with the best of them. . . . Many are the suckers we roped in, and many the large rolls of bills we corralled. . . . Bill never weighed over 130 pounds, and was always complaining of pains in his head." [17]

It was never necessary for Canada Bill to disguise himself in order to make the proper contacts with suckers whom he had chosen for the kill, but he did so anyway at every opportunity, for he had the small boy's love of make-believe. His favorite

[17] *Forty Years a Gambler on the Mississippi,* by George Devol; 1926 edition; pages 185–86.

impersonation was that of an uncouth hog-drover, and when thus made up he must have been a fearful spectacle. Mason Long, one of the many reformed gamblers who flourished on the lecture platform after the Civil War, capped for a Monte hangout which Canada Bill operated at Utica, N.Y., during the harness races there in 1876, and described the sharper, in the guise of a hog-drover, as "a rustic looking creature . . . munching a huge piece of pie . . . a large man dressed in coarse clothes, with a sunburned countenance, a nose highly illuminated by the joint action of whisky and heat, and an expression of indescribable greenness and freshness about him." [18] Incidentally, Canada Bill's stay in Utica netted several thousand dollars in cash and a half-bushel of watches, most of which he sold back to the men who had lost them.

Canada Bill made a great deal of money in the thirty or forty years in which he was active as a Monte thrower, but he was nearly always broke, for he was cursed by a veritable passion for gambling; he would play any game proposed and bet on any proposition, and he seldom won except at his own specialty, at which he never lost. "He loved gambling for its own sake," said George Devol, "just as the moralists love virtue for its own sake. No man that I ever came in contact with ever struck me as being so fond of gambling. I have seen him give parties two points in Casino and Seven-Up, and they would play marked cards on him . . . he was a fool at short cards. I have known men who knew this to travel all over the country after Bill, trying to induce him to play cards with them. He would do it, and that is what kept him poor. . . ." In Canada Bill's inordinate love of gambling and his willingness to play any game regardless of the odds against him, originated a story which has become the most popular of all gambling anecdotes.

[18] *Mason Long, the Converted Gambler,* Written by Himself; Cincinnati, 1884; pages 118–21.

Compelled to spend the night in a small Louisiana town, Canada Bill finally found a Faro game in the back room of a barber-shop and began to play. His partner saw at once that the dealer was using a two-card box, and urged Canada Bill to quit.

"The game's crooked," he declared.

"I know it," Bill replied, "but it's the only one in town!"

Canada Bill worked the railroads after the Civil War had virtually stopped traffic on the Mississippi and driven the sharpers off the river, and found suckers so plentiful that he offered to pay one of the Southern systems $25,000 a year for the right to operate Monte and confidence games on its lines without molestation, promising to victimize only preachers. The offer was refused. During the 1870's Canada Bill made a grand tour of the race tracks, and with Three-Card Monte and other swindles made so much money that he could have retired a dozen times—if he had kept away from Faro and short cards. He died a pauper at Reading, Pa., about 1880, and was buried by the Mayor of that city, who advanced money for the funeral expenses. He was afterward repaid by a group of Chicago gamblers. The story goes that when the body of Canada Bill was being lowered into the grave one of the gamblers present offered to bet $1,000 to $500 that Bill was not in the box. "Not with me," was the reply. "I've known Bill to squeeze through tighter holes than that!" Mason Long, who described Canada Bill as "the most notorious and successful thief who ever operated in this country," declared that the gambler had drunk himself to death, but George Devol indignantly denied this version of Canada Bill's death. "He did not drink whisky at all," Devol wrote. "His great drink was Christian cider, and it was very seldom I could get him to drink wine."

For all of his dangerous way of life, Canada Bill was an arrant physical coward—"he would not fight a woman if she said

242

boo." But there was never any need for him to fight as long as he traveled with Devol; the latter was fully competent to attend to that phase of the business. In his autobiography Devol boasted that he had "fought more rough and tumble fights than any man in America," and described himself as "the most daring gambler in the world." So far as gambling was concerned he may have taken in a little too much territory, although few sharpers of his time were more successful. As a Monte thrower he was second only to Canada Bill, and the pair formed a combination calculated to make the sucker clutch his wallet and scream in terror. In addition to his gifts in this field, Devol was an adept at dice and short cards, especially when it came to ringing in cold decks and "laying the bottom stock." His *bête noire* was Faro; he was always scolding Canada Bill for losing his money at Poker, Casino and Seven-Up, and at the same time was himself succumbing to the fascinations of the tiger. Devol was a professional gambler for almost forty years—he began about 1844 at the age of fifteen, a few years after he had run away from his home at Marietta, O., and retired in the early eighties—and in that time at least $2,000,000 passed through his hands, most of it going to enrich crooked Faro dealers. "It is said of me," he wrote in 1886, "that I have won more money than any sporting man in this country. I will say that I hadn't sense enough to keep it; but if I had never seen a Faro bank, I would be a wealthy man today."

As a rough and tumble fighter Devol was in truth one of the mighty men of the Mississippi. He had scores of fights, but he was never beaten, although for some twenty years the sports of New Orleans, St. Louis and other river towns tried to find a man who could take his measure; it is doubtful if even the bullies of the flatboats could have made him cry "enough." Devol was a good man with his fists, but his most formidable weapon, with which he won most of his fights, was his head;

he butted his opponents into submission with his massive, dome-shaped cranium, backed by the weight of his powerful two-hundred-pound body. "He was a terrible rough and tumble fighter," said a writer in the Cincinnati *Enquirer,* "and many a tough citizen have I seen him do up. George was a great 'butter.' He could use his head with terrible effect. He can kill any man living, white or black, by butting him. Although over fifty years of age, I don't believe there is a man living who can whip him. New Orleans sporting men will go broke on that." [19]

Devol's most memorable feat as a butter was performed in 1867, when he engaged in a friendly butting match with Billy Carroll, one of the attractions of Robinson's Circus, who was billed as "The Great Butter" and "The Man with the Hard Head." Carroll's act consisted in smashing barrels and heavy doors with his head, and in butting all comers. He had never been knocked off his feet until he met Devol. The gambler and the circus star came together just once in New Orleans, and when Carroll recovered consciousness he said, "I have found my papa at last!" According to doctors who examined Devol when he was working the steamboats, his skull above the forehead was more than an inch thick. "It must be pretty thick," wrote the gambler, "for I have been struck some terrible blows on my head with iron dray-pins, pokers, clubs, stone-coal and bowlders. . . . I never have my hair clipped short, for if I did, I would be ashamed to take my hat off, as the lines on my old scalp look about like the railroad map of the state in which I was born."

A great many of Devol's fights were forced upon him by ambitious and optimistic young squirts eager to gain renown by defeating the famous butter, but all any of them ever got out of such an encounter was a headache. The gambler never

[19] Quoted in Devol's autobiography, 1926 edition, pages 287–88.

dodged a fight when he was opposed by no more than two men, but when his enemies attempted to overwhelm him by force of numbers he had sense enough to run. For several years he was hunted up and down the river by a gang of ruffians known as the Arkansas Killers, who dominated the country around the Arkansas towns of Helena and Napoleon. Both of these communities were noted for the brawling proclivities of their inhabitants, and during the 1850's were the toughest settlements on the Mississippi, "where it was not safe for any man to do the bluff act, for they would kill him just to see him kick." As a matter of fact, Napoleon's reputation was not built up in that decade alone; it was notorious as a tough town in the days of the flatboats, and appears to have been the birthplace of one of America's classic stories of fighting. Said Thomas Bangs Thorpe in *Harper's New Monthly Magazine* for December, 1855:

"The story is familiar of the man who took passage in a flatboat from Pittsburg bound for New Orleans. He passed many dreary, listless days on his way down the Ohio and Mississippi, and seemed to be desponding for want of excitement. . . . In course of time the raft upon which he was a passenger put in to Napoleon, in the state of Arkansas, 'for groceries.' At the moment there was a general fight extending all along the 'front of the town,' which at that time consisted of a single house. The unhappy passenger, after fidgeting about, and jerking his feet up and down, as if he were walking on hot bricks, turned to a used-up spectator and observed:

" 'Stranger, is this a free fight?'

"The reply was prompt and to the point:

" 'It ar'; and if you wish to go in, don't stand on ceremony!'

"The wayfarer did go in, and in less time than we can relate the circumstance he was literally 'chawed up.' Groping his way down to the flat, his hair gone, his eye closed, his lips swollen, and his face generally 'mapped out,' he sat himself down on a chicken coop and soliloquized thus:

" 'So this is Na-po-le-on, is it?—upon my word it's a lively place, and the only one at which I've had any fun since I left home.' "

The Arkansas Killers were determined to catch Devol and "do him up," a euphemism, current in those days, for gouging out his eyes, pulling his ears off, and stamping his face into an unrecognizable mass. But the gambler always managed to keep away from them, although he had several narrow escapes. Once when he was throwing Monte, disguised as a countryman, on the steamer *Fairchild,* twenty-five of the Killers came aboard at Napoleon. Instead of hiding, the gambler, confident that they could not penetrate his disguise, opened up his game and cleaned out the whole twenty-five, taking their money, watches and other valuables. For a while the Killers made no complaint, although they realized that they had been trimmed by a professional sharper, but after a few drinks at the bar one of them said:

"Let's kill that damned gambler who got our money!"

They scattered to their staterooms to get their guns, and Devol hastily left the Social Hall. "Well," he wrote, "they hunted the boat from stem to stern—even took lights and went down into the hold—and finally gave up the chase, as one man said I had jumped overboard." While the search was in progress Devol was hiding under the pilot house. He gave the pilot $100 in gold, "as I had both pockets filled with gold and watches," and the pilot promised that at the first point of land he would run the steamboat close inshore so Devol could jump.

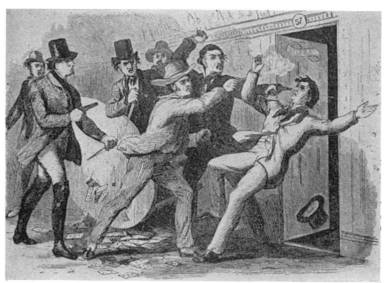

From an old print

THE EXPOSURE OF "CHARLEY BLACK EYES"

From an old print

"CANADA BILL" TRIMMING A SUCKER AT THREE-CARD MONTE

Presently the pilot told him to get ready, and the gambler slipped from his hiding place and climbed to the top of the wheel-house, where he waited until the boat came close to shore. "Away I went," he wrote, "but it was farther than I expected, so I went down about thirty feet into the river, and stuck in the soft mud clear up to my waist. Some parties who were standing on the stern of the boat saw me, and gave the alarm, when the 'killers' all rushed back, and commenced firing at me, and the bullets went splattering all around me. The pilot threw her into the bend as quick as he could, and then let on she took a sheer on him, and nearly went to the other side." Devol was pulled out of the mud at the end of a long pole by some Negroes, and waited on the bank for another boat to come along. "I was always very stubborn," he said, "about giving up money if anyone wanted to compel me to do it."

On another occasion Devol was compelled to get off a steamboat at Helena, "as things had gotten a little too warm for me on the boat." Hearing that he was in town, and knowing that he would catch the next boat out, a dozen of the Killers assembled at the landing. There they found several gamblers, and thinking Devol was among them, beat them unmercifully. Meanwhile Devol was in a crowd of townspeople watching the fight. As the crew of the steamboat got ready to pull in the gangplank, Devol charged the Killers, butted his way through their demoralized ranks, and rushed safely aboard the boat.

6

Although the sure-thing artists were vastly in the majority, there were a few gamblers on the Mississippi in those days—notably John Powell, Dick Hargraves, Major George M. White, and Napoleon Bonaparte White, better known as Poley—who were notorious among the sharpers as "square players;" they depended upon luck and skill rather than trickery and dishonesty. And it is perhaps significant that most of them appear to have died in poverty, while hundreds of sharpers who never drew an honest breath amassed fortunes and retired to enjoy the rich rewards of a misspent life. The career of John Powell, as honest a gambler as ever dealt a Poker hand, provides a case in point. A Missourian who maintained a home in New Orleans during the period of his activity on the Mississippi, Powell was a fine figure of a man—tall, handsome, distinguished, well-educated, and possessing a personality and charm which won him the friendship of such men as Stephen A. Douglas and Andrew Jackson. He is said to have spent considerable time at Jackson's home, near Nashville, during the old hero's last years. Powell himself had been destined for a political career, but as a young man had declined a nomination for Congress in Missouri to become a professional gambler. He was active on the Mississippi for some fifteen years, and during most of that time was recognized as the best Poker player on the river—a daring plunger always willing to back his judgment to the limit.

His success was extraordinary. On his fiftieth birthday, in 1858, he reckoned that he had acumulated, entirely through gambling, a fortune of approximately half a million dollars. Among other properties, he owned a theater and several houses in New Orleans, a plantation and many horses and slaves in Tennessee, and valuable real estate in St. Louis. His friends urged him to retire, but he refused, and within a few months after this decision his career as a gambler, so far as success was concerned, had ended with a triumph and a tragedy. In the late summer of 1858 he won $50,000 in a three-day Poker session on the steamer *Atlantic,* during which the four players ran up a bar bill of $791.50. A month or two later Powell got into a

Poker game with a young English traveler, and won $8,000 and all of the young man's luggage. The Englishman didn't appear to be particularly disheartened, but when he came into the dining-saloon next morning he shook hands ceremoniously with all of the passengers and then shot himself. Badly shaken by the suicide, Powell sent the money and baggage he had won to the Englishman's family, and was seen no more on the Mississippi for a year. When he returned to the river he was both inept and unlucky, and within another year had lost everything he owned. Shabby and desperate, he hung around the New Orleans gambling houses until a year or so after the beginning of the Civil War. Then he went to Seattle, where he died in 1870.

The career of Napoleon Bonaparte White, who followed the river with considerable success from about 1845 to the Civil War, had an even more tragic ending than did that of John Powell. Poley's misfortunes began during the early years of the carpet-bag regime in Louisiana, when he begat two sons and opened a gambling house on St. Charles Avenue in New Orleans. His partner, Sam Williams, made a fortune from the venture, but Poley's share of the profits was spent trying to save his sons, who seem to have been scalawags almost from birth, from the consequences of their crimes. One of the boys, Benny, died of alcoholism in jail; and in the fall of 1889 Poley learned that the other, Jimmy, had killed two men in California and was a fugitive. On the day he received this distressing information, Poley was also notified that the New Orleans police intended to enforce a new anti-gambling ordinance. Broke and desperate, Poley borrowed five dollars, bought a revolver and some poison, told his friends good-bye, and then went home and killed himself.

Both Dick Hargraves and Major George M. White appear to have saved at least a part of their winnings, and were in comfortable circumstances when they died. Major White was a professional gambler for sixty-two years; he played his first game in New Orleans in 1825, and his last in San Francisco in 1887, thirteen years before his death in 1900 at the age of ninety-five. His most prosperous year on the Mississippi was 1857, when he made a clear profit of $30,000, which in those days was an enormous income for such a period. For several years Major White is said to have been paid $400 a week for dealing Faro in New Orleans, and it seems reasonable to assume that while thus engaged his squareness was in abeyance, for as has been pointed out, no Faro artist was ever paid that much money simply for pulling cards out of a box.

Hargraves, a slim, handsome Englishman who was almost as popular as John Powell, won renown on the river as a duelist and an adventurer as well as a gambler. He came to the United States as a boy of sixteen about 1840, worked as a bartender in New Orleans for a few years, and became a professional gambler about 1844, after he had won $30,000 in a Poker game with a rich Louisiana sugar-planter. If legend be true, or even half true, Hargraves was the most successful of all river gamblers—he is said to have won $2,000,000 at the card table in less than twelve years' activity on the steamboats. Hargraves was a notorious lady-killer and was involved in many amours, several of which resulted in duels with lovers and husbands whom he had supplanted. The most serious of these affairs occurred in the early 1850's, when he became infatuated with the wife of a New Orleans banker, and killed the latter in a meeting under The Oaks, the city's famous dueling ground. A year or so later he met the wife's brother, who had sworn to kill him on sight, in a gambling house at Natchez-under-the-Hill. Hargraves killed the brother after a desperate fight with knives, but when he returned to New Orleans his mistress stabbed him and then committed suicide. When Hargraves recovered from his wounds he married a girl whom he had rescued from a fire in Mobile, but soon tired of wedded bliss and joined a filibustering expedition to Cuba. At the outbreak of the Civil War his military experience won him a commission as Major in the Union Army. When the War ended he went to Denver, where he died of tuberculosis sometime in the early 1880's.

7

Four of the many well-known gamblers who left the river for the river's good when the Vigilantes went on the warpath at Vicksburg—Isaiah Rynders, Charles Legate, Colonel J. J. Bryant, and Charles Cora—were destined to achieve fame of a sort in other fields. Rynders went to New York, where he called himself Captain, eschewed gambling, and went into politics as a shoulder-hitter and ward heeler for Tammany Hall. The adeptness with which he discouraged anti-Tammany voters with a blackjack earned him the posts of leader of the famous Five Points gang and Democratic boss of the Sixth Ward; and after that he was successively a saloon-keeper, founder of the notorious Empire Club, member of the Tammany Central Committee, and United States Marshal. He was a candidate for the Legislature in 1850, but was defeated; during the campaign Philip Hone, in his diary, referred to Rynders as "a notorious bandit." One of Rynders' claims to fame is that he was the principal instigator of the Astor Place riots in 1849, when twenty-three persons were killed and more than 125 injured. Ostensibly this disturbance grew out of the professional jealousies of the American actor Edwin Forrest and the English actor William C. Macready; actually it was the result of the manipulation, by Rynders and other politicians, of the Irish element which has always been powerful in New York.

Legate was a Canadian by birth, a handsome "black-muzzled

villain," sometimes called Charley Black Eyes. He was known up and down the Mississippi, and in Vicksburg and Natchez-under-the-Hill, not only as an expert playing sharper, but also as an "itemer" of rare talent. He left Vicksburg at the first sign of trouble, and was far up the river, traveling as Charles L. Montford of New Orleans, when the five gamblers were hanged in the barbecue grove. For the next few years Charley Black Eyes lived in St. Louis, posing as a banker and speculator, moving in the best sporting society, and carefully avoiding all who had known him on the lower Mississippi. Meanwhile he was developing latent gifts as a forger and an all-around swindler, and soon was as expert at these trades as at card playing and "iteming." About 1840, disguised variously as a banker, a planter and a merchant, Charley Black Eyes began to appear on the steamboats and in the larger river towns, forging checks and swindling firms and individuals, and gradually returning to his first love, gambling. Within a few years he was in bad odor with the police of almost every town south of St. Louis, and particularly of New Orleans, where a reward of $2,000 had been offered for his arrest. To escape the hue and cry, Legate went to New York, which was a mistake, for when he swindled a New York merchant out of $50,000 his victim put on his trail George S. McWatters, a famous private detective of the period, who was afterward a shining ornament of the New York police force and the Secret Service. No criminal ever escaped Officer McWatters; he practically admitted as much in his autobiography.[20]

The defrauded merchant gave the detective a good description of Legate, and recalled that the tip of the swindler's left little finger was missing—it had been hacked off in a brawl at

[20] *Knots Untied, or, Ways and By-Ways in the Hidden Life of American Detectives,* by Officer George S. McWatters; Hartford, 1871. Republished in 1883, with a few changes and additions, under the title of *Detectives of Europe and America, or Life in the Secret Service.*

Natchez-under-the-Hill. Since McWatters couldn't find Legate in New York, he cleverly deduced that Charley Black Eyes had returned to his old stamping ground on the Mississippi, and himself went to St. Louis. There he learned that Legate had left for New Orleans several months before, so he embarked on the steamer *Continental* for the passage down the river. Luck was with McWatters, as it frequently was, for when the *Continental* stopped to "wood up" at Napoleon, Ark., who should come aboard but Legate! Officer McWatters didn't recognize Charley Black Eyes, for the sharper called himself Colonel Jacobs, posed as "a well-to-do planter of middle age," and had an apparently complete left little finger, upon which he wore a heavy seal ring. Nevertheless, the detective felt at once that Colonel Jacobs was not what he pretended to be, and suspicion became certainty that evening when gambling began in the Social Hall. To the observant eye of McWatters it was obvious that Colonel Jacobs was a sharper, and that he was in cahoots with another passenger, "large and quite comely," and disguised as "a Stranger from the North," who had also joined the boat's company at Napoleon. Colonel Jacobs played a few stiff hands of Poker with the Stranger, and the latter was so inept that when the Colonel decided to quit there was a great clamor among the passengers as to who should take his place. A four-handed game was organized, and immediately the Stranger began winning heavily—for the very good reason that Colonel Jacobs had posted himself in an advantageous position and was iteming the hands of the opposing players.

Presently the Stranger was accused of cheating, a few minutes later Charley Black Eyes was detected iteming, and a cry arose that "That black-muzzled wretch is worse than the big one!" The Stranger slipped away, but Colonel Jacobs was set upon by the passengers and severely beaten. He was carried to his stateroom, where McWatters noticed that his left little finger and seal ring were gone. Both were found at the scene of the fracas. "I took charge of the finger, which was made of hardened wax, as my trophy," wrote McWatters, "and someone, I knew not who, took the ring." McWatters took Legate to a private hospital when the *Continental* reached New Orleans, and the gambler avoided prosecution by returning $50,000 to the New Yorker whom he had swindled and $25,000 to the New Orleans firm which had offered the reward for his arrest, and paying McWatters' fee and expenses. There is no record that Legate again operated on the river; when he left the hospital he said he intended to abandon gambling and raise "niggers and cotton."

Colonel J. J. Bryant, for many years the best known gambler on the Mississippi, who acquired his military title by the easy method of usurpation, attempted to follow Isaiah Rynders' example and carve out a new career in politics, but his success was negligible, although he gained a certain distinction as the first Democratic candidate for Sheriff of San Francisco. A native of Lynchburg, Va., the Colonel's first venture into public life was at the age of eighteen, when he ran away from home and joined a traveling circus, in which he performed acceptably for several years as a sword swallower and a slack wire artist. In his early twenties he married and settled in Jackson, Miss., opening a grocery store and later a hotel. Neither prospered, and the Colonel tried his hand at dealing in Negroes, and after that at a dozen other businesses. In all of these commercial undertakings Colonel Bryant had partners who were invariably left holding the bag, while the Colonel, who, as one of his biographers said, "had more assurance than twenty men ought to be entitled to," gracefully withdrew with whatever profits might have accrued to the firm.

Throughout his business career Colonel Bryant spent at least as much time at the card table as in attending to his legitimate

OFFICER GEO. S. MC WATTERS

affairs, and during the middle 1820's he abandoned all pretense, became an avowed professional gambler, and enjoyed several prosperous years on the steamboats and in the river towns. He specialized in Brag, Poker, All-Fours and Old Sledge, although he often financed and roped for Faro banks in New Orleans, Mobile and other cities, and sometimes dealt a game. He was never a first-rate Faro artist, but few could equal him at short cards, even when the game was honestly played. About 1832 Colonel Bryant established himself at Vicksburg, and in less than a year was the most important gambler in the town, and the financial backer of several Roulette houses and six or eight Faro banks, into which he roped prospects whom he was unable to trim at short cards. A few of his enterprises were at the Landing, but most of them were on the Hill, where the Colonel himself made his headquarters. They were frequented by some of Vicksburg's leading citizens, prime suckers who also participated in Bryant's Brag and Poker games and admired him tremendously for his heavy betting and lavish entertainment. For the Colonel "understood the advantages of display, and spent his money freely with those who were rich, more especially when he had designs on their pockets." He was never caught cheating, and it is doubtful if any other gambler of his time had more influential friends. Apparently he had no connection with the Clan of the Mystic Confederacy.

In all probability Colonel Bryant would not have been molested had he remained in Vicksburg, but he didn't dare put friendship to such a test, and was one of the first to leave when the gamblers were ordered out of the town. During the next few years the Colonel traveled in Alabama and Louisiana, winning a great deal of money at short cards and losing most of it at Faro and *Monte,* which was just beginning to be popular in that part of the country. In 1839, at Huntsville, Ala., the Colonel had a memorable short card session with Allen Jones, a prosperous saddler and a Poker player of considerable local renown. Bryant let Jones play along until he had pledged his business and every cent he owned, and then dealt the saddler four kings and himself four aces. Jones was so impressed by the ease with which he had been trimmed that he implored the Colonel to teach him the tricks of the trade, the upshot being that the two men became partners. For the next ten years they were inseparable companions living on a common purse. They spent the summers at the fashionable watering-places of the South, and the winters at New Orleans and Mobile, and at Jackson, Miss., where they operated a Faro bank and Poker house during the sessions of the Mississippi Legislature.

Colonel Bryant dissolved the partnership in the fall of 1849 and went to San Francisco, where within a few weeks he won $75,000 playing *Monte*. He sent a third of this fortune to his wife in Mississippi, and with the remainder bought a hotel called the Ward House, which he renamed the Bryant House. Under the Colonel's management the Bryant House was more a gambling-joint than a hotel, but it produced a large revenue, which the Colonel spent freely to further his political ambitions. When he was nominated for Sheriff of San Francisco in 1850 the Bryant House was literally covered with flags and bunting, free drinks were served at the bar to all comers, and the Colonel made a speech from the balcony every few hours. On election day the Bryant forces paraded Portsmouth Square with signs and banners, companies of gaudily-clad horsemen, and bands of music in carriages. But the independent candidate, Colonel Jack Hayes, was an even better showman than Colonel Bryant. Unable to equal the latter's display, he appeared in the Square alone, astride a magnificent black stallion, and wearing the uniform in which he had won fame during the War with Mexico. The voters promptly abandoned Bryant's circus for the stern warrior, and elected Colonel Hayes by a large majority.

The embittered Colonel Bryant sold his hotel soon after the collapse of his political career, and was preparing to seek greener pastures when he was offered a third interest in one of the Faro banks at El Dorado, early San Francisco's most celebrated gambling house. He was supposed to rope for the game and give it the benefit of his effulgent presence. In three months the Colonel's share of the profits was large enough for him to send his wife $30,000—all told, during his few years' stay in California, he provided for his family to the extent of $110,000, and still was able to maintain himself in an extremely extravagant style of living. He quit El Dorado when the game entered upon a losing streak, and confined himself to short card trickery in San Francisco and various mining camps. About 1854 he suddenly left California, his departure probably being hastened by the arrival in San Francisco of Charles Cora, one of his cronies of the old days at Vicksburg, to whom he owed $35,000. The Colonel was next heard of in New Orleans, where he was more or less concerned in the operation of several gambling houses.

Cora, a foundling reared by the keeper of a brothel at Natchez-under-the-Hill, was a professional gambler at sixteen, and before he was forty had achieved a permanent place in California history as one of the miscreants hanged by the San Francisco Vigilance Committee of 1856. In gambling annals he deserves renown as one of the few sharpers who could beat the other man's game. Like all professional cheats of his time, Cora was a Faro addict, and when he wasn't operating his own bank he was bucking the tiger from the other side of the layout. But unlike his fellows, he was a consistent winner against some of the most expert tricksters who ever practiced their mysterious arts in America; he seemed to possess the uncanny knack of being able to guess whether the Faro artist had prepared the cards to win or lose, and made his bets accordingly. His entire career, until it ended abruptly at the end of a rope, was an almost continuous run of good luck. In one period of about six months he performed the well-nigh incredible feat of winning $85,000 from Faro banks at New Orleans, Vicksburg and Natchez-under-the-Hill, while his total gains from his comrades in skulduggery are said to have approximated $300,000.

By the time he was eighteen, in 1834, Cora had a stake of $10,000, which he had won at Faro in Natchez and New Orleans. Early in 1835 he went to Vicksburg, and within two months had devastated half a dozen Faro banks, most of them controlled by that courtly scalawag Colonel Bryant, and thereby added $40,000 to his bankroll. Greatly perturbed by the spectacle of an eighteen-year-old boy on the loose in Vicksburg with $50,000 in his pockets, Colonel Bryant evolved a somewhat complicated scheme intended to reduce Cora to his proper status. He began by paying considerable attention to the young gambler, entertaining him at dinner and publicly congratulating him on his victory over Faro banks. Presently he broached the subject of a loan, and Cora, flattered at being noticed by such a famous personage as the Colonel, readily parted with $10,000, with which one of Bryant's associates opened a Faro game. The Colonel then roped Cora in to play against his own money, and the boy won the $10,000 in a few deals. Next day the Colonel borrowed another $10,000 and Cora won that also, as well as $15,000 which the Colonel talked him out of a week later. Colonel Bryant then owed Cora $35,000, which he had no intention of paying, as one of the guiding principles of his life was never to discharge a debt if it could be avoided. To rid himself of the importunate Cora, who had at last realized what the Colonel was trying to do, Bryant employed a noted ruffian to run him out of town. Properly frightened, the boy went to Natchez-under-the-Hill, and was there when the crusade against the gamblers began. He fled with the rest of the Natchez sharpers.

After a few years in New Orleans and Mobile, and a successful whirl at gambling on the steamboats, Cora turned his steps toward the East, and finally landed in Baltimore, where he seduced Arabella Ryan, daughter of a Baltimore clergyman, who thereafter called herself Belle Cora. Together they went to San Francisco, and while Cora made life miserable for both the suckers and the Faro dealers, she quickly amassed a comfortable fortune by operating a brothel on Pike Street, now Waverly Place. On November 18, 1855, Cora shot and killed General W. H. Richardson, United States Marshal for the Northern District of California, during a quarrel which had begun three days previously, when General Richardson objected to Belle Cora's presence at the American Theater. Cora was arrested and tried for murder, but the jury disagreed after deliberating forty-one hours. He was still in jail, awaiting a new trial, when the Vigilantes gained control of San Francisco in May, 1856, and was executed by the Vigilance Committee on May 20. An hour before he was hanged he and Belle Cora were married, and after his death she remained in her room for a month. When she emerged she sold her brothel and devoted herself to good works, becoming widely known for her gifts to charity. She died in comparative poverty on February 17, 1862.

8

There was a great influx of river gamblers into New Orleans when Federal and Confederate gunboats began operating on the Mississippi and the navigation of passenger steamboats virtually ceased. In a great burst of patriotic enthusiasm the gamblers organized a military company, officially called the Wilson Rangers but known among the sharpers themselves as the

Blackleg Cavalry, which was one of the best-equipped units, and the most nearly useless, in the Confederate Army. In a glowing account of their fine horses and handsome uniforms the New Orleans *True Delta* optimistically judged the Rangers "to be a valuable addition to our army of gulf coast defense," but according to George Devol, who was a member of the company, the gamblers were strictly peace-time soldiers. They rode out to drill every day, but instead of maneuvering under the hot sun they devoted the time to sitting under shade trees and skinning one another at Poker and Seven-Up. The Rangers' first and only experience in actual warfare came in April, 1862, when Farragut's fleet began to bombard Forts Jackson and St. Philip, the most important of New Orleans' defenses. The gamblers' company was sent down the river to harry the Yankee land forces under General Benjamin F. Butler, and the townspeople cheered the Rangers as they rode through the streets, but as Devol said, "there was but little cheer in that fine body of gamblers." Some six miles below the city a Yankee ship fired at them, and the doughty sharpers retreated at full speed. When they reached New Orleans they cut the brass buttons off their uniforms, buried their sabers, and forthwith discharged themselves from the Army. "We had enough of military glory," wrote Devol, "and were tired of war."

General Butler prohibited all gambling after the Yankee Army had taken possession of New Orleans on May 1, 1862, but a few weeks later he notified the sharpers that they might open houses if they would pay a stiff license fee and take his brother, A. J. Butler, in as full partner. A dozen gamblers accepted this arrangement, but several who attempted to operate without paying tribute to the Butlers, among them Price McGrath, were imprisoned. During most of the Butler regime George Devol ran the old Oakland race track, giving the suckers fixed races to bet on and skinning them with Faro and

Monte games in the grandstand. This was one of the most prosperous periods of Devol's career, but it came to an end when he began trimming Yankee officers and Army paymasters. Butler warned him to stop, but he persisted, and Butler put him in jail and confiscated all the horses at the race track, which were worth about $50,000. A little later the General's brother took the animals across Lake Pontchartrain and sold them to the Confederate Army. When Devol was released he resumed operations in New Orleans, but afterward went to Mobile, where he ran two gambling houses until the end of the War. The New Orleans gamblers ceased their payments to the Butler brothers when the General was transferred in December, 1862, and the gambling houses were not molested until early in 1864, when they were again closed by order of General A. Hulburt. They remained closed until the carpet-baggers took over the civil government of Louisiana.

9

At the conclusion of the Civil War hundreds of sharpers attempted to revive the good old days on the Mississippi, but they found that conditions had undergone a radical change. Comparatively few steamboats were making regular trips, travel was light and the travelers poor and suspicious, and the rich slaveowner and cotton planter, who had been the mainstay of river gambling, had vanished altogether. Moreover, the professional gambler was no longer regarded with amused tolerance by the officers of the steamers; instead, he was looked upon and treated as an ordinary crook. States on both sides of the Mississippi began to pass laws calculated to harass and suppress the sharper, and more often than not he was turned over to the authorities ashore and clapped into jail. By the middle 1870's river gambling had declined to such an extent that a sharper on a steamboat was a rarity instead of a commonplace. Most of the old-time river gamblers drifted into the big cities or followed the post-war wave of immigration into the cow and mining towns of the Western frontier, while many took to the railroads. For a few years the trains of the South and Southwest were almost as crowded with gamblers as the steamboats had been in the days of their greatest popularity. Railroad gambling, however, never reached really important proportions for several reasons. In the main the train-crews were extremely hard-boiled, while the rate of travel was so fast, and the average railroad journey so short, that the sharper had insufficient time to work up his games and bring his sucker to fever heat.

CHAPTER X

THE MIDDLE WEST AND
MIKE MCDONALD

D URING the period in which the professional gambler was
establishing himself in New York, Washington and
other cities of the Atlantic seaboard, his brethren who had
pursued the wandering sucker up the Western rivers and across
the Alleghenies were spreading throughout the valleys of the
Ohio and the upper Mississippi. By the early 1840's virtually
every settlement of any consequence in the Middle West had
its "nest of gamblers," many of which eventually became sizable rookeries and were prime sources of lawlessness and political corruption. Cincinnati, St. Louis, and especially Chicago,
were the great centers of mid-Western gambling, but at various times from about 1850 to the early 1890's Milwaukee, Indianapolis, St. Paul and Minneapolis enjoyed more than local renown, partly owing to the power and prosperity of their own
sharpers, and partly because they served as training grounds
for Chicago, whither they sent a steady stream of cornfed
tricksters.

Of lesser importance, but still more widely known than the
average town, were Cleveland and Fort Wayne, Ind. Cleveland produced one gambler of national stature in George
Randall, who owned two hells there and one in Saratoga; but
the city's reputation among sporting men was due almost entirely to the sweat shop conditions which prevailed in its half
dozen resorts. As late as the 1880's, even in the best places,

dealers and croupiers were compelled to work eight to sixteen hours a day, under close supervision, for wages ranging from twenty to thirty dollars a week, while other employes were paid an even lower scale. Mason Long, a Faro dealer and short card cheat who forsook the green cloth for religion and the lecture platform in 1877, wrote in his autobiography that during the middle 1860's Fort Wayne was "a paradise for gamblers . . . and some of the largest games in the United States were maintained." [1] The best known resorts were the Lodge, a saloon and Faro house; and a Keno dive operated by Tim McCarthy, champion billiard player of Indiana, where the cards were sometimes sold for as high as twenty dollars each. McCarthy made a fortune, but squandered it in a few years, and finally shot himself before a mirror in a Chicago saloon. The Lodge was kept by John Sterling, "a good-natured, warm-hearted man always ready to help the needy or skin a sucker," and Billy Grunauer, who "dressed in the extreme of fashion, wore the costliest clothing and the rarest diamonds, smoked imported cigars, drank the most expensive wines, and drove a thousand dollar team." Curiously enough, the principal suckers at the Lodge and other Fort Wayne houses were the members of the gangs of confidence men captained by Dad Ryan and a Chicago swindler known as Little Casino. When these gentry were driven out gambling in Fort Wayne immediately began to decline.

2

Milwaukee was the first of the minor metropolises to attract the sporting element—a gambler named Martin Curtis opened a Faro game there in 1843, when the population of the town was less than 3,000, and prospered for almost a decade. He

---

[1] *Mason Long, the Converted Gambler,* Written by Himself; Cincinnati, 1884; page 53.

made a great deal of money by investing his Faro gains in real estate and in building houses, among them a row of residences which stood for many years in Broadway opposite Police Headquarters. He is said also to have helped finance Milwaukee's first real hotel, the Kirby House, which was erected about 1845 by Mayor Abner Kirby. In 1865, when Milwaukee had become an important city of more than 50,000 inhabitants, the old Kirby House was replaced by a more pretentious structure, the 136 rooms of which were given names instead of numbers. The bridal suite was called "Paradise," while drunken guests were assigned to a meagerly furnished chamber known as "Hell." Occasionally an itinerant sharper wandered into Milwaukee and started a Faro snap, but otherwise Curtis had no competition until 1848 or 1849, when Tom Wicks opened a first-class house with his two brothers. Wicks was Milwaukee's most powerful gambler; he ran his place almost without interference for some twenty-five years, and was so influential in politics that no other gamester could start a game without obtaining his permission. During much of his career Wicks carried on his business in a building owned by General Lucius Fairchild, who was Governor of Wisconsin for six consecutive years, from 1866 to 1872. "As showing the pull which Wicks had on politicians and public men," said the reformed gambler John Philip Quinn, "it may be of interest to record the fact, that although Governor Fairchild went through four bitter political campaigns as a candidate, there was never a word said in any paper in reference to the fact that while Governor of Wisconsin he knowingly rented his property for gambling purposes." [2]

In addition to his Wisconsin enterprises, Wicks was interested in two or three skinning houses in Chicago, which were staffed by artists and croupiers who had been trained in the

[2] *Fools of Fortune, or Gambling and Gamblers,* by John Philip Quinn; Chicago, 1892; page 479.

Milwaukee establishment. The end of Wicks' reign came in 1872, when he made a disastrous foray into the wheat market and was forced to sell everything he owned in order to pay his losses. His experience as a sucker at another man's game changed his whole attitude toward gambling. He declared publicly that all gamblers were cheats, and that he intended to drive them out of Milwaukee. He succeeded in procuring a few indictments, but his crusade collapsed when the gamblers threatened to prove that he was merely trying to extort money from them. As an indirect result of Wicks' disclosures, however, the police within another year or two closed the gambling houses, which numbered about half a dozen, and to some extent put a stop to the Poker, Rondo and other games which were the great features of life in the back rooms of the saloons. Since that time there have been brief intervals of more or less open gambling in Milwaukee, but the vice has never been as widespread, nor the sharpers as powerful, as in the days of Tom Wicks.

3

John Philip Quinn wrote in 1890 that "from time immemorial, the capital of Hoosierdom has been recognized among sporting men as a poor locality in which to attempt to conduct a gambling house, not so much because of the higher morality of the inhabitants, nor on account of the rigid enforcement of the laws against gaming, as for the reason that the authorities, from the patrolman on the beat up to the officials of high rank, have been wont to levy such heavy assessments upon keepers of resorts of this character." [3] Nevertheless, Indianapolis was the foremost gambling town of its size in the Middle West from about 1855 to the late 1870's, during which time it increased in population from about 10,000 to approximately 75,000, and

[3] *Ibid.*, page 545.

supported from two to twenty gambling houses and a hundred professional sharpers. Dan Mortland, who was killed in a fall from his buggy; George Basey and his son-in-law, Major Russell, both of whom committed suicide, were probably the best-known of the pre-Civil War gamblers. As Martin Curtis had done in Milwaukee, Mortland put his money in buildings and real estate. When he died he owned a fine business structure on Illinois Street, part of which was occupied by his gaming resort, and several valuable city lots. Basey and Major Russell ran a Faro house, but the latter, popular because of his wit and genial manner, made his biggest killings in the Poker Room of the Bates House, one of the famous old hotels of the Middle West, and a favorite rendezvous of members of the Indiana Legislature. The statesmen were the main support of the game, which was in almost continuous operation at the Bates House for thirty years.

Some of the gambling resorts which were opened in Indianapolis during and immediately after the Civil War are said to have been among the finest in the Middle West—they were well furnished, served excellent suppers, and in many respects were equal to the big establishments of Chicago and St. Louis. The most elaborate was Charley O'Neill's house in Canal Street. O'Neill catered particularly to the young bloods of the town and other gulls of high social and business standing, and occasionally admitted the higher orders of professional gamblers, for whom he courteously ran an honest game. He prospered until the 1870's, when he opened a Keno game and made the mistake of refusing the demand of the police for more graft. In consequence he was indicted for keeping a gaming house, and his place was raided several times by policemen who destroyed his equipment and frightened away his suckers. After a few months of this treatment O'Neill closed his establishment and left Indianapolis for Washington, where he ran a small Faro house for several years. Only slightly inferior to O'Neill's resort were Howard Barnes' Maison Dorée, Bill Snow's House of Lords, and the Dollar Store, which was run by a syndicate of gamblers and was supposed to have a minimum limit of one dollar. Lower in the scale were six or eight Poker rooms, and half a dozen brace Faro dens in which such worthies as Jake Fidler, Sock Riley, Little Walter Ellworthy, French Joe, Big Kendrick and Scarface Ed Brown displayed their skill with a two-card box. Most of the sharpers who ran the brace games were also confidence men, and when gambling was slack operated various swindles in and around the Union Depot.

4

There was little or no public gambling in Minneapolis before the Civil War, but St. Paul was a favorite summer rendezvous of many Southern sharpers, and as early as about 1851, when the population was less than 2,000, harbored three or four small resorts. The most pretentious was a "club house," with a single Faro bank and two billiard tables, which was operated by Cole Martin and Cole Conant, otherwise known as King Cole, who were well known on the Ohio and Mississippi Rivers, where Martin was regarded as one of the cleverest of Faro artists and Poker players. One of the first victims of Martin's expert dealing in St. Paul was the famous steamboat sharper George Devol, who arrived in the Minnesota capital about 1852 with $2,000 and lost his entire bankroll within a few hours. A few days later Devol asked Martin for a loan of $300 with which to open a Keno game, and Martin gave him the money without question.

"Pay me when you are able," said Martin, "as I like to help a young man who tries to help himself."

Devol set up his Keno apparatus on one of Martin's billiard

tables, and Martin and King Cole helped start the game by closing the Faro bank and suggesting that their suckers play Keno. "They commenced playing at $1 per card at twelve o'clock," Devol wrote in his autobiography, "and at six in the morning they were playing at $10 per card. I was taking out ten per cent. They all got stuck. That night my receipts amounted to $1,300. The result was that they put the carpenters at work to fit up a nice room for me, and in eight months my part of the game was $33,000." With a small fortune in his pocket Devol went to the little Minnesota river town of Winona, which was becoming an important disembarkation point for immigrants bound into the Northwestern country. There he hurriedly built half a dozen houses, so flimsily constructed that "you could stand outside and throw a big dog through the cracks." But they were filled every night with travelers who provided their own bedding and slept on the floor at a dollar a head. Devol then opened a saloon and a Keno game, and as he put it, "was making money like dirt, when one day a man walked in with a bucket of water and commenced pouring it on one of my billiard tables, that I got in Chicago and which cost me $500." The gambler promptly butted the vandal until he was unconscious, and that night he died. Devol escaped down the Mississippi in a canoe, and was hiding in Dubuque when he heard that he had been exonerated; the doctors had performed an autopsy, and had decided that the man would have died anyway within a few days of delirium tremens. "They sawed open his skull," Devol wrote, "and found his brain a jelly in the center. So I went back and found his wife, gave her one of the houses which I had built and $700 in money . . . and went back to St. Paul, where my Keno games were still going on." [4]

Devol departed for other fields within another month or so,

[4] *Forty Years a Gambler on the Mississippi*, page 14.

as did King Cole, who died penniless in Chicago a few years
later; but Cole Martin, except for occasional ventures upon the
Mississippi, remained in St. Paul, and was one of the town's
principal sporting men for many years. During the 1870's and
the 1880's both St. Paul and Minneapolis experienced such phenomenal growth that the population of the capital increased
from 20,000 to 135,000, and that of Minneapolis from 13,000 to
almost 165,000. From about 1870 to the late 1880's gambling
was at its peak, and the two cities were the headquarters of
some of the best known gamblers of the Middle West, who
varied the monotony of life in their gaming houses with frequent forays against the suckers of Brainerd, Moorhead, Iron-
ton and other towns along the line of the Northern Pacific
Railroad. Among those who favored St. Paul, besides Cole
Martin, were Jack O'Neill, Dave Mullen, Shank Stanfield, and
Dan Shumway. All of these men more or less worked together,
and for years met for a drink every afternoon at Dave Crum-
my's saloon. Between Shumway and Stanfield, however, enmity
arose which in 1872 culminated in a pistol battle at Moorhead
in which Shumway was killed.

In Minneapolis during this period gambling was dominated
by a syndicate, known as "the combination," which operated
two first-class houses in Nicollet and Hennepin Avenues, and
controlled several other resorts of a lower type. This group of
sharpers was organized soon after the Civil War by John Flan-
agan, who retained his interest until the late 1880's, when he
retired with a modest fortune. His associates included Pat
Sullivan, Colonel Bill Tanner, Bill Munday, Mike Shelley, and
Frank Shaw, who afterward ran a big pool room in St. Paul
called the Turf Exchange. Before he joined "the combination"
Colonel Bill Tanner, with Munday as a partner for a few years,
kept the Elite, a skinning den in Nicollet Avenue, which was
as well known in that part of the country as the Tapis Franc

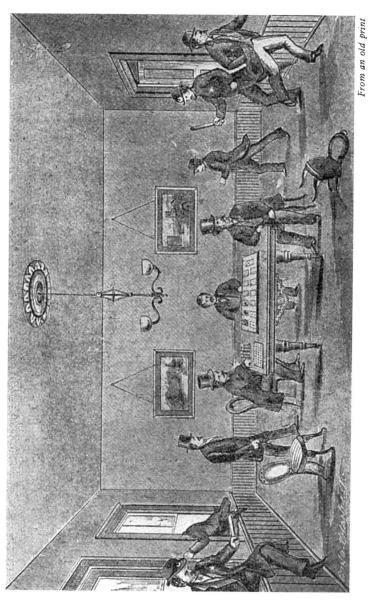

From an old print

A RAID ON AN EARLY GAMBLING HOUSE AT FORT WAYNE, IND.

had been in the East. Ostensibly the Elite was a saloon, but upstairs were brace games of every description, to which the suckers were introduced by a trio of very gifted ropers, Sammy Barrett, Charlie Dean and Jerry Desmond, who are still remembered by old-timers in Minneapolis for the skill with which they cajoled visiting suckers. Another who sometimes roped for the Elite was George W. Post, a notorious confidence man and one-time associate of Tom O'Brien, of Banco fame.

5

The people of early Cincinnati proudly called their town "The Athens of America" and "The Queen City of the West," but it was better known throughout the country as "Porkopolis" —it was the center of the pork-packing industry until superseded by Chicago in 1863, and for some forty years hogs and Cincinnati were so nearly synonymous in the public mind that pigs-feet were called "Cincinnati oysters," and in many places were so listed on restaurant menus. In addition to its pork products, and the $3,000,000 worth of Monongahela whisky which poured from its distilleries every year, Porkopolis made at least one unique contribution to American gambling in the Wolf-Trap, of which No. 98 Barclay Street and the Tapis Franc, in New York, were such shining examples. No record remains of the date upon which the first of these dens opened its doors, but it was probably between 1825 and 1830, when Cincinnati was already the most important port on the Ohio River, and with approximately 25,000 inhabitants was the largest city west of Philadelphia and north of New Orleans, a distinction which it retained until the rise of St. Louis and Chicago in the decade of the Civil War. By 1832 half a dozen Wolf-Traps were in operation in Cincinnati, most of them near the steamboat landing and designed especially to ensnare the river men. Others were opened in 1835 by refugee sharpers from Vicksburg and Natchez, many of whom remained in Porkopolis despite the warning proclamations of the Mayor and the threat of summary action by the respectable citizens. John O'Connor found twelve or fifteen Traps running full blast when he was in Cincinnati in 1836 or 1837, and thus described a dive run by one Robbins, "a little dried-up fellow, about fifty years of age, of a swarthy visage and small black eyes, and bushy hair of the same raven hue":

". . . a long, narrow and excessively dirty room, which could be divided at pleasure into two apartments by sliding-doors. The whole was carpeted with a dilapidated straw-matting, and decorated with several rough wooden boxes, which, being filled with sawdust, served as spittoons, when the patrons desired to indulge in expectoration. The front windows, which looked upon the street, were protected by green Venetian blinds, the walls had at some remote period been papered, but were now so smoked that the original pattern was undecipherable. They were adorned at intervals by various penny pictures tacked to the walls, as well as several in frames, representing celebrated racers, distinguished generals and statesmen, steamboats, fishing and hunting scenes, etc., etc. The furniture included a few dozen of cane-seated chairs, a poker-table covered with a discolored green cloth, and at the furthest end of the room, a large faro ditto, also covered with the usual green cloth, on which now reposed a layout, a set of chips, and a card-box. Against one side of the front room stood a strong oaken side-board, which had long since seen its best days, and on it rested a wooden pail filled with water, in which a gourd swam invitingly for those who desired to quench their thirst—the only entertainment which the establishment offered to its patrons. . . .

"I now amused myself by scanning the patrons of the place, who were fast filling the room, and a motley gathering they were, both in dress and personal appearance. . . . The majority were men occupying various positions on the steamboats plying on the river; for instance, cooks, stewards, mates, pilots, and engineers. There was also to be seen a considerable sprinkling of residents of the place representing the rowdy element in force, besides some mechanics, loafers and pot-house political spouters, and others of like grades and callings. The better-behaved amongst them sat looking quietly about them, or reading the newspapers, while the younger and better-dressed portion of the crowd gathered about the faro-table, where they discussed their own bad luck, the merits of fast women, fighting men, race-horses, river steamers, and a hundred kindred subjects. Their conversation was garnished by many terrible oaths and obscene expressions. 'Who'll open a snap?' was the oft-repeated question of the crowd, . . . At length their patience was rewarded by the appearance of a slight, dandified-looking individual, who was received with a yell of delight from the delectable crowd assembled around the faro-table, while several screamed at the tops of their voices, 'Here's Marks; we'll have a bank now.'

"The gentleman whose arrival had raised this ebullition of feeling . . . was dressed in a rather genteel manner, and wore around his neck a heavy gold chain, and a fine brilliant sparkled in his elaborately embroidered shirt-front. He held in his hand a small gold-headed cane, and advanced into the room and up to that end of it occupied by the faro table and its appurtenances, with a perfectly blank face, and took no more notice of the yelling, screeching audience, than if he had been the sole occupant of the room. Without bestowing on any person the smallest sign of recognition, he coolly divested himself of his coat, folded it carefully, and handed it to Mr. Robbins. . . . He then moved with a kind of shuffle towards the dealing-chair, and having fixed himself there to his satisfaction, he took with his thumb and finger, from his vest pocket, a half eagle, which he tossed on the table with the utmost *sang froid,* at the same time crying out, 'Here, Robbins, give us fish for this.' According to custom, that worthy counted out from the pile of checks on the table five dollars, issuing them at five cents apiece. When he had set Mr. Marks' bank aside, he handed him a dealing box and a pack of cards. The latter shuffled these according to the most approved method, and placed them in the dealing box, and during this operation neither spoke, nor in any way noticed, even by so much as a look, any one around him. . . . When ready to receive company, he addressed his audience in the following polite strain: 'Gentlemen, I don't want no fightin' at this 'ere game, nor no 'queer' played in on me. Steal everybody's checks but mine, and now, ye d—n rascals, pitch in!' . . .

"The bank struggled hard for an existence, but was finally obliged to succumb to capital. Without allowing his ill success to ruffle his temper, Mr. Marks quietly took out what money was in the card-box. . . . When he had redeemed his checks, Robbins handed him his coat, which he put on, seized his gold-headed cane in his left hand, and, with a flourish of his right, thus addressed the patrons: 'Gentlemen, as my term of office has now expired, allow me to thank you for your generous patronage, and also to carry away with me the remembrance of the happy moments I have passed in your society.' This speech was received with boisterous cheering, during which Mr. Marks shuffled himself out of the room." [5]

[5] *Wanderings of a Vagabond,* page 354–58.

274

O'Connor wrote that in no other city did Wolf-Traps "flourish so extensively, or were the resort of so many ruffians and lawless characters" as in Cincinnati. That was true enough for twelve or fifteen years, in which these places, as far as banking games were concerned, virtually monopolized the town's gambling. But the police and the politicians absorbed more and more of the meager earnings of the Traps, and when the graft was not forthcoming subjected the keepers, dealers, and customers to the danger and annoyance of frequent raids, on the ground that the dives were the rendezvous of criminals and the breeding places of crime and disorder, which, as a matter of fact, they were. Unable to withstand such persecution, the Wolf-Traps gradually decreased in numbers, and by the early 1850's, when they were at the height of their popularity in other towns, dens of this character had well-nigh vanished from the city of their origin. Thereafter the ruffians, river men and others who had supported the traps gambled in a few third-rate resorts where the games were banked by the house and dealt by house artists, who made certain that the profits were large enough to satisfy the police and leave something over.

First-class gambling in Cincinnati appears to have been confined to occasional games of Poker and All-Fours until the middle 1840's, when the sharpers began to fit up rooms in which the suckers of a higher social standing could play in comfort if not in luxury. By 1851, when the town had passed the 100,000 mark in population and was growing so fast that patriotic citizens boldly predicted a million inhabitants in ten years, Cincinnati harbored nine Faro houses, of which only one or two were Wolf-Traps; seventy-two Bagatelle games; thirty billiard rooms; twenty-seven Rondo and Keno halls, and 420 places where short card games were played. One of the Rondo establishments, founded by Joseph and Daniel Smith in

Fifth Street about 1845 or 1846, is said to have been the largest
and most prosperous in the United States, with "hundreds of
dollars changing hands every hour, both day and night."
George Devol went to work for the Smith brothers in 1847,
when he was eighteen years old, at a wage of $18 a week, but
was taken into the firm within a few months, and for almost
a year he and his partners divided the profits which averaged
about $600 a day. Eventually, however, they got into trouble
with the police, who began to raid the place and fine Devol
and the Smiths fifty dollars each once a month. "Then they
raised it to $100," wrote Devol, "and next to $500. That was too
much, so we had heavy oak and iron doors put up; but the
police would batter them down, and get us just the same. One
night they surrounded the house, broke down the door, and
arrested my two partners; but I escaped by the roof. The next
day I went up to the jail to take the boys something to eat,
when they nabbed me and locked me up also. They fined us
$500 each, and let us go, and that broke up Rondo." Devol re-
turned to the river after this adventure, but the Smiths were
permitted to reopen their Rondo game after a few weeks, and
ran it with great success for several years.[6]

The preponderance of short card resorts in early Cincinnati
was due to the great popularity of Poker, which was the favorite game of the town's suckers until about the time of the
Civil War. Almost every saloon maintained a Poker room,
while others were operated by river gamblers, who found Cincinnati so much to their liking, and their natural prey so

[6] Rondo, also spelled Rondeau, is played with a stick and nine small ivory
balls on a pool table, or any table with pockets. The balls are rolled across
the table with the stick to the pocket diagonally opposite the roller. Bets are
called for by the banker on *inside* and *outside,* and the stakes on each side
must balance. As soon as they do so, the banker says, "Roll, the game is made."
At least one ball must go into the pocket, and at least one must remain outside,
otherwise the roll is made again. The number of balls left outside the pocket,
odd or even, decides whether the inside or outside bets win. The banker takes
ten per cent.

276

abundant, that hundreds of them spent about as much time ashore as they did on the steamboats. For a few years the biggest Poker games were played in the Burnet House, where Grant and Sherman planned Sherman's march to the sea, and which, when it was opened in May, 1850, was described by the London *Illustrated News* as the "best hotel in the world." Late in 1853, however, the big-time sharpers transferred their allegiance to the new Spencer House, which provided a large soundproof room for the exclusive use of professional gamblers, a sort of de luxe Wolf-Trap furnished with tables and apparatus for banking games as well as for Poker. During the War the Spencer House was known as a "copperhead hotel," and the soundproof room was frequently used for meetings of Southern spies and sympathizers.

As more gaming resorts were opened, Faro gradually supplanted Poker in the affections of Cincinnati's sporting men, and was the most important game during the twelve or fifteen years, from about 1860 to the middle 1870's, in which gambling was at its peak, and when "there were pool rooms in many of the saloons, gambling houses were as open as dry goods stores, policy was openly played, and lottery tickets were apparently legitimate articles of commerce." Throughout this period the business was in the hands of eight or ten sharpers, who paid from $50,000 to $60,000 a year for police protection, and in return were given dictatorial powers over their fellow gamblers. Their authority didn't extend to the pool rooms and policy shops, but they drove out the undesirables who attempted to open Faro, Roulette, Poker and Keno houses, and regulated the number of these resorts according to the capacity of the available suckers. They seldom permitted more than a dozen first-class places to operate, and as a result everyone made money.

The best known of Cincinnati's boss-gamblers were Bolly Lewis, Tom Mead, Ephraim Holland; and Blackie Edwards, who was an honorable man, as gamblers went, and ran one of the town's few honest Faro games. In consequence he was the poorest of the lot, although even he managed to retire on a competence. Bolly Lewis settled in Cincinnati after a brief career on the Ohio and Mississippi Rivers, and for almost ten years operated one of the finest houses in the Middle West. In the end, however, remorse destroyed his business. An Army paymaster dropped into the resort one night late in 1865, and before daylight had been fleeced of $40,000 in government money. The desperate plight of the officer so affected Lewis that he resolved to mend his ways. He returned the $40,000, closed his gambling house, joined a church, and made several large donations to charity. He retained for himself, however, most of the considerable fortune he had accumulated at Faro, and with this money entered the hotel business, becoming part owner of the famous old Gibson House. At the time of his death Lewis was one of Cincinnati's most respected citizens.

Tom Mead was described by a contemporary as "a quiet, apparently inoffensive gentleman, dressing moderately, fond of good horses and devoted to his wife." He started for San Francisco in 1849, but was so impressed by the number and prosperity of the fortune-hunters going and coming across the Isthmus of Panama that he stopped at Panama City and opened a gambling house, from which he extracted more gold than most men ever found in California. He returned to the United States a very wealthy man in the late 1850's, and after a year or so in Boston came to Cincinnati and bought shares in three gambling houses in Vine, Fifth and Longworth Streets. His large earnings were invested in real estate, and when the gaming resorts were closed he was able to live handsomely on the income from his properties. One of Mead's partners for a few years was Ephraim Holland, better known as "Eph," another

278

of the river gamblers who had found a haven in Cincinnati when the Civil War drove them off the steamboats. Holland was the payoff and political front man for the sharpers; he collected and disbursed the graft, and maintained the necessary contacts with the police and the politicians. In so doing he acquired a great deal of influence, and during the early and middle 1870's was an important figure in local politics; in getting out the vote and manipulating a nominating convention he is said to have been one of the most skillful men of his time. Finally, however, he went too far. Seeing that an election was going the wrong way, he stuffed a ballot box, and when the hullaballoo had subsided found himself serving a jail sentence.

The public feeling against Holland extended to all gamblers, and the reform elements of Cincinnati took advantage of the situation to compel the enactment and enforcement of stringent anti-gambling ordinances. The gambling houses, together with the pool rooms and lottery offices and most of the police shops, were closed in 1878 despite the plaintive protests of the sharpers, who argued that they usually fleeced only strangers, and that they were performing a civic duty in attracting money to Cincinnati and keeping it there. Some of the houses reopened in 1884 when a liberal administration came into power, but were closed again in 1886. The last of the old-timers to succumb was Marshall Wooden, who left the town late in 1886 and opened a place in Hot Springs, Arkansas. Eph Holland also resumed his career in Hot Springs when he was released from prison. After the second cleansing Cincinnati suckers threw their money away in the Faro and Keno houses of Newport and Covington, across the Ohio River in Kentucky. One of the Newport resorts was a "resplendently gorgeous gaming place," backed by Cincinnati capital, which was a gold mine for many years.

6

The most remarkable feature of gambling in early St. Louis, and the true measure of the town's importance as a gaming center, was the number of famous gamblers who either learned their trade in the Missouri metropolis or operated there before or after gaining renown elsewhere—in this respect St. Louis was excelled only by New Orleans. The roster of these distinguished sharpers included such celebrities of the green cloth as Henry Perritt, Allen Jones and Price McGrath of New Orleans; Gabe Foster, Ben Burnish and Johnny Lawler of Chicago; Johnny Chamberlin of New York; Tom Wicks of Milwaukee, and Bob Potee of Kansas City. And a score of noted river gamblers, among them Cole Martin, Star Davis, the elegant Jimmy Fitzgerald, the boastful Colonel Charles Starr, and that shining knight of the Poker table, John Powell. A few of the river gamesters ran Faro snaps when ashore in St. Louis, but most of them concentrated on Poker and other short card games, as the sharpers of the Ohio did in Cincinnati. Their favorite rendezvous was the Planters Hotel, one of the most famous houses in America, which was opened on April 1, 1841, at a time when St. Louis, with a population of about 18,000 was the commercial center of the Mississippi Valley and next to Cincinnati the largest town in the Middle West. The management of the Planters proudly advertised that it had 215 rooms and "the largest ballroom west of the Alleghenies," but its fame was due chiefly to its cuisine, in particular fried chicken, waffles and candied sweet potatoes; and the bar, where America's greatest bartender, Professor Jerry Thomas, invented the Tom and Jerry sometime in the early 1850's.[7]

No part of the Planters Hotel was ever operated as an open

[7] This was the second Planters Hotel. The first was a tavern which opened in 1817. The second was torn down to make way for the third, which was opened on September 16, 1894. It was closed in 1924.

gambling resort, but nevertheless it was the center of the business for many years—Poker and other short card games were played in its rooms, and within a radius of three of four blocks were clustered most of the city's first-class Faro houses, which varied in number from half a dozen in the 1840's to fifteen or twenty during the Civil War. Four were directly across the street, three of them controlled by George Griffen, a Bostonian who arrived in St. Louis without a penny and in less than two years owned interests in several resorts. The fourth was operated by Gabe Foster and Ben Burnish, and is said to have been the most luxurious place in town. In the 1850's Foster and Burnish employed a case-keeper named Bill Fisher, member of a good New England family and well educated, who was a curious sort to be found in a gambling house. He never gambled, although he kept cases faithfully night after night, and was a natural card player, particularly expert at Boston, Whist and Cribbage. His failing was liquor, and in return for whisky he would sometimes sit in a game of cards at the behest of professional gamblers, who made a great deal of money backing his play. Fisher lived in the gambling house, and usually drank himself to sleep after the place had closed for the night. He finally died of alcoholism.

Johnny Lawler, who probably achieved greater notoriety than any other St. Louis gambler, was one of Griffen's partners for a few years. Lawler began in St. Louis as a roper, and whatever actual gambling he did in those days was from the wrong side of the Faro layout. He was an amiable, jovial fellow when he wasn't bucking the tiger, but as soon as he began to play he developed an irascible disposition, and was a hard loser. When a turn went against him he would throw whatever he happened to have in his hand—on one occasion it was a bucket of oysters—at the dealer; and if his bad luck continued he would scream, butt his head against a wall, and try to pull his ear off.

Lawler had many ups and downs in St. Louis, but finally scraped together enough money to open a Faro bank in partnership with George Griffen. He made money for a few years, but about 1867 sold his part of the business and went to Chicago, where he enjoyed his greatest prosperity and experienced his greatest misfortunes. His prosperity was due to the fact that he became friendly with Mike McDonald, Matt Robbins, and other leading Chicago sharpers, and was associated with them in several lucrative enterprises. At the time of the Chicago fire he owned a Faro house and the lease of the Southern Hotel in Wabash Avenue, which he had refitted at a cost of $20,000, and had a bank roll of $40,000. His troubles in Chicago grew out of an encounter with George Devol. One version of the affair is that Devol knocked Lawler into a mud puddle for insulting a woman friend of the great butter. Devol, however, said that he quarreled with Lawler in a gambling house and "slapped him in the face." In any event, Lawler went home and got a pistol, and began shooting when he met Devol at Clark and Madison Streets later in the day. His first shot struck Devol in the arm, but the others missed because Devol found shelter behind a lamp post. Lawler was arrested, tried, convicted of assault with intent to kill, and sentenced to three years in prison, but eight months later obtained a new trial and was acquitted. While he was in jail his hair turned from black to snow white, and after he had paid his lawyer he was penniless. Thereafter luck went against him. Several Faro banks in which he became interested were soon broken, and the police closed a handsomely furnished "club house" which he had opened in Clark Street. He saved a hundred dollars from the wreckage and with it bought a ticket to the Pacific Coast. When last heard of he had quit gambling, and was doing fairly well in the real estate business in Tacoma, Washington.

In addition to the sharpers who scaled the heights of gambling fame in other cities, St. Louis harbored, at various times, twenty or more gamblers who were almost as notorious as the Lawlers, the McGraths and the Chamberlins, although their activities were not so extensive. Perhaps the best known of this local talent were Dick Roach, Bob O'Blennis, Count Sobieski, Charley Teenan; Jack Silvia, who lost everything he owned and then pawned his gold teeth and dropped the proceeds into the insatiable maw of the tiger; and Coal-Oil Johnny Hall, a brace game dealer who was finally killed at Terre Haute, Ind., when his wife caught him with another woman. Dick Roach came to St. Louis from Detroit about 1863, when still in his teens, and immediately displayed unusual gifts both as a Faro artist and as a player against the bank—he possessed the same sort of gambling instinct that had proven so helpful to Charles Cora. Roach won a big stake within a year, opened a Faro bank, and was worth half a million dollars almost before his whiskers began to sprout. He was probably St. Louis' richest gambler. Bob O'Blennis was noted for his pugnacity; he would not only fight at the drop of a hat, but would drop the hat. He was paralyzed and helpless during the last few years of his life, and went about in a wheel chair attended by a Negro servant, who delivered his challenges and helped him place his bets at Faro. Count Sobieski was a Faro banker in the John Law tradition. He maintained a magnificent apartment, and entertained at dinner every Sunday evening. At the conclusion of the feast Sobieski would produce a dealing box and a layout and teach his guests the mysteries of Faro. He prospered for several years, but drank so much that his wife finally left him, and he wandered about the West until he died in Salt Lake City. Charley Teenan, as expert an artist as ever pulled two cards out of a dealing box, died a hero in the burning of the

283

Southern Hotel on April 11, 1877. He was at work behind a Faro table across the street when the fire started, and immediately abandoned his deck of cards and dashed into the building. He made four daring rescues of guests who had been overcome by smoke, but fell from a window ledge while attempting a fifth. He was still conscious when picked up, and was carried into the gambling house and laid upon a Faro table, where he died with the dealing box in his hand.

Gambling in St. Louis was divided into three periods—the first before the Civil War, when most of the Faro banks were square; the second during the War, when the sure-thing players were in the ascendancy; and the third from about 1870 to 1882, when brace games were operated almost exclusively. Throughout the 1870's the situation in St. Louis was much the same, on a somewhat smaller scale, as it had been in New York in the days of the "very splendid hells." The hotels, the railroad stations, and the steamboat landings fairly crawled with ropers and steerers, and the gamblers ran their resorts wide open, to the great profit of themselves and of the police and politicians who permitted and encouraged the skinning houses as long as protection money was promptly paid. "Squeals from victims were of daily occurrence," wrote John Philip Quinn, who was roping for a St. Louis dive at the time, "and the authorities found themselves compelled to take notice of the complaints . . . when the officers of the law found themselves compelled to make a raid upon one of these resorts the descent was accomplished in a most perfunctory manner. The common practice was to send notice to the proprietors in advance that they might 'expect visitors' at an hour named. The gamblers being thus forewarned, the police rarely found anything to justify stringent measures. The paraphernalia was generally stowed away out of sight; and if, by chance, any gambling instruments were captured, their owners were generally privately advised as to where, when and how they might recover their property." [8]

By the late 1870's the gamblers not only dominated the municipal government of St. Louis, but exercised considerable influence in the state capitol at Jefferson City, and controlled many members of the General Assembly. Their aim was the enactment of a law legalizing their business, and that they didn't succeed was due almost entirely to the efforts of Charles P. Johnson, who had been City and Circuit Attorney of St. Louis and Lieutenant-Governor of Missouri, and was the foremost criminal lawyer of his time, with a practice that extended over half a dozen states.[9] Johnson was elected to the General Assembly in 1880 on his promise to work for an anti-gambling law which would make the keeping of a gambling house a felony. The statute was passed in 1881, and as soon as it went into effect Johnson returned to St. Louis, and with the aid of the newspapers and interested citizens compelled the police to enforce it. Within a few months the sharpers were in retreat, and by the end of 1882 the last gambling house had been closed. The few resorts which have sprung up from time to time since then have operated strictly under cover, and in great fear and trembling.

7

The population of Chicago was less than six hundred when "the mud-hole in the prairie," as envious St. Louisans called the new settlement, was incorporated as a town in 1833, but already it contained a leavening of gamblers large and fermentitious enough to cause grave concern among the respectable citizens. One of the first public outbreaks against the sharpers was a crusade instigated in 1833 by the Rev. Jeremiah Porter,

[8] *Fools of Fortune,* page 411.
[9] One of his clients was Frank James.

the town's first resident preacher, which resulted in the closing of two "nests" and the imprisonment of their keepers. The success of the movement, however, was ephemeral; only a few months later, on December 31, 1833, a letter in the Chicago *Democrat* called attention to the prevalence of gambling and demanded that the laws against it be enforced. And in October, 1843, a mass meeting appointed a committee of nine to study the situation and devise means of eradicating the vice. The members of this committee adopted resolutions which pledged them to refuse their friendship to gamblers and to wage unremitting warfare against "sharpers and blacklegs," and urged the people not to patronize public houses where gambling was permitted. "Cost what it may," said the committee's report, "we are determined to root out this vice, and to hunt down those who gain by it an infamous subsistence." But threats of social ostracism and economical boycott were not sufficient to curb the excesses of the gamblers or to keep them out of the saloons and taverns. A "season of prayer" held by the religiously inclined in 1835 was scarcely more efficacious, even though it did send two gamblers to jail and reclaim several young men from the way of evil.

For the gambler, as well as for the honest settler, all roads in the Middle West led to Chicago. By the late 1840's, although no more than half as large as St. Louis or Cincinnati, the town had more first-class gaming resorts and big-time gamblers than either the Missouri city or Porkopolis. Short card games predominated, the favorites being Brag, Poker, Seven-Up and Whist, although Checkers, Chess, Cribbage and Backgammon were also frequently played for large stakes. There were only two or three small Faro banks in operation during the first fifteen years of Chicago's existence as an organized municipality, and Keno, Roulette and Chuck-a-Luck, which eventually became enormously popular, appear to have been unknown until about 1850. The principal gambling houses, all of which exacted a ten per cent rakeoff from every pot, were run by George Rhodes, Walter Winchester, John Sears; the three Smith brothers, Charles, Montague and George, better known as One-Lung; and Cole Martin and King Cole Conant, of St. Louis and the Mississippi, who were prominent in Chicago sporting circles from about 1845 to 1851, when they went to St. Paul. One-Lung Smith was the last of the old-timers to quit the business; he ran a popular and well-furnished house in State Street until the early 1880's, when he sold out and went to New York. But he was never very successful in the metropolis; after a long run of bad luck he died in a Faro house while playing with borrowed money. John Sears was the outstanding figure of early Chicago gambling. He played Poker almost exclusively, and is said to have been so expert at the game that he never found it necessary to cheat, and in consequence was highly respected as a square player. Naturally, he died a poor man. Even more than for his skill at Poker, Sears was noted for his elaborate wardrobe and his good looks—for years he was considered the handsomest and best-dressed man in Chicago—for his gifts as a story-teller, and for his love of poetry. He was especially fond of Burns and Shakespeare, and sometimes startled his opponents at the Poker table by interlarding his comments with apt poetical quotations.

Most of the gambling in the resorts operated by Sears and his contemporaries apparently was honest, the keepers of the resorts contenting themselves with the usual ten per cent cut, and in general discouraging bottom dealing and the use of cold decks, reflectors, hold-outs and other devices for cheating. Sure thing players began to work on a large scale in Chicago during the early 1850's, when Faro increased in popularity and Keno, Roulette and Chuck-a-Luck were introduced by a gang of Eastern and Southern sharpers which included Bill McGraw,

Dan Oaks, Billy Buck, Dutch House, and Little Dan Brown, veterans of the skinning dens of New York and New Orleans. For a year or so they ran their games in the low hotels and the back rooms of saloons, and in a few gambling houses which admitted them on a percentage basis. Soon, however, they opened resorts of their own, and were so successful in roping and fleecing fat suckers that sharpers of this class flocked into Chicago from all parts of the country. In the late 1850's, when Chicago could, and did, boast of almost 100,000 inhabitants, and was in the early stages of the great boom which brought a growth unequaled by any other city in the world, there were so many crooked gamblers in town that skinning houses were the rule rather than the exception. The more elaborate of these dens ran wide open in State, Lake and other principal streets; while the worst, including a few Wolf-Traps, were for the most part concentrated in the Sands, a vice-ridden area which lay north of the Chicago River, and in squalor and viciousness rivaled the Five Points section of New York and the Swamp district of New Orleans. "A large number of persons, mostly strangers in the city," said the Chicago *Tribune* of April 21, 1857, "have been enticed into the dens there and robbed, and there is but little doubt that a number of murders have been committed by the desperate characters who have made these dens their homes. The most beastly sensuality and the darkest crimes have had their home in the Sands."

Several attempts were made to clean up the Sands and disperse the hoodlums, thieves, prostitutes and sharpers who infested the district, but none succeeded until John Wentworth, owner of the Chicago *Democrat,* and called Long John because of his great height, became Mayor in 1857. An advertisement of a dog-fight lured most of the able-bodied men away from the Sands, and on the afternoon of April 21, 1857, a deputy

288

sheriff and thirty policemen invaded the quarter and pulled down nine of the ramshackle buildings. Six more were destroyed by fire later in the day. The newspapers praised the Mayor for ridding the town of a plague-spot, but actually Long John had done nothing except raze a few unsightly houses. The criminals who had made their lairs in the Sands simply scattered to other parts of Chicago, and as far as they were concerned business went on as usual. But with the Sands disposed of to his own satisfaction, Long John turned his attention to the gamblers, warning them in the *Democrat* that they would be summarily dealt with unless they mended their ways and showed a decent respect for the city's laws. When they ignored the warning, Mayor Wentworth proceeded to carry out his threats, himself leading a raid upon Dave Burrough's establishment in Randolph Street. Several policemen entered the resort from the roof of an adjoining building, and chased the employes and players downstairs into the street, where they were captured by other officers under the command of the Mayor, and marched to the city jail. Meanwhile the police inside the building confiscated and hauled away in carts everything movable, including the rugs and carpets. Everyone who had been in the place was heavily fined. Even to the arrogant gamblers it was apparent that Mayor Wentworth was in earnest, and no other raids were necessary. As John Philip Quinn said, "Open gambling ceased at once, and the 'hole and corner' variety of the vice was soon hunted out. Banking games were no longer to be found, and the few Poker rooms that were started in out-of-the-way places were speedily discovered." An interesting development of this period of suppression was the so-called "traveling game," which is such an important feature of modern gambling. Quinn wrote that "occasionally a game of Faro was dealt . . . but when an adjournment was had, it was 'sine die'; and no two consecutive games were played at the same place." [10]

Throughout his first administration Long John Wentworth kept the gambling houses closed and the sharpers on the run; probably at no other time in its history has Chicago been so nearly free of the vice. But the Civil War had begun when he entered upon his second term, and he was concerned with weightier matters than the protection of suckers. In consequence, the bars were let down and the gamblers began to return, their numbers augmented by tricksters from the Mississippi steamboats, and from St. Louis and other towns along the river. And with them came the riffraff and criminals of a dozen cities—prostitutes and fancy men, sneak thieves and pickpockets, race-track touts and confidence men, burglars and foot-pads, garroters and safe-crackers, all attracted to Chicago by its riches and opportunities for plunder. During the Civil War and until the great fire of 1871, while the one-time "mud-hole in the prairie" was tripling in population and expanding in every direction, the underworld literally ran wild, with almost no interference from the authorities. For at least ten years Chicago richly deserved its reputation of being the wickedest and toughest place in the United States. Brothels, saloons, and dives of an even more vicious character crowded such important streets as Clark, Monroe, State, Randolph, Adams and Polk; two thousand *nymphes du pavé* maintained rooms on the upper floors of office buildings and walked the business district both day and night; and the slums along the Chicago River swarmed with thugs and thieves, called by the police "as desperate a class of men as ever disgraced a city."

Hundreds of gambling houses of every size and type, from the palatial skinning house with a Keno room, half a dozen Faro tables and as many Roulette wheels, to the hovel where

---

[10] *Fools of Fortune*, pages 391–92.

the only equipment was a board and a pack of greasy cards, were scattered all over the city, and in not more than a dozen did the sucker receive an honest run for his money. The best known of the very few places in which square games were dealt at all times was operated at No. 167 Randolph Street by Colonel Wat Cameron, a Virginian who was distinguished for his courtly manners and his generosity. He managed to make a good living for a few years without recourse to a two-card box, but about 1863 took into partnership Gabe Foster and Ben Burnish, who had arrived in Chicago from St. Louis a few months before. They soon rid themselves of Colonel Cameron, and transformed the house into a skinning den which became one of the most notorious resorts in Chicago. Burnish eventually retired with a fortune, but Foster became an opium addict and squandered his money in dissipation. He finally went to Little Rock, Ark., and one night, after smoking opium for several hours, wandered into the woods near the town. Next morning he was found dead.

Most of the first-class gaming resorts of war-time Chicago were in Hairtrigger Block—Randolph Street between Clark and State—so called because of the great number of shooting affrays which occurred there; and in Gamblers' Row—Clark Street from Randolph to Monroe—where they clustered so thickly that there was room for no other business except a few saloons and an occasional brothel. All sorts of games and swindles ran full blast in these places at all hours, but the favorite was Faro, although Keno was so popular in the early 1880's that crowds of would-be players stood for hours in front of the packed Keno rooms, waiting for a chance to get inside and buy cards. Since the sharpers paid heavily for protection, the police seldom invaded Hairtrigger Block or Gamblers' Row, and when they did it was frankly for the purpose of adding to the city's revenues, and a gesture for the benefit of the newspapers and the godly. The raiding squads were careful not to damage furniture or equipment, and policemen obligingly guarded the resort while the gamblers and their employes and suckers rode in hacks to the office of the nearest Magistrate and deposited small sums as bail, which was usually forfeited. This formality completed, they returned in their carriages to the gaming house, the police retired, and play was resumed.

There was no nonsense about the Chicago gambler of those days. He was after the sucker's money, and he got it as quickly as possible and let the squawks fall where they might. He saw no reason to coddle his victims, to bewilder them with luxurious surroundings and obsequious servants, or to stupefy them with fine liquors and rich foods. As a result of this realistic attitude the houses which flourished before the great fire were in the main crude and poorly furnished, provided only with the bare necessities of gambling. Only a few were in any way comparable to the magnificent establishments of New York, Washington and New Orleans. The finest was the Senate, run by Frank Connelly. It was the show-place of Hairtrigger Block, but only in minor respects was it superior to the skinning houses run by Jew Hyman, Matt Robbins, Nellis Adams, Johnny Lawler, Hugh Dunn, the Smith brothers, Bill Foster, Johnny Molloy, Hank McGuire, George Trussell, Theodore Cameron, who was not related to the Colonel, and a dozen others. Theodore Cameron ran two places, one at Clark and Madison Streets, and another at No. 68 Randolph Street which was famous for its bird suppers and the quality of its liquors, all of which were free to suckers. Cameron is said to have made a million dollars in Chicago, but as John Philip Quinn said, "he was a man who, had he made a hundred thousand dollars in a night, would have contrived to get rid of it during the next twenty-four hours, even if he had to burn it up." When he finally left Chicago in the middle 1870's he had less than five hundred dollars.

George Trussell, who was described by John O'Connor as "a shrewd, cunning Yankee from Vermont" and by Quinn as "a man of fine physique, scrupulous in his dress, and extravagant in his tastes and habits," was a bookkeeper in Chicago for several years before he turned gambler. He began in a small way as a roper and capper for a skinning house on Hairtrigger Block, but by about 1862 owned several establishments in partnership with Old Bill Leanord, Otis Randall, and "an all-around sport" named Judd, who was an expert at all games. Judd had got his start in California, where he went from one mining camp to another with a Roulette wheel on his back and a Faro layout in his pocket. To bring victims into their houses, Trussell and his partners employed a gang of ropers whose tactics caused much ill-feeling among the keepers of the few honest games. It was the custom of these slickers to sneak into the hallway of a square house and turn out the gas, and then when a sucker came along tell him that the place had been closed, and steer him to a den controlled by Trussell's syndicate. Naturally, Trussell soon became rich. John O'Connor said of him that "this fellow had full sway over the gambling privileges of the city, which his compeers and himself turned into a stealing privilege, for which they feed the accommodating police most munificently." This estimate of Trussell's influence was somewhat exaggerated, but it was unquestionably greater than that of any other Chicago gambler of his time; he paid high for protection, and while he couldn't prevent the opening of a house, the sharper who incurred his enmity, or attempted to seduce his suckers, soon found himself the object of a destructive raid. And he was almost as important in horse-racing circles, for he was interested in the Chicago Driving Park, and was part owner of the famous trotter Dexter, which later came into the possession of Robert Bonner, a New York publisher.

In the late summer of 1866 the attention of American racing enthusiasts was centered upon the Driving Park, where Dexter, which had stepped a mile under saddle in 2: 18,[11] was matched against Cooley, Medoc, General Butler, and other celebrated trotters. Trussell's mistress at this time—some said he had married her—was a handsome young prostitute known as Mollie Trussell, whom the gambler, in 1864, had installed as Madame of a luxurious brothel in Fourth Avenue. Until he acquired an interest in the great trotter, Trussell was devoted to Mollie; he appeared with her at the theaters, loaded her superb figure with jewels and fine raiment, took her for a daily ride in his carriage, and otherwise flaunted his generosity and excellent taste in women. But when Dexter came into his life, his interest in Mollie declined. More and more she sat alone among her strumpets, while Trussell spent his time at the stables admiring his share of the horse, and gossiping in the saloons with the race track crowd. The crowning insult was his failure to take her to the grand opening of the Driving Park early in September; he was one of the lions of the occasion, but she was a deserted mistress, making change in a brothel. As she reflected upon her wrongs her jealousy mounted, and her rage increased at being compelled to play second fiddle to a horse. On the night after the opening she donned her finest gown, described by the papers as "a gorgeous white moiré dress," hid a pistol in its voluminous folds, and went down to Hairtrigger Block. She found her errant lover in a saloon, drinking a toast to Dexter. As she began to describe his ancestry and speculate upon his upbringing, he told her to go home and started to lead her roughly to the door. But she jerked away, drew her pistol,

[11] At Buffalo, N. Y., on August 18, 1866. Dexter's best time in harness was 2:17 ¾, made on August 14, 1867. This was the record until August 14, 1874, when Gloster trotted a mile in harness in 2:17. This time was reduced to 2:14 by Goldsmith Maid about two weeks later, on September 2nd.

From the New York World. Courtesy the Press Publishing Co.

THIS ELABORATE ESTABLISHMENT FLOURISHED FOR A YEAR OR SO AROUND 1900

and fired. Trussell fell to the floor, mortally wounded, and she flung herself upon his body, screaming:

"Oh my George, my George! He is dead!"

And as Lloyd Lewis said in his admirable book about Chicago, "it was an early sign of the chivalry of Cook County juries when Mollie went free." [12]

8

With the death of George Trussell began the rise of Michael Cassius McDonald, politician, newspaper owner, prince of sharpers, traction magnate, central figure in a series of extraordinary marital difficulties, right-hand man of Mayor Carter Harrison, and friend of Illinois' greatest Governor, John Altgeld. As a gambler, McDonald was the most powerful ever to operate in Chicago, and one of the three or four most important that have yet appeared to harass the American sucker. But a niche in the gambling hall of fame would have been reserved for him if he had been the most insignificant of tinhorns, for it was Mike McDonald, according to Chicago legend, who coined that sagest and truest of aphorisms, "There's a sucker born every minute."

McDonald was born near Chicago in 1839, and started his life work at an early age—at sixteen he was a swindling news butcher on a railroad train, selling fake prize packages to verdant passengers, and roping and capping for any train gambler who would give him a few dollars. At eighteen he was a lively young sport with a thousand dollar bankroll and an extensive knowledge of trickery, though not yet a professional sharper. About 1857, soon after Long John Wentworth had closed the gambling resorts in Chicago, young McDonald went by train to St. Louis, and from there voyaged down the Mis-

[12] *Chicago, the History of its Reputation*, by Lloyd Lewis and Henry Justin Smith; New York, 1929; page 101.

sissippi to New Orleans. He was so greatly impressed by the glamorous gamblers of the steamboats, and by the rich and influential sporting men of New Orleans, that he resolved to dedicate his life to the despoliation of the sucker, and to become the greatest gambler in the world. He began by aping the mannerisms of the river sharpers and copying their dress—he discarded the gaudy attire which had seemed so elegant in Chicago, and thereafter never wore anything but solid black, with snow white linen. At the same time he evolved a code of ethics which consisted of two precepts, "Stick to your friends," and "Keep your word once given." To both he adhered without deviation or compromise for almost half a century.

Thus equipped, Mike McDonald returned to Chicago and set out along the road he had chosen. He was successful from the beginning. By the outbreak of the Civil War he had become such a prominent figure in Chicago sporting circles that the newspapers referred to him as "the well-known gambler"; and in 1861 the twenty-two-year-old sharper was important enough to be one of the signers of a poster which called upon all Irishmen to join the Irish Regiment of Volunteers for service with the Union Army. Mike himself, however, didn't join. During the Civil War decade and until the great fire of 1871, McDonald was an increasingly influential factor in the life of Hairtrigger Block and Gamblers' Row; in partnership with others he owned several houses, and he was known as a cagey and successful player against the bank in the resorts where the games were square. He didn't reach full stature as a gambler, however, until Harvey D. Colvin, whom he had supported, was elected Mayor on a liberal platform in 1873. Under Colvin's predecessor, Joseph Medill, the gambling houses had operated, but the police made frequent raids and some of the sharpers were heavily fined. But with Colvin in power Hairtrigger

Block and Gamblers' Row bloomed anew, and conditions soon became at least as bad as they had been before the fire. "The Mayor manifested utter indifference to the enforcement of the laws," wrote John Philip Quinn. "Dance halls, concert saloons, and disreputable houses of every description abounded and flourished. Toughs of every grade walked the streets without fear; and the bunko men, brace dealers, Monte players and crooks of high and low degree openly plied their vocations. . . . Of all the free and open cities in the Union, Chicago was at this time the worst." [18]

Mike McDonald's principal contribution to this saturnalia was a grand new gambling house at Clark and Monroe Streets, which was one of the most magnificently equipped and furnished "palaces of chance" that ever dazzled the suckers of the Middle West. He called it "The Store," and in conjunction with it operated a saloon and a hotel. For almost twenty years The Store was the leading resort of Chicago, the favorite rendezvous of city and county officials, important politicians and professional gamblers, and rich suckers from the upper classes. For their education and his own profit, McDonald maintained a dozen Faro banks and half as many Roulette wheels and Chuck-a-Luck cages, as well as facilities for all kinds of dice and short card games. He always insisted that his wheels and dealing boxes were honestly handled, but actually he used the system that Pendleton had employed with such success in Washington—the degree of squareness depended upon the standing of the player. Officials and high ranking politicians, and professionals who would have been able to spot trickery, often won respectable sums, but fat suckers from private life were dealt with as ruthlessly at The Store as anywhere else.

In the 1870's The Store stood virtually alone in Chicago, and as far as influence and popularity with the right people were

[18] *Fools of Fortune*, page 402.

concerned, in the 1880's also. But during the latter decade the actual dollar and cent business of the resort suffered somewhat from the opposition of the palatial houses operated by Pat Sheedy, Curt Gunn, Ed Wagner, the Hankins brothers; Harry Varnell, who kept his place open twenty-four hours a day and employed a force of fifteen croupiers, twenty-five Faro dealers and from forty to fifty ropers and cappers; and Billy Fagan, in whose famous House of David one room was never used for gambling. According to a sign on the door, it was reserved for "Prayer Meetings and Gospel Services." Pat Sheedy, a Poker player of rare skill and one of the most prominent of Chicago gamblers for several years, might have succeeded Mike Mc-Donald as the boss sharper of the town if he had taken full advantage of his opportunities. He went to New York in the 1890's, however, and became a sort of unofficial stooge to Richard Canfield; he was a familiar figure in Canfield's gambling houses, and was always eager to tell newspaper reporters what a great man Canfield was. Sheedy also acquired considerable notoriety around 1900 by acting as go-between in the restoration of stolen works of art and other property. His most notable exploit in this respect was in connection with Gainsborough's painting of the Duchess of Devonshire, which had been cut from its frame in an English art gallery by Adam Worth, famous fence and bank robber. The picture lay hidden in a Brooklyn warehouse for years, but was finally produced when the owners, through Sheedy and Pinkerton detectives, paid Worth $25,000. Later the painting was sold to J. P. Morgan for $125,000.

Over a period of eight or ten years the Clark Street establishment of the Hankins brothers is said to have earned net profits of $20,000 a month. Professional gamblers were never admitted into the domain of the Hankinses; they catered exclusively to the "dinner pail brigade"—amateurs with comparatively small incomes and an incurable passion for the gaming table. In the 1880's the Hankins brothers and Harry Varnell were associated with Mike McDonald in a bookmaking syndicate which dominated the gambling at the Chicago and Indiana race tracks. In one season at the old Garfield track the syndicate made $800,000, which up to that time at least was the largest profit ever taken at a single track. About the only independent bookmakers of any importance who prospered in Chicago while the syndicate was in existence were McDonald's old-time friends. Big Jim O'Leary, whose mother owned the cow which is supposed to have started the Chicago fire; and Silver Bill Riley, who rigorously excluded miners from his place and permitted no card playing or cigaret smoking. Riley, a native of Brooklyn, was a camp follower of the Union Army during the Civil War, and landed in San Francisco in the late 1860's with $1.50. He made $1,500 in ten days exhibiting a red-whiskered miner as the "Wild Man of Ceylon," and then went back to Chicago. There he opened a pool room with the backing of Mike McDonald, and made book on elections, horse races and sporting events. He was also a popular stake-holder; in the Blaine-Cleveland campaign of 1884 he was custodian of bets amounting to $250,000. At the height of his career Riley was worth several million dollars, but when he died in the summer of 1912 he was penniless.

Most of the big-time gamblers who flourished in Chicago during the two decades that followed the fire were either partners of Mike McDonald or were in business at his pleasure, and remained unmolested only so long as they gave liberally to a slush fund which he collected periodically and distributed where it would do the most good. McDonald was rich and powerful by the middle 1870's, but by 1880 he was a millionaire, and was the most powerful politician in Chicago with the exception of Carter Harrison. Apparently he was never concerned with prostitution, but if any man wanted to pander to the more respectable vices it was necessary to "see Mike." And Mike's decisions were final. McDonald's rise to political power began with the election of Mayor Colvin, and increased rapidly when he became a friend of Carter Harrison, then a member of the Cook County Board of Commissioners, and later a member of Congress and Mayor of Chicago for many years. Harrison, known to the people as "Our Carter," was a consummate politician and a rabble rouser second to none; his speeches were gems of demagoguery, and his antics were those of a clown. "Every day on the streets," wrote Lloyd Lewis, "people cheer the 225-pound Mayor as he thunders by on his galloping horse, his slouch hat and big beard rakish in the Chicago winds. The masses love his hot, witty head, his habit of listening to their woes, his private and eternal ambition to catch a burglar some night in his mansion—and kill him." [14] Once on a vote-getting tour of the city, at mass meetings in the foreign districts, Harrison successively claimed Irish, Jewish, German, Hungarian and Polish descent. Finally he arrived at a Negro meeting, and gave this thought to the sea of worshiping black faces:

"I regret that the blood of your glorious race does not flow in my veins, but ladies and gentlemen, I say to you that I am proud of the fact that in childhood I was nursed at the breast of a dear old Negro mammy."

As Harrison climbed the ladder, Mike McDonald was at his elbow, proffering sage advice and delivering the votes of the underworld. The gambler was one of Harrison's principal advisers during the latter's four consecutive terms as Mayor, from 1879 to 1887, and when "Our Carter" ran again in 1892 his campaign was organized and managed by McDonald, who by this time was leader of the Cook County Democratic ma-

[14] *Chicago, the History of its Reputation*, page 158.

chine and an important factor in state politics through his friendship with John Altgeld. In the 1880's, with his gambling interests well organized, and their safety assured by the presence of Carter Harrison in the Mayor's chair, McDonald extended the scope of his operations and took a whirl at legitimate business. He speculated heavily in downtown real estate, bought the Chicago *Globe* and ran it for several years, and was associated with Charles T. Yerkes in the development of Chicago traction lines, in particular the Lake Street Elevated. In all of these enterprises McDonald made money. He made more, not quite so legitimately, in 1888, when a gang of politicians, of which he was one, grafted a fortune out of Cook County building contracts. Several of the crooks went to jail. McDonald, however, not only escaped punishment, but presented and collected a bill of $67,000 for painting the buildings. But the feeling engendered by the steal destroyed whatever chance he might have had of being elected to Congress, an ambition which he had cherished for years.

The Chicago police were active against the gambling houses for two or three years after Harrison went out of office in 1887, but only the resorts run by the smaller fry were actually closed. In 1892 Harrison was elected Mayor for the fifth time, and his platform, like those of his previous campaigns, pledged a wide-open town. During his last administration he more than made good on his promises. After his victory at the polls, and during the period of the World's Fair in 1893, the lid was off in Chicago as it never was before and never has been since. Not even Mike McDonald and his efficient organization could keep track of the horde of sharpers who swarmed into the city and set their traps for the money-laden suckers who had come to gape at the wonders of the Fair. "America has never seen a gambling orgy on such a scale," said Hugh S. Fullerton, a well-known magazine writer. "Tens of thousands of dollars an hour poured over the tables." [15] But these halcyon days came to an end when Carter Harrison was assassinated on the night of October 28th, 1893, by a disgruntled office-seeker. The sound of eulogies had scarcely subsided before the Civic Federation, formed by clergymen, bankers and business men largely as a result of exposures by the British journalist William T. Stead, who had found Chicago reeking with vice and corruption, had compelled Harrison's successor to close the gambling houses. At the same time the political power of Mike McDonald began to decline. By 1895 he was through as a politician and as a gambler, and had retired to enjoy his illgotten riches.

9

Mike McDonald the gambling house keeper was renowned only in sporting and political circles, but Mike McDonald the wronged husband was known to newspaper readers all over the United States. He had two wives, and both got into the headlines and dragged him in with them. The first was the wife of his youth and the mother of his two children, Mary Noonan McDonald. She received her first taste of publicity in the middle 1870's, when she shot a policeman who had blundered into her kitchen during a shake-down raid on The Store. McDonald's influence was sufficient to bring about her arraignment before a judge who held that she was justified in killing the invader of her home, and to guard against the possibility of more trouble Mike took her out of The Store and installed her as mistress of a fine mansion which he had built in Ashland Avenue near the home of Carter Harrison. Within a year, however, Mrs. McDonald again made news by eloping with Billy Arlington, a minstrel singer who had come to Chicago

---

[15] In a series of articles in the *American Magazine* for February, March and April, 1914.

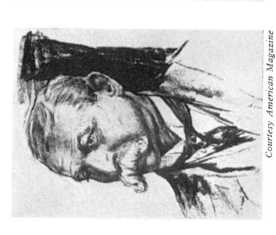

MIKE MC DONALD

TWO FAMOUS CHICAGO GAMBLERS: SILVER BILL RILEY (LEFT) AND JIM O'LEARY

as a member of the famed Emerson Troupe. McDonald set out in pursuit of the guilty pair, and columns in the newspapers kept the world informed of his progress across the country. He finally traced them to the Palace Hotel in San Francisco, and was in front of the hotel, waiting, when they returned from a drive into the country. He stopped the horses, but before he could do anything else his wife had jumped from the carriage and flung her arms about his neck.

"Don't shoot, Mike, for God's sake!" she cried. "It's all my fault! Take me back, for the love of God!"

Without a word to the trembling minstrel, McDonald led his wife to a railroad station and put her on a train bound for Chicago. There she resumed her place in the house on Ashland Avenue, and for several years she and Mike apparently lived happily enough. But McDonald was very busy, and she was much alone. With little to occupy her mind, she turned to religion, and had a magnificent private altar built into her home. She was frequently assisted in her devotions by the Rev. Joseph Moysant, Assistant Rector of the Church of Notre Dame, and McDonald never suspected that his wife and the stalwart young priest were celebrating an even more ancient mystery than the Mass until a day in 1889, when he came home to find that they had run away to Europe. In a fit of rage Mike smashed the altar and renounced Catholicism, not to return to the fold until he lay dying. Then he divorced his wife and declared that he was through with her forever. Mrs. McDonald and Father Moysant lived together in Paris for a few years, but the repentant priest at length entered a monastery, and she returned to Chicago and opened a rooming house.

In 1884 one of the playmates of Mike McDonald's children was a ten-year-old Jewish girl, Dora Feldman, for whom the gambler had a great but fatherly affection. He watched her grow to womanhood, when she removed from the neighbor-

303

hood and married Sam Barclay, a baseball player. She soon left Barclay and went on the stage, and McDonald saw her again in the chorus of a musical show in 1895, when she was twenty-one years old and he was fifty-six. He was overwhelmed by her lush beauty, and madly infatuated, embraced the Jewish religion and married her according to the rites of her faith. He built a grand new home for his bride on Drexel Boulevard, and they lived there until early in 1907, when McDonald was in his sixty-eighth year and scarcely a fit mate for a lusty young wife of thirty-three. On February 21st of that year Dora McDonald walked into the downtown office of Webster Guerin, a young commercial artist, and shot him dead with a revolver. When the police arrived she said that Guerin had been her lover, and that she had killed him because she "loved him so much."

"I told him I knew where his heart was," she said, "and I didn't miss it an inch."

At first Mike McDonald believed that Guerin had been blackmailing his wife, and that the shooting had been the hysterical outbreak of a frightened woman. But his faith in her was shattered when evidence began to pile up that Dora had become infatuated with young Guerin when he was still a boy in high school, and had pursued him so relentlessly that his mother had begged her to let him alone. Nevertheless, Mike McDonald provided for her defense, and engaged two of Chicago's ablest lawyers, A. S. Trude and James Hamilton Lewis, now United States Senator from Illinois.

"I don't ever want to see the —— —— again," he is said to have told Trude, "but save her if it costs every dollar I've got."

The skill of eminent counsel prevailed, and Dora McDonald was acquitted early in 1908, after a jury had deliberated for six and one-half hours. But Mike McDonald was not there to hear the verdict. He had died, a true Catholic once more, in the

304

Hospital of St. Anthony of Padua on August 9, 1907, with only his first wife at his bedside. His will, disposing of about $2,000,000, left one third of the estate and a special defense fund of $40,000 to Dora, and the remainder to his son and daughter.

And the *Police Gazette,* that candid recorder of human frailties, sagely remarked that "As Mike McDonald might have expressed it himself—a sucker has to die every minute to make room for the one that is born."

10

The Chicago gambling houses which had been closed at the behest of the Civic Federation after the murder of Carter Harrison were again in operation early in 1894. The Mayor, John P. Hopkins, said that "certain business men" had asked that the resorts be allowed to reopen; he believed with these captains of industry that gambling in the open, where it could be watched and regulated by the police, was less objectionable than "in secret and lawless places." To the Civic Federation this reasoning was specious; wide open or under cover, gambling was a vice to be extirpated. A special sub-committee was appointed under the chairmanship of the Rev. W. G. Clarke, and an active campaign was begun. When argument failed to influence the Mayor, the committee resorted to direct action, and in September of 1894 employed a raiding force of forty special constables. Attacks were made upon Harry Varnell's, John Condon's, and Billy Fagan's House of David. At Varnell's the raiders battered down the doors, surmounted a barricade of chairs and tables—and were arrested on warrants issued by an Evanston Justice of the Peace. At Condon's they seized the gambling equipment, but a writ of replevin compelled them to return it intact. They succeeded, however, in bringing Billy Fagan's paraphernalia into court before Judge Theodore Brentano, and when that able jurist refused to recognize a replevin issued by the Coroner they burned Fagan's wheels and tables in the furnace of City Hall.

Many of the first-class houses soon went out of business rather than submit to the continual harassing by the Civic Federation, and those that didn't were operated on a much smaller scale behind barred doors. Until the election of Fred Busse as Mayor in 1907, gambling was largely confined to betting on the races, and naturally Chicago became the biggest handbook and poolroom town in the country. The shining lights of the profession during this era were Big Jim O'Leary, Hot Stove Jimmy Quinn, Mont Tennes; and John Condon, an erstwhile Indiana barber who was better known as "Johnny Fix-'Em." Hot Stove Jimmy was king of the North Side, and for a year or so Mont Tennes was his prime minister. But Tennes was ambitious and wanted a realm of his own. He set about organizing the remainder of the city, and within two years was head of a syndicate which had absorbed Quinn and dominated gambling, especially the handbooks, all over Chicago. For years Tennes led the forces of the combine in a destructive war aginst the independents, in which dwellings, saloons and gambling houses were bombed and several men killed. The police finally announced that they had stopped the carnage, but actually the gamblers became quiet because they had patched up a truce and divided the territory.

Johnny Fix-'Em Condon was one of Mike McDonald's protégés, and first appeared in Chicago as handy man and fixer for the McDonald–Varnell–Hankins syndicate. He opened his own house, with McDonald's blessing, in the late 1880's, but was always more interested in horse racing than in Faro or Roulette. His most successful period began in the middle

1890's, when he became the owner of the Harlem Race Track. For many years, according to the New York *World* of October 6, 1901, he was "the real power behind the throne in the Western Jockey Club," which controlled all of the Western and Southern tracks. To run a race course and dominate the racing of half a continent was not, in those days, incompatible with the operation of handbooks and pool rooms. Condon lost his eyesight by disease in 1899, and thereafter was led about by a man-servant, but his zest for gambling remained unimpaired. Two of his biggest enterprises were organized and carried through after this misfortune occurred. In 1900 he and Big Jim O'Leary ran a club house in Hot Springs, Ark., from which they took profits of $250,000 in one season. A year later Condon headed a syndicate—O'Leary was a member—which established a placed called "Chicago's Monte Carlo" at Long Beach, Ind., twenty-three miles from the Chicago City Hall and thirty minutes from the city by special train. The opening of the resort was announced to the sporting world of Chicago by an elegantly engraved invitation:

"You are invited to the finest equipped and only Monte Carlo in America, delightfully situated in Lake County, Ind., near the Standard Oil Company's Works at Whiting. No 'interference' from county or State officials. Open the year around."

Accompanying the invitation was a handsomely printed booklet which contained a map of the Monte Carlo district, the time of special trains, a description of the interior of the $32,000 building, pictures of the various gambling devices, and, on the inside cover, this blurb:

"This place is delightfully located on the south shore of Lake Michigan, the surroundings being picturesque, the

307

rooms large and airy, having a gallery on the four sides of the building where you can enjoy the cooling breezes off the lake. Ample accommodations for 5,000 people. Why go to the race tracks when you can come here and play all the races at the tracks named below? Washington Park, Brighton Beach, Fort Erie, Newport, St. Louis, Harlem and Hawthorne.

"All the finest brands of wines, liquors and cigars."

In the blue prints at least, for many of the main features never got beyond that stage, Chicago's Monte Carlo was probably the most extraordinary gambling house ever projected in the United States—a castle protected by stockades, barbed wire and picket fences, armed lookouts in sentry boxes, alarm boxes, ferocious bloodhounds described as veritable man-eaters; and with tunnels leading outside the grounds and arrangements for setting fire to the place if the police succeeded in gaining an entrance. But as the New York *World* said, "Visitors noticed the great divergence between the plans outlined in the map and the actual surroundings of the place."

Condon and his associates made many mistakes in planning their resort, but their worst blunder was in advertising that there would be no interference. This put both state and county officials squarely on the spot, and aroused the clergymen of Indiana to screaming fury. The former promptly disavowed any knowledge of the scheme, and the latter scattered over the state a facsimile of the booklet, together with a statement of their own calling upon the Governor to demolish the place and characterizing the gamblers as "those vipers and corrupters of public morals who would debauch the youth of our state by their glowing invitation to visit this hell-hole."

The Monte Carlo never had a chance. It was opened on a small scale early in the spring of 1901, but closed after a few

308

months partly because the authorities were preparing to proceed against it, and partly because of unexpected opposition from the Chicago race tracks. There was another grand opening in the fall of 1901, but little business was done, and the enterprise was soon abandoned. It was probably the biggest flash in the pan in the history of American gambling.

CHAPTER XI

WESTWARD HO!

THE third and final phase of the expansion of gambling in early America was the westward movement of sharpers which began with the establishment of the Texas Republic and increased in intensity during the California gold rush and the era of development which followed the annexation of Texas and the territories of the Pacific Coast and the Southwest. The invasion reached its peak with the rise of the frontier cattle towns and mining camps and the building of the trans-continental railroads which the gamblers followed step by step, carrying on their thieving business in every mushroom town that sprang up along the route. John O'Connor wrote in 1873 that at one time during the construction of the Union Pacific, "at least three hundred sharpers were operating along the line of this road, with their ropers, cappers and other stand-bys, all of whom were engaged in conducting such games or frauds as waxed card *Monte,* snapper roulettes, marked cards *Vingt et Un,* red and black lottery, and Three-Card Monte." [1] By the middle 1870's, in all the vast area from the Rio Grande to the Canadian border and from the Mississippi to the Pacific Ocean, conditions were almost precisely the same as they had been in the East and South forty years earlier. The entire country swarmed with itinerant Faro artists, *Monte* dealers, short card cheats and Three-Card Monte swindlers, many of whom were notorious outlaws and gunmen as well; while every town and hamlet, from Podunk-at-the-crossroads to cosmopolitan San Francisco, was infested by pro-

[1] *Wanderings of a Vagabond,* page 213.

fessional gamblers, and harbored skinning-houses and occasional square games in numbers according to the population, the prosperity and gullibility of the suckers, and the venality of the politicians and office-holders.

Of all the towns west of St. Louis, however, only San Francisco, Denver and Kansas City reached the status of first-class gambling centers and held it for any considerable time. And by far the most important was San Francisco. No other American community has ever experienced such a carnival of gambling as reigned in the California city during the fabulous days of Forty-niners. For almost ten years after the discovery of gold on a fork of the American River in 1848, the gaming resorts of San Francisco seldom closed their doors, and were crowded with eager suckers at all hours of the day and night. As the town's first historians said, "gambling was *the* amusement, *the* grand occupation of many classes, apparently the life and soul of the place . . . around the tables themselves the players often stood in lines three or four deep, everyone vieing with his neighbor for the privilege of reaching the board, and staking his money as fast as the wheel and ball could be rolled or the card turned. Judges and clergymen, physicians and advocates, merchants and clerks, contractors, shopkeepers, tradesmen, mechanics and laborers, miners and farmers, all adventurers in their kind—everyone elbowed his way to the gaming table, and unblushingly threw down his golden or silver stake." [2] Another observer of the period, the British artist J. D. Borthwick, found gambling so widespread in early San Francisco that in a typical resort could even be found "little urchins, or little scamps rather, ten or twelve years of age, smoking cigars as big as themselves, with the air of men who were quite up to all the hooks and crooks of this wicked world (as indeed they were), and losing their hundred

---

[2] *The Annals of San Francisco,* by Frank Soulé, John H. Gihon, M.D., and James Nisbet; New York, 1855; pages 248–50.

dollars at a pop with all the nonchalance of an old gambler." [3]

The first and most renowned gambling house established in San Francisco after the beginning of the gold stampede was El Dorado, which was opened in the spring of 1848 in a canvas tent fifteen by twenty-five feet, on the present site of the Hall of Justice at Washington and Kearny Streets. The operators of the resort paid rental for the tent, and for a large square building of rough boards which soon replaced it, at the rate of $40,000 a year. This may seem a fantastic sum for such quarters, but it was not so considered in San Francisco at a time when an apple or a boiled egg cost from one to five dollars, tea or coffee four to five dollars a pound, bricks a dollar each, whisky thirty dollars a bottle, lumber $500 a thousand feet, and common tacks approximately $192 a pound. For a very brief period El Dorado had a monopoly of first-class gambling in San Francisco, but scores of other places were quickly opened as adventurers from all strata of society, and of virtually every nationality, continued to pour into the town; and as miners began to return from the diggings with their pokes filled with gold dust and their hearts yearning for the flesh pots and the excitement of the gaming tables. By the spring of 1850, when an overwhelming majority of the 25,000 inhabitants were men under forty, and a woman was so rare a spectacle that the sight of one daintily picking her way among the mudholes was enough to cause a suspension of business, San Francisco harbored no fewer than a thousand regularly established gambling resorts. The largest and most prosperous were on Portsmouth Square, the Plaza of the old Mexican town of Yerba Buena, and for many years the heart of the city. "The whole of the eastern side of Portsmouth Square," said *The Annals of San Francisco,* "three-fourths of the northern, and a portion of the southern sides were occupied by buildings specially devoted to gambling." In addition, every saloon and

[3] *The Gold Hunters,* by J. D. Borthwick; page 67.

hotel bar-room contained two or more tables of Faro, *Monte* and Chuck-a-Luck, while outside in the muddy streets roamed a horde of free lance Thimble-Riggers and Three-Card Monte throwers. Some of these latter swindlers were mere children—Borthwick describes one as "a precocious little blackguard of fourteen or fifteen," who scornfully refused to pitch a broad for a bet of less than a hundred dollars.

The best known of the Portsmouth Square houses, besides El Dorado, which was owned during most of its existence by Thomas J. A. Chambers, were Dennison's Exchange; the Empire; the Mazourka; the Arcade; the Varsouvienne; the Ward House, afterward renamed the Bryant House and operated by Colonel J. J. Bryant of Vicksburg fame; the Parker House, where a syndicate of gamblers headed by the appropriately named Colonel Jack Gamble paid $60,000 a year for the second floor; the Fontine House; La Souciedad; the St. Charles; the Alhambra; the Verandah; the Aguila de Oro; and the Bella Union, which in later years became San Francisco's most celebrated music hall. Of equal importance, though not on the Square, were Bill Briggs' house in Montgomery Street, and a resort in Commercial Street operated by Steve Whipple, who sometimes worked the steamboats which ran between San Francisco and Sacramento on the Sacramento River. Bill Briggs was probably the most picturesque, as well as the most popular, of gold rush gamblers. His idiosyncrasies are still recalled in San Francisco, and so are his benefactions; he gave thousands of dollars to stranded miners and gamesters, and to charities of every description. He held the fixed opinion that the possession of any coin smaller than a silver dollar was unlucky, and every morning at four o'clock he collected all the small change which had been taken in over his tables during the night. If the weather was bad, he simply tossed the money into the street; if the weather was good, he walked down to the vegetable market and flung the coins among the boys who gathered the refuse of the market to feed their goats. Briggs and Colonel Jack Gamble were the last of the old-timers to abandon gambling in San Francisco. Colonel Gamble, whose final venture was a roadhouse on the San Jose highway fourteen miles from the city, quit in 1873, but Briggs kept his Faro game going until 1880, when he succumbed to repeated raids and destruction of his furniture and gaming apparatus by the police. Briggs died about 1891.

All of early San Francisco's gambling resorts were periodically destroyed by the great fires which devasted the town half a dozen times in 1849 and the early 1850's, but after each conflagration they were quickly rebuilt, with little or no change in exterior design or interior arrangement or equipment. Thus a description of any given establishment applied with approximate accuracy to all succeeding houses of the same name. The first-class places seem to have been as alike as peas in a pod—a large square or rectangular room with a row of pillars down the center, a bar at one side, an elevated platform at one end, the floor of rough boards crowded with gaming tables and a profusion of gilded furniture, the walls covered with gaudy hangings and exotic pictures, and many lamps blazing from the ceiling. Compared to the magnificent houses which flourished in New York, Washington and New Orleans at the same time, they were crude and tawdry. That a contrary impression prevailed in the East was due to the imaginative tales of travelers, and, in New York, to statements made in the second annual report of the Association for the Suppression of Gambling, which was published in 1852 and had a wide circulation. Quoting from an unidentified source, the report declared that "the gambling saloons of San Francisco are the most splendid in the world," and that "the saloons of London, Havana, New York or New Orleans are far beneath them in splendor of decoration and magnitude of dealings." The report continued:

"The hells are fitted up with superb furniture and appointments. On the gilded walls, often painted in fresco, are grouped copies of the most beautiful gems of modern and ancient art. . . . The couches, lounges, divans, etc., scattered along the sides of these temples of chance, heaped with cushions of crimson, green and gold, purple and azure, are of every graceful and lovely shape. . . . Upon the marble tables are scattered flower-shaped vases of alabaster or Bohemian glass of every hue, and quaint jars of costly porcelain. The lamps are veiled, until their light softly floats in the air, and mysteriously reveals the surrounding objects."

Borthwick's account of a gold rush gambling house was more restrained, and apparently more in accordance with the facts. "On entering a first-class gambling-room," he wrote, "one found a large well-proportioned saloon sixty or seventy feet long, brilliantly lighted up by several very fine chandeliers, the walls decorated with ornamental painting and gilding, and hung with large mirrors and showy pictures. . . . There were a dozen or more tables in the room, each with a compact crowd of eager betters around it, and the whole room was so filled with men that elbowing one's way between the tables was a matter of difficulty. The atmosphere was quite hazy with the quantity of tobacco smoke, and was strongly impregnated with the fumes of brandy . . . it was the fashion, while standing betting at a table, to have a lot of dollars in one's hands, and to keep shuffling them backwards and forwards like so many cards. . . . The people composing the crowd were men of every class, from the highest to the lowest." [4] The well-known California journalist John P. Young, in his two-volume history of San Francisco, wrote that "we may trust the description of the gambling saloons up to a certain point . . . but there is reason to believe that the

[4] *The Gold Hunters*, pages 65–66.

showiest were tawdry affairs despite the almost uniform testimony of the argonauts to the contrary." He concluded that if reproduced today the finest of the gaming resorts "would hardly be considered an attractive addition to the water front of a sea port."

The extraordinary scarcity and high cost of food prevented the serving of the rich suppers and free liquor which were such important features of public gambling in the East and the South, but the keepers of the San Francisco houses titillated the visiting suckers in other ways. Every first-class resort had a band of music which performed throughout the hours of play, and many provided a special table at which, as an enraptured German visitor said, "a real living, pretty, modest-looking young girl, in a close-fitting black silk dress, her slender fingers adorned with rings," sold tea, coffee, chocolate, cakes and preserves. As added attractions to the band and the real, living girl at the tea and cake tables, some of the Portsmouth Square houses offered variety shows and special musical numbers by harpists and violinists, among them a woman who received two ounces of gold dust for an hour's fiddling at the Alhambra each evening. The most popular of the variety performers, however, was not a woman, but a ballad signer named Charley Schultze, the star of the Bella Union. His best number, and a sure tear-jerker, was *You'll Never Miss Your Sainted Mother Till She's Dead and Gone to Heaven,* sung to the tune of *Aloha.*

The principal gambling games in San Francisco, in the order of their popularity, were *Monte,* Faro, Roulette, Chuck-a-Luck, *Vingt et Un* and *Rouge et Noir.* During the first few years of the gold rush *Monte* was dealt almost exclusively by Mexicans, while Americans handled the cards at the tables devoted to the tiger. Borthwick said that because of its apparent simplicity, *Monte* was largely played by novices, but that as dealt in San Francisco it was "a game at which the dealer has such advantages, and

316

which, at the same time, gives him such facilities for cheating, that anyone who continues to bet at it is sure to be fleeced." Faro was the favorite game for heavy betting, and "was generally played by systematic gamblers, who knew, or thought they knew, what they were about." San Francisco legend has it that all of these games were square, and that the sharper who attempted to operate a crooked house was invariably killed by indignant suckers or driven from the town by an outraged citizenry. As a matter of fact, there were hundreds of brace games throughout the town, and even in the largest establishments, though none were run as out-and-out skinning houses, skullduggery on the part of the artists and croupiers was common. The two-card Faro box and the magnetized Roulette wheel were used in San Francisco as they were everywhere else in the United States.

In the aggregate, enormous sums were won and lost, principally the latter, by the multitude of suckers who frequented the early gambling houses. The daily turnover in such resorts as El Dorado and the Bella Union is said to have often exceeded $200,000, and for months on end was seldom less than $100,000. But the individual bets were comparatively small, ranging from fifty cents to ten dollars and averaging less than five dollars. Even the great plungers rarely risked more than two or three thousand dollars at a time, and then only "when the rich gamester was getting desperate, or a half-tipsy miner had just come from the diggings with a handsome pile." Occasionally, however, very large amounts were ventured upon a single turn at Faro. At the Bella Union in 1850 a miner staked an eighty-five pound sack of gold dust, worth $16,000, and won; but a week later another gold-digger lost $20,000 in an attempt to perform a similar feat. A free-lance professional gambler named Jim Rynders won $89,000 in three days' play at Steve Whipple's place, but Whipple won it back within a week, and $11,000 besides. San Franciscans still like to tell how the famous Lucky Baldwin once won $200,000 on a single turn at El Dorado, but the tale is of extremely doubtful authenticity. In the first place, Baldwin was a poor man until long after El Dorado had closed its doors; in the second place, Baldwin's important gambling was done at the race tracks. He played Poker frequently with his friends, but seldom for more than a fifty-cent limit.

The largest single bet ever turned for at Faro in San Francisco, as far as the records show, was $60,000, and was made and lost by Ed Moses, who owned shares in several gambling houses, in the course of an eight-hour tussle with the Tiger at El Dorado which cost him a total of $200,000. Soon after Moses' memorable game a nineteen-year-old boy, playing in the same house, won $22,000 on three successive turns of the ace, and had sense enough to walk away with his gains. "He was followed by a miner," said the report of the New York Association for the Suppression of Gambling, "a rough, reckless, hardy yet honest-looking fellow, who placed his bag of dust, recently acquired, upon the card which had thus proved so lucky for the youth. He won also, and doubling the bet, he won again. Elated by his success, he placed the whole on the same card, and was followed by at least a dozen others. All around, and on the card were heaps of gold, money, dust, ore and counters. . . . Slowly the cards went forth —not a sound was heard until an ace was revealed, favorable to the bank. Curses and imprecations, shouts of 'foul! foul!' with hoarse threats and expressions—until the two dealers coolly produced their revolvers, declared everything fair, and the bank a winner of $95,000."

The men who owned the first-class gambling houses—the Bryants, the Gambles, the Whipples and the Briggses—were for the most part veterans of a thousand gaming ventures in the East and the South, and were typical of their class; they were among the richest, most popular and best dressed men in San Francisco as their brethren were in New York, Washington and

EL DORADO IN 1850

A GAMBLING HOUSE IN SANTA FÉ, 1859

New Orleans. But the small fry gambler, and in particular the artist and croupier who dealt Faro and *Monte* and spun the Roulette wheel, appear to have been of a new and distinct type, *sui generis* in California. Certainly he was unknown in other parts of the country, and since he could not have been born and grown to manhood in San Francisco, his origin remains a mystery, unless perchance he sprang full-panoplied from the brow of Old King Faro. Almost without exception historians of the gold rush describe him as tall, thin and cadaverous, clad in funereal black from head to toe and apparently tottering slowly and dejectedly to the grave. He was utterly emotionless, he made no friends and trusted no man, and in all circumstances he was taciturn and self-sufficient. Hubert Howe Bancroft, California's most eminent historian, wrote that "the character of the typical gambler of the flush times is one of the queerest mixtures in human nature. . . . Supreme self-command is his cardinal quality; yet, except when immersed in the intricacies of a game, his actions appear to be governed only by impulse and fancy. . . . He is never known to steal except at cards; and if caught cheating he either fights or blandly smiles his sin away, suffers the stakes to be raked down without a murmur, treats good-humoredly, and resumes the game unruffled. . . . He accustoms himself to do without sleep, and if necessary can go for several days and nights without rest. . . . He deals his game with the most perfect *sang froid,* and when undergoing the heaviest losses there is no trembling of fingers or change of expression." [5]

This master of the dead pan customarily went armed to the teeth, a double-barreled derringer at his elbow and his pockets bulging with pistols and bowie-knives. He flashed into action with these weapons on very little provocation, but as Bancroft said, "his swiftest vengeance and cruelest butchery seem rather the result of policy than passion. . . . He is as ready with his

[5] *California Inter Pocula;* San Francisco, 1888; pages 705–6.

pistol as with his toothpick, but he never uses it unless he is right; then, he will kill a man as mercilessly as he would brush a fly from his immaculate linen." [6] The speed and efficiency with which the gambler fulfilled his lethal obligations gave him such a fearsome reputation in early San Francisco that, according to Borthwick, "In the forenoon, when gambling was slack, the gamblers would get up from their tables, and, leaving exposed upon them, at the mercy of the heterogeneous crowd circulating through the room, piles of gold and silver, they would walk away, seemingly as little anxious for the safety of their money as if it were under lock and key in an iron chest." Borthwick put it mildly when he said that "it was strange . . . in a city where robberies and violence were so rife, that, when out at night in unfrequented quarters, one walked pistol in hand in the middle of the street, to see money exposed in such a way as would be thought madness in any other part of the world." [7]

2

The great era of public gambling in San Francisco was from 1848 through 1851. By the middle of 1852 the town had assumed an aspect of permanence and showed clearly signs of future greatness, thousands of immigrants had established homes and businesses, and the gaming table was no longer the only place where a man could find amusement. In consequence, the influence of the professional gambler and the popularity of the gambling house had definitely begun to wane. As early as April 7, 1852, the San Francisco *Herald* declared that while the gaming places were still "a prominent feature of life in San Francisco," public opinion was in the main opposed to their existence, and "they are tolerated for no other reason, that we know of, than that they are charged heavily for licenses." The ordinance under

[6] *Ibid.*
[7] *The Gold Hunters,* page 71.
320

which they were permitted to operate without interference so long as the license fees were paid was supplanted in the winter of 1854 by a state-wide law which made gambling and keeping a gambling house a felony. Although this law was never rigidly enforced, together with the Vigilante activities in 1856 it afforded a clear indication of the trend of public feeling. Moreover, by removing the cloak of legality it put the gamblers wholly at the mercy of the politicians, and several houses were closed partly as a reform gesture and partly because they refused to pay tribute. The statute was repealed in 1859 as a result of efficient lobbying at Sacramento by Colonel Jack Gamble, but the revival of gambling which followed, in volume of play and in number of houses in operation, was trivial in comparison with the halcyon days of the gold rush. Another law passed in 1873, and reinforced by local ordinances, completed the rout. A few old-timers continued to run their games for half a dozen years or so, but repeated raids by the police eventually compelled them to quit. Since Bill Briggs closed his doors in 1880, it is doubtful if three banking games of any consequence have been in operation in San Francisco at any one time, even during the wide-open period in which the city was controlled by the notorious Abe Reuf and his corrupt political machine.

Another factor which contributed to the decline of the gambling house in San Francisco was the gradually increasing importance of Poker. For various reasons, among them lack of facilities in the hells of Portsmouth Square and the fact that the suckers of the period were too impatient for anything but the quick action of a banking game, Poker was virtually unknown during the gold rush, and was not played to any great extent until the late 1850's. It didn't become really popular until about 1870, but since that time it has been the favorite gambling game of San Francisco, although in recent years its supremacy has been seriously threatened by Craps. From the early 1870's to the middle 1890's, however Poker had no serious rival, and as a Poker-playing town San Francisco was second only to Washington. Scores of Poker rooms, many of them elegantly furnished, were in operation all over the city, and were especially numerous in the business and financial districts. As late as 1891, according to the reformed gambler John Philip Quinn, "all the cigar stands along Market Street have back rooms for Poker parties. . . . The games are small, a twenty-five dollar pot being considered a bonanza." [8] Theoretically, these and similar places were public; actually, each had its regular clientele and was seldom visited by strangers. All varieties of Poker, from Show-Down to Spit-in-the-Ocean, were played, but Draw was the most popular except for a few years around 1880, when Stud had a great vogue. It was checked by the California Legislature, which in 1884 passed a law specifically prohibiting Stud Poker anywhere in the state.

The finest of San Francisco Poker rooms was probably the ornate establishment kept in Kearny Street during the 1870's by Charles Felton, who afterward became prominent in California politics. Felton, himself a famous Poker player, barred professional gamblers and required no contributions to a kitty. Instead, he depended for his profit upon his own winnings and the sale of liquor. More typical of the Poker places, however, was the Market Street resort of Mose Gunst, which was in its heyday in the late 1880's. Gunst deducted fifty cents from every pot of a dollar and a half or more, and maintained a staff of salaried pluggers who sat in the games and turned their winnings over to the house. "While the direct charge of cheating cannot be made against the establishment," wrote Quinn, "the cards are played very close, and the visitor finds it an exceedingly hard game to beat." [9]

---

[8] *Fools of Fortune,* by John Philip Quinn; Chicago, 1892; page 443.
[9] *Ibid.*

The biggest Poker games ever dealt in San Francisco were not played at the public rooms, but at private sessions in the old Baldwin Hotel, which also had rooms specially equipped for dice games; in the famous Cinch Room of the Palace Hotel; [10] and at the Pacific Club, one of the city's oldest social organizations, which later merged with the Union Club. The participants in these battles were ten or a dozen of the richest men in the West, among them James C. Flood, one of the original owners of the fabulously rich Big Bonanza mines of Nevada; William C. Ralston, president of the Bank of California and the foremost San Franciscan of his time, who was drowned in the Pacific Ocean the day after his bank failed in 1875; and four Nevada Senators—James G. Fair, John Percival Jones, William Sharon, and William M. Stewart, all of whom had amassed enormous wealth through the ownership and manipulation of mining properties on the Comstock Lode. These men probably played for consistently higher stakes than any other group of Poker addicts in the history of the game—with them a $50,000 pot was a common-place, and one of $100,000 was not unusual. Sharon was probably the best player of the group, or at any rate the luckiest—over a period of some fifteen years his winnings at the Pacific Club alone are said to have amounted to a million dollars. They would have been greater if he had never played with Ralston, for the banker could always beat him. One of the games in which Ralston triumphed over Sharon was thus described by a collector of Poker lore:

---

[10] The Cinch Room was an out-of-the-way annex to the billiard room of the Palace, and was established for the especial use of visiting Nevadans when the hotel was opened in 1875. It was equipped with easy chairs, innumerable brass spittoons, many decks of cards, and a long table covered with books, magazines and newspapers. At first the Nevadans used the room principally as a place in which to play Cinch, a variation of All-Fours which was also known as Double Pedro or High Five, but after a few years it was devoted almost entirely to Poker.

"Five of the big fish were in the game and they were playing jack pots. Sharon opened and Ralston and two others stayed. There was some light chipping of $100 and $200 several times around, when Ralston strengthened his play and began raising by thousands. Sharon and Ralston soon had the play to themselves, and it was not long before there was $150,000 in the pot. Then Sharon met a raise with a $50,000 counter. Ralston studied only a moment and then came back with a raise of $150,000. Sharon did not take long to decide his play.

" 'I quit, Bill,' he said, and shuffled his cards into the deck.

"Ralston was so delighted over having made his bold partner lay down that he spread his hand, disclosing a pair of tens. Sharon never told what he held in his hand until after Ralston's death. It was a pair of jacks." [11]

3

Denver's period of importance as a frontier gambling center began almost a decade after the California gold rush. In the summer of 1859, about a year after the town had been laid out on the banks of Cherry Creek, Denver's population consisted of fewer than a thousand men and half a dozen women, all housed in some three hundred buildings of hewn pine logs. A few of these structures were covered with hand-split shingles, but most were roofed with logs spread with prairie grass and dirt. Only three or four had glass windows or board floors, and chairs and other comforts were virtually unknown. Hearths and fireplaces were of adobe, and the chimneys were constructed of a framework of sticks plastered with mud. Albert D. Richardson, a New York journalist who in 1859 visited Colorado in company

[11] *Jack Pots, Stories of the Great American Game,* by Eugene Edwards; Chicago, 1900; page 177.

with Horace Greeley, described the town as "a most forlorn and desolate-looking metropolis," and wrote that Denver society was a strange medley of "Americans from every quarter of the Union, Mexicans, Indians, half-breeds, trappers, speculators, gamblers, desperadoes, broken-down politicians and honest men. . . . The men who gathered about our coach on its arrival were attired in slouch hats, tattered woolen shirts, buckskin pantaloons, and moccasins; and had knives and revolvers suspended from their belts." The settlement and its inhabitants reminded Richardson of the story of the sailor who was asked to describe the manners and customs of savages among whom he had been shipwrecked. "They have no manners," replied the sailor, "and their customs are disgusting." A great change came over Denver, however, with the discovery of gold on Clear Creek and elsewhere in the Pike's Peak region. Returning to the town after an absence of four months, Richardson found that it had "developed wonderfully. . . . Frame and brick edifices were displacing mud-roofed log cabins. Two theaters were in full blast, and at first glance I could recognize only two buildings. . . . The population was improving, for more families had settled here. . . ." [12] Within another two years Denver boasted more than 3,000 inhabitants; stores, hotels, newspapers, churches, banking-houses and other enterprises had been established, and the city limits had been extended to embrace 5,000 acres of building lots. By 1865 some of these lots, which in 1859 had been traded even up for revolvers, were selling for as high as $12,000 each.

[12] *Beyond the Mississippi,* by Albert D. Richardson; Hartford, 1869; pages 177–78, 186, 279. Richardson, one of the best-known journalists and war correspondents of his time, was the victim in a famous New York murder case. On November 26, 1869, he was shot and mortally wounded in the office of the New York *Tribune* by Daniel McFarland, an Assistant City Assessor, whose wife had divorced him and announced her engagement to the journalist. She and Richardson were married a few days before the latter's death on December 2, 1869. McFarland was tried in April, 1870, and acquitted.

Despite the primitiveness of living conditions in early Denver, the ubiquitous professional gambler was on hand almost from the time the first settler swung his ax against a pine tree. But for the first year or two of the town's existence the sharpers were few in numbers, and virtually all of their operations were carried on at the Denver House, one of the most famous of pioneer hotels, a low, one-story log building 130 feet long and thirty-six feet wide, with glassless windows and a dirt floor which was frequently sprinkled to keep down the dust. Horace Greeley and the journalist Richardson engaged lodgings at the Denver House, and "true to the national instinct," wrote the latter, "the occupants of its great drinking and gambling saloon demanded a speech. On one side the tipplers at the bar silently sipped their grog; on the other the gamblers respectfully suspended the shuffling of cards and the counting of money from their huge piles of coin, while Mr. Greeley, standing between them, made a strong anti-drinking and anti-gambling address, which was received with perfect good humor." [13]

The "great drinking and gambling saloon" of the Denver House was approximately forty feet long and extended the entire width of the building. Richardson wrote that the resort was "always crowded with swarthy men armed and in rough costumes," and that one of their common amusements was shooting at the bartender. "At first he bore it laughingly," said Richardson, "but one day a shot grazed his ear, whereupon, remarking that there was such a thing as carrying a joke too far and that *this* was 'about played out,' he buckled on two revolvers and swore he would kill the next man who took aim at him. He was not troubled afterward." Besides the long bar, the furnishings of the Denver House saloon comprised a few rough benches and half a dozen tables at which the gamblers held forth from noon to early morning seven days a week. The principal swindles were

[13] *Ibid.*, page 178.

DENVER, 1859

Monte, Faro and Three-Card Monte, and men of every class
crowded into the Denver House to buck the games—Richardson
said that he saw "the probate judge of the county lose thirty
Denver lots in less than ten minutes," and "afterward observed
the county sheriff pawning his revolver for twenty dollars to
spend in betting at Faro." [14] The stakes in the Denver House
were small, but play was virtually continuous, and at many of
the tables the total was very large—Richardson commented on
the fact that one sharper, "in woolen shirt and jockey cap, drove
a thriving business at Three-Card Monte, which netted him
about one hundred dollars a day." The journalist recorded the
come-on spiel of this prosperous "broad pitcher," which is of
interest as showing how little the methods of the Monte men
have changed; it was used in the South and Southwest twenty
years before Denver was founded, and it can still be heard, almost word for word, wherever the game is played:

"Here you are, gentlemen; this ace of hearts is the winning card. Watch it closely. Follow it with your eye as I
shuffle. Here it is, and now here, now here, and now—
where? If you point it out the first time you win; but if you
miss you lose. Here it is, you see; now watch it again. This
ace of hearts, gentlemen, is the winning card. I take no bets
from paupers, cripples, or orphan children. The ace of
hearts. It is my regular trade, gentlemen, to move my hands
quicker than your eyes. I always have two chances to your
one. The ace of hearts. If your sight is quick enough, you
beat me and I pay; if not, I beat you and take your money.
The ace of hearts; who will go me twenty? It is very plain
and simple, but you can't always tell. Here you are, gentlemen; the ace, and the ace. Who will go me twenty dollars?" [15]

[14] *Ibid.,* page 188.
[15] *Ibid.,* pages 187–88.

The Denver House remained a favorite rendezvous for the gamblers for several years, but the facilities of the "great drinking and gambling saloon" were inadequate to accommodate the sharpers who swarmed into the town after the discovery of gold had started Denver on its first boom. Two or three gambling houses, magnificent establishments by frontier standards, soon made their appearance in Blake Street, where almost every building housed a saloon or a liquor store, and a few smaller places were opened in other parts of the town; while Thimble-Riggers, Monte throwers, and short card cheats operated in the streets and in the bar-rooms. Both the houses and the independent gamblers flourished despite the opposition of the respectable element of the population and the vigorous campaigns waged against them by William M. Byers, editor of the *Rocky Mountain News*. The sharpers and their allies, the rowdies and the desperadoes, made so many attempts to destroy the *News* printing plant— they set it afire several times and burned down Byers' home— that the editor and his employes worked with revolvers buckled about their waist and loaded shotguns standing beside desks and type-cases. On one occasion, following the publication of an especially vitriolic editorial, four armed gamblers surprised Byers in his office and dragged him through the streets to a saloon where only the strategy of a friend saved his life. "After his escape," wrote Albert D. Richardson, "the enraged gamblers rode back to the *News* office and fired several bullets into it. The typos returned the fire, killing one of the assailants. By this time half a dozen armed citizens reached the scene and chased the flying gamblers through the streets. One of the latter named Steele, galloping along Blake Street, met Thomas W. Pollock, whose horse was also upon a full run. Neither checked his speed. Both fired at the same instant. Pollock was unhurt; Steele fell dead with a charge of buckshot in his brain. Another of the gamblers was captured and barely escaped hanging. By a close vote in a popular assembly, he was permitted to leave the country." [16]

The early history of Denver, as far as gambling was concerned, in general paralleled that of San Francisco; but the activities of the sharpers were on a much smaller scale, for the Colorado metropolis failed to experience the spectacular growth which quickly transformed San Francisco from a mudhole into the most important American city west of St. Louis. Not until the late 1870's did Denver's population exceed 30,000, and the 100,-000 mark was not reached until about 1890, when the town entered upon its era of greatest development. Throughout the long pioneer period suckers were never plentiful enough to support as many gamblers and gambling houses as flourished in San Francisco during the gold rush. But San Francisco soon outgrew the blatant lawlessness of the early days, and within twenty-five years after the beginning of the gold stampede had reduced gambling to almost negligible proportions; while Denver retained many of its frontier characteristics for more than half a century, and except for a few brief periods of suppression, was a wide-open gambling town until the early 1920's. The palmy days of the sharper in Denver were from the late 1860's until about 1900, when the city seldom harbored fewer than a score of tough skinning houses, most of them operated in connection with dance halls, saloons and low variety theaters, and all sending a steady stream of Faro artists and short card swindlers into other parts of the West. Among these houses were such notorious resorts as the Palace, the Bucket of Blood, the Morgue, the Tivoli, the Chicken Coop; and Murphy's Exchange, better known as the Slaughter House, where more shooting affrays are said to have occurred than anywhere else in Denver.

Ed Chase, the celebrated Soapy Smith, and Lou Blonger were probably the dominating figures of Denver gambling. Chase was

[16] *Ibid.*, page 293.

the earliest of the trio; he was an important gambling house keeper for almost forty years. During a large part of his career he ran the Palace, with a saloon, a gambling den and a dance hall all in one big room. The Palace was a rough and boisterous dive, but there was seldom any real trouble, for during business hours Chase sat on a high stool above the bar with a double-barreled shotgun across his lap. In later years, about 1894, Chase abandoned the saloon and dance hall features of his business, and bought a private mansion in Curtis Street near Fifteenth. There he opened the Inter-Ocean Club, which is said to have been Denver's swankiest gambling house, and the only one which compared at all favorably with the great casinos of the East. It was also the only place where the stakes were consistently high. The sucker had no more chance at the Inter-Ocean than anywhere else, however, for in the long run he paid for the handsome furniture, the rich Oriental rugs, the fine paintings and engravings, the reading and lounging rooms, the free drinks at the bar, and the salaries of the club's forty employes.

Soapy Smith, who was born in Georgia in 1860 and christened Jefferson Randolph Smith, earned his nickname by his skill at a swindle known as "the soap game," which was invented in the early 1880's by a sharper in Leadville. To operate the soap game the swindler made a pitch on a street corner, with tripod and keister in the day time and in a buggy with gasoline torches at night, and attracted a crowd by playing on a musical instrument or making an interesting spiel. In the presence of the suckers he apparently wrapped cakes of soap in five, ten and twenty dollar bills, and then sold them for from one to five dollars each, the victims being allowed to choose their own cakes. Needless to say, it was all done by sleight of hand, and no one but the swindler's cappers ever received anything but soap. In addition to his gifts at this business, Soapy Smith was probably the cleverest of Thimble-Riggers, and was also an expert cheat at short cards. He ran a skinning house or two in Denver—the Tivoli was his best known establishment—and maintained "club rooms" where suckers were fleeced at Poker and Seven-Up; but primarily he was a confidence man, and his connection with gambling in Denver was mainly parasitic. As boss of the underworld—a position which he attained soon after his arrival in the town in 1888 and held for half a dozen years— Smith collected tribute from all of the gambling house keepers except Ed Chase and two or three others who were powerful enough to defy him, and allowed no con man or unattached gambler to operate unless he received a fat share of the profits. In return, Smith protected them from interference by the police and the politicians, who from Denver's earliest days appear to have been as corrupt a gang of office-holding crooks as ever infested an American city. In their dealings with Soapy Smith, and later with Lou Blonger, the only stipulation they made was that residents of Denver should not be victimized.

Smith's influence in Denver began to wane in the summer of 1893, after his brother Bascom had killed a California thief and gambler known as Shotgun Smith, and it definitely came to an end in the fall of the same year when a reform Governor reorganized the Denver Fire and Police Commission and dismissed several of Smith's friends. Smith left the town soon afterward, and for more than two years wandered about Texas and the Southwest, working the soap and Thimble-Rig games and attempting to organize a Foreign Legion for service with the Mexican Army. Denver was again wide open when he returned late in 1895, but Lou Blonger, a French-Canadian who had first appeared in Denver in 1880 as the owner of a combination dance hall, saloon and gambling den, was in control of the underworld, and was so deep in the good graces of the politicians that a private telephone line ran from his office to Police Headquarters. Smith was unable to dethrone Blonger, and the best he could do was to operate his soap game under Blonger's protection, with Blonger pocketing half the take. In the fall of 1897 Smith and a few numbers of his gang sailed for the Klondike, where Smith opened a saloon and gambling joint at Skagway and for some six months enjoyed greater power than he had ever been able to achieve in Denver. He was shot and killed at Skagway on July 8, 1898, by City Engineer Frank H. Reid, when he attempted to break up a meeting of citizens which had been called to consider ways and means of ridding Skagway of Soapy Smith and his kind.

Lou Blonger continued to dominate gambling and other swindles in Denver until 1922, when his gang was broken up by District Attorney Philip S. Van Cise. Blonger and a score of his associates, including Kid Duffy, his principal lieutenant and a former member of the famous Maybray gang, were sent to prison, where Blonger died after serving a few months of a seven to ten year sentence. He was seventy-three years old, and had been a crook for more than half a century. Much of the evidence upon which Blonger and his gangsters were convicted was provided by J. Frank Norfleet, a Texan who, having been twice swindled by confidence men, spent several years and a fortune bringing them to justice.

4

Kansas City's early renown was confined principally to the 1870's and the early 1880's, when the town's thirty or forty gambling houses included two of the finest hells in the West —the Main Street resort of Major Albert Showers, an old gentleman of great dignity and imposing presence who had once dealt Faro for Henry Clay and Daniel Webster in the Hall of the Bleeding Heart in Washington; and the establishment in

Missouri Avenue operated by Bob Potee, a cultured Virginia gambler in the Pendleton tradition, who drowned himself in the Missouri River when luck finally turned against him. Potee's place was probably the best known and most luxurious gambling house in the history of Kansas City; local legend says that it was wondrously furnished with velvet carpets, French mirrors, lace and damask curtains, wickedly comfortable divans and lounges, and Faro tables of glistening mahogany inlaid with mother-of-pearl.

Many of Kansas City's sharpers fled across the state line into Kansas City, Kan., in 1881, when the Missouri legislature passed a stringent anti-gambling law. Banking games were scarce in the Missouri city for the next quarter of a century, but the town's reputation as a sporting center was maintained by a score of "social clubs," where prosperous and unwary suckers were trimmed at short cards. One of the classic stories of Western gambling concerns a Boston merchant who was inveigled into one of these traps to play Poker with a group of Kansas City "business and professional men." He was soon convinced that he was being cheated, but he was unable to discover the *modus operandi,* and remained in the game until he had lost several thousand dollars. When he finally quit he still had insufficient evidence to justify a direct accusation, but in order that the sharpers might know that at least he suspected what had happened, he made this parting speech:

> "Gentlemen, I was assured that I should find this a gentleman's game. You are all gentlemen, and I know it. I appreciate the way in which I have been treated. I appreciate it thoroughly. I've got a few dollars left, and if one of you gentlemen will be kind enough to tell me where I can sit in a horse thief's game, I believe I'll go around there."

The most important of the gamblers who transferred their activities to Kansas City, Kan., were Gus Galbaugh, Clayton Maltby, Joe Bassett, George Frazier, and Tom Wallace, all of whom opened new houses near the border and maintained roping staffs on the Missouri side of the line. None suffered any loss of patronage. The biggest game was operated by Maltby, who once kept an accurate record for thirty days of all the money which passed over his Faro tables in return for chips. Although only one man bought as much as $100 worth at a time, the other buys ranging from one to fifty dollars, the total for the month was $63,843.75. Since at least two-thirds remained in Maltby's cash drawer, his Faro games had an annual gross income of approximately half a million dollars. A small portion of Maltby's winnings, and those of the other gaming-house keepers, went into the municipal coffers under a sort of licensing-by-fines system which is still used to regulate gambling in many American cities, and which for many years was employed virtually everywhere in the country. The operation of the system in Kansas City, Kan., where it is said to have been first developed, was thus described by a Kansas City newspaper on August 2, 1889:

"Three gambling houses in Kansas City, Kansas, were raided by the police last night. . . . The Chief of Police, accompanied by several officers, went to C. Maltby's place and found thirty or more men gambling. Their names were taken down and the proprietor was required to deposit $10 apiece for his visitors and $100 for himself as security for their appearance in the police court today. The police then went away and the gambling was immediately resumed. At G. F. Frazier's twenty-six men were playing, and the proprietor paid $300 to the officers. This morning Frazier, Galbaugh and Maltby appeared in the police court and were formally fined the amounts they had deposited. This is the manner in which gambling houses are, to all intents and purposes, licensed in Kansas City, Kan."

5

With the exception of the games in San Francisco and Denver, the biggest gambling in the West and the Southwest before the Civil War was carried on in El Paso and Santa Fe. The journalist Albert D. Richardson who traveled in southern Texas in 1859, reported that among El Paso's four hundred inhabitants "habitual gambling was universal, from the boy's game of pitching *quartillas* (three-cent coins) to the great saloons where huge piles of silver dollars were staked at *Monte*. In this little village," he continued, "a hundred thousand dollars often changed hands in a single night through the potent agencies of *Monte* and Poker." [17] A few weeks later Richardson was in Santa Fe, where he found "fifty American 'sporting men,' as professional gamblers are politely termed." Most of these sharpers had set up their tables in the hotel bar-rooms, at one of which Richardson "often saw three *Monte* banks in operation from daylight until midnight. . . . Enormous piles of silver weighed down the tables, and frequently ten thousand dollars changed hands in ten minutes. Business men would publicly lose or win a thousand dollars with the greatest nonchalance." [18] Richardson told of one man who won thirty thousand dollars at *Monte* in thirty days, and then lost it all, and more besides, within a week.

Santa Fe remained a center of Southwestern gambling for many years, but El Paso, which didn't begin to develop much as a city until after the turn of the twentieth century, and as late as 1880 had a population of less than eight hundred, failed to carry out its early promise, although it was wild enough in other

[17] *Beyond the Mississippi,* page 238.
[18] *Ibid.,* pages 251–52.

respects. As the rendezvous of Texas sporting men, El Paso was outstripped after the War by Austin, Fort Worth and San Antonio, which were wide open to cheating games of every description throughout the 1870's and most of the 1880's. Austin was the most important of the three, mainly because it was the capital of Texas, and for several months each year was the temporary home of those prime suckers, the members of the State Legislature. The statesmen were taught the finer points of Faro, *Monte,* Roulette and Poker in three first-class skinning houses which were the best equipped resorts on the western frontier. Austin's principal contributions to American gambling, however, were Phil Coe, a native of the town; and Ben Thompson, who was born elsewhere but always claimed Austin as his home, and who was so well liked in his early days that he served a term as City Marshal.

Thompson earned his living as a saloon-keeper and a professional gambler, but his talent as a sharper was mediocre—he was clumsy at short cards, and usually dealt Faro honestly because he wasn't clever enough to deal it otherwise. His great fame in the West is based entirely upon his exploits as a gun fighter. Bat Masterson once said that of all the bad men he had known on the frontier, Ben Thompson was the most dangerous; and other authorities agree that as a handy man with a gun Thompson was second only to that other Texan, the greatest killer since John A. Murrel—John Wesley Hardin, a preacher's son who had killed six men before he was sixteen, and by his twenty-fifth birthday had forty-odd notches on his pistol butt. The record of the Austin gun-slinger never approached that of Hardin, but at least a dozen men died at his hands during the decade in which his blazing guns, his inept Faro dealing, and the crude trickery at short cards which few were bold enough to denounce, were known and feared from the Dakotas to the Rio Grande. Thompson finally passed in his own checks on the night of March 11, 1884, when he and King Fisher, another Texas bad man who had become a Deputy Sheriff of Uvalde County after the dispersal by Rangers of his gang of road agents and cattle rustlers, were shot down in a variety theater in San Antonio. A Coroner's jury found that they had been killed by Joe Foster, a gambler, and a policeman named Coy, and returned a verdict of justifiable homicide. But the presence of five bullets in the top of Thompson's head, which could only have been fired from above, appeared to confirm the general belief that he and Fisher had been ambushed by riflemen hidden in the theater boxes.

Phil Coe was a sharper of a type frequently met with in San Francisco and the East, but seldom encountered on the frontier —tall, handsome, invariably neat and well-dressed, and possessing a charm of manner comparable to that of the distinguished Pendleton of Washington. But another peculiarity set Coe apart from the great majority of his fellows even more than did his dress and charm. He nearly always went unarmed. In fact, he is said to have carried a gun but once, and on that occasion went on a spree and fired the weapon in the streets of Abilene, Kan., where he and Ben Thompson were running the Bull's Head Saloon and Gambling House. Unfortunately for the gambler, Wild Bill Hickok was Marshal of Abilene at the time, and shooting off his a pistol was a violation of an Abilene ordinance. And Wild Bill was a stickler for law enforcement. He cautioned Coe, and when the sharper became quarrelsome and flourished his gun Hickok killed him with a double-barreled derringer.

Another Texas gambler of the Phil Coe stripe was Nat Kramer, who was well known in Austin but who was really Fort Worth's gift to the gaming table. Kramer began his career on the Red River, and later worked the steamboats between New Orleans and Shreveport. After the Civil War he returned to Fort Worth, and thereafter operated in that town, Austin and Colorado City, with frequent invasions of Abilene, Dodge City and other frontier settlements. In manner gentle and benign, Kramer's guiding philosophy was the ancient proverb "A soft answer turneth away wrath." He was a professional gambler for more than fifty years, and in all that time is said never to have taken a drink, engaged in a quarrel, or carried a weapon of any sort. He was probably the only frontier gambler of whom that could be said. Luke Short, a noted gambler and one of the famous "Fighting Marshals" of the cattle country, once said of Kramer: "He is the most mysterious success I ever saw. How he does it I would like to know, because I am tired of this business of packing a gun." Kramer died in Fort Worth in October, 1905, and a few minutes before the end a friend asked:

"What will you tell St. Peter?"

"Well," replied the old gambler, "I am just going to tell him that I have helped some and I have skinned some. Those I skinned could afford it, and those I helped needed it, maybe."

Despite the fame of Thompson, Coe, Kramer and the three elegant houses in Austin, neither Fort Worth, San Antonio nor the Texas capital ever attained the heights of blazing glory briefly enjoyed by such celebrated frontier hell-holes and railroad "end towns" as Abilene, Hays and Dodge City in Kansas; Tombstone in Arizona, Cheyenne in Wyoming, Virginia City in Montana; Leadville, Creede and Cripple Creek in Colorado; Virginia City in Nevada, and Deadwood in the Black Hills of South Dakota. Cheyenne and Virginia City, Mont., were probably the first of these settlements to attract the sharpers and scalawags of every degree who swarmed throughout the West, and were at their liveliest during the early days of the frontier. The latter, which had a comparatively short but turbulent existence after it was founded in 1862, was especially renowned for the combination saloons, dance halls and gambling joints called hurdy-gurdy houses. Western tradition has it that these resorts, where whisky was sold for fifty cents a drink and champagne

338

for twelve dollars a bottle, were the wildest dives on the frontier, frequented by gamblers and other desperate characters who caroused and cheated to the accompaniment of roaring revolvers and flashing knives. But the journalist Albert D. Richardson, who visited the Montana town in 1865, told a different story. He found the hurdy-gurdy houses "filled with visitors ranging from judges to black-legs, in every costume from broadcloth to buckskin," and thus described the debauchery, which appears to have been something less than riotous:

"At one end of the long hall, a well-stocked bar, and a *Monte* bank in full blast; at the other, a platform occupied by three musicians; between, many lookers-on, with cigars and meerschaums. The orchestra leader shouted: 'Take your ladies for the next dance!' Half a dozen swarthy fellows fresh from the diggings, selected partners from the tawdry, bedizened women who stood in waiting. After each dance the miners led their partners to the bar for whisky or champagne; then after a short pause, another dance; and so the sorry revelry continued from nine o'clock until nearly daylight, interrupted only by two fights. For every dance each masculine participant paid one dollar, half going to his partner and half to the proprietor. This latter functionary, who was dealing *Monte,* with revolver at his belt, assured me that his daily profits averaged one hundred dollars. Publicly, decorum was preserved; and to many miners, who had not seen a feminine face for six months, these poor women represented vaguely something of the tenderness and sacredness of their sex." [19]

Cheyenne, probably the most notorious of the "end towns," was settled when the Union Pacific Railroad reached there in

[19] *Ibid.,* page 480.

1867, and for two or three years was so tough that it was generally known in the West as "Hell on Wheels." Gamblers, desperadoes, prostitutes and their hangers-on comprised at least half of the population, and lawlessness was kept in check only by the activities of Vigilance Committees. As a visitor noted in 1869, these Committees "now and then purified the atmosphere," and hanged or expelled evil-doers after giving them scrupulously fair trials before impromptu juries. Sometimes the juries thus impaneled produced unusual verdicts. On one occasion, having heard the evidence against a man accused of theft, the jurors reported that "We find the prisoner not guilty, but if he is smart he will leave this town within twenty-four hours." The need for Vigilantes in Cheyenne began to pass about 1869, when the town was incorporated and chosen as the capital of Wyoming, but gambling was openly carried on for many years. During the 1870's at least one Faro or *Monte* bank was in operation in virtually every bar-room. The biggest play was in Greer Brothers' Gold Room Saloon, where George Devol, the famous Mississippi River sharper, dealt Faro for several months about 1872. This game was run by a gambler named Bowlby, who prospered until Wild Bill Hickok visited Cheyenne in 1874. Bowlby's artist attempted to swindle Hickok, whereupon Wild Bill knocked him down with a cane, wrecked the Faro table, and walked out with the contents of the cash drawer.

Abilene, Hays and Dodge City, most celebrated of Western cow towns and the stamping ground of Bat Masterson, Wild Bill Hickok, Luke Short, Jack Bridges, Billy Tilghman, Wyatt Earp, Mysterious Dave Mathers, and other famous frontier peace officers and gun-fighters, were in the heyday of their unsavory renown in the late 1860's and in the 1870's. The largest and farthest west, and also the worst, was Dodge City, the principal shipping point of the trail herds from Texas; and, in later years, when the town had fallen on evil days, headquarters of an extensive traffic in buffalo bones, which were hauled in from the prairies and shipped by the hundreds of carloads to Eastern factories to be converted into fertilizer. During the first year of Dodge's existence twenty-five men were killed in shooting affrays, and for almost a decade it was probably the most disorderly community in the United States. It was described accurately enough by a railroad conductor in 1872. To a drunken passenger who said he wanted to go to hell, the conductor replied, "Get off at Dodge!"

For several years after the discovery of gold in the Black Hills in 1874, Deadwood was almost as turbulent a place as Dodge City, but the Dakota town's chief claim to fame is as the scene of the murder of Wild Bill Hickok, and as the birthplace of a phrase which has probably been used at least once in every Poker game played in the United States in the past fifty years. Wild Bill arrived in Deadwood about the middle of June, 1876, and during that month and July located several claims and made a few prospecting trips into the hills. In his leisure time he played Poker, at which he is said to have been an expert, although he was never a professional. On August 2, 1876, he was playing with three friends in Carl Mann's saloon, and for the first time in his career sat with his back to the door. Late in the afternoon a young tin-horn gambler, Broken-Nose Jack McCall, entered the room and sauntered carelessly toward the group of card players. Wild Bill had just drawn cards, and was busy arranging his hand, when McCall suddenly drew a revolver and shot the famous frontiersman in the back of the head. Wild Bill's cards slipped from his fingers, and friends who picked them up saw that he had held two pair—aces and eights. And since that time aces and eights have been known among Poker players as the "dead man's hand."

There was no organized government in Deadwood, and hence no legal court, but McCall was tried before a jury chosen by a hastily formed committee of citizens. He was acquitted, ostensibly upon his own testimony that Wild Bill had killed his brother and had threatened to kill him. Not until McCall had left Deadwood was it learned that he had been paid $200 by gamblers who feared that Hickok might be appointed Marshal of the town, and that the sharpers had influenced the verdict with the expenditure of two hundred ounces of gold dust. McCall went to Laramie, Wyoming, and while drunk boasted that he had lied about his brother and Wild Bill's threats. He was arrested and sent to Yankton, South Dakota, and in the fall of 1876 was tried before a legal court and found guilty of murder. He was hanged on March 1, 1877.

Leadville, which is described by even the conservative *Encyclopædia Brittanica* as having been "one of the most turbulent, picturesque and in all ways extraordinary, of the mining camps of the west," was at its best, or worst, in the late 1870's and the early 1880's. At one time, about 1880, Leadville had 35,000 inhabitants and was the largest city in Colorado, as well as the most lawless. But as far as violence and disorder were concerned, Leadville had begun to decline by the early 1890's, when Creede and Cripple Creek appeared to carry on the traditions of the frontier and to become the last symbols of the wild and woolly west. Creede's boom began with the discovery of the silver deposits of Mineral County by N. C. Creede in January, 1892. Within two weeks after Creede had shouted, "Holy Moses! Rich at last!" and had thus given the name of Holy Moses to the richest of his claims, the town boasted a population of 10,000 persons, at least half of whom were there for no other reason than to prey on the other half. Creede's period of lawlessness and gambling glory was brief, but it was made memorable by the presence of two men who had already won great distinction in their chosen fields —the notorious Soapy Smith, and Bob Ford, "the dirty little coward who shot Mr. Howard, and laid Jesse James in his grave."

THE FAMOUS HURDY-GURDY HOUSE IN VIRGINIA CITY, MONTANA, 1865

Ford had dealt Faro and operated saloons and gambling dens in various parts of the West since the assassination of the Missouri outlaw at his home in St. Joseph, Mo., on April 3, 1882, and he was first on the ground at Creede with a resort called Ford's Exchange, where suckers danced with prostitutes from San Francisco's Barbary Coast, paid exorbitant prices for cut and adulterated liquor, and were robbed at Faro, *Monte,* Roulette and Chuck-a-Luck.

When the great silver strike was reported and the rush to Creede began, Soapy Smith was riding high in Denver. But he quickly realized the possibilities of a new and wide-open mining camp, and hurried to Creede with a dozen of his ablest henchmen. For a few days Smith spied out the land and consulted with those who knew him personally or by reputation, meanwhile operating a Thimble-Rig game on a street corner. When his plans were perfected he opened a gambling joint called the Orleans Club, and as soon as the place was running full blast played his trump card—he proclaimed himself boss of Creede, and calmly announced that thereafter he would be the sole dispenser of gambling, vice and swindling privileges. Curiously enough, the underworld and sporting elements accepted his sovereignty almost without question, and emboldened by the success of his *coup,* Soapy Smith made an even greater seizure of power by organizing a municipal government. He called a mass meeting of citizens, which he packed with gamblers and saloon-keepers, and the meeting ordered an election, which Smith manipulated. A few offices were given as a sop to reputable men, but the key positions were filled by adherents of Soapy Smith. The result was an administration which decreed a wide-open town for the dictator, and expulsion or worse for all who questioned his supremacy or attempted to muscle in on his rackets.

Except for a few feeble squawks from honest miners and

business men, the only dissenting voice heard in Creede while Soapy Smith was carrying out his ambitious program was that of Bob Ford, who had fancied himself the biggest frog in the Creede puddle. But Ford reluctantly submitted to Smith's authority after a conference with some of Soapy's gangsters, and agreed to play second fiddle to the great Thimble-Rigger. He did so without any outward show of rebellion, although he secretly tried to hatch a scheme that would topple Smith from the throne. But Ford soon ceased to be a menace, for on June 7, 1892, he was killed in his own Exchange by Ed O'Kelly, a mysterious stranger who had arrived in Creede a few days before wearing the garb of a cowboy. O'Kelly refused to tell why he had shot Ford, but it was generally believed that he had been hired to do the job by friends of Jesse James. There was also a widely-held theory that Soapy Smith was responsible, based partly upon the fact that Smith was nearby when the killing occurred, and saved O'Kelly from being lynched by Ford's infuriated friends.[20] In any event, the providential removal of "the dirty little coward" eliminated all opposition to Soapy Smith, and for the next several months he was the absolute monarch of Creede; probably no other American town had ever been so completely dominated by one man. But in the fall of 1892 the merchants and other respectable citizens began to express dissatisfaction with conditions, and many of them bluntly told Soapy Smith that in the new deal they contemplated for Creede there would be no place for dictatorship by the underworld. With rare perspicacity, Smith recognized that the end of his reign was at hand, and he wisely decided to get out of Creede before the inevitable revolution occurred. So late in 1892 he closed the Orleans Club, aban-

[20] O'Kelly was tried at Lake City a month or so after the shooting of Ford, and was convicted of murder and sentenced to prison for life. He was pardoned in 1902, and two years later was killed by a policeman in Oklahoma City.

doned his other enterprises, and returned to Denver. A few years later Smith attempted to invade Cripple Creek, but he was too late; the politicians had the situation well in hand there, and were administering the town for their own benefit. Their agent and front man was the Chief of Police, James Marshall, a gambler and gun-fighter known as Three-Fingered Jim. When Smith and his henchmen arrived in Cripple Creek they were met at the railroad station by Marshall and a posse of gunmen, who disarmed the invaders and sent them back to Denver on the next train.

Perhaps the toughest of all mining camps, Tombstone was founded in the spring of 1879 after the discovery of silver deposits in the Dragoon Mountains of southern Arizona, and within a few years was the metropolis of the territory—a hell-roaring town of some 15,000 population, with banks, hotels, newspapers, theaters, saloons, bawdy houses, gambling dens, and other appurtenances of civilization. Tombstone's extraordinary position in frontier history is due partly to the fact that it was the favorite playground of Curly Bill, John Ringo and other celebrated Arizona outlaws; but principally to the exploits of Wyatt Earp and his brothers Virgil and Morgan, whose feud with the Clanton and McLowery clans forms one of the bloodiest and most picturesque chapters in the annals of the West. As a gambling center Tombstone overshadowed the New Mexico towns of Las Vegas and Albuquerque, which flourished about the same time, and supplanted Santa Fe as the headquarters of Southwestern sharpers. In Tombstone's palmy days, during the early 1880's, there were facilities for public gambling in every building on one side of Allen Street, the main thoroughfare, as well as in many places on Fremont and Tough Nut Streets. None of these places ever closed their doors, no limits were imposed on the games, and ten and twenty dollar gold pieces were commonly used as chips.

Tombstone began to decline about 1887, and by another decade had become a ghost town, in which fewer than seven hundred inhabitants struggled for existence and dreamed of the glories of the past. But in the meantime Phoenix, Prescott and Tucson were increasing in population and importance, while in New Mexico, Albuquerque, Las Vegas and Roswell had shaken off their frontier swaddling clothes, and even old Santa Fe was enjoying a mild boom. In these and other towns the frontier gambler made his last stand, under the protection of laws which levied an annual tax of $500 upon every gambling device or layout. Half of the money thus raised went into the general funds of the territories, and half was applied to the support of the county and district schools. During the first half dozen years of the twentieth century Arizona and New Mexico each harbored from 700 to 1,000 gambling resorts, nine-tenths of which were skinning dens of the worst sort. Herbert J. Hagerman, who was Governor of New Mexico in 1906 and 1907, said in a message to the Territorial Council that "some of the games as played here afford the player 250 per cent less chance of winning than similar games afford in the larger gambling establishments of Europe, which pay enormous dividends to their stockholders." All of these dives were abolished, legally at least, when the politicians began to clean house in 1907 preparatory to the admission of both territories into the Union. The New Mexico anti-gambling law, passed in February, 1907, was one of the most stringent ever enacted in the United States—it imposed a $500 fine and imprisonment for six months upon the gambler, the sucker, and the owner of the premises in which the game was played. The Arizona law, adopted about the same time, was less severe, but it was strengthened by local ordinances. For example, Prescott not only closed its forty public games, but prohibited the playing of Euchre, Whist, Cinch, Five Hundred, Hearts and Forty-five in private homes.

6

Probably the most noted of the hundreds of gamblers who operated in the old Southwest were Doc Holliday and John Dougherty, both of whom were prominent figures in Tombstone. Holliday, a Georgian, had been educated as a dentist, but abandoned the staid life of a tooth-puller in the early 1870's to become a professional gamester. He was a sharper of the Ben Thompson type—more of a gunman than a gambler, but withal more proficient at the card table than the Austin killer ever was; he dealt a very tricky game of Faro, and at short cards was regarded as a veritable wizard. His fame, however, came from the muzzle of a gun rather than a Faro box or a deck of cards. Holliday was in Dodge City during the two years from 1877 to 1879 in which Wyatt Earp was Marshal of that decaying cow capital; and late in 1879 accompanied Earp to Tombstone. There he dealt Faro in the Oriental Saloon and Gambling House, of which Earp was part owner, and served as Earp's principal gunman and main reliance in battle. He was always the first to be deputized when Earp, as Marshal of Tombstone, had need of assistance, and appeared on the scene of trouble carrying that deadliest of short range weapons, a sawed-off shotgun, in addition to his regular armament of two revolvers and a long knife, which he wore slung down his back under his coat. For more than two years Holliday was accounted the most dangerous man in Tombstone, and with the exception of Buckskin Frank Leslie, the quickest and most accurate with a gun. He left Tombstone with Wyatt Earp early in 1882, after a street fight in which three of the Clanton-McLowery faction were killed, and drifted about the West until about 1897, when he died of tuberculosis in Colorado. The exact number of his killings was never computed, but was certainly no less than ten.

John Dougherty followed the well-nigh universal custom of

carrying a revolver, but he was no gun-fighter; he attended strictly to his own business, which was gambling, and as far as the record shows he died without a single notch on his pistol butt. He was an expert at all games from Faro to Craps, but in Tombstone and the Southwest he was renowned for two things —the smallness of his feet, of which he was inordinately proud, and the bigness of the stakes in his Poker games. He commonly carried a roll of $100,000, played only no limit games, and refused to join a session unless the other players could show at least $10,000. When he bought a drink, he paid for it with a five dollar bill, and was insulted if change were offered him. If Southwestern tradition is to be credited, Dougherty in one of his games made the biggest raise ever risked on a Poker hand anywhere. This historic event occurred in 1889, when Dougherty and Ike Jackson, a rich cattle owner of Colorado City, Texas, met in Bowen's Saloon in Santa Fe and agreed to play a square, no limit game for the Poker championship of the West. A hundred prominent citizens of Sante Fe, including L. Bradford Prince, Governor of New Mexico, crowded into the saloon to watch the battle. For a few hands the play was desultory, but soon both men drew good hands at the same time, and the betting immediately became heavy. In a few minutes $100,000 in coin and currency was piled on the table between the players. Jackson was then short of cash, so he wrote out a deed to his ranch and 10,000 head of cattle, and with this document raised Dougherty a hundred thousand. Dougherty hadn't money enough either to call or to raise, but he was equal to the emergency. He called for paper and pen, wrote rapidly for a moment or two, and then handed the paper to Governor Prince, at the same time drawing a revolver.

"Now, Governor," he said, "you sign this or I will kill you. I like you and would fight for you, but I love my reputation as a

348

Poker player better than I do you or anyone else."

Without reading what Dougherty had written, Governor Prince hastily signed, and with a smile of triumph Dougherty flung the paper into the pot, saying impressively:

"I raise you the Territory of New Mexico! There's the deed!"

The Texan threw down his cards with a mighty curse.

"All right," he said, "take the pot. But it's a damned good thing for you that the Governor of Texas isn't here!"

7

The unique features of gambling on the frontier were the universality of the vice; the employment of women as dealers and croupiers, and the picturesqueness of the suckers. The sharpers of no town east of the Mississippi could boast that their clientele comprised virtually the entire population of the community; it is doubtful if a woman ever dealt Faro or spun a Roulette wheel in an Eastern gambling house except in those operated exclusively for females; and the East could provide nothing to match the bewhiskered miner, the grizzled ranchman and cattle baron, the death-dealing gun-fighter, and the dashing cowboy with his jingling spurs and ornamental pants. But in every other respect gambling in the East was far superior to the Western brand, the principal reason being more and richer suckers. Despite their mushroom growth and the great fame they acquired, the mining camps and cattle towns were in reality little more than villages; the population of only a few ever exceeded 10,000 even in boom times, and even these lost most of their inhabitants as soon as the brief flurries of mining or cattle shipping had subsided. The best of the frontier towns in their liveliest days, except perhaps Leadville and Tombstone for a year or two, could never have supported a Hall of the Bleeding Heart, an 818 Broadway,

Price McGrath's house in New Orleans, or any of a hundred such establishments which flourished in the cities of the Atlantic seaboard.

Gambling accommodations in the West were usually of the most primitive description, and everywhere outside of San Francisco, Denver and Kansas City there was an entire absence of the luxury and elegance with which first-class gaming was surrounded in the East. There were scarcely any houses in which gambling was the sole or even the principal business; the typical gambling resort of the frontier was operated as an adjunct to the more important saloon or dance hall, or both. Such a dive seldom contained more than a single Faro layout, a *Monte* bank, a Poker table and a Roulette wheel, and occasionally a Chuck-a-Luck cage, a table of *Vingt et Un,* and a Three-Card Monte pitch, all in the same room with the bar and the dance floor. Thus a town which is heralded in frontier history as having harbored a hundred gambling houses might have had, by Eastern standards, proper equipment for not more than a dozen. About the only Western resort comparable in size to the big houses of the East was a place in Pueblo, Colorado, which was famous in the 1880's and the early 1890's, when the city had a population of approximately 25,000. This establishment, which Pueblo sporting men proudly declared was the largest in the United States, enticed the suckers with six Faro banks, four Roulette wheels, one Hieronymus bowl,[21] four tables for Hazard and Craps, two for Stud Poker, two for Draw Poker, one for Short Faro, one for *Vingt et Un,* and one for High Suit. All of this apparatus was in one large

[21] Hieronymus was a dice game somewhat similar to Chuck-a-Luck, played with three dice and two wooden bowls, the smaller ends of which were connected by a hollow tube. Bets were made on a numbered layout. The dice were then placed in the upper bowl and permitted to fall through the tube and fall upon a tambourine upon which the lower bowl had been inverted. The operator paid even, two and three to one, according to how many figures on the dice corresponded to those on which bets had been made. The percentage in favor of the bank was so enormous that the game was usually played honestly.

room, opening directly off the street, which also contained a bar and a lunch counter. In the rear were two other rooms where Policy drawings and Keno games were held daily, and upstairs was a lodging house. The resort was open twenty-four hours a day, and employed about fifty men who worked in three eight-hour shifts. In most gambling houses it was customary, when a sucker went broke, to give him a small sum of money before turning him into the street. But in the Pueblo establishment he received instead a brass check, which could not be played at the gaming tables, but was good for a night's lodging, a drink at the bar, or a meal at the lunch counter.

There are no records on which to base an estimate of the total daily or annual take of the frontier gambling places, but they were very large because everybody gambled. The individual stakes, however, were small. The no limit games at Tombstone in the early 1880's, and at Leadville during the same period, were exceptions rather than the rule, as were the big Poker sessions in which such gamblers as John Dougherty engaged. More often that not the Poker games were one and two-dollar limit, while the usual bets at Faro and *Monte* ranged from twenty-five cents to a dollar. A bet of a hundred dollars at Faro was unusual enough to attract considerable attention, and when a plutocratic sucker risked a thousand on a single turn, as happened once in a while, it was talked about all along the frontier. About the only place on the frontier where the stakes compared favorably with those in the big Eastern resorts was a celebrated house operated by Gentry & Crittenden at Virginia City, Nev., metropolis of the Comstock Lode district, and the town where young Samuel L. Clemens worked as a newspaper editor and first used his pen name of Mark Twain. During the two great periods of pro-ductivity of the Comstock Lode, in the middle 1860's and again in the middle 1870's, hundreds of miners who had made fortunes almost over night flocked into Virginia City demanding action on their great piles of gold dust. They found it at the Gentry & Crittenden house, where a famous Faro dealer named Hamilton Baker would turn the cards for any amount the player cared to put upon the layout. Bets of $5,000 were common, and quite often a plunger risked $10,000 on a single card. The highest bets recorded in this house were $18,000 and $30,000, both risked on a single turn. Baker became so well known as a dealer that at one time half a dozen Eastern gambling houses offered him a job. He finally came to Saratoga and handled the Faro box for John Morrissey for two or three seasons at a wage of $4,500 a month. For several years Baker's average annual earnings were about $70,000, but his income stopped suddenly when his right side was paralyzed as a result of a railroad accident, so that he could no longer deal. When he died he was a poor man.

The games themselves ranked in popularity about the same in the West as in the East. Faro was king, although in some parts of the frontier country, especially in the Southwest where the Mexican influence was strong, its position was threatened by *Monte*. At short cards Poker was supreme; it was the game most favored by the few professional gamblers who played square, and by Wild Bill Hickok and the other great gun-fighters in their hours of relaxation. Many of the superstitions which are still religiously observed by dyed-in-the-wool Poker players originated in the games which were always in progress in the frontier saloons—Western Poker addicts were the first to convince themselves that it was bad luck to count chips or to play with a kibitzer looking over the shoulder, that the player who drew a pat hand of jacks full on red sevens would not leave the game alive, and that luck could be improved by walking around a chair. Perhaps the commonest belief in the West, however, was that bad luck would forever dog the footsteps of a man who played Poker with a one-eyed gambler, a superstition which gave rise to the expression, "There's a one-eyed man in the game," meaning "look out for a cheat." The bad repute of the one-eyed player is said to have come about in this fashion:

"A little game of draw was in progress in Omaha, and among its participants was a one-eyed man. He was playing in rather remarkable luck, but no one could very well find fault with that. Presently, however, there came a jackpot, and it was the one-eyed man's deal. He opened the pot, and while he was giving himself cards a certain bellicose gentleman named Jones thought he detected the one-eyed man in the act of palming a card. Quick as a flash, Jones whipped out a revolver and placed it on the table in front of him.

" 'Gentlemen,' he said, decisively, 'we will have a fresh deal; this one doesn't go.'

"The players were surprised, but as none of them had bettered his hand save the opener, who made no sign of disapproval, they willingly consented.

" 'And now that we start on a new deal,' pursued Mr. Jones, carelessly toying with the revolver, 'let me announce that we are going to have nothing but square deals. I am not making any insinuations or bringing any charges, and I will say only this, that if I catch any son-of-a-gun cheating I will shoot his other eye out.' " [22]

8

The presence of women dealers and croupiers in the gaming resorts of the West was not a recognition of superior skill on the part of the ladies, for few of them ever became really expert at manipulating a deck of cards or a Roulette wheel. It was due almost entirely to the sense of showmanship possessed in some degree by all professional gamblers. Women were scarce in the frontier country, and the sharper who was fortunate enough to

[22] *Jack Pots*, by Eugene Edwards; page 321.

have a mistress exhibited her at his gaming tables for much the same reason that he would have exhibited an elephant—she aroused comment and speculation and attracted crowds. The woman-starved suckers of the West fairly fought for the honor of losing their money to a lady gambler; and whereas a man caught operating a two-card Faro box or a snapper Roulette wheel was mowed down without compunction, a woman could use the same apparatus and safely be as clumsy as she pleased. As a rule the chivalrous frontiersman felt that being cheated was a small price to pay for the privilege of watching dainty feminine hands rake in his coin and gold dust. The lady trickster was regarded a cunning little rascal rather than as a common cheat.

In the Mexican towns along the Rio Grande women *Monte* dealers, who incidentally knew the Gringos as "los God dammes," were common as early as 1840. But there is no record that any operated in an American gambling house until the spring of 1850, when Mme. Simone Jules, a handsome young Frenchwoman who was renowned for her enormous black eyes, startled the habitues of the Bella Union in San Francisco by taking over the croupier's job at the Roulette wheel. Madame Jules was an instantaneous success, and her table did such an enormous business that El Dorado, the Verandah and other resorts were compelled in self-defense to follow the Bella Union's example. The *Alta California,* principal newspaper of the town, fulminated mightily against the innovation on the ground that a woman's place was in the home and not in a gambling house, but to no avail; within a month after Madame Jules had first spun the wheel in the Bella Union women gamblers were on duty at virtually every first-class house in San Francisco. The custom spread to other parts of the West when the development of the frontier began, and during the great days of the gunfighters there was scarcely a cattle town or a mining camp which couldn't point with pride to at least one lady sharper. A few of these women broke away from the men who had trained them and drifted about the West as free-lance gamblers, playing short cards and both dealing and bucking Faro. Among them were Poker Alice, who finally settled in Deadwood and was a local landmark for many years; Kitty the Schemer, who was around in the 1870's claiming to be Queen of the Gamblers of the Barbary Coast and chatelaine of a big house in Hong Kong; and Buckskin Alice, one of the heroines of Leadville. Little was heard of Buckskin Alice after about 1890, when she visited New Orleans wearing a gaudily decorated buckskin costume and proclaiming that she was the greatest Faro player in the world, and had once won $2,000 on a single turn. She was invited to display her skill at one of the under-cover houses of New Orleans, and the slick Southern sharpers stripped her to the buckskin.

The queenpin lady gamblers of the frontier were a Frenchwoman known as Madame Moustache, and a four-foot firebrand called Minnie the Gambler, who was famous as a *petité maîtresse* and for her skill at the gaming tables. Minnie did a man's work in a gambling house and commanded a man's wages; she is said to have been a real artist with a Faro box, and at short cards was a bottom dealer of rare talent. In later years she became the sweetheart of Colorado Charley Utter, who is chiefly remembered as having accompanied Wild Bill Hickok to Deadwood, and dealt Stud Poker for him in El Paso until 1904, when the reform elements of the Texas city put a stop to public gambling. Minnie and Colorado Charley then organized a medicine show with which they traveled through Mexico and Central America. Colorado Charley died on the tour, but Minnie returned to the United States and retired to Southern California with a comfortable fortune.

Madame Moustache always said that her real name was Eleonore Dumont, but it is not improbable that she was the veritable Simone Jules, pioneer lady sharper of the West; she came from

355

San Francisco, resembled the descriptions of Madame Jules which had been broadcast by her proud victims, and appeared to know everyone with whom Madame Jules would naturally have come in contact. In 1854, when she was about twenty-five years old and only slightly worried about a bit of fuzz on her upper lip, Madame Moustache appeared in Nevada City, which in those days was one of the wildest of California mining towns, and opened a game of *Vingt et Un* in a vacant store. Her resort was very popular from the beginning, and to accommodate the rush of suckers she took in as partner a young tinhorn gambler named Billy Tobin, who ran Faro, Keno and Poker games while the Madame continued to preside at the *Vingt et Un* table. Tobin remained in Nevada City for a year or so, and then went to New York, where he is said to have accumulated a fortune with a skinning house.

Madame Moustache started to travel when Nevada City began to decay in 1856, and for the next two decades was a familiar figure throughout the West, where she was as well known for the looseness of her morals as for her activities as a gambler. She was more successful at the gaming tables, however, than in the field of amour, for she soon became corpulent and untidy, while the growth of hair on her lip blossomed into a large and un-sightly moustache. During the years of her itinerancy Madame Moustache operated gambling houses and brothels in San Francisco, Cheyenne, Boise and Bannock in Idaho, Eureka in Nevada, and Bodie in California, and followed the Union Pacific Railroad through Wyoming with a gambling outfit and a troupe of girls. One of her young ladies was a fifteen-year-old redhead named Martha Jane Canary, who is better known in Western history as Calamity Jane. Occasionally Calamity Jane took a hand in a Poker game or attempted to manipulate the Faro box, but she was much more adept at another business even more ancient than gambling. Madame Moustache's most ambitious establishment was at Bannock, where in 1864 she installed her troupe in a seven room log house. Downstairs was a bar, a dance hall, and rooms for Faro, Keno, *Vingt et Un,* and Poker; and upstairs were three girls and a spare room to which dancing couples could retire for a cosy chat. The Madame's last and most disastrous venture was at Bodie, where she operated in increasingly bad luck until a night in September, 1879, when a gang of professional gamblers broke the bank in her Faro game. Next morning her body, with a bottle of poison beside it, was found in the road near the town.

CHAPTER XII

JOHN MORRISSEY AND HIS TIMES

NEW YORK continued to develop as the principal gambling center of the United States throughout the Civil War and the few years immediately following, when William M. Tweed and his Tammany ring were plundering the city with a thoroughness unequaled by any other American politicians; and during the so-called Flash Age of the 1870's, when the public ideals were gaudy display and vulgar ostentation, and a man's worth and standing were judged by the size of his diamond stud and the voluptuousness of his mistress. With the connivance of a corrupt police force which found a measure of justification in the fact that gambling was the favorite pastime of the nation's leaders in politics and business, hundreds of gaming houses ran wide open, from the Thimble-Rig and Three-Card Monte dens of the Bowery to the "day houses" of the financial district and the palatial establishments farther uptown, many of which were superior to the ornate resorts which had flourished in the palmy days of Reuben Parsons and Pat Herne. A writer in *St. James' Magazine* declared in 1867 that there was "scarcely a street without a gambing house," while some five years later a metropolitan journalist professed to have personal knowledge of ninety-two first-class Faro houses alone, with a total playing capital of $1,000,000. There were even a few resorts exclusively for women, forerunners of the modern Poker flat and Bridge parlor, where the ladies could be cheated at Faro, Roulette and various short card games by artists of their own sex. Some of these resorts were still in operation as

358

late as 1890. A newspaper reporter who in company with an habitué visited one of them in 1888 said that the place was "fairly packed with women" every Saturday night, and "pretty well filled" every night. "They come in coaches, too," he wrote, "for some of those who go there are said to be wealthy." He continued:

"After passing through two heavy doors the young lady and the writer were ushered through the hallway, and from there into a large parlor which was handsomely furnished. A long table occupied the center of the parlor, on which was set a supper of ordinary excellence. In the front part of the room . . . a half dozen women were clustered about a table playing a private game of cards with checks for $1, $2.50 and $5. Near the folding doors was a Roulette table, and in the back room was the Faro bank, around which seven or eight richly dressed women were engaged in losing money. . . . Then the reporter was shown upstairs. . . . Three rooms on this floor were moderately furnished. . . . Smoking seemed a favorite pastime with the majority of the females on this floor. . . . The rooms above were fitted up luxuriously . . . in fact, were the most handsomely furnished in the establishment. In a corner of the room stood a marble-top table with many bottles and glasses upon it. Here the women treated themselves to sherry. . . . The front hall bedroom was a resting place for dizzy girls who had gone broke downstairs. . . . There was nothing vulgar about any of the women found upstairs, good breeding being visible on all sides. The language used was the most refined." [1]

[1] *Wonders of a Great City; or the Sights, Secrets and Sins of New York,* edited by Matthew Hale Smith, Prof. Henry L. Williams, and Ralph Bayard; Hartford, 1888, pages 363–64.

359

Many of the feminine Faro artists and cold deck manipulators varied the monotony of gambling house life by occasionally working the trains and the Hudson River steamboats, impartially fleecing both men and women. The usual procedure was to make the acquaintance of a likely gentleman, bring the conversation around to card playing, and invite him into her state room or drawing room to teach her Poker and Seven-Up, which the sucker did in the hope that it would lead to other two-handed games. But "the result is said to be very one-sided," commented a writer who exposed one of these hussies in 1879, "the fortune of the game being invariably with the fair one. The young man who 'calls' on her . . . usually finds himself at the end of his journey as lean in pocketbook as if he had followed Jay Gould's advice in speculating in stocks." [2]

2

For almost twenty years during and after the Civil War the dominating sound in the city-wide clatter of Roulette wheels and Faro chips was the voice of John Morrissey, the most picturesque figure, and in many respects the most important, that American gambling has yet produced. Morrissey not only became the best-known gambling house keeper in America and the boss of gambling in New York; he was also champion heavyweight pugilist, a famous rough-and-tumble fighter known in his brawlsome nonage as Old Smoke, founder of the Saratoga Race Track, a member of Congress and of the New York State Senate, and a power in Tammany Hall in the reign of the original Honest John Kelly. As a politician, Morrissey was a typical Tammany product; as a gambler, he was neither better nor worse than his contemporaries. He was an expert Poker player, and in private sessions with his friends was noted

[2] *Snares of New York; or, Tricks and Traps of the Great Metropolis,* Anonymous; New York, 1879; pages 25–26.

for scrupulous fairness. But in his public games he was not so particular; his resorts were operated as skinning houses except when honesty brought greater returns, and the sucker had no more chance there than anywhere else. As the New York *Tribune* said at the time of his death, "he employed the most skillful rogues in the profession, and his Faro, Roulette and French Pool games were known to all experts as swindles."

Morrissey was born in Ireland, but was brought to the United States by his parents in 1834, when he was three years old. The family settled in Troy, N.Y., where John's father devoted himself for many years to raising game cocks and carrying on a feud with a neighbor named Heenan, which had begun in an argument over the relative merits of a pair of bantam roosters. John went to school for a few months when he was about eight years old, but was nineteen before he learned to read and write. Except for brief periods when he worked on a Hudson River steamboat and as a moulder in a stove foundry, Morrissey spent his undisciplined boyhood on the streets of Troy. Before he was eighteen years old he had been indicted twice for burglary, once for assault and battery, and once for assault with intent to kill, and had served sixty days in jail. For several years in the middle and late 1840's Morrissey was the leader of a band of young ruffians called the Downtowns, who were almost constantly embroiled with another Troy gang known as the Uptowns. He began to think of pugilism as a career in 1848, after he had whipped half a dozen Uptown bullies in a single afternoon, but did nothing to further his ambition until about the middle of 1849, when he sent a challenge to Dutch Charley Duane, a well-known New York prize fighter and a henchman of the notorious Captain Isaiah Rynders.[3] But Dutch Charley only laughed at the effrontery of the upstate boy, and Morrissey

---

[3] Duane went to San Francisco later, and was one of the ruffians expelled by the Vigilantes in 1856.

went down to New York to deliver his challenge in person and teach the pugilist some manners. He walked into Rynders' Empire Club in Park Row and asked for Dutch Charley, but was told that the bruiser had gone to the races.

"Are there any prize fighters in the house?" asked Morrissey.

"Not today," replied Rynders, whereupon Morrissey threw his cap on the bar, spat on his hands, and said:

"I can lick any man here!"

Half a dozen of Rynders' sluggers immediately rushed upon the brash youth and smote him hip and thigh with fists, bottles, chairs, slung shots, and other weapons. Morrissey held his own for a time despite the heavy odds against him, but was finally floored when Big Tom Burns hit him behind the ear with a spittoon. Captain Rynders was so impressed by Morrissey's courage and ability that he put the young bruiser to bed and nursed him until he was able to return to Troy. There Morrissey ran a saloon for a few months, but was again in New York in 1850, working as a shoulder-hitter for Captain Rynders, and as an immigrant runner for a Cherry Street boarding house. He systematically sought out and thrashed each of the men, except Rynders, who had attacked him in the Empire Club, and was soon recognized as a rough-and-tumble brawler of exceptional merit. Although he was less than six feet tall and seldom weighed more than 180 pounds, Morrissey was extraordinarily powerful, with huge, gorilla-like hands and arms, extremely broad shoulders, a deep chest, and a large head crowned by a shock of bushy black hair. In battle he asked no quarter and gave none, and his stamina was well-nigh incredible. "John never seemed to know when he was licked," said one of his opponents, "and just as you got tired of thumping him he kind of got his second wind, and then you might as well tackle the devil as try to make any headway against him."

Morrissey won his sobriquet of Old Smoke in a fight which grew out of his efforts to supplant Tom McCann, a noted hoodlum of the period, in the affections of Kate Ridgely, who ran a popular brothel in Duane Street. The two men met in Sandy Lawrence's saloon at Broadway and Leonard Street, and Morrissey agreed to McCann's suggestion that they fight to a finish for Madame Ridgely's favors. When the combat began McCann rushed at Morrissey and threw him heavily to the floor. As they fell a stove was overturned, and a great mass of glowing coals rolled out of the firebox. McCann forced Morrissey onto the coals and held him there until his flesh began to burn, meanwhile attempting to gouge out Morrissey's eyes. But when the floor caught fire also Lawrence threw water on the coals, and McCann was temporarily blinded by the smoke and steam. Despite the pain from his burns, Morrissey got to his feet and kicked and slugged McCann into submission.

The one rough-and-tumble battle in which Morrissey was beaten was the outcome of bitter political animosities and the natural rivalry between Old Smoke and Butcher Bill Poole, whose reputation as an "anything goes" fighter was at least equal to that of Morrissey. Besides his interest in a meat stall, Poole owned a saloon, and was the leader of the rougher element of the Native American or Know Nothing Party. His shoulder-hitters included the members of his Washington Market gang and the bullies of Red Rover Engine No. 34, the company of which David C. Broderick was foreman before he went to California; and such famous fighters as Smut Ackerman, Tommy Culkin, the pugilist Tom Hyer; and Theodore Allen, better known as "The" Allen, a well-known gambler and political heeler, and in later years owner of the notorious *Bal Mabille,* a favorite resort of fancy men and fast women. Among Morrissey's satellites, all staunch Tammany men, were Blacksmith Dan Edgar, Wally Patrick, Charley Vosburgh, and

Bill Mike Murray, who had followed Old Smoke to New York from Troy; Lew Baker, Jim Turner; Paudeen McLaughlin, a terrible little thug whose nose had been chewed off in a fight; and a second-rate prize fighter known as Awful Gardner, whose real name was Orville.

While many of Poole's followers were eminent in other fields, of Morrissey's corps of eye-gougers only Awful Gardner and Bill Mike Murray achieved enduring fame apart from their exploits as sluggers. Awful Gardner reformed in the late 1850's, opened the Fourth Ward Temperance Coffee-House, and organized an anti-liquor society called the Dashaways. Every member of the Dashaways, as *Frank Leslie's Illustrated Newspaper* said on January 14, 1860, was required to "take the pledge for a month, a year or any time he thinks his moral force is adequate to sustain." A New Year's Watch Party given in the Temperance Coffee-House by Awful Gardner and the Dashaways was described by *Leslie's* as "a very interesting occasion. Prayers were said, hymns sung, speeches made, and coffee drank by those who had been in the habit of drinking rum and swearing." [4]

Bill Mike Murray was a fairly important figure in the skinning house division of New York gambling in the 1870's. He remained on Morrissey's pay roll as a bouncer and a slugger for several years in the 1860's, and during that period also served a prison sentence and ran a Faro skin game in partnership with John C. Heenan. Early in 1871 Murray put all of his capital into a house in Eighth Street east of Broadway, which he called the House of Bill Mike Murray; and which "for comprehensive gambling," said a journalist of the times, "is unequaled in New York, and probably not surpassed anywhere." In this establishment, which occupied all of a five-story and basement

[4] Awful Gardner was a familiar figure at temperance meetings for many years. He was instrumental in converting Jerry McAuley, founder of one of New York's most famous rescue missions.

structure, Murray attempted to put gaming on a sort of department store basis, with separate rooms for Faro, Roulette, *Rouge et Noir,* Chuck-a-Luck, *Vingt et Un, Monte,* Poker, and even Keno, every game dealt or operated by an expert artist. But the house failed to attract the high-class trade which had been expected, and, moreover, proved too big for effective management; Bill Mike was robbed and cheated on all sides by his own employes, and many opulent suckers escaped through sheer carelessness on the part of the staff. Murray abandoned the venture after a year or so, and opened a smaller but elegantly furnished establishment at No. 13 West Twenty-eighth Street. Because of his influence with the police, of which he frequently boasted, Murray was able to operate the house, despite its notoriety as a skinning den, for more than six years. His downfall began early on the morning of August 3, 1877, when a professional gambler named Jim Murphy, described by the New York *Tribune* as "a desperate character," but who nevertheless was very sentimental and fond of quoting poetry, walked into the resort and began to buck the Faro game. Murphy played for an hour or two, and then sat down in an easy chair, drew a revolver, and blew out his brains. A note found in his pocket asked the police to notify his mother in Elgin, Ill., and said that he owned property at Hollister, Calif., and had $2,300 on deposit in a San Francisco bank. The suicide gave Murray's house a bad name, the police began to interfere with his business, and Bill Mike soon passed out of the picture.

3

For a year or more after the enmity between Bill Poole and John Morrissey began to develop, there were frequent encounters between groups of the warring factions, but no meeting of the champions occurred until the night of July 26, 1854, when

Poole entered the City Hotel at Broadway and Howard Street and found Old Smoke drinking at the bar. Challenges were issued and accepted, and the two men agreed to meet next morning at the Amos Street dock and fight to a finish for a side bet of $100 and the glory of being the kingpin bruiser of New York. The titanic struggle was thus described by Theodore Allen, who was one of Poole's principal seconds:

"Five o'clock in the morning Poole came up to the Amos Street dock in a coach, accompanied by Smut Ackerman, Tommy Culkin, and myself. . . . Numerous admirers of Poole had already put in appearance and they had cleared a place for the fight. . . . Morrissey had not yet got uptown. A number of his friends, however, had started up Hudson Street in coaches. Poole's friends were laying in wait for them and every carriage that appeared was stopped and either upset or emptied of its inmates. A fight invariably ensued, which ended in Old Smoke's supporters making their departure for home or a hospital. It was nearing 7 A. M., before news, which traveled ahead of him, apprised that Morrissey was driving up with a friend in a light wagon. He came with Johnny Lyng, proprietor of the Sportsman's Headquarters at Canal Street and Broadway, and they walked toward us arm in arm. . . .

"There was no ring, but by general consent the throng had kept a space open for the combat. Poole, in his undershirt . . . was ready. It did not take Morrissey long to peel. Throwing off his coat and white shirt, he stood in his red flannel undershirt, as brawny a young bruiser as the most enthusiastic admirer of muscle could desire to see. . . . The fight began with some light sparring, Poole holding himself principally on the defensive as his opponent

366

circled about for a chance to close. For about five minutes this child's play of the giants lasted. Then Morrissey made a rush. But Poole was too quick for him. As Old Smoke made his lunge Bill the Butcher ducked with remarkable agility and seized him by the ankles. In a flash Poole threw his opponent clean over his head and as Old Smoke went sprawling he had only time to roll over when Bill pounced on him like a tiger. Then followed terrible minutes of fighting.

"Clutching each other in grips of steel they butted and pounded their heads together, tearing at each other's face with their teeth and gouging for the eyes with talon-like fingers. It was sickening to watch, for in no time they were frightfully punished. There was a long gash in Poole's cheeks where the flesh had been torn by his opponent's teeth. The blood was streaming from Morrissey's both eyes. They never changed positions while the struggle went on, for the minute they were down the crowd closed in on them and the surging bodies of the combatants pressed against the feet and legs of the surrounding onlookers. The wonder is that the two on the ground were saved from being trampled to death. Not a hand was raised to interfere or favor either contestant during the two or three minutes this inhuman struggle lasted. But Morrissey was underneath, and was doomed to defeat. And soon his voice was heard, hoarse, breathless and suffocating with blood.

" 'I'm satisfied,' he gasped. 'I'm done.'

"A cheer went up from the crowd, and the shout rang out and repeated till it swelled into a roar that carried through the streets half a mile away.

" 'Poole's won! Poole's won!' " [5]

[5] From an article written by Theodore Allen for *The Police Gazette* in 1880.

Butcher Bill's victory established his supremacy as a mayhem expert and greatly increased his prestige, but instead of bringing peace it only intensified the bitterness between the Poole and Morrissey factions. Morrissey was attacked by some of Poole's bullies even before he had left the scene of his downfall, but with the aid of others who thought he had been punished enough managed to make his way to the Bella Union Saloon in Leonard Street. An hour after the fight Smut Ackerman, attempting to show how Poole had thrown Morrissey, fell and fatally fractured his skull. A few nights later Theodore Allen and two other Poole adherents were cornered in a saloon in Bayard Street by a band of Morrissey's sluggers, and in the fight which followed a policeman was beaten to death and both of Allen's eyes were gouged from their sockets and hung down on his cheeks. A surgeon put them back in place, but Allen was blind for several weeks, and ever afterward his eyesight was poor. Battles of equal brutality and viciousness were of daily, almost hourly, occurrence until the night of February 24, 1855, when Poole was shot by Lew Baker in Stanwix Hall, a popular Broadway saloon opposite the Metropolitan Hotel where, at the time, William M. Thackeray, the English novelist, was a guest. Baker escaped, hid in a Broome Street saloon for a few days, and then shipped as a common sailor aboard the brig *Isabella Jewett,* bound for Teneriffe. But George Law, a New York capitalist and one of the principal backers of the Know Nothing movement, sent his clipper yacht *Grapeshot* in pursuit of the brig, and the *Isabella Jewett* was overhauled and boarded on the high seas. Baker was brought back to New York and three times tried for murder, but each time the jury disagreed, and the state finally abandoned the prosecution. Morrissey and seven other men were indicted for complicity in the crime, but were never tried.

Bill Poole's funeral on March 11, 1855, three days after his death, was probably the most extraordinary event of its kind ever seen in New York. "The sidewalks all along the route of the procession," wrote Theodore Allen, "were jammed, and every housetop and window were clustered. The very trees, awnings and projecting signs were seized on as points of vantage and the air was alive with the great roar of the multitude. Opposite the dead man's residence [in Christopher Street] was a carpenter shop owned by a man named Onderdonk. It was a sturdy two-story frame building with a stairway on the outside giving access to the upper floor. The spectators packed this stairway as one solid mass and every inch of roof space was also taken up. The structure began to creak ominously, then the roof and stairway gave way, and the people and the timbers fell together in one common wreck. Four people were killed and thirty injured. To add to the excitement, the firebells were set ringing and several companies were called to the scene of the casualty. It was amid this turmoil that the funeral cortege got under way." The procession was led by a detachment of several hundred policemen, and then came the Poole Association two thousand strong, twice as many members of the Order of United Americans; hose and engine companies from New York, Philadelphia, Boston and Baltimore; thousands of citizens, and, surrounding the hearse as a guard of honor, two military companies, the Poole Guards and the Poole Light Guards, which had been named in honor of the dead man. "The course lay through Christopher and Bleecker Streets on to Broadway," wrote Allen, "and every foot of the way had to be cleared as the cortege slowly made its way downtown. At Grand Street, a body of five hundred men in the familiar attire of working butchers knelt with their heads uncovered as the procession passed." [6]

After impressive ceremonies at Greenwood Cemetery in Brooklyn, most of the various organizations returned to New

[6] *Ibid.*

York separately. The Poole Guards and the Poole Light Guards, however, marched together, and late in the afternoon reached Broadway and Canal Street. On one corner of the intersection a house was being demolished, and work had been stopped for the day because of Poole's funeral. "Behind the brick and timber barricades made by the wreck and that lined the gutter," wrote Allen, "a strong party of Morrissey followers had ambuscaded themselves. They consisted of members of the 36th Engine, known as the Original Hounds, reinforced by a gang of Butt-enders and Short Boys, led by Larry Aiken and Dan Linn. As the Poole volunteers came within range a volley of stones and bricks darkened the air. Another and another followed. The attack was so sudden and unforeseen that the spectators who were gathered in the street watching the parade had no time to get out of the way and a woman on the other side of the street was killed, while a number of men and women were badly wounded. Five of the Poole Guards were included in the list of the injured. They were not long in recovering their order and Canal Street soon became the scene of a pitched battle. . . . The fight continued for an hour, when the Morrissey men, having used up pretty much all of their barricades for missiles, were left without cover and the Poole Guards proceeded to charge them with their bayonets. The Morrisseyites had no stomach for cold steel and they scattered just as the 7th Regiment . . . appeared on the scene. The assailing party had a number of its members disabled and two lay dead. . . .

"That night the Hounds were gathered around the stove in their engine-house discussing the events of the day, when a menacing murmur fell upon their ears. In a moment more there came a crash which shook the building and split the doors. Another and another followed until the doors fell open. Then, dropping the beam that had been used as a battering-ram, the besiegers poured in upon their demoralized foes. The assailants were the Poole Guards which had come down bent on vengeance. . . . When they got through there was nothing left of the engine-house but four blackened and smoking walls. The Hounds narrowly escaped with their lives. After which the Poole Legion . . . celebrated long into the night. Bill Poole's burial had certainly been a grand and exciting occasion." [7]

4

Morrissey's jobs as boarding-house runner and shoulder-hitter for Captain Rynders weren't very remunerative, and several times during his first year or so in New York he actually went hungry. Nevertheless, he managed to save enough to pay his passage to California, and arrived in San Francisco late in 1851 with $13 in his pocket. Unable to find a job tending bar, which was the only sort of work he knew how to do, Morrissey opened a cheap Faro game in partnership with a stranded artist, and soon amassed a sizable bank roll. One of the victims of his game, Jim Hughes, challenged him to a duel, but fled in terror when Old Smoke appeared on the field of honor with a pair of butcher's cleavers under his arm. During his stay in California, besides making his debut as a gambler, Morrissey also appeared for the first time in the professional prize ring, defeating George Thompson, better known as Pete Crawley's Big Un, in nineteen minutes at Mare Island in August, 1852, for a purse of $4,000 and a side bet of $1,000. After this victory Old Smoke called himself the Champion of America, but his claim to the title was not generally recognized until he had beaten Yankee Sullivan in 1853 at Boston Corners, N.Y. His last encounter was with John C. Heenan, son of his father's old enemy in Troy, who won re- nown in later years as the Benecia Boy and as the husband of the famous actress, Adah Isaacs Menken. Morrissey defeated

[7] *Ibid.*

Heenan in twenty-one minutes at Long Point, Canada, in October, 1858, for a side bet of $5,000.[8] Immediately after the fight Morrissey announced his retirement from the ring, declaring in a letter to the New York *Tribune* that he had been actuated in this decision by "an honest desire more becomingly to discharge my duties to my family and society," and that "my duties to my family and myself require me to devote my time and efforts to purposes more laudable and advantageous." So he became a politician and a professional gambler. Heenan claimed the championship when Morrissey ignored his demand for a return bout, and defended it successfully for several years. His most famous fight was a forty-two round draw with the British champion, Tom Sayers, near Aldershot, England, on April 17, 1860.

Morrissey embarked upon his first business venture in New York soon after his return from California, opening the Gem Saloon in Broadway and becoming part owner of the Bella Union in Leonard Street, named after a famous resort in San Francisco. He sold both places in 1855, and thereafter, except for a disastrous invasion of the stock market in 1869, confined himself to politics and gambling. With the bet he had won from Heenan, and the profits from the sale of his saloons, Morrissey early in 1859 opened a gaming place at Broadway and Great Jones Street in association with Matt Danser. The partners prospered, and soon afterward started another establishment at No. 12 Ann Street, next door to the notorious Tapis Franc. After two or three years, however, Morrissey withdrew from the partnership and took over the resort at No. 8 Barclay Street, which had been opened as a gambling house about 1859 by Charles Ransom, a native of Connecticut who, incidentally, was one of the most expert tenpins bowlers of his time. Ransom had previ-

---

[8] All of Morrissey's fights were with bare knuckles under London Prize Ring rules. A round ended when a fighter fell or was knocked or thrown to the ground, and a fight ended when one of the bruisers failed to come up to scratch, i. e., a mark in the center of the ring, at the beginning of a round.

ously been one of Tom Hyer's and Frank Stuart's partners in Jack Harrison's old establishment in Park Place, and in later years was associated with Morrissey in various enterprises. His most popular resort was at No. 11 West Twenty-fifth Street, which he operated with great success from 1865 to 1885, when he died of tuberculosis. According to Richard Canfield's biographer, Ransom "was known as the squarest, quietest, most cool-headed gambler in New York," and his house at one time had "the reputation of being the biggest and squarest game east of San Francisco." The New York *Tribune* of August 13, 1877, however, said that Ransom was poor, and was gaining a precarious living "by carrying on a 'skin game' in West Twenty-fifth Street. . . . His fondness for fast horses and his dissolute tastes wasted his once large fortune."

The building at No. 8 Barclay Street had a longer life as a gambling house than any other place in the history of the city; it was so occupied continuously until 1902, though not always as a first-class resort. Under Morrissey's management, however, the establishment was one of the finest in New York, and soon became very popular among politicians and sporting men, as well as with a multitude of suckers who were attracted by Old Smoke's fame as a prize fighter. Morrissey banked a net profit of $1,000,000 in five years, and then sold the house to Matt Danser, believing that the future of New York gambling lay farther uptown. With eight other sharpers Old Smoke opened a richly-appointed resort at No. 5 West Twenty-fourth Street, and himself purchased Joe Hall's place at No. 818 Broadway, which he ran for eight years. During this period his profits from this establishment alone are said to have exceeded $700,000, including $35,000 which an opulent sucker lost on a single turn at Faro; while his share of the take at the West Twenty-fourth Street house amounted to almost half a million. Morrissey attempted to carry on the Joe Hall tradition at No. 818 Broadway, but never achieved the master's touch in entertainment, although he maintained the exclusive character of the house and catered only to suckers of wealth and position, and to the upper grades of professional gamblers. A visit to the resort was thus described in 1868 by the anonymous author of *Asmodeus in New York:*

"We went through an elegantly furnished parlor, in which were many frequenters of the house, either conversing or reading newspapers. We next entered a large room lighted by numerous gas-jets. In the center of this apartment was a long table covered with green cloth. The room was crowded with persons busily engaged in gambling. Different games of chance are in vogue in the United States; but the favorite game of European gamblers, roulette, was not tolerated in the establishment we were then visiting. . . . Besides the table in the center of the room, there were half a dozen others in remote corners, and also in adjoining rooms, and which, as Asmodeus had observed, were occupied by persons engaged in some favorite game. Around the large table stood an anxious crowd. There was evidently an exciting game in operation. Near the center of the table was seated a banker or dealer, with a large quantity of checks at his right hand, of the denomination of five, ten, twenty dollars, and upward. . . . I took him, at first, for the proprietor of the establishment. 'You are mistaken,' said Asmodeus, 'the host is that stout man whose necktie is pinned with a large diamond, and who is playing *écarté* near yonder window, with a constant frequenter of his house. A few years ago he was one of the most renowned pugilists in the United States. With the profits derived from his victims in the manly art, he purchased a fine house. . . . He gradually withdrew himself from the noisy companions of his younger years, and soon had the satisfaction to behold

374

PLAYING AT THE GAME FARO

From Under the Gaslight—Dec. 1879

FAIR ONES AT FARO—A WOMEN'S GAMBLING SALOON ON THE WEST SIDE IN NEW YORK

bankers, brokers, merchants, and men belonging to the wealthy classes flock to his establishment. As his business rapidly increased, he purchased this handsome house, situated in one of the most fashionable streets of New York. It has become a favorite resort for many persons of good standing in society, and for 'the fancy' of New York. . . . The landlord is married, and very careful that everything is carried on in an orderly manner. Women are not admitted into the gaming rooms, or even into the parlors of the house. An elegant supper is served up, every evening, to frequenters and visitors." [9]

When Morrissey abandoned all outward connection with New York gambling, about 1877, the establishment at No. 818 Broadway passed into the hands of a syndicate of sharpers headed by Mike Eaton and Steve Whipple. Ferdinand Abell, in later years the owner of a resort at Newport which he sold to Richard Canfield, acquired control about 1879, at which time the house itself was "owned by a wealthy widow lady who receives $5,000 per annum rent for the same." Abell called the house the Central Club, and after a few years took in as partners Lucien O. Appleby, and Davy Johnson, who afterward operated houses of his own in New York and Saratoga. The place finally closed voluntarily on July 10, 1890; by that time it was so far downtown that profitable operation at night was no longer possible, while the daytime business was absorbed by the "day gambling houses" in Ann, Fulton, Liberty and other downtown streets in or near the financial district. Like Sherlock Hillman's resort of an earlier day, these places were open only from about 11 A. M. to six or seven o'clock in the evening.

Throughout the Morrissey regime No. 818 Broadway was raided but twice—once in 1867, when the anti-gambling society

[9] Pages 131–34.

was revived and began a crusade which was quickly checked by the judicious expenditure of a fund of $25,000 raised by the gamblers; and again in 1873, when a member of the Board of Police Commissioners had a grudge against Morrissey. After Old Smoke's retirement, however, the resort was frequently raided by the police and by agents of reform organizations. The most spectacular of these invasions occurred in January, 1880, when D. J. Whitney, secretary of the Law Enforcement Committee of the Society for the Prevention of Crime, marched into the place at the head of forty policemen—and marched out again empty-handed, having found neither players nor gambling apparatus. But when Whitney threatened to repeat his visit and refused to surrender his warrants, Abell and several members of his staff voluntarily came into court, where they were described by the New York *Times* as "a delegation of beefy, rosy-cheeked, cleanly groomed sporting men. . . . All of them wore gold studs, faultless linen and glossy beaver hats, and most of them twirled ivory or gold-headed canes." Four were indicted, but were never tried.

There was always a great deal of comment in the newspapers upon the failure of raiding parties to find any gambling paraphernalia in No. 818, but the mystery was not solved until March, 1900, when workmen drilling in the cellar discovered, built into the brick wall, a secret vault which had obviously been used as a hiding place for the resort's gambling tools whenever danger threatened. "The vault is ten feet in length and three and one-half feet in width," said the New York *Herald* of March 15, 1900. "The door is about six feet high and three feet wide, and is made of iron. Over the door and hiding it, there is a wall of brick and mortar. When the door is closed, this false wall has the appearance of being a part of the real wall. If a wire running along the ceiling is pulled, a clasp over the door will be raised, and if the door is then kicked vigorously it will fly open."

Morrissey's first partner, Matt Danser, is said to have been a silent partner in the syndicate which purchased No. 818 Broadway from Old Smoke, but as far as the record actually shows, Danser's last gambling enterprise was the house at No. 8 Barclay Street. Danser was one of the few professional gamblers who amassed great riches and kept them. The New York *Tribune* said in 1877 that "Matt Danser's continued prosperity was a notable exception and almost without precedent," and that Danser, Reuben Parsons and Henry Colton "were considered for years to be the richest men of their disreputable class." Danser retired from active gambling in 1872 with almost $1,000,000, and his fortune was virtually intact when he died. Legend has it that Danser was the squarest gambler who ever turned a card in New York, so honest that suckers frequently entrusted him with large sums to bet against his own game. But George W. Walling, who was Superintendent of Police in the metropolis during a part of Danser's career and knew the gambler well, wrote in his reminiscences:

"Danser was one of the shrewdest men in his mode of living. He was after the 'main chance' all the time. Some persons have said that he never 'ran a square game,' and that in the early days of the War he thus laid the foundations of a vast fortune. . . . In justice to him, however, it should be said that despite the way in which he made his money he kept his family aloof from his transactions. No one could be more devout than his wife and daughter. Matt tried hard to 'get religion,' but, to all outward appearances, signally failed. That fact, however, did not interfere with the piety of his family. He was the most extraordinary man I ever saw in respect to facial development. A slight stroke of paralysis had affected one side of his face, so as to draw his mouth sideways into a pucker, and when he talked or swore it was hard to keep one's countenance when looking him in the eye." [10]

In common with most gamblers, Danser handled his money with great carelessness. When he retired his fortune was converted into stocks and bonds, but instead of renting space in a safe deposit vault he kept about $500,000 worth of negotiable securities at his home, 50 West Eleventh Street, in an old trunk with a flimsy lock. This fact was well known, and thieves soon accepted the invitation to plunder. In April, 1875, a week or so after Danser's pocket had been picked of a $1,000 bill in Union Square, Mrs. Danser engaged as a servant one Mary Logan, "a sly, repulsive-looking woman." She soon learned where the bonds were kept, and having forced the lock of the trunk, carried a bundle of securities into the coal cellar. By the light of a candle she clipped coupons amounting to $21,640, putting about $16,000 into her own trunk, and hiding the remainder, together with about $200,000 worth of unclipped bonds, under the coal. Before she could return to her scissoring she became ill and was taken to St. Luke's Hospital, where she died on May 29, 1875. The next day her trunk was claimed and taken away by her relatives, Michael and Ann O'Farrell. A month later Danser discovered his loss, and a search of the house unearthed the bonds and coupons which had been secreted in the cellar. The police immediately suspected Mary Logan and the O'Farrells, and the latter were finally found on Ninth Avenue, where they had recently established a clothing manufactory, with a dozen sewing machines and a large number of hands. O'Farrell said that he had found in Mary Logan's trunk a lot of little pieces of paper with printing on them and not knowing their value had burned them. He stuck to this story until detectives found about $8,000

[10] *Recollections of a New York Chief of Police,* by George W. Walling; New York, 1887; page 383.

in coupons under the plates of the sewing machines, and then confessed. He was convicted of receiving stolen property and sentenced to five years in Sing Sing, but his wife, who had also been arrested, pleaded coverture and was released.

Before the O'Farrells were brought to trial another attempt was made to steal the Danser fortune. On July 12, 1875, Danser went downtown after breakfast, and his daughter went to church, leaving Mrs. Danser alone in the house. Fifteen minutes after Danser's departure three men rang the bell at the basement door and told Mrs. Danser that they had come "to see about the water." Concluding that they were plumbers or sanitary inspectors, she unbarred the door, whereupon they seized her and rushed her upstairs to a small bedroom on the third floor. There she was bound and threatened with death if she made an outcry. Then the thieves made a hurried and bungling search of the building, damaging some of the woodwork and furniture with hatchets, and left in a few minutes with a packet of Virginia City bonds worth about $17,000. Mrs. Danser was afraid to call for help, and the alarm was not given until her husband came home about noon and released her. The police believed that the robbery was planned by Big Jim Brady, a member of the gang of burglar and safe-blowers captained by the famous George Leonidas Leslie, but sufficient evidence to justify an arrest was never obtained. No one was punished for the crime.

These adventures so affected the Dansers that no member of the family was ever again in good health. Danser died in August, 1876, his wife followed him to the grave in November of the same year, and their daughter died in February, 1877. Miss Danser left $30,000 to her fiancé, a telegraph operator at Police Headquarters, but bequeathed most of her father's fortune to religious organizations, so that, as Superintendent Walling said, "what had been gained through the instrumentality of the devil went, in the end, to the service of God."

5

Not the least of John Morrissey's claims to a permanent place in American sporting history is the part he played in the development of gambling and horse racing at Saratoga Springs, which for almost a hundred years was the most celebrated wateringplace in the United States. In common with other American summer resorts, Saratoga in its early days was a welter of piety and hypocrisy, and everyone who went there was either ill or pretended to be. The town was the headquarters of the antiliquor movement—the first temperance society in America was organized at the Springs in 1808—daily prayer meetings and Bible readings were held at the hotels and boarding-houses, which permitted no arrivals or departures on Sunday; and the only amusements available were hymn singing, buggy riding before dark, listening to sacred music, and drinking water from the famous mineral springs. Although as late as 1843 one of Saratoga's principal hotels, the Union Hall, was described by a New York newspaper as "a sort of moral place of entertainment, where they every morning read the Bible, say prayers and drink spring water," the resort in general began before 1820 to cater to the gayer elements of New York society, and to the Southern planters, hundreds of whom visited the Springs every summer until the Civil War. During the 1830's Saratoga became the favorite vacation resort of social and political bigwigs, as well as the great summer playground of *hoi polloi*. "All the world is here," wrote Philip Hone in his diary in 1839, "politicians and dandies; cabinet ministers and ministers of the gospel; officeholders and office-seekers; humbuggers and humbugged; fortune hunters and hunters of woodcock; anxious mothers and lovely daughters." Hone said of a reception at Saratoga in honor of Henry Clay that "Eight hundred persons were present, comprising a greater number of distinguished men and fine women than have probably ever been collected in this country."

Dancing, billiards, bowling and card playing were introduced at Saratoga about 1825, and within the next thirty years were followed by public gambling, horse racing, and "a great variety of amusements, such as cosmorama, solar telescope, carousal, swinging boat. . . ." A guide book of the late 1820's declared that "the mineral waters of Saratoga and the healing virtues of the springs are not the only nor the principal objects which draw to its sands the thousands who annually flock thither," and a Saratoga poet of the same period thus limned the glories of the Spa:

> Of all the gay places the world can afford,
> By gentle and simple for pastime adored,
> Fine balls and fine singing, fine buildings and springs,
> Fine rides and fine views, and a thousand fine things,
> (Not to mention the sweet situation and air)
> What place with these Springs can ever compare?
> First in manners, in dress, and in fashion to shine,
> Saratoga, the glory must ever be thine!

Visitors to Saratoga, especially the rich and reckless Southerners, were gambling privately in the hotels before 1825, but apparently there were no facilities for public gaming until the early or middle 1830's, when a few of the billiard halls and bowling alleys began to install Faro and Chuck-a-Luck games. The first house exclusively for gambling was a small, modestly furnished place in an alley near the old United States Hotel, and was opened by Ben Scribner about 1842. Although Scribner's resort was never patronized by the big-money suckers, he was moderately successful for many years. Eventually, however, competition destroyed his business, and he ended his days working for John Morrissey. Several houses somewhat more pretentious than Scribner's were established during the 1850's, but gambling at Saratoga was on a comparatively small scale, and very much under cover, until John Morrissey entered the field backed by the prestige of his name and the experience which he had gained in the operation of his New York houses. Several attempts to close Morrissey's place and drive him out of Saratoga were made by reform elements, but Old Smoke met these attacks with gifts to the town, to the churches, to civic organizations, and to politicians and officials. As a visitor to the Spa remarked in 1871, Morrissey "divides the profits of his sinning with the good people of the village with a generous hand."

Before the end of the Civil War gambling had been established as one of the main attractions of Saratoga, and by 1870 about fifteen luxurious hells were running wide open throughout the season. The town remained an important center of gambling until the collapse of Richard Canfield's enterprises a few years after the turn of the twentieth century. For several years in the early 1890's the gamblers were the most powerful faction in Saratoga, and so completely dominated the town that they succeeded in electing one of their number, Caleb Mitchell, to two terms as Village President.

Morrissey's first gambling house at Saratoga was in Matilda Street, later Woodlawn Avenue, and was opened in 1861, about the time that François Blanc abandoned Baden Baden, obtained a concession from the Prince of Monaco, and began to build a casino at Monte Carlo which was destined to become the world's most renowned gambling resort. The Matilda Street establishment was very successful, but Morrissey was dissatisfied with the location; it was in one of Saratoga's principal thoroughfares, and Old Smoke felt that a gambling house should be less conspicuous. However, he remained there six years, meanwhile carefully building up a reputation as an honest and orderly gambler, and as an open-handed philanthropist who always had at heart the best interests of the town and the politicians. By 1867 Morrissey's position as Village Santa Claus, and as the undisputed

From an old print

A GAMBLING HOUSE IN WASHINGTON IN THE 1870'S

VAULT CLOSED. VAULT OPEN.

Courtesy N. Y. Herald-Tribune

SECRET VAULT IN THE GAMBLING HOUSE AT NO. 818 BROADWAY,
NEW YORK

boss of gambling, was secure; and in that year he bought and filled in a swamp on Congress Street, where he erected a red brick building which he called the Saratoga Club House. Soon after this structure had been completed he built a race track, which superseded the course established by the Saratoga Association in 1863, and which is still one of the important tracks of the country.[11]

The Saratoga Club House was Morrissey's major achievement, as far as gambling was concerned; within a few years it was universally recognized as America's finest gaming establishment, and was being favorably compared with the great gambling casinos of Europe. "More like Baden Baden every year becomes Saratoga," wrote a visitor in 1871. "John Morrissey has added still another building to his old establishment, making it a fair rival of the Kursaal at the Badens. The rooms now include a beautiful club *salon*. . . . Gorgeously furnished toilet rooms, Faro parlors, and drawing rooms carpeted with soft carpets and decorated with rich carvings and bronzes, hold the *blasé* and allure the *naive*. . . . It is dreadful to think that the descendants of Miles Standish are some day to follow in the footsteps of the gambling Badeners, but year by year the curtain is lifted a little higher and higher, until now we begin to see the beautiful figure of vice without shrinking." During the first year this palatial sucker-trap was in operation, Morrissey established two rules, rigidly enforced by later owners of the Club House, which were at least partly responsible for the long-continued success of the establishment and the almost complete absence of suicides of ruined suckers, which had proved so distressing to François Blanc at Baden Baden—no resident of Saratoga was allowed to gamble, and women were not admitted to the gaming rooms.

---

[11] The first race track in Saratoga was opened on July 4, 1848, and races were held two or three days a week for purses of from fifty to two hundred dollars. Racing was never really important there, however, until Morrissey's track was established.

The ladies, however, were welcomed to the *salon* and the drawing rooms, and flocked there by the thousands—25,000 in the summer of 1871 alone—to be entertained while their husbands and sweethearts bucked the tiger or broke themselves upon the Roulette wheel. All of the current banking games were available in the Club House, the most popular, of course, being Faro and Roulette, and private rooms were available for Poker and other short card games. Throughout the late 1860's and the 1870's, and again under the management of Richard Canfield, the Club House was a favorite gambling rendezvous of the richest men in the United States.

Morrissey was worth at least a million dollars when he built the Club House and the race track at Saratoga, and the first two years' operation of the gambling resort netted him another half million. His fortune might eventually have reached dizzy heights if he hadn't undertaken a foray against the stock market under the treacherous guidance of old Commodore Cornelius Vanderbilt. He left a great deal of his cash in Wall Street, and in addition saddled himself with debts which he was unable to pay in full until a year or so before his death. Morrissey first met Vanderbilt, who customarily spent several weeks of each summer at Saratoga, late in 1868. "His best friends," said the New York *Herald's* obituary account of Old Smoke, "state that from that time Morrissey went on the downward road . . . the visions of Wall Street dazzled his eyes. Black Friday in 1869 found him possessed of a large amount of New York Central and on that eventful day he was cleaned out of $500,000. Again on another day his relations with the commodore being exceedingly friendly he held a long line of Harlem stock. The commodore, as runs the report, went for his friends and cleaned them all out. . . . It was said by those who best knew Mr. Morrissey's affairs that if he had never known the commodore or never taken his advice he would have fared better and died a rich man."

A considerable part of the fortune that remained to Morrissey after he had been dusted off by Vanderbilt was expended in vain attempts to gratify his own ambition to be known as a gentleman, and that of his wife to be recognized by Society. They began their campaign in Troy, where Morrissey tried to buy a house in the aristocratic part of the town. But his prospective neighbors, aghast at the effrontery of the gambler and former prize-fighter, formed a syndicate and bought the property. This bit of snobbery so incensed Old Smoke that he purchased a lot in the rear of the district and built a soap factory, which produced more vile odors than it did soap. After a few weeks the Trojan aristocrats were glad to buy the factory at a high price. Soon after Morrissey opened the Club House he braved the ribald jeers of his henchmen and began to appear in public clad in a swallow-tail coat, striped pants, patent-leather boots, and white kid gloves, with beaver hat and accessories to match; while Mrs. Morrissey, who was already considered one of the most beautiful women in New York, now became equally famous for the magnificence of her appointments. One of the sights of the town, during the winter season, was Mrs. Morrissey, blazing with jewels, in her box at the theater, viewing the play through opera glasses of solid gold set with diamonds and monogrammed with matched pearls. But all this display went for naught; despite Old Smoke's eminence as a politician, a gambler, and a retired heavyweight champion, the Morrisseys failed to make the social grade.

6

Morrissey's political career ran parallel with his career as a gambler; they complemented one another, and each made the other possible. Old Smoke was the most powerful gambler of his time because he used his political strength to dominate and levy tribute upon his fellow-gamesters; and he was politically important for so many years because of the great following he had acquired as a gambler and a prize fighter. William M. Tweed, probably the most efficient grafter that even Tammany Hall has ever produced, once said that as an organizer of repeaters Morrissey had no superior; and from the time he returned to New York from San Francisco Old Smoke commanded Tammany's battalions of shoulder-hitters and engineered miracles of dishonest balloting. In 1866 the organization rewarded these labors with a seat in Congress, and re-elected him in 1868 despite the fact that he was no longer in good standing with Tweed. Throughout both of his terms Morrissey kept the House of Representatives in an uproar; if another member disagreed with him he wanted to fight, and once in the heat of debate he offered to whip any ten men in the house.

At the conclusion of his second term in Congress Morrissey became one of the leaders of the Young Democracy, which was formed in 1870 to fight against the domination of Tammany Hall by Tweed and his gang of looters, and for this heresy Old Smoke was expelled from the organization. He was reinstated when Honest John Kelly reorganized the Hall after Tweed's downfall, and for several years he and Kelly were virtually co-leaders. He was again expelled in 1875 when his growing strength and popularity threatened Kelly's political existence, and never returned to the fold. Thenceforth he was as violently anti-Tammany as he had previously been pro-Tammany. He announced his candidacy for the State Senate from Tweed's old district, the Fourth, was elected despite Kelly's opposition, and at Albany worked and voted against all legislation introduced or favored by the Tammany delegation. Annoyed by Kelly's statement that only the district which had elected Tweed to office would have sent "a vicious thug, a rowdy prize fighter, and a notorious gambler" to the Senate, Morrissey ran for re-election from the most reputable district in the city, the Seventh. He was victorious by a considerable majority, although Tammany concentrated its strength against him and put up as his opponent the Grand Sachem of the Hall, Augustus Schell. Morrissey's triumph was short-lived, however, for he had become ill during the campaign, and died of pneumonia on May 1, 1878. He was popularly believed to be still a rich man at the time of his death, but when his estate was settled his once great fortune was found to have dwindled to less than $75,000.

7

John Morrissey's immediate successors in the ownership of the Club House and race track at Saratoga were Charles Reed and Albert Spencer. In a brief account of their activities the New York *Tribune* said in 1877 that Reed's adventures "have been many and varied," and that "because he cannot trust himself he does not drink;" while Spencer was described as "a man of some education, and quiet and unobtrusive manners," with "a reputation among his fellow gamblers as a saving and avaricious man." In his latter years, after gambling and frugality had made him rich, Spencer was an amateur art critic of some distinction, and as a hobby collected fine paintings and sold them at auction. Reed's cultural ambitions never lifted him higher than the gambling house and the race track, although he did spend many years analyzing and attempting to develop the game of Casino. He began his career as a gambler in New Orleans, where he was an associate of Allen Jones and Price McGrath, but was not accounted a big-time sharper until he came to New York. Soon after the capture of New Orleans by Federal troops and warships in 1862, Reed killed a man named

McCullough, and was sentenced to death. He was pardoned by
Major-General Benjamin Butler at the request of the General's
brother, Andrew J. Butler, to whom all of the New Orleans
gamblers were paying tribute. When the gambling houses were
finally closed by the military authorities, Reed left New Orleans, and sometime in 1865 appeared in New York. There he
met Spencer, who for several years had been interested in several small resorts in the metropolis, and the two men formed a
partnership which endured until the late 1880's. Their first important venture was membership in the syndicate, headed by
John Morrissey, which established the gambling house at No. 5
West Twenty-fourth Street, destined to become one of New
York's most celebrated resorts; it was operated continuously,
first by the syndicate, then by Reed and Spencer, and finally by
Reed alone, until 1904. Besides their interest in this establishment, Reed and Spencer also ran, during the 1870's, another
resort at No. 21 West Fifteenth Street known as the Cottage,
which was distinguished by handsome Gothic windows, a gable
roof and ornamental chimneys. In cuisine and high play it
ranked among the first half dozen gambling houses in New
York. In 1877 they closed the Cottage despite its great popularity, bought out the other members of the Morrissey syndicate, and confined their labors to Twenty-fourth Street until
Old Smoke's death, when they took over the property at Saratoga.

The partners shuttered their New York establishment during
the Saratoga season, and both spent the summers at the Springs.
The management of the Club House and the race track, however, was almost entirely in the hands of Spencer, for Reed
built a fine residence at Saratoga and devoted himself to a
Society-crashing campaign. But the best people ignored his as-
pirations, although he dutifully attended the Episcopal Church
and subscribed liberally to religious charities. By adhering to

Morrissey's policy of frequent largesse to the village and regular gifts to politicians and officials, Reed and Spencer enjoyed virtual immunity from interference, a pleasant condition which applied to other Saratoga gambling houses as well. Only two serious attempts to close the Club House were made during the fifteen years that elapsed between the death of Morrissey and the acquisition of the resort by Richard Canfield. The first was engineered by Anthony Comstock, who slithered into Saratoga in August, 1886, and with several assistants spent a week gathering evidence and raiding gambling places. None of the gamblers, however, was brought into court. In his report to the New York Society for the Suppression of Vice Comstock declared that twenty gambling houses had closed their doors, but admitted that most of them "resumed business as soon as our agents left town." As a matter of fact, the wheels were turning and the tiger growling in the Club House long before the departure of the great Smut-Hound.

The second attack upon gambling in Saratoga during the Reed-Spencer regime was made in 1889 by Spencer Trask, a New York broker who owned the Saratoga *Union,* a daily newspaper. Trask's campaign was vigorously opposed by most of the villagers, who recognized the fact that the presence of large, free-spending crowds was due principally to horse racing and open gambling, and the newsdealers refused to handle the *Union* when it published a map showing the location of the gaming resorts. Trask thereupon recruited a small army of uniformed boys to distribute the paper, which they did with considerable difficulty, for the people of Saratoga were disinclined to accept the *Union* even as a gift. Private detectives imported from New York obtained sufficient evidence to compel the issuance of warrants, and Trask procured the arrest of Spencer and half a dozen other gamblers, including Caleb Mitchell. They were released on bail to await the action of the

Grand Jury, and reopened their houses as soon as they left the courtroom. Their victory was complete when the Grand Jury refused to return indictments. Trask had spent $50,000, and had succeeded only in annoying the gamblers and destroying the prestige of his newspaper.

Spencer withstood Trask's crusade alone, for Reed had given up his interest in the Club House in 1887 and returned to New York. When the house in West Twenty-fourth Street was closed, Reed retired to his stock farm in Tennessee, which he had established several years before, and where he had at stud the famous racing stallion St. Blaise. Reed had paid $100,000 for this animal, but his progeny never came up to expectations. Spencer remained in Saratoga only a few more years. In 1880 he sold his ninety per cent interest in the race track for $375,000 to Gottfried Walbaum, who had operated a notorious race course at Guttenberg, N.J., and who in later years was said by the New York police to be one of the owners of the famous gambling house in West Thirty-third Street known as the House with the Bronze Door. Walbaum in turn sold the racing plant in 1901 to a syndicate headed by William C. Whitney, and it was never again controlled by gamblers. Three years after he had disposed of the track Spencer took Richard Canfield in as a partner in the Club House, and in 1894 Canfield became sole owner. Spencer went to France to live, and died there in 1907, a year or so after Reed's death in Tennessee.

8

John Morrissey's most important rival in New York, and one of the few who refused to acknowledge Old Smoke's overlordship, was Johnny Chamberlin. A native of Pittsfield, Mass., Chamberlin followed Horace Greeley's advice and went west in the middle 1850's, and as John O'Connor said, "his first ap-

From an old print

THE FEMALE GAMBLER AND HER LITTLE GAME IN A PULLMAN
STATE-ROOM

pearance in public life was made as bar-tender on one of the numerous steamboats running from the port of St. Louis." Chamberlin learned the rudiments of sharping from the river gamblers, for whom he acted as custodian of cold decks and other cheating paraphernalia, and after a year or two on the Mississippi began to serve as roper-in for a skinning house whenever his boat was in her home port. "In his mind's eye," O'Connor wrote, "he marked out each passenger on the boat, during her trip to St. Louis, whom he thought likely to prove a profitable subject to him, and after showing him the sights of the city, would bring him up standing before a 'brace game,' have him robbed, and afterwards receive half the plunder." [12] Having acquired a considerable stake in this fashion, Chamberlin abandoned the river when the Civil War began, and opened a skinning house of his own in St. Louis, a disreputable dive which he operated with great success until 1864. In the summer of that year Price McGrath, who only a little while before had been released from a New Orleans military prison, arrived in St. Louis, and he and Chamberlin decided that their future lay in New York, which harbored more suckers to the square mile than any other city in the country. Accordingly Chamberlin sold his skinning den, and the precious pair set out for the metropolis with a joint capital of more than $100,000. They landed in New York about the time that John Morrissey began organizing the syndicate which established the house in No. 5 West Twenty-fourth Street, and immediately subscribed to the project. They performed prodigies of roping among the Southern and Western suckers who swarmed into New York immediately after the Civil War, and much of the extraordinary early success of the house was due to their efforts. In 1867, however, Chamberlin quarreled with Morrissey, and both he and McGrath withdrew from the syndicate. With almost half a

[12] *Wanderings of a Vagabond*, page 203.

million dollars in his pocket, McGrath returned to his native Kentucky, and near Lexington established a stock farm, which he called McGrathiana. For many years he was prominent as a breeder of thoroughbreds which carried his colors at most of the important race meets in the East and the South. Also, he became a very influential citizen, and at McGrathiana entertained the great and the near-great of Kentucky. Said a Kentucky newspaper of May 5, 1872:

"McGrath, of beautiful and princely McGrathiana, Sunday last gave a dinner to his many friends gathered at Lexington with the object of attending the races. Report says the day was lovely and the dinner was a grand success. Among the gentlemen who gathered round the tables spread on the blue-grass lawn, under the stately locust trees, were . . . ex-Governor Robinson, General A. Buford . . . General John C. Breckinridge [13] . . . General Basil Duke, General James F. Robinson, Jr., . . . General William Preston . . . Colonel Robert Wooley. . . . Hospitality at McGrathiana is as princely as the estate is lordly; and it is not necessary to add that the distinguished gentlemen thoroughly enjoyed themselves. Not to know McGrath and McGrathiana is not to know all the splendors of the blue-grass country." [14]

Chamberlin remained in New York after his break with Morrissey, and at No. 8 West Twenty-fifth Street opened a gambling house which for elegance and magnificence outshone No. 818 Broadway and the house in West Twenty-fourth Street, and in at least one respect excelled even the Club House at Saratoga. A French chef, said to have been the first ever employed in an American gaming resort, presided over the

[13] Vice-President of the United States in Buchanan's administration.
[14] *Wanderings of a Vagabond*, pages 261–62.

kitchen in Chamberlin's establishment, "and on every night, except Sunday, a table might be found there, which, for the rarity, diversity, and the choiceness of its viands, wines and liquors, the elegance of its appearance, and the excellence of its cuisine, could not be surpassed by any in the world." Morrissey frequently tried to have Chamberlin's place closed by the police, and otherwise attempted to discipline the defiant gambler, but all of his efforts were unsuccessful, for Chamberlin's first care had been to form friendships with men who were able to protect him. Also, he was very careful to keep them away from his two-card Faro boxes and his crooked Roulette wheels. He numbered among his gambling intimates such powerful politicians and officials as Superintendent of Police James J. Kelso, William M. Tweed, Honest John Kelly, Peter B. Sweeney, Slippery Dick Connolly; and, among other influential private citizens, James Fisk, Jr., most famous of early New York's playboys. When Fisk lay dying after he had been shot by Edward S. Stokes in 1872, Chamberlin was among the group of friends gathered at his bedside.

Saratoga's most ambitious rival as a gay watering-place for some fifteen years after the Civil War was Long Branch, N.J., the summer home of President Ulysses S. Grant in the 1870's, the vacation playground of Jim Fisk and his crowd, the Mecca of horse-owners who could drive as fast as they pleased on the smooth beaches; and, as an advertisement said in 1875, "a cheap and easy release from the narrow streets of the city, and equally narrow pursuits of gain, to the soul-saving worship of the great and good God through the never-quiet, never-ceasing roar of the mighty ocean." But gambling and horse racing, with Johnny Chamberlin as their prophet, actually played a greater part in the development of Long Branch as a summer resort than did the "soul-saving worship of the great and good God." In 1869 Chamberlin made himself even more obnoxious to John Morrissey by building at Long Branch a palatial gambling house which attracted many suckers who might otherwise have gone to Saratoga. A year later he established the Monmouth Park race track, which competed successfully with the Saratoga track, and drew larger crowds because of its nearness to New York. The gambling house is said to have cost $90,000 to build and equip, while in the track Chamberlin put $150,000 of his own money, and another $100,000 subscribed by his friends, among them Fisk, Tweed, Price McGrath, and Pierre Lorillard, head of one of New York's most noted families.

Chamberlin's gaming establishment, which he called the Monmouth Park Club House, occupied a commanding position in the center of an imposing fifty-acre lawn, the only other buildings being an ice house and a stable, both of which were roofed with variegated slate and capped with golden vanes and rods. "The Club House itself," wrote a reporter for the Chicago *Tribune* in 1870, "was of a pale yellow color frame, and three stories high; the upper story in a tipped Mansard roof of beautiful inlaid slate, and the whole was tipped with a gilded balustrade of peculiar iron work. A piazza surrounded the first story of the house, of a light and beautiful construction—green trellis-work below, the columns painted red, with gilt Corinthian capitals, and the balustrade above was also yellow and gilt. There was but one entrance, and that a grand one, with a drive meandering up to it. The whole edifice was a gem of carpentry, standing high and gracefully, and I guessed its proportions to be eighty feet square. . . . We passed into an elegant house, rather extravagantly bedecked with mirrors, and yet upholstered in places with as much taste as cost. Copious supplies of gas filled the many softly enameled globes of the chandeliers, and these lights were reproduced in the mirrors; while yet the rich carpets were of subdued patterns, and the wall paper would have done credit to an educated lady's eye. The furniture was as unique and solid [it included a famous sideboard, made entirely of inlaid wood, which had cost $1,200] as the workmanship of the day can afford. The time has gone by when we can describe a master gambler by his gaudy surroundings. The arts can find no better patrons in our time than successful gamblers. . . . [Chamberlin] at once led the way to the supper room.

"'Take seats,' he said, 'here is about everything—frogs, woodcock, quails, robins, trout, soft-shell crabs, and terrapins. William, some wine.'

"A black man, of deferential manners, gave me a plate of frogs and robins, and filled a glass with such wine that all previous vintages of my acquaintance seemed mere cider to it. The table was epicurean in every part. . . ."

As for the happy owner of all this magnificence, the *Tribune* reporter thus described him:

"Chamberlin was a good-looking man under forty years of age, with the blackest eye one can see in a man's head, large, piercing and animal-like, and at once beautiful and dangerous. His forehead was good, and with large developments over the eyebrows, so strong that I was not mistaken to see some instances of a wonderful memory, so necessary to a gamester. The lower part of his face and nose were coarser, and his mustache appeared to be dyed, while his hair was glossy black as the crow's wing. He had a laughing manner, a good smile, and in his features the gentleman and the outlaw were blended. His shoulders were broad and square, and his frame was over-powerful, and he stood upon his feet in that posture approaching bowleggedness, which is natural in the sporting man and the sparrer. Withal, he looked his part, a man of wild instincts stricken with a commercial ambition, and erecting his vices into a business interest; a young man, still unmarried, but consoling himself with the temporary possession of one of the most voluptuous actresses in America. . . ."

Chamberlin's house in West Twenty-fifth Street retained its popularity for some ten years, and with the aid of Price Mc-Grath he kept the establishment at Long Branch going almost as long. McGrath raced his horses at Monmouth Park every year, and also roped for the Club House, receiving a substantial percentage of the profits. He remained a familiar figure at Long Branch until he died there on July 5, 1881. Chamberlin enjoyed extraordinary prosperity for several years, but he bought a stable of thoroughbreds about 1875, and thereafter his downfall was rapid; he backed his horses heavily, and lost so much money that he was compelled to close the resort in New York and sacrifice the Club House at Long Branch and his interest in the race track. "It is supposed," said the New York *Tribune* in 1877, "that Chamberlin has won altogether $1,000,-000, but . . . in spite of the 'snapper' roulette wheel and many mechanical devices for cheating he has failed utterly unless, as is supposed by some, his brother holds his property to defraud his creditors." Chamberlin saved enough from the wreckage of his gambling career to make a new start in Washington in the early 1880's, establishing a restaurant which became one of the most celebrated eating places in the history of the city. Some years later Congress voted him a grant of land on the military reservation of Fortress Monroe, in Virginia, and among his friends in politics and society Chamberlin raised a fund of $1,500,000, with which he built the Chamberlin Hotel at Old Point Comfort. It was the finest and best known seashore resort in that part of the country until it burned soon after the end of the World War.

9

During the long period in which John Morrissey was cock of the walk in New York and Saratoga, both Washington and New Orleans, as far as the East and South were concerned, retained their ante-bellum rank as next in importance to the metropolis, although neither city ever regained the reputation it had enjoyed in the great days of Edward Pendleton and the Hall of the Bleeding Heart, and of John Davis and Price McGrath. The flurry of gambling in Boston in the late 1860's was of short duration, dominated by John Stuart and his chain of second-class skinning houses, and of no particular importance; while the few good establishments opened from time to time by the sedate sharpers of Philadelphia failed to arouse any great excitement among either gamblers or suckers. Richmond harbored scores of Southern gamesters while the Virginia city was the capital of the Confederate States, but the houses they operated were makeshift resorts hurriedly equipped to trim the officials and employes of the new government. After Lee's surrender and the collapse of the Confederacy most of Richmond's gamblers fled, some going to New York and New Orleans and others crossing the Alleghenies and beginning new careers in Chicago and the West. Baltimore failed to fulfill her promise of the early days, and was never nationally prominent as a gambling town despite the Herculean efforts of a syndicate of gamesters in the 1870's and the 1880's.

A few sharpers, notably George Devol, Charley Bush and Colonel J. J. Bryant, prospered in Mobile during the early years of the War, but their houses were closed when a Federal Army captured the city in 1865. After the cessation of hostilities the development of gambling in Mobile was halted by harsh laws and an almost complete stoppage of economic and population growth—not until 1890 did the town have as many as 30,000 inhabitants—which was at least partly due to the rise of Birmingham as the chief city of Alabama. Unable to produce or attract big-time suckers, Mobile was naturally shunned by big-time sharpers, and gambling was confined to Keno and Rondo parlors, an occasional cheap skinning house, and, of course, Policy and the Lottery. From the viewpoint of the professional gamester, Mobile's only claim to renown in post-bellum times was as the birthplace of Bud Renaud, who was probably the best known gambler in the South in the 1870's and the 1880's, and was as celebrated for his good looks and courtly manners as for his gifts at Faro and short cards. He backed several houses in New Orleans, plunged heavily against any honest Faro bank he could find, and around 1880 attempted to revive first-class gambling in Mobile, but without much success. In the latter years of his career Renaud's main interest was in pugilism, and he promoted, among other famous fights, the last professional bare-knuckle battle on American soil—the contest between John L. Sullivan and Jake Kilrain at Richburg, Miss., on July 8, 1889, which was awarded to Sullivan on points at the end of the seventy-fifth round.

For a decade of John Morrissey's reign Mobile's former place in Eastern and Southern gambling was occupied by Buffalo, which for some twenty years prior to the Civil War was notorious as one of the toughest towns in the United States, the rendezvous of prize-fighters and their attendant ruffians, and the playground of Great Lakes sailors and the boatmen of the Erie Canal. The latter especially were just as hardy and quarrelsome as the bullies of the Mississippi, and when ashore demanded the same sort of entertainment. It was lavishly provided by a double row of dives in Canal Street, "then in the zenith of its prosperity and debauchery," among which were many cheap gambling dens. As an old-time Buffalonian once said, "Faro rooms, Keno rooms, Poker rooms, and general gaming rooms, were as thick as sand flies, and ran in all their glory, in full blast day and night." Gambling facilities for suckers of a more substantial class were introduced into Buffalo in the early 1850's, and a dozen first-class houses were in continuous operation for almost fifteen years. None of these establishments approached the resorts of New York and Washington in pretentiousness, but the furnishings and equipment were adequate and the play high, and they were accounted very comfortable places in which to lose money. They enjoyed their greatest prosperity during the war period, when the weekly profits of each of the principal houses ranged from $5,000 to $20,000, against running expenses of from $1,500 to $3,500. The first move by the authorities against the gamblers was made in 1866, when every house in Buffalo was closed by the newly-organized Niagara Frontier Police. Many reopened within a few months, but all except two or three, which managed to maintain an existence for almost forty years, were once more suppressed in 1870. In later years lenient city administrations occasionally permitted a few houses to operate, but gambling never again reached important proportions.

Considering the size and comparative isolation of the town and the fact that first-class gambling flourished there for such a short time, Buffalo produced a remarkably large number of celebrated gamblers. Perhaps the best known were Gentleman Bill Carney, Timothy Glassford, Oat Forrester, Reed Brockway, Oliver Westcott, Jim McCormick, and Adam Clark, the last named an English Jew who owned a large tract of land in Main Street. After Clark's death this property was turned into an amusement park known as Spring Abbey, while the handsome brick house in which the gambler had lived and run his games became a Home for the Friendless. Clark's greatest asset as a gambling house keeper was his credit; not only his fellow-gamesters, but bankers and merchants as well, frequently lent him large sums on no other security than his verbal promise to pay. He was worth about $100,000 in 1860, but when he died his affairs were so involved that lawyers got most of the estate. Forrester was the dandy of the Buffalo gamblers—he wore a set of diamond jewelry which had cost him $30,000, and never paid less than $75 for a suit of clothes, in those days an enormous price. McCormick was a famous Faro dealer, well known in New York and Chicago, who commanded the fabulous wage of $1,000 a week and a percentage of the profits. He abandoned gambling in the 1870's and put his money into a stable of trotting horses, with which he made a fortune. Reed Brockway, an intellectual sharper who studied mathematics as a hobby, is said to have been able to keep the run of cards at Faro without the aid of a case-keeper, and never make a mistake. His success at naming winning cards was sometimes uncanny. Once in 1867, with six cards left in the box, he bet $2,000 that the case king would be the last winning card, which it was. Oliver Westcott was widely known as a plunger, never betting less than $1,000 on a single turn at Faro, and often backing his judgment with ten times that amount. After he had won $60,000 in two months Faro dealers throughout the country placed a limit of $5,000 on his bets. He was rich half a dozen times, but eventually luck deserted him, and he ended his career running a small game in Colorado.

Carney and Glassford were the king-pin gamblers of Buffalo for many years. The latter was well educated and spoke several languages, and at one time, in the 1870's, exercised considerable influence in both city and state politics. His Faro game, which he usually dealt himself, is said to have been strictly honest, and since he imposed no limit it attracted Faro plungers from all over the country. In 1867 Glassford's fortune was estimated at $200,000, but at the time of his death in the middle 1880's it had dwindled to about $80,000, including three parcels of real estate in Main and Eagle Streets. Gentleman Bill Carney was a member of a respectable and well-to-do Buffalo family. He began gambling professionally in his 'teens, and by the time he was twenty years old was considered one of the most expert Faro dealers in the country. He made a fortune of half a million dollars with his gambling house, but drink and dissipation took their toll, and he was a poor man when he died about 1890.

10

From 1860 to 1867 more than six hundred professional gamblers made their headquarters in Washington, and the suckers of the national capital supported at least a hundred gaming houses, of which about one-third were first-class establishments. All were frequented by government officials and departmental employes, members of Congress, politicians and lobbyists, Army and Navy officers and paymasters, and others who had access to the public funds. Said Edward Winslow Martin in a book called *Behind the Scenes in Washington,* published in 1873:

"Here you may see the 'great men' of the country, as they are called, men high in position and authority in the land, men charged with the handling of the funds of the nation. . . . Sad as is the assertion, it is nevertheless true, that the greatest men this country has ever produced, have been frequenters of these fashionable hells. . . . It makes you feel nervous to see paymasters and financial agents of the government clustering around the tables. . . . It is a well known fact in Washington, that during a certain memorable session of Congress, the proprietor of a noted gambling house received from the Sergeant-at-Arms nearly all the salaries of a large portion of the members of the Lower

House, upon presenting orders made payable to him by said members. . . ." [15]

The number of gambling houses decreased rapidly after the War; in 1872 Washington was said by the police to harbor only seventeen such resorts, all but four of which were skinning dives of the worst sort. By the middle 1880's first-class places were unknown in the capital, and big-time gambling was confined almost entirely to the private Poker games of rich Senators, Representatives, lobbyists, and government officials. Many of the big sessions of this character were held in Chamberlin's restaurant, for while Chamberlin had no facilities for public play, he did provide private rooms, with no kitty for the house, which men of sufficient social or political standing could use for short card games. At some of these sessions, especially those in which Senator E. O. Wolcott of Colorado was concerned, the stakes were very high, and frequently as much as $100,000 changed hands in a single evening. During the 1880's and the early 1890's Senator Wolcott was generally regarded as the ablest Poker player in the capital, and with the possible exceptions of Henry Clay and General Robert C. Schenck, was probably the greatest that Washington has ever produced. A few years later, at Richard Canfield's house in New York, Senator Wolcott acquired a reputation as a Faro plunger second only to that of John W. Gates.

One of the hundred gambling houses in war-time Washington was the resort opened about 1853 by Joe Hall. It remained in continuous operation until October, 1870, but was not as successful, after Hall had begun to devote most of his time to horse racing, as when it was competing with the Hall of the Bleeding Heart. Another was the Congressional Faro Bank, so called because of the character of its clientele, which occupied

[15] Pages 506–7. Edward Winslow Martin was the pseudonym of James Dabney McCabe, a Virginia author and dramatist.

the second and third floors of a brick building in Pennsylvania Avenue near Fourteenth Street, and in which John Morrissey owned an interest when he was a member of Congress. More popular and prosperous than either of these, however, was a gaudy den in Pennsylvania Avenue which, during the three years from 1863 to 1866, made an annual profit of $500,000. It was operated by a small syndicate of gamblers headed by Bill Parker, who had arrived in Washington from the South a year or so before the Civil War; and Jim Kirby, later a dealer at No. 818 Broadway in New York, who was described by the New York *Times* in 1880 as "a benevolent-looking old party . . . with long, silver-gray beard and puffy countenance indicative of good feeding." A third member of the syndicate was an extraordinary young man, a New Yorker, named Florence Scannell, who unquestionably would have won great fame both as a gambler and as a politician if a bullet hadn't cut his career short before he was twenty-five years old. Like Bill Poole, young Scannell was a butcher by trade, and owned a valuable stand in Poole's old stamping ground, the Washington Market. He also followed the Poole traditions in the matter of fighting, and was a noted rough-and-tumble bruiser before he was twenty. With his five and one-half feet of height Scannell was a pigmy compared to other great sluggers of his time, but what he lacked in inches was made up in agility and strength—a description of him published in 1869 said that he had "a chestal and muscular development such as the writer never saw equaled." Politically he was "an unadulterated Democrat of unbounded pluck and rare political strength."

Scannell's ability as a fighter and his great popularity among the roughs made him invaluable to Tammany Hall, and despite his youth he was of great assistance in the handling of repeaters and shoulder-hitters. Although he could barely write his name and read print only with difficulty, Scannell was elected to the

City Council in 1866, soon after his twenty-first birthday, and repeated his victory in 1869, although in the meantime he had quarreled with Tweed and had been marked for the slaughter as an enemy of the Tammany ring. He was involved in the registration and naturalization frauds which were uncovered by a Congressional Committee early in 1869, and told the investigators that they could bet their lives he was "coming down there to Congress some day." He was there sooner than he had anticipated, for when he refused to answer the Committee's questions he was arrested and haled before the bar of the House of Representatives. Persisting in his refusal, he was fined the costs of his arrest, and in default of payment was imprisoned for five weeks in makeshift quarters in the basement of the Capitol.

The gambling activities of this brilliant young ruffian were less spectacular than his exploits as a politician, but it is doubtful if they have been equaled by any other American sharper of his age. He was collecting tribute from the skin games in his own district before he was eighteen years old, and he was only about nineteen when he became one of the backers of Washington's principal gambling house. Besides this venture he owned, during the War, shares in other capital resorts, and in two or three small Faro games in Alexandria, Va., which had been occupied by Federal troops soon after the outbreak of hostilities. After his election as a member of the New York City Council, about the time that John Morrissey was establishing the Club House at Saratoga, Scannell opened a Faro bank in Fourth Avenue near Twenty-seventh Street, which netted him about $1,600 a month, a very handsome income for a boy of twenty-two. He was climbing upward with great strides, determined to control Tammany Hall and supplant John Morrissey as boss of New York gambling, when in December, 1869, he was shot by a saloon-keeper named Tom Donahue in the latter's barroom at Second Avenue and Twenty-second Street.

Scannell died on July 9, 1870, and on November 2, 1872, Donahue was killed by his victim's brother, John Scannell, Deputy Sheriff and owner of a hotel in Third Avenue. John Scannell was acquitted on a plea of self-defense. In later years he became politically powerful, and was a trusted adviser of the famous Tammany chieftain, Richard Croker.

Florence Scannell retired from the Washington syndicate when he opened his own place in New York, and Parker and Kirby closed the house in the capital about 1868, after the yearly take had dwindled to less than $50,000. The record is silent concerning the further activities of these accomplished sharpers until early in 1870, when they became associated with Robert J. Slater, better known as Doc Slater, who was destined to become Baltimore's most celebrated gambling house keeper and a more or less prominent figure in the political machine controlled by Senator Arthur Pue Gorman and I. Freeman Rasin. Slater was born in East Baltimore in 1838, and as a youth was trained as assistant to his father, a prosperous butcher and bacon cutter. But he soon abandoned the cleaver and the sausage grinder for the gayer life of a rowdy, becoming the leader of a band of Plug-Uglies and rendering yeoman service to the politicians. During this period of his career Slater was widely known as an expert at Quoits, and was recognized as the best tenpins bowler in Baltimore. He began gambling professionally a year or two before the Civil War, and about 1862 started a Faro bank with an open limit of $6.25, in partnership with two other young sports. They established themselves in the building at No. 10 South Calvert Street, which had been first opened as a gambling house about 1832, and which was used continuously for that purpose for some seventy years, until it was destroyed in the great fire which devastated Baltimore in February, 1904.

Despite the smallness of the limit and the fact that it was

patronized almost exclusively by poor suckers, Slater's game made a net profit of $40,000 in its first year of operation. At the end of that time he bought out his partners, raised the limit to $25 open, and within another year had doubled his stake. He now renovated and refurnished the establishment, served free liquors and meals, and began to cater to the best suckers of Baltimore, announcing that he would accept bets up to a limit of $5,000 on a single turn. His good luck was phenomenal, and convinced that a Faro bank could not lose, he enlarged his operations, backing houses in Washington, Annapolis, and Cape May, then the gayest of American seashore resorts. He also emulated Brother Elijah Skaggs and sent half a dozen artists through the country to search out Faro addicts. But Slater's luck began to turn early in 1868. The game in Calvert Street began to lose consistently, profits from his other houses decreased and finally stopped altogether, and his traveling sharpers either lost their bankrolls or absconded with them. Within two years Slater had lost all of his own money and $25,000 which he had borrowed from friends, including $5,000 from Parker of Washington. He approached Parker for another loan, but that stern realist said he had no more money to throw away on an honest Faro bank. He offered, however, to put $100,000 into the Calvert Street house if Slater would agree to throw the element of chance out of the window and let the Faro dealers and the croupiers "protect the bank." Slater had turned down several such propositions in the days of his prosperity, but now he perforce agreed, for it was either that or financial ruin.

Jim Kirby joined the syndicate, and the result of much planning and a lavish expenditure of money was the Maryland Gentlemen's Club House, which was thrown open to the enraptured suckers of Baltimore with a grand dedication banquet attended by more than one hundred and fifty guests. Among

JOHN MORRISSEY

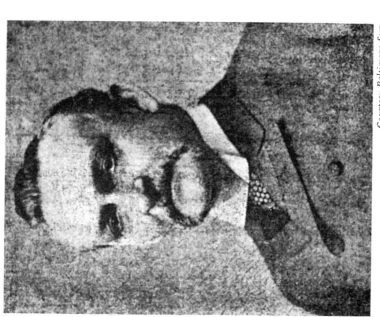

ROBERT J. (DOC) SLATER

them, as John O'Connor said in his *Wanderings of a Vagabond,*
were "many of the most distinguished men of Maryland, members of the State Legislature, Judges of the higher courts, and
a score or so of representatives of the city government, contractors, etc.," all in full dinner costume of black coat and pants,
white vests and white neckties. "Speeches were made by prominent gentlemen, laudatory of the enterprise of the management in enacting so fine a club house. . . ." The artists employed by Messrs. Slater, Parker & Kirby apparently lost no time
in getting down to business, for "after dinner the play ranged
high, the bank beginning its career with a run of luck, winning
about $20,000, half of which was lost by a well-known City
Hall contractor." The surroundings in which the chivalry of
Baltimore disported itself on this memorable occasion were
almost unbelievably elegant, for the Maryland Gentlemen's
Club House was not only the grandest gambling establishment
in Baltimore's history; it was also one of the finest that had
ever opened its doors anywhere in the United States. If this
description of the resort, published in *Wanderings of a Vagabond* in 1873 and quoted from the New York *World,* is even
half-way accurate, it lost nothing in comparison with the gilded
palaces of John Morrissey and Johnny Chamberlin:

> "The building itself . . . has undergone a complete
> renovation, the floors in the upper part being raised four
> feet each, the rooms in the second story thrown into one,
> and connected with a large dining hall in the rear, through
> folding doors, and the ground floor being devoted exclu-
> sively to kitchen and store-room purposes. A large cellar
> extends the length of the building underground, and a pri-
> vate entrance leads out into the open lot on a back street,
> through which the visitors can pass if desirous of shunning
> the main entrance.

REGARDLESS OF EXPENSE

"In making these extensive preparations, no regard has been paid to their cost. . . . The total cost, I am told, of furnishing the house, amounted to fifty thousand dollars. This does not include various costly works of art, such as rare paintings and statues, and the dinner service, for which the round sum of twenty thousand dollars was paid to one European firm alone. . . .

A GORGEOUS VESTIBULE

"The hall door which faces Calvert Street, about half a block from Baltimore Street, the principal thoroughfare in the city, opens into a small vestibule, from the ceiling of which hangs a large bell-shaped chandelier lined with silver, and with the jets so arranged, that the light streams down and outward in a soft flood, revealing oak-paneled walls in etchings of gold, and a lofty ceiling frescoed with groups of sporting naiads. Immediately beyond, and dividing the hall into two parts, stands another and a more massive door of solid walnut. . . . The inner hallway is larger than the outer, and once over its threshold, the visitor is at liberty to explore the mysteries above, to which a flight of steps winds slowly upwards. The same paneled walls and a similar chandelier mark this second hall, which has, however, the addition of a velvet carpet, thick enough to stifle the heaviest footfall.

MAGNIFICENT FURNITURE

"The main saloon, to which the hall stairs conduct, occupies the entire front of the second story, and is about sixty feet long and thirty wide. It is gorgeously fitted up. A seamless dark blue velvet carpet, like that in the east room of the White House, covers the floor, over which are scattered articles of furniture of the most massive description. On the right, as you enter, an étagère of rose-wood that reaches up to the ceiling; two bronze statues of Richard Coeur de Lion and Philippe Auguste rest on its lower shelves, flanking a famous equine bronze representing a stallion teasing a mare. A mirror forms the backing of this piece of furniture, which was imported at a cost of three thousand, five hundred dollars. On the left stands a sideboard on which are ranged all sorts of decanters and glasses, the former of cut glass, and filled with various kinds of wines and liquors; these are at the gratuitous use of the visitors. All along the room are placed various articles of furniture, made wholly of walnut and rose-wood; sofas, chairs, foot-stools, massive round tables for the convenience of short card parties, writing desks, lounges, etc. Two mantels of Parian marble, surmounting ranges of the most approved and costly make, are set in the west wall, over which hang two mirrors of French plate glass set in walnut frames, with an intertwining of gold leaves and vine work. . . .

AN ARTISTIC CHECK BOOK

"The check book for the use of persons who, having no ready cash, are yet desirous of playing, together with other writing materials, is kept in a large book-case in one corner of the saloon. This book-case is filled with private compartments of various sizes. . . . It also contains a number of secret drawers, used to keep 'collateral' in until redeemed.

BLUE AND GOLD

"The walls of this saloon are paneled similarly to those of the entry, except that the background is of blue, and there is a freer use of gold. The contrast between this and the frescoes on the ceiling is very striking and effective. . . . The windows are curtained by fine lace drapery, backed by heavy damask curtains, pendant from cornices of rosewood with gold borders.

THE GAMING TABLES

"Are three in number. At two of these Faro is played; at the other, Roulette. . . . Immediately behind the Faro tables hang two pictures of Rubens, representing Sunrise and Sunset at Sea. A third of a French Peasant Girl, returning home laden with fruits, is the production of a clever French artist. . . . The dealers, of whom there are five, are men well known in the profession.

MORE SPLENDOR UPSTAIRS

"The upper story comprises seven chambers, three of which are used as club rooms. Appurtenances for playing all sorts of games can be found in them, and the furniture is of the richest possible description. Back of these rooms are three bed-chambers elegantly furnished. The beds are importations, and cost five hundred dollars each. These rooms are for the use of players who wish to leave the city by an early morning train, or who, from too free libations of champagne, are disinclined to walk home. A bathroom, with hot and cold water, is attached to each chamber. The kitchen and store-room run the whole length of the ground-floor. The former is larger than any hotel kitchen in the city, and has a range able to cook provisions for one hundred persons at a time; its cost was three thousand, five hundred dollars. . . . The wine-cellar . . . is under ground. . . . Twenty thousand dollars worth of wines and liquors are stored here already, and a large importation, I am informed, is *en route*.

THE CLIMAX OF ENCHANTMENT

"Of all the various departments of the house, however, it is reserved for the dining hall to stand forth as the Alpha and Omega of its many splendors. The entrance to it is from the main saloon, and it is through folding doors of stained box-wood, the panels of which are carved to represent various scenes of the chase. They move on noiseless wheels an inch and a half deep, made so on account of the great superincumbent weight. . . . The table is an immense affair, and is capable of seating eighty persons. It is made of black walnut, supported by heavy dragon-legs of the same material. The chairs are also of black walnut, with soft cushions, covered with green morocco. The appointments of the table are dazzlingly magnificent. In the center rests an enormous silver ice-holder, which can also be used as a flower stand. Its sides are of solid silver, with an embossed net-work of branches and fruits in virgin gold; the inside is also of the same metal. . . . All glass used in this establishment is cut, and of European importation, and stamped with the initial 'S.' . . . The rest of the dinner-service is of solid silver, lined with gold. Among other things are two silver pitchers, two feet high, which were made in Geneva at a cost of one thousand dollars each. The room is brilliantly lit by two chandeliers and various side jets. . . . The walls are unlike those in the main saloon, being box-wood paneled with etchings of scarlet and silver to match the doors. . . . The floor is laid with a red velvet carpet, so thick and soft that the foot falls noiselessly upon it. . . ." [16]

[16] Pages 189–94.

Parker is said to have sold his share of the Maryland Gentlemen's Club House to Slater after a few years, but Kirby retained his interest, and the building still stood in his name when it was finally sold on May 2, 1902. Kirby was also associated with Slater in the operation of the Ocean Club at Long Branch, and similar resorts at Cape May and White Sulphur Springs, from all of which Slater retired during the middle 1890's. The active management of the Calvert Street establishment was in Slater's hands from the beginning, and for more than thirty years it was known all over the country simply as "Doc Slater's place." It enjoyed its greatest popularity in the 1870's and 1880's, when it was "the headquarters of some of the most widely known sporting men in the country, including the Lorillards, the Belmonts, Tom Ochiltree, and many others," and when "the turn of a card meant the changing hands of from $15,000 to $25,000 every few minutes." Although John O'Connor declared that the Club House was opened as a *de luxe* skinning-den, Baltimore legend has it that the Faro and other games played there were fair, and that Doc Slater was an honest gambler from start to finish. "In all the games of chance in which he played or which he backed," said the Baltimore *Sun's* obituary account of his career,[17] "there was never a whisper or a suspicion of anything that was not perfectly straight."

Slater's income from the Club House and other enterprises was enormous, but when he died on May 3, 1902, in his sixty-fifth year, he was a comparatively poor man. The bulk of his fortune had been squandered at the race track, but a considerable portion had gone to charitable purposes, for like many another professional gambler, Slater was extremely generous. According to the Baltimore *Sun* he supported seven families, paid the funeral expenses of fifteen or twenty destitute sporting men, endowed three beds at the old St. Agnes Hospital and com-

[17] May 4, 1902.

412

pletely furnished one room, and contributed largely to the support of St. Vincent's Orphan Asylum; while "for many years a crowd of pensioners living upon his bounty were wont to appear regularly every Saturday afternoon at his Calvert Street place to receive their weekly allowance." If the obituaries are to be believed, Slater's private life was beyond reproach—he was a good Catholic, devoted to his family, and a teetotaler, while his lips were never sullied by even the mildest of oaths. In appearance he bore no resemblance to the gaudy gamblers of New York and other cities. "Mr. Slater was always one of the most neatly dressed men in the city," said the *Sun*. "He spent a large amount of money on his clothes and took considerable pride in them. They were, however, never flashy. It is said that he got as many as twenty pairs of trousers at once from one of the most fashionable tailors in the city. Many of his clothes he had made in New York, and many more in London. He did not wear rings or pins, and even a watch chain was rarely seen on him." [18]

II

Public gambling was unknown in New Orleans for some two years after the gaming houses were closed by the Federal Army of Occupation in 1864, but the sharpers began to emerge from their hiding places early in 1866, and appeared in New Orleans in rapidly increasing numbers as the carpet-baggers superseded the military in control of the city and the state. Among the first of the old-timers to return were Charley Bush and Colonel J. J. Bryant; and Allen Jones, who had spent most of the war-time period on his plantation in Mississippi. Bush established a new house in Royal Street, while Jones fitted up his old rooms in St. Charles Avenue directly opposite the St. Charles Hotel. Colonel Bryant had won a million dollars in Mobile during the

[18] *Ibid.*

War, but it was all in Confederate money, and he arrived in New Orleans with no assets but a trunkful of worthless currency. For old times' sake Jones took him in as partner, and the Colonel acted as the establishment's principal roper-in. He made the St. Charles Hotel his base of operations, and to lighten his labors suggested that the hotel management build an enclosed passageway above the street, leading from the second-floor parlors to the gambling house. But the hotel failed to see eye to eye with the Colonel in this matter. Although the Faro players among whom Colonel Bryant had always been most successful, the rich merchants and the planters, could no longer afford to buck the tiger, Bryant managed to bring in enough wealthy suckers to enable him to live in the manner to which he had accustomed himself, and to provide a good profit for the house. In the winter of 1868, however, the Colonel roped in his last sucker, a Texan who was fleeced of all of his money and a hundred dollars more which he had bet on markers. Bryant found the Texan in the lobby of the St. Charles a few days later, and when he attempted to collect an altercation began, in the course of which the Colonel made a sudden motion toward his hip pocket. Believing his life to be in danger, the Texan drew a revolver and shot the gambler dead. Later it was found that all Colonel Bryant had in his pocket was a handkerchief. The death of the Colonel was an irreparable loss to Allen Jones. He kept his house open for another year or so, but business fell off immediately; no other roper-in of Bryant's class was available, and when Jones himself attempted to corral the elusive sucker he was robbed by the men to whom he had entrusted the actual management of the gambling house. By 1870 Jones had lost all of his property except the Mississippi plantation, which was in his wife's name, and was plunging desperately against other Faro banks in the forlorn hope of winning enough to make a new start. He dropped out of sight about 1872.

414

Early in 1869, when control of the city and the state governments had passed into the hands of the carpet-baggers and the looting of the South in the name of reconstruction had fairly begun, gambling in New Orleans was legalized by the Louisiana Legislature for the third time in the city's history. An annual tax of $5,000 was levied upon each establishment, and no restrictions were placed upon the number which might be opened, nor upon the character of the men who operated them. The result of this law exceeded all expectations. Hundreds of sharpers hurried to New Orleans from every large city in the Union, and gambling houses were opened on all the principal streets; and though relatively few paid the license fee, all submitted to blackmail by the police and city officials. Many resorts occupied the whole of three-story buildings, with Faro on the first floor, Roulette on the second, Keno and Rondo on the third, dice and short card games on every floor, and limits ranging from five cents to the roof. On St. Charles Avenue alone, in the few blocks between City Hall and Canal Street, there were forty gambling places, some with special tables for boys, which were open night and day seven days a week. The sidewalks of St. Charles Avenue, Royal, Canal and Chartres Streets, and other important thoroughfares both in the American section and in the so-called French Quarter, were a jostling mass of cappers, steerers, ropers-in and pickers-up, fighting over the suckers and literally dragging their prey into the gambing houses. And working almost shoulder to shoulder were the mobs of Thimble-Riggers and Three-Card Monte men, who made their pitches on folding tables and packing-cases and carried on their swindles without molestation.

The new license law aroused great resentment among the respectable people of New Orleans, but curiously enough the first active opposition to the measure was provided by the men who had been instrumental in procuring its enactment—the operators of the first-class gambling houses. These deluded sharpers had expected to enjoy a monopoly under the protection of the law, but instead found themselves involved in such cut-throat competition that several were forced out of business, and even the most popular houses could barely make expenses. Led by Bill Franklin, a Cincinnati gambler who had opened an ornate resort at Common Street and St. Charles Avenue, the gamblers organized a committee and subscribed funds, and at the next session of the Legislature New Orleans witnessed the unusual spectacle of the gamblers working for the repeal of the law which had rendered them immune from interference. They succeeded, and with gambling once more illegal the big-time gamblers were able to arrange with the police and the politicians to drive out the new-comers. Thereafter for some ten years gambling in New Orleans was conducted quietly, the sharpers dutifully paying tribute to greedy officials, and the latter in return keeping out the undesirables. The only new resort of much importance established in this period was a fine skinning house opened in Royal Street by S. A. Doran, who claimed to have been a Major in the Confederate Army, was known to have killed one man in Texas and another in Memphis, and always carried a pair of big revolvers. Doran ran his place with great success until late in 1883, when he sold out and went to Hot Springs, which was becoming prominent as a health resort, and where gambling was ruled by the three Flynn brothers, Frank, John and Bill. They warned the Major to leave the Springs, but Doran defied them and established a skinning house, whereupon they told him that he must close it or he would be killed. But Doran didn't wait for the Flynns to carry out their threats. He polished up his pistols, organized a body guard of four men, whom he armed with rifles and shotguns, and sent word to the brothers that he was ready for battle. On February 9, 1884, the Major and his henchmen opened fire

416

on the Flynns as they drove down the main street of Hot Springs in a hack, killing Frank Flynn and the hackdriver and wounding John and Bill Flynn. Major Doran escaped trial on his plea of self-defense, and as neither John nor Bill Flynn ever fully recovered from their buckshot wounds, he remained the undisputed gambling king of Hot Springs for several years.

When Joseph Shakespeare became Mayor of New Orleans in 1880, the city harbored eighty-three large gambling resorts, most of which were first-class skinning houses, and all of which were regularly blackmailed by the police and the politicians. Shakespeare advocated the licensing of a few establishments and the rigorous suppression of all others, but the City Council refused to pass the necessary ordinances. Early in 1881 the Mayor ordered the police to close all gambling houses except those in the area bounded by Camp, Gravier, Carondelet, Bourbon, St. Louis and Chartres Streets, and then summoned the operators of the unmolested resorts, which numbered about sixteen, to a conference in his office. He told them that thereafter they would be permitted to operate without competition and without fear of blackmail by the police, on condition that they ran honest games, employed no ropers-in or cappers, barred minors from their premises, and paid to his private secretary $150 a month for each house. The gamblers agreed to the plan, and the initial payments were made in May, 1881. For the first year the total was $30,000, and the annual average approximated that amount during the six years the plan was in operation. Most of the money thus raised was used to build and maintain the Shakespeare Almshouse, an institution which had been needed in New Orleans for years, but enough was withheld to pay the expenses of a few private detectives who periodically inspected the gambling houses and saw to it that the gamblers observed the regulations which had been agreed upon.

The Shakespeare Plan, which was continued through most of

417

the two succeeding administrations, was successful as long as it was honestly administered. It kept gambling within reasonable bounds, and gave to the suckers of New Orleans an opportunity to lose their money in honest games. But in 1885, when J. Valsin Guillotte was Mayor, a few skinning houses were allowed to operate, and the politicians began to divert the fund—of more than $20,000 collected in that year, only $4,875 went to the Almshouse. The remainder, as a Grand Jury put it after an investigation of the situation, was used by city officials "as a sort of contingent or secret service fund." The continued diversion of the gamblers' contributions resulted in a scandal which was taken up by the newspapers, and in March, 1887, the Grand Jury indicted thirty-five gamblers. The cases against them were *nol-prossed* by the District Attorney, but they refused to make any further payments, and the Shakespeare Plan was abandoned. Thereafter New Orleans depended upon the system of control used in most American cities—toleration under corrupt administrations, and suppression when reform elements were in power.

CHAPTER XIII

THE CANFIELD ERA

THE last of the famous gambling house keepers of the nineteenth century was Richard A. Canfield of New York, Newport and Saratoga, who dominated the scene for more than a decade after the retirement of Mike McDonald in the early 1890's. Whether Canfield was also the greatest depends upon the point of view. Considered purely as the operator of a gaming resort, he probably was, for his houses surpassed all others in luxury and magnificence, the play at his tables was for higher stakes than anywhere else in the world, and he was the only American of his class whose renown was truly international. But his influence upon gambling was probably less than that of either John Morrissey or McDonald. He was never powerful in the sense that these eminent sharpers were powerful; he had no interest in politics, and his association with the police and the politicians was confined to the prompt payment of protection money. His business methods were far more honorable than those of the great majority of his contemporaries, and of most of the great gamblers who had preceded him. In none of his resorts did he ever employ ropers and cappers, he never welshed on a bet, and the squareness of his games was never questioned except by the District Attorney and disgruntled police officials who were obviously trying to work up feeling against him in the newspapers. None ever produced proof of such charges. Canfield often declared that it was unnecessary for a gambler who ran banking games to use crooked paraphernalia. "The percentage in favor of a gambling house," he once said, "is sufficient to guarantee the profits of the house. All any gambler wants is to have play enough for a long enough time and he'll get all the money any player has."

Canfield was a gambler of the type of Pendleton of Washington and John Davis of New Orleans; with Morrissey and Mike McDonald he would have had little in common—they were Irish roughnecks, and the veneers of gentility which they acquired failed to conceal their origins. Although his formal education ended with grammar school, Canfield read and studied to such purpose that in his heyday he could pass in any company as a cultured and educated man with a special knowledge of art, Latin and the classics. As a New York newspaper once said, "a stranger who did not know his calling would be at a loss to determine whether the man was an art critic, a man of letters, or a financier . . . but of gambling one would never know he had the remotest knowledge." Outside of his gaming houses, and the Stock Market, in which he won and lost a fortune, Canfield's main interest was in art. He was a connoisseur of considerable distinction, and his opinion was listened to with respect at Christie's and other great auction rooms. He was a charter member of the exclusive Walpole Society, formed by art lovers and men of letters; and for several years was an intimate friend of James McNeill Whistler, who painted his portrait. His collection of Whistler's work was second in value and importance only to that formed by Charles Freer of Detroit.

The height of Canfield's career as a gambler was reached in 1899 when he opened the Saratoga Club in East Forty-fourth Street, the most famous of his houses. At that time he was forty-four years old, five feet and eight inches tall, with brown hair and gray eyes, and weighed about two hundred pounds. His weight increased by forty pounds before his death, and during his last years he wore corsets to keep his abdomen within reasonable bounds. His jowls were heavy and his face was clean-shaven except for a few years in the 1890's, when he wore a small mustache. He arose each morning between six and seven o'clock, ate a comparatively light breakfast of eggs, rolls and coffee, and after looking over his mail took a walk before settling down to the business of the day. In New York he usually dined at Delmonico's, and in Saratoga at the Clubhouse, and nearly always dressed. He ate heavily of rich foods, smoked immoderately, and drank large quantities of wine, often to the point of intoxication. His evenings were spent at his gambling house, but he seldom appeared in the gaming rooms, and was usually in bed by midnight. He slept in an old-fashioned night-shirt. He never gambled, except in the Stock Market, and permitted none of his employes to gamble. He told everyone who asked him that it was impossible to win consistently against the bank, and insisted that no man should play unless he could afford to lose. He liked to be recognized in public places, and maintained his early reputation as a good dresser with an elaborate wardrobe, of which the chief items were forty suits and fifteen pairs of shoes. He was an omnivorous reader, especially of history and books on art and religion, although his interest in the latter subject was purely academic. His favorite literary work was Gibbon's *The Decline and Fall of the Roman Empire.*

2

Canfield was born in New Bedford, Mass., on June 17, 1855, the son of a printer who in his youth had made several voyages aboard a New Bedford whaler. His maternal ancestors came to America on the *Mayflower,* and his father's family was in this country long before the Revolution. In common with many other great American gamblers, Canfield was still a boy when he succumbed to the lure of the playing card and the fascination of the spinning Roulette wheel. He was fourteen years old when he obtained his first job in a Boston department store, but he quit it within a year, and except during a brief period when he was a hotel clerk and manager, never held another. At eighteen, in 1873, he was part owner of a small Poker room in Providence, R.I., which was equipped with a table, a few chairs, and half a dozen packs of cards. Only a ten-cent limit game was played. The Providence police closed the place after a few months, but Canfield's share of the profits had been large enough to confirm his resolution to become a professional gambler. For the next few years he made a good living playing against Faro banks and Roulette wheels in the Providence gambling houses, and early in 1876 ended a long run of good luck with a bankroll of almost $20,000. With this small fortune in his pocket he sailed for Europe, and for several months gambled in a small way at Monte Carlo and other celebrated casinos. He had very little money when he returned to the United States, but he had accumulated a store of very useful knowledge, not the least item of which was that in the long run the only winner at any game of chance is the man who holds the bank.

For four or five years after his European trip Canfield was in the hotel business, first as night clerk at the old Union Square Hotel in New York, where his cousin was landlord; and later as day clerk and manager of summer resort houses at Spring Lake and Seagirt, N.J. During the winters he lived in Pawtucket, R.I., and in association with a young gambler named Bob Kendall ran a small Poker room of half a dozen tables. The game was twenty-five cent limit, with a ten per cent kitty for the house. Coffee and sandwiches were served free to the players, and it was characteristic of Canfield that he insisted upon compounding them of the finest ingredients obtainable. Pawtucket had fewer than 20,000 inhabitants in those days, but it was a busy and prosperous town, and wide open as far as gambling was concerned. A score of Faro and Roulette houses and

Courtesy the N. Y. Sun

THE HOUSE WITH THE BRONZE DOORS—A FAMOUS NEW YORK
GAMBLING PLACE OF THE 1890's

Poker rooms competed for the dimes and quarters of Pawtucket suckers, and in some of them considerable sums passed over the tables every night. The Canfield-Kendall establishment was one of the smallest, but its earnings enabled Canfield to live at the best hotel in Pawtucket, and to indulge his fondness for good food and fine raiment. Unlike that of most of his fellow gamblers, however, Canfield's attire was never flashy, neither in his salad days nor afterward when he was the best known gamester in the world. He wore the best clothing he could buy, but it was dignified and conservative in cut and pattern, and he always had a horror of ostentatious jewelry.

Canfield was married in Pawtucket in the late summer of 1882, and a few months later removed with his bride to Providence, where their two children were born and where Mrs. Canfield lived during the remainder of her life. Canfield had $5,000 in cash and was in his twenty-seventh year when he arrived in Providence, and he felt that the time had come to abandon the picayune profits of the Poker room and invade the more lucrative fields of Faro and Roulette. One of the Providence resorts in which Canfield had made his first big killing in 1876 was a Faro house operated by Thomas Sprague at Union and Eddy Streets, near the business district of the town. Sprague had been greatly impressed by Canfield's skillful playing, and especially by his personality, and several times had suggested that Canfield buy an interest in the place. When Canfield came to Providence with his wife he accepted Sprague's offer, and entered the business in the spring of 1883 as a full partner, and so began his first connection with a regular gambling house. The game played in the Sprague-Canfield establishment was trivial compared with that in Canfield's later houses in New York and Saratoga, but it was the largest in Providence, and the place was very popular with the richest of the Providence suckers. The partners prospered until the night of April 26, 1884, when the police descended upon the place in a raid which was believed to have been instigated by a business man with whose wife Canfield had been accused of being a little too friendly. The raiders caught Sprague dealing Faro and Canfield acting as lookout, and both were arrested and indicted. They were at length brought to trial on June 17, 1885, and pleaded guilty in the hope of escaping with fines. Instead, they were each sentenced, on Canfield's thirtieth birthday, to serve six months in the Providence County jail. They were released on January 16, 1886.

Both Canfield and Sprague agreed that it would be folly to open another gambling house in Providence, and the latter went into temporary retirement. Canfield finally determined to try his luck in New York, and left Providence for the metropolis in June, 1886. During the next eight or ten months he did nothing except gamble occasionally and attempt to get a job dealing Faro in the famous house at No. 818 Broadway, which at that time was operated by Ferdinand Abell and Lucien O. Appleby. Canfield became a familiar figure in the New York gambling houses, but he had no luck at No. 818, although Abell and Appleby took his name and repeatedly told him that he would be notified if a vacancy occurred. When the spring of 1887 had arrived, and there was still no opening at No. 818, Canfield began to make plans for the establishment of his own house. His bankroll had dwindled to less than $1,000, but he borrowed from his cousin and Sprague, and in partnership with a pawnbroker named William Glover fitted up a Poker room in Broadway between Eighteenth and Nineteenth Streets, with six or eight tables and a fifty-cent limit game. Within six months the place was earning average weekly profits of about $300. In Pawtucket, or even in Providence, this would have been important money, but in New York it was chicken feed, and Canfield soon saw that he would never make a fortune from a Poker room. He was trying to raise enough money to equip the gambling house of

424

his dreams when he met David Duff, who for several years had been dealing Faro in the resort at No. 5 West Twenty-fourth Street, run by Charley Reed. Several of Reed's wealthy suckers had become interested in Duff, and had offered to back him if he wished to open a place of his own. Duff suggested that he and Canfield join forces, and Canfield sold his share of the Poker room to Glover and again borrowed from Sprague, and his cousin, who had just inherited $200,000. Sprague, realizing that here was the great opportunity, mortgaged his home in Providence and turned the entire proceeds over to Canfield. A year or two later he came to New York, and thereafter dealt Faro for Canfield until the master gambler retired, when he was pensioned. Canfield also brought to the metropolis two other young men, David Bucklin and Jimmy Levens, with whom he had been associated in Providence. Bucklin was general manager of Canfield's gambling properties until 1905, when he bought the resort at Newport in association with Billy Coe. Levens, an expert bookkeeper, worked for Canfield until his suicide in 1898.

In May of 1888 Duff and Canfield, under the firm name of Duff & Company, opened the Madison Square Club in a four-story brownstone house at No. 22 West Twenty-sixth Street. The resort was admirably located to attract the proper type of big-money sucker. Delmonico's celebrated restaurant was nearby, and so was Madison Square, then the heart of the retail and amusement districts, while within a radius of a few blocks were half a dozen of New York's finest hotels, among them the St. James, the Albemarle, the Brunswick, the Fifth Avenue, and the Hoffman House. The two upper floors of the Club were used as living quarters by Canfield and by Duff and his wife. Tables for Poker and other short card games were on the second floor, and on the first was a large reception hall and two rooms for Faro and Roulette. After a year or so, however, the Poker tables were removed and the entire second floor was devoted to banking games, while the first was given over to reception and lounging rooms, and a dining hall in which were served the best suppers provided in any New York gambling house of the period. The task of furnishing and decorating the resort was entirely in Canfield's hands, and the result of his work was an indication of what he would do in later years when the funds at his disposal were virtually unlimited. He created in the Madison Square Club an atmosphere of comfort and dignity, so that the house formed a pleasant and welcome contrast to the gaudy palaces which had been the rule in New York for so many years. The cost of operating the Club ranged between $2,000 and $6,000 a month, and included rental of $600, salaries and wages of the staff, and the protection money paid to the police. At first the latter was $200 a month, but it was soon doubled, and as the resort increased in popularity and prosperity the police also took a percentage of the profits. During the first two years the Faro limits were $25 on case cards, and $50 on the double, triple and quadruple cards. In 1890 these limits were doubled, and in the course of the next few years were increased tenfold. At all times the safe of the house in Twenty-sixth Street held a cash reserve of from $25,000 to $100,000, to insure payment of possible losses.

The Madison Square Club was an important gambling house almost from the beginning, and the profits were larger than Canfield had anticipated. Canfield was unchanged by his good fortune, but Duff couldn't stand such sudden prosperity. Apparently he began to suffer from delusions of grandeur. He drank heavily, lost large sums in other houses and paid with checks drawn on Duff & Company, which Canfield patiently honored, and frequently annoyed the suckers and frightened the servants in the Club by boisterous talk and rowdy actions. Canfield often remonstrated with Duff, but went no further for more than a year. But in September of 1890, when Duff went on an especially violent spree, he found himself barred from the

Club by Canfield's orders. Enraged at being locked out of his own house, Duff smashed a first-floor window with a stone, whereupon Canfield immediately closed the place and kept it shuttered for a week. Meanwhile he negotiated with Duff and finally bought the latter's interest for something less than $50,-000. The house was reopened about October 1, 1890.

At the age of thirty-five, for the first time, Canfield was sole owner of a New York gambling house, and was fairly started on his amazing career.

3

John Morrissey had been dead ten years when Canfield and David Duff opened the Madison Square Club, but the evil that he had done lived after him; the gambling machine which he had been instrumental in fashioning still functioned, and the corruption he had helped to foster in the police department had reached new heights and had permeated every branch of the service, as was fully brought out by the Lexow and Mazet investigating committees in 1894 and 1899. Despite the activities of the Parkhurst Society, the Committee of Fourteen, and other reform agencies, vice and crime were even more widespread in New York in the 1880's and the 1890's than they had been during the reign of the king of bruisers. Gambling resorts were everywhere—day houses in the financial and business districts, five-cent Faro and Roulette dens and penny card games in the poorer sections; a dozen grades of Poker Flats, which the New York *Mercury* in 1886 described as "the newest racket in gambling"; hundreds of Policy shops and Lottery offices and scores of pool rooms all over the city, and from twenty to fifty first-class houses in which brace games were played more often than not. The *Mail and Express* declared in 1892 that the metropolis harbored 250 Faro banks alone, but John Philip Quinn, writing in 1891, estimated that there were fewer than a hundred. Said Quinn:

"The Faro banks of New York have as capital a little less than one million dollars, which is very unequally divided, as the ninety-two houses vary from $2,000 to $50,000, although only three or four have the latter amount, and the average banking capital is about $10,000. It is impossible to say what amount of money changes hands upon this basis. It is asserted that the average yearly winnings of all the banks taken together is about fifty per cent over and above the expenditure required to keep up the establishments, so that every year these gamblers absorb about $500,000, while the gross profits are more than one hundred per cent. These figures are conclusive that the way of the transgressor, if he be an occasional player rather than a dealer, is hard." [1]

Quinn's estimates were probably too low in every respect. There were many gambling houses in New York which were backed by bankrolls exceeding $100,000, and the money taken from the metropolitan suckers every year totaled well into the millions. A sizeable share of this enormous gross was paid to the police and the politicians as protection money; their charges ranged from ten dollars a month for a small Poker room or Policy shop to a thousand dollars and half the profits for a big house which catered to rich gulls. In addition, special assessments were frequently levied upon all classes of sharpers. It was small wonder that political heelers retired with fortunes, and that poorly paid policemen owned yachts and country estates.

From about 1880 to the middle 1890's, when they began to creep into the Roaring Forties, the most important of the first-class houses, with the exception of No. 818 Broadway and two or three places in Ann and Barclay Streets, were concentrated in the old Tenderloin district, which was a part of the Twenty-ninth Police Precinct and comprised, roughly, the area from

[1] *Fools of Fortune,* page 424.

Madison Square to Forty-second Street between Broadway and Fifth Avenue. Except for two years, the Tenderloin was ruled by the man who had named it, that extraordinary policeman Alexander S. Williams, sometimes known as Clubber Williams, and the author of the famous dictum, "There's more law in the end of a policeman's nightstick than in a decision of the Supreme Court." Williams rose in the department from patrolman to Inspector, and amassed a fortune in spite of the low pay of most of the grades of which he was an ornament. Eighteen times he was brought before the Board of Police Commissioners on charges of graft and misconduct, and each time the Board solemnly found him not guilty. Several policemen testified before the Lexow Committee that they had collected money from the gambling houses and other resorts and paid it over to Williams; and Williams himself admitted that he had half a dozen large bank accounts, and that he owned a yacht, a house and other property in New York, and an estate at Cos Cob, Connecticut, on which the dock alone cost $39,000. With a perfectly straight face Williams told the Committee that he had made his money speculating in building lots in Japan. No action was taken against him as a result of these disclosures, but he resigned from the force in 1895 and entered the insurance business, which was a good field for the politically connected in those days as it is now. When he died in 1910 Williams was several times a millionaire.

Another picturesque police official who shared in the protection money paid by the gamblers was William S. Devery, commonly called Big Bill, a huge man, almost illiterate, who gained a certain fame by the frequent and pompous use of the phrase, "touchin' on an' appertainin' to." The evidence adduced by the Lexow Committee against Devery was so conclusive that the Board of Police Commissioners dismissed him from the force. A few months later he was indicted for extortion, but was acquitted by a jury in 1896. Meanwhile a court order had restored his police job—he had been a captain—and so great was his political influence that he was appointed Inspector. Within six months he had become Chief of Police, and remained at the head of the department until the Legislature abolished the office of Chief in 1901. He was demoted to Deputy Commissioner, but soon resigned and became interested in the real estate business. He died in 1919, a rich man.

Despite the demands of the police and the politicians, virtually all of the big gamesters who operated in the old Tenderloin appear to have made enough money to maintain their resorts in the style to which the New York sucker had been accustomed by Herne, Parsons, Chamberlin, Morrissey, and other giants of the old days. The journalist Matthew Hale Smith, writing in 1887, said that the first-class houses of the period were "superb in all their appointments." He continued:

"A brownstone front or marble building is selected, and kept in grand style. The door is set off by a broad silver plate, usually bearing the name of some club, and rich heavy blinds or curtains at the windows hide the inmates from prying eyes. If one wishes to enter he rings the door bell. This is answered by a finely dressed colored doorman, for all the servants are black. . . . The elegance of the establishment dazzles you. The doors are of rosewood. The most costly carpet that can be imported lies on the floor. No tawdry frescoing, but costly paintings by the first artists, adorn the walls and cover the ceiling. The richest of gold, gilt and rosewood furniture in satin and velvet abound. . . . The front parlor is used for dining. The dinner is served at six o'clock. Nothing in New York can equal the elegance of the table. It is spread with silver and gold plate, costly china ware, and glass of exquisite cut, and the viands embrace all the luxuries of the season served up in the richest

430

style. Fruits, home and foreign, fill the sideboards, and wines and costly liquors are to be had for the asking.

"The rooms are open to all comers. All are welcome to the table and sideboard. No questions are asked, no price is paid, no one is solicited to drink or play. . . . To the rear of the dining room or front parlor is the principal gaming room. It will contain one or more Faro layouts, owing to the demands of the play, and a Roulette or *Rouge-et-Noir* table. The Baccarat tables and Poker rooms are usually on the third floor. None but men who behave like gentlemen are allowed the entree of the rooms. . . . Gentlemen well known on 'change and in public life, merchants of a high grade, whose names adorn benevolent and charitable associations, are seen in these rooms, reading and talking. . . . To one not accustomed to such a sight, it is rather startling to see men whose names stand high in church and state, who are well dressed and leaders of fashion, in these notable saloons, as if they were at home. . . . Some play lightly; they lose five or ten dollars and then stop. Many play deep, and losses are heavy. From ten to fifty thousand dollars frequently change hands in a night. . . . Recently one man lost three hundred thousand dollars. . . ." [2]

Of the scores of gaudy hells which flourished in New York during the two decades that elapsed between the death of John Morrissey and the rise of Richard Canfield to unquestioned supremacy, the best known and largest contributors to the police were those operated by John Daly, Bret Haines, Sam Emery, Bob Hughes, Morey Isaacs, John Traphagen; Charley Reed, in Morrissey's old house at No. 5 West Twenty-fourth Street; Ferdinand Abell, who went in with Joe Doyle at No. 141 West Forty-second Street when No. 818 Broadway closed in 1890, and later founded

[2] *Wonders of a Great City,* pages 339–44.

the Nautilus Club at Newport which he sold to Canfield; Billy Bennett, a prominent Tammany heeler and one of the backers of John L. Sullivan; Shang Draper, who turned to gambling after a turbulent career as a bank robber and a saloon and dive keeper; Dave Gideon, also well known on the race tracks; Davy Johnson, who once offered to bet $100,000 against a Rembrandt painting and to let the issue be decided by a single turn at Faro; French Red Bellenger, a minor power in Tammany Hall; George Costigan, whose place was in Ann Street near the site of the old Tapis Franc; Pat Gallagher of No. 3 Barclay Street, described by the *Mail and Express* as "the meanest and closest gambler in New York"; Honest John Kelly, who in his palmy days often boasted that his wardrobe contained twenty pairs of pants, nine overcoats, forty-four fancy vests, and a hundred morning, afternoon and evening coats; Dink Davis, who had been one of Mike McDonald's boys in Chicago; Ed Stokes, the murderer of playboy Jim Fisk; Lon Maynard, "a protégé of the police department for ten years"; Pete Downey, once a partner of the notorious Bill Mike Murray; and Colonel Thomas Darden and Willard Fitzgerald. Colonel Darden was a Washington banker who, about 1890, inherited the resort at No. 6 West Twenty-eighth Street from his brother. He took Fitzgerald in as partner, and operated the house with great success until 1895, when he sold out and returned to Washington. In later years the place was run by Shang Draper. One of Colonel Darden's Faro dealers was a young man named Billy Coe, who afterward had his own house and was also manager of Canfield's resort at Newport. He purchased the latter place with Dave Bucklin in 1905.

Honest John Kelly's chief claim to distinction lay in the fact that he was the last of the old guard to surrender; despite many setbacks, he continued to run a gambling house in New York until 1921, when he finally abandoned the metropolis for Florida and the Bahama Islands. Kelly was not related to the Tammany Hall leader of the same name, and his sobriquet had nothing to do with his gambling resorts, which were no more honestly conducted than any others. He was a baseball player in his youth, and later an umpire. In 1888 he umpired a game between Boston and Providence on the result of which depended the league championship, and a coterie of gamblers offered him $10,000 to favor Boston in his decisions. He refused, the story got around, and thereafter he was known as Honest John. In the 1890's Kelly refereed several prize fights, and was the first American referee to assume the prerogative of calling off all bets whenever there seemed to be something fishy about a contest. He did this in the Corbett-Sharkey fight in 1898, although he had been warned not to interfere by Big Tim Sullivan, a Tammany politician who had bet $13,000 on Sharkey. Next day Kelly's gambling house was raided and wrecked by the police.

Kelly's first business venture in New York was a saloon, with a Faro game upstairs, which he opened at Sixth Avenue and Thirty-first Street about 1890 in partnership with Mike Kelly, a famous baseball player. Five or six years later Honest John disposed of his share of the saloon, and opened a new gambling house at No. 141 West Forty-first Street, which he ran for some fifteen years. Kelly was often in the bad graces of the police; he resented the necessity of paying protection money, and never did so except under compulsion. As a result his house was frequently subjected to disciplinary raids, and finally, in 1912, the place in Forty-first Street was invaded by policemen who battered down the doors, smashed the windows, and pounded the furniture and gambling equipment to bits with axes, fire hatchets and crowbars. Kelly announced that he was through, but within a month had opened an elaborate place at No. 156 West Forty-fourth Street, which he called the Vendome Club. This house also was on the police blacklist, but Kelly kept it going until 1922, when he sold the property to a Republican political organization. During the last three or four years of Kelly's occupancy, Police Commissioner Richard E. Enright kept a uniformed policeman on duty in front of the premises day and night. Nevertheless, according to a statement made by Kelly in 1925, suckers slipped past the policeman in such numbers that the gross take of the house for the final eighteen months was more than $1,000,000. Most of this money came from Stud Poker, for Kelly was always a very cautious gambler, and preferred the certainty of a Poker kitty to the hazards of Faro and Roulette. After getting out of West Forty-fourth Street Honest John ran gaming places at Nassau in the Bahamas, and at Palm Beach in Florida, where he died in March, 1926, at the age of seventy. There was much talk in some of the newspapers about Kelly having been a gambler of the Canfield type, but the New York *Sun* provided the proper slant on Honest John when it said that "He was as much the inheritor of the Canfield tradition as the Automat is the inheritor of the Delmonico tradition."

The kingpin gambler of New York throughout the 1880's, and in the 1890's until Canfield relegated him to second place, was John Daly, one of the Troy, N.Y., sporting men who had been induced to come to New York in the early years of the Civil War by the success of John Morrissey and John C. Heenan. Daly was a competitor of Johnny Chamberlin's at Long Branch during the 1870's, and early in that decade opened his first New York house in Broadway between Thirteenth and Fourteenth Streets, only a block or so from No. 818. A few years later he and Dave Gideon acquired a controlling interest in the old Morrissey house at No. 8 Barclay Street, and about 1880 took in another partner, young Dink Davis, whose phenomenal luck against the bank had caused a great sensation. Fresh from Chicago, Davis walked into No. 8 with $1,900 in his pocket, and in a two-day bout with the tiger ran his bankroll up to $85,000.

He stopped playing long enough to buy a fourth interest in the resort, and then returned to the Faro table, winning another $18,000 before his partners barred him from the game. Afterward Davis operated a house at No. 57 West Twenty-eighth Street, and when Canfield moved uptown in 1899 Davis stepped into his old place in West Twenty-sixth Street and ran it for three years, but on a very small scale compared to that of the old master. When it was closed in 1902 the clientele consisted almost entirely of clerks and mechanics, and the play was trivial.

Daly's best known house was at No. 39 West Twenty-ninth Street, in the heart of the Tenderloin, which he opened in 1878 after selling his place in Broadway. With the exception of No. 8 Broadway, and later Canfield's and the House with the Bronze Door, the Twenty-ninth Street place was probably New York's most magnificently equipped gambling house. The play, however, was not as large as in many less pretentious places; only an occasional plunger used the Faro limits of $50 on case cards and $100 on doubles. Daly is said to have paid more for protection in Twenty-ninth Street than any other gambling house keeper of his time. The exact amount was never divulged, but in the 1890's rumor said that it was $100,000 a year. In any event, Daly was able to keep his business going for almost a quarter of a century. The only serious interruption occurred in the late 1880's during the reform administration of Mayor Abram S. Hewitt, when Daly was so alarmed by the threatening gestures of the police that he closed No. 39 and transferred his gambling paraphernalia to a house in West Forty-second Street. There he operated his games for several months, admitting only his most trusted suckers, until the uproar subsided. Mayor Hewitt's war against the gamblers began with a typical police raid upon Bud Kirby's Faro house at No. 1 Ann Street, which was thus described by one of Kirby's clients:

"I had just 'coppered' $5 on the queen to the intense disgust of half a dozen fellows who were playing her to win, when the 'nigger' who kept door came bounding upstairs, three steps at a time, fairly pale in the face, and whispered to the proprietor:

" 'Boss, there's some men at the door that won't go away, and say they'll break down the door if I don't let 'em in.'

" 'Quick!' answered the proprietor, 'open the door and ask 'em to step right up.' The words were not out of his mouth before he had slipped the bank roll into the safe, gathered up all visible chips of the banks, and asked the players to gather up theirs, saying, 'Boys, put your chips in your pockets and come around this afternoon and I'll cash 'em in for you.' In a flash all evidence of present gaming were wiped out. There were only a couple of tables, a dozen or so players, the proprietor, smiling blandly, and—a policeman in sight.

"In less time than it takes to tell all this the still shivering doorkeeper had ushered in three 'plain clothes' men from headquarters. At the same time the police officer, in full uniform, who was already in the room—and who had been playing with the rest of us, mind you—edged towards the door so as to seem to have come in with and after the raiding officers. He was the worst frightened man in the crowd. But, with quite remarkable presence of mind, considering the strain on him, the officer in uniform stepped promptly back into the foreground, with a pitying smile on his face, and seizing the beard of the proprietor of the game, said to the raiding officers, who looked as if they wondered where he had come from:

" 'Gentlemen, this is Mr. Bud Kirby'—

" 'And sorry I am, gentlemen,' Bud interrupted, with a bow and a smile, 'to make your acquaintance under such unfavorable circumstances! What will you have to drink?'

"You could have knocked me down with a feather. 'This then,' thought I, as all hands stepped up to the sideboard and took a friendly drink, 'this then, is one of those terrible raids we read so much about.'

"The players, fortunately for me, were not molested in the least. They melted away into the early morning gloom (it was then about 2 o'clock), and the officers who carted away the cards, the Faro layout and the Roulette wheel, melted away to headquarters and made their report, and that afternoon we all went back and Kirby cashed our chips—and everything was lovely. No officer thought of touching the safe which contained the 'roll,' the only thing of any great value about the establishment, and nobody suffered any great loss or discomfort." [3]

Daly closed the house at No. 8 Barclay Street in March, 1902, and in September of the same year the last card was turned at No. 39 West Twenty-ninth Street. His last gambling venture was a resort in West Forty-fourth Street near Broadway, which he and Dave Gideon fitted up early in 1903, and which was managed for them by Billy Busteed, Shang Draper, and Al Adams, the Policy King. It was closed in 1904, and Daly died two years later.

4

Richard Canfield remained a comparatively minor star in the gambling firmament for two or three years after he had kicked David Duff out of the Madison Square Club, but day by day his light shone brighter, and by 1895, when the Club had been under his sole ownership for five years, he had made almost half a million dollars and was the foremost gambling house keeper

---

[3] *Fools of Fortune,* page 426.

in America, although he didn't reach the apogee of his fame for another five or six years. But in the middle 1890's the play in his Twenty-sixth Street house, where the Faro limits had been raised to $500 on the cases and $1,000 on the doubles, was already consistently higher than anywhere else in the country, and not even John Daly's place was more popular among the rich suckers. They admired the restrained splendor and luxurious comfort of Canfield's appointments, enjoyed his rich suppers and choice liquors, appreciated his dignity and graciousness as a host and the smooth efficiency of his staff—and remained to fling their money into the capacious maw of the tiger or fritter it away in fruitless essays against the Roulette wheel.

As his fortune increased at every turn of the cards and every spin of the wheel, Canfield began to consider enlarging his operations, and to look about for suitable investments. For several years he had felt that Albert Spencer, who was running John Morrissey's old Club House at Saratoga, was neglecting his opportunities; Canfield was convinced that with proper management the resort could be made to pay enormous dividends. In the fall of 1892 he went to Saratoga and made an offer for the property, and after lengthy negotiations Spencer took Canfield into the business as a partner. Spencer managed the place in 1893, but in the spring of 1894 Canfield became sole owner, and operated the house alone until it was finally closed in 1906. Three years after he had acquired the Club House, Canfield further increased his holdings by buying the Nautilus Club at Newport from Ferdinand Abell, who had purchased a controlling interest in the Brooklyn baseball team of the National League and was more interested in the so-called national game than in gambling. Canfield paid $65,000 for the Nautilus Club, and in less than eight years took from it about $500,000 in profits. But he always regarded it as a white elephant, and he was glad to sell the place for almost nothing in 1905 to Dave Bucklin and

From the New York World. Courtesy the Press Publishing Co.

THE CANFIELD GAMBLING PALACE

Billy Coe, especially as it had ended the season of 1904 with a net gain of one hundred dollars.

On the other hand, the house at Saratoga was even more of a gold mine for Canfield than it had been for John Morrissey. The profits of the 1894 season alone almost equaled the $250,000 he had paid Spencer, and in the twelve years of Canfield's operation the total take was between $2,500,000 and $3,000,000. These profits would have been enormous for a gambling house running day and night seven days a week; they become really extraordinary when it is considered that the Saratoga house was seldom opened before the last week in July, and was always closed by the first of September; and that there were several years in which reform administrations refused to permit Canfield to operate his games at all. The longest time the Club House was open in any one year was two months, and it is doubtful if it was in active operation for business more than ten or twelve months altogether, so that Canfield's net earnings from the place averaged approximately $250,000 a month.

Canfield made no changes in the physical appearance of the Club House property until 1902, when at a cost of several hundred thousand dollars he built an Italian Garden, which at that time was considered a masterpiece of charm and beauty; and added a commodious kitchen and a magnificent dining room in which was installed the first system of indirect lighting used in America. For the Garden Canfield imported marble fountains and some sculptures of nymphs and satyrs, which are still to be seen leering on the Club House grounds. Throughout the Canfield regime the restaurant was the finest in the United States, and one of the really great eating places of the world. The prices were much higher than those of the best New York restaurants, but they were not too high for the class of trade Canfield was after, and no better food and service could be found anywhere. Canfield paid his chef at Saratoga, a Frenchman named Columbin, $5,000 for the season; and during the remainder of the year Columbin traveled in Europe at Canfield's expense, searching for new dishes with which to tempt the appetites of the Club House patrons. Columbin's creations were served by fifty waiters to whom Canfield paid a dollar a day and railroad fare from New York to Saratoga. But they actually fared much better than this might indicate, for their tips averaged about fifty dollars a day. Canfield lost money on the restaurant, although the daily receipts were more than $5,000, but it was an admirable puller-in, and as such served its purpose.

The gambling arrangements of the Club House under Canfield's ownership remained substantially the same as in John Morrissey's day, but the only article of furniture reminiscent of the earlier lord of Saratoga was his massive iron desk, which is still on exhibition in the main hallway. The public gaming room was on the first floor, and contained from eight to ten single-end Roulette wheels, and from two to four Faro layouts. In private rooms upstairs, where the biggest plungers played, were two double-end wheels and another Faro box. There was no provision for dice or short card games, although occasionally Canfield permitted old friends to use one of the private rooms for Poker or Bridge. The gambling apparatus was handled by thirty croupiers, dealers, lookouts and case-keepers, whose wages ranged from $500 to $1,000 for the season. The Roulette limits, ranging from $50 on single numbers to $5,000 on even chances, averaged more than twice as high as those at Monte Carlo. The limits at Faro were the same as in the New York house, $500 and $1,000, but any responsible player who wanted to plunge could always go higher by applying to Canfield or Bucklin. The highest limit ever requested at Saratoga, and granted, was $5,000 and $10,000. All gambling was done with chips, which varied in value from one dollar to one thousand dollars, and if the bank lost payment was made by check. However, cash was available if the player preferred, for in the Club House there was always one million dollars in fifty, one hundred, five hundred and one thousand dollar bills, which Canfield reckoned was enough to meet any emergency. There is no record that anyone ever tapped this roll to any great extent.

The front door of the Club House was never closed during business hours, and the resort was public in every sense of the word except to women and residents of Saratoga, who were barred from the gaming room although the restaurant was open to them. Restrictions were imposed upon other visitors only when the temper of the village authorities was uncertain and trouble might be expected. Then the doors between the restaurant and the main gambling room were closed, and only trusted suckers were allowed access to the wheels and the Faro banks. At all times half a dozen private detectives from New York were on duty at the doors to keep out known crooks, and throughout the season the grounds were patrolled by squads of Saratoga policemen. It was never necessary for Canfield to make regular payments of protection money in Saratoga, but he often made loans to politicians and police officials, which amounted to the same thing. As John Morrissey and Spencer had done, Canfield kept himself and his establishment in good standing with the townspeople by large and frequent donations to hospitals, churches, and various civic and charitable institutions. This species of bribery kept the reform element fairly quiet for many years.

5

While Canfield was busy at Saratoga transforming the Club House into the greatest gambling asset the United States has ever known, conditions were changing in New York. From the middle 1890's the trend of the city's night life had been northward,

away from Madison Square and the old Tenderloin and into the
Forties north of Forty-second Street. By the turn of the century the transition had virtually been completed, and Longacre
Square, now Times Square, had become the center of the theatrical and sporting district. Delmonico's Restaurant had moved uptown to Fifth Avenue and Forty-fourth Street, there to encounter unexpected opposition from Louis Sherry across the avenue.
At Broadway and Forty-fourth Street George Rector had established a restaurant and cabaret which was destined to become
the most famous of lobster palaces. Only slightly less renowned
was Shanley's at Broadway and Forty-third Street, where the
Paramount Theater now stands; and, a little later, Considine's
Café, Murray's Roman Gardens, Churchill's, and Reisenweber's
on Columbus Circle. Shanley's Grill was famous for its thick and
juicy steaks, but for several years it possessed an even greater
attraction—it was the favorite loafing place of the celebrated
Bat Masterson, ending his career as a sports writer for the *Morning Telegraph* in the days when the *Telegraph* was the Bible of
the show business and the racing crowd. Every night the old-
time gun fighter, resembling nothing so much as a huge spider,
presided over a big steak in a corner of Shanley's grill, holding
a crowd of admirers spellbound with tales which were about
as wild and wooly as the West he was describing.

As early as 1896 Canfield saw that the real future of gambling
in New York, assuming that the police would continue to look
upon it with favor, lay uptown; but not for two years was he able
to obtain a place which would be satisfactory in every respect.
He finally found what he wanted in a brownstone front, twenty-
seven feet wide, with four stories and a basement, at No. 5 East
Forty-fourth Street, one door from Delmonico's and a hundred
feet or so from Sherry's, and only a few blocks from Times
Square. Early in 1898, in the name of his mother-in-law, Maria
Martin, he bought the property for $75,000; and in the summer

of the same year Clarence Luce, a noted architect, began the work of transforming the interior of the drab old residence into what was probably the finest gambling house ever opened anywhere. It has always been customary to refer to a first-class gaming resort as "palatial," although except for perhaps half a dozen places the term, in America at least, has been a misnomer. But if such houses as Pendleton's in Washington, McGrath's in New Orleans, No. 818 Broadway in its best days, Doc Slater's in Baltimore, and Johnny Chamberlin's in Long Branch, deserved to be so called, then Canfield's establishment in Forty-fourth Street can only be described as "super-palatial." By comparison it was nothing less. Luce spent $400,000 before the place was ready for occupancy in the fall of 1899, and Canfield put at least as much more into paintings, etchings, tapestries, bronzes, Chinese porcelains, peach-blow vases, of which he had several that cost from $8,000 to $12,000 each; and Chippendale furniture, including a famous set of twelve chairs for which he is said to have paid about $60,000. From basement to roof the house was finished and decorated with a magnificent disregard of cost. For example, in one of the private gaming rooms the floor was of teakwood and the walls were covered with Spanish leather hand-tooled in gold; another room, which Canfield used as a private office, was paneled in white mahogany inlaid with mother-of-pearl. By the time the first card was turned and the wheel spun for the first time, the establishment represented an expenditure of at least $1,000,000.

The massive front door of No. 5 East Forty-fourth Street, the only outward sign of the glories within, was of bronze, and is said to have cost $1,000. It opened into a vestibule, from which another door equally strong and heavy led into the house. All visitors were carefully scrutinized, through a peep-hole, by a Negro doorman, and if he was not satisfied, by one of the croupiers or dealers. Both doors were operated by electricity, and it was impossible to open one without closing the other. On the first floor were Canfield's offices and the reception rooms; the public casino occupied the whole of the second, and on the third were several rooms for private bouts with Roulette or the tiger. On the fourth floor were Canfield's library and living quarters, where the gambler took his well-earned repose. The only gaming equipment in the house was a double-end Roulette wheel of hickory inlaid with ivory, and a Faro layout with a solid silver dealing box, on the second floor; and a single-end Roulette wheel which was used in the private rooms. There were no facilities for short cards or dice. Supper was served every evening at eleven o'clock, and consisted of the finest of cold cuts, salads and desserts, all of which were prepared in the house. If a player wished anything more it was ordered from Delmonico's and served without cost to him. The best cigars, for which Canfield paid a dollar each, were free for the asking, and so were the wines and liquors from the gambler's $75,000 cellar, which was frequently replenished with rare vintages.

The Forty-fourth Street house probably cost as much to operate as any two other gambling resorts in New York. At least $40,000 a year was spent on entertainment, and the other expenses were proportionately large. As Manager, Dave Bucklin received ten per cent of the profits besides his large salary, and from fifteen to twenty-five per cent went to the police for protection, in addition to a regular fee of $1,000 a month. The protection money was paid in cash at regular intervals by Canfield in person, usually over a table in Delmonico's. Despite the terrific overhead, Canfield's net return from the house in a little more than two years was about $1,500,000. The greater part of this profit, if not all of it, came from Roulette, always the mainstay of a big gambling resort, in which a fixed percentage of between five and six operates against the player every time the wheel is spun. It is doubtful if Canfield ever did better than

444

break even at Faro; at all of his houses the biggest winnings were made against the tiger.

The ivory chips used in the Forty-fourth Street house possessed the same value as in Newport and Saratoga, and officially the usual Canfield limits prevailed at Roulette and Faro. Many of the men who gambled there regularly, however, had special limits up to $10,000 at Roulette, and from $2,500 to $5,000 at Faro, and were allowed to go even higher upon request. A half million dollars was kept in the safe in Canfield's office, but unless a player expressed a preference for cash house losses were paid by check, as at Saratoga. The clientele of the place was small—there were seldom more than five or six men playing at one time— but almost without exception the regular patrons were multimillionaires to whom the loss of a few hundred thousand dollars was a trifling matter, and the amount of money that changed hands in the course of a night was sometimes stupendous. It was a common occurrence for one of Canfield's suckers, after dallying with the Faro bank or the Roulette wheel for a few hours, to walk out of the house a hundred thousand dollars poorer than when he entered. Many of the players gambled on credit, giving I.O.U.'s for their losses and taking them up at regular intervals. Several, however, welshed on these obligations. When Canfield retired he had something like $250,000 in I.O.U.'s which he was never able to collect.

The backbone of Canfield's business was the group of famous plungers who flourished in the 1890's and for a few years after the turn of the present century. Among them were Colonel Isaac Ellwood; John A. Drake, son of an Iowa Governor and owner of a racing stable; Senator Edward O. Wolcott of Colorado, whose special limit at Faro was $2,000 and $4,000, and who frequently bucked the tiger for two days and two nights at a stretch; State Senator Patrick McCarren of Brooklyn, who in one day lost $100,000 at Faro; Phil Dwyer, the race track king, who

445

pursued a streak of luck at Roulette until it turned on him and left him $90,000 in the hole; Reginald Vanderbilt, who gave Canfield an I.O.U. for $300,000 and finally settled it for $130,-000; Theodore Hostetter of Chicago, who gambled away $1,-000,000 in a few months, part of it at Canfield's and part matching pennies with Davy Johnson at $1,000 a turn; and a score of others of equal wealth and prominence. And, finally, John W. Gates, known to the public as Bet-a-Million Gates and to his intimates as the Big Stiff—a multimillionaire by virtue of his market operations and the part he played in the organization of the American Steel and Wire Company and the United States Steel Corporation; and a resplendent figure for many years, with three diamonds in each suspender buckle and three more blazing in his shirt front.

If a distinction can be made between gambler and gambling house keeper, Gates was one of the great gamblers of the world, and the greatest that America has yet produced or is likely to produce. Gates would gamble on anything and on either side. He would hold the bank at Baccarat with no declared capital and accept any stake his opponents wished to fix. He would play Poker for a limit of one dollar or $50,000 or with no limit at all, and Bridge for anything up to a thousand dollars a point. He would match pennies for $1,000 a turn; once in Memphis, when he was asked to play Poker with a group of local sports who had raised a purse of $35,000, he offered to flip a coin for the entire amount. He would bet on the speed of raindrops sliding down a window pane; in 1897, on a train between Chicago and Pittsburg, he won $22,000 at this fantastic game. But his favorite methods of gambling were Faro, Poker and horse racing. He took terrific punishment at the race tracks, even though in a single afternoon in England he won $500,000 backing a plater named *Royal Flush* to beat Richard Croker's celebrated *Americus;* but at Faro and Poker he probably finished on the right side of the ledger. In any event, he was a consistent winner at Canfield's. In both the Saratoga and Forty-fourth Street houses he had a special Faro limit of $2,500 on the cases and $5,000 on the doubles, and would sometimes play for three days without sleep and with infrequent pauses for food. From these Gargantuan gambling jousts he nearly always emerged winner of from $50,-000 to $100,000. When he returned to his hotel after such a gaming spree Mrs. Gates was invariably waiting for him. If he had lost, they quarreled violently, and next day Gates made his peace with a diamond ring or necklace. If he had won, she would don an apron and beat up a batch of flapjacks and cook them on a small range that was kept in their suite.

One of the games of Faro in which Gates made the tiger squeal was the biggest of which there is authentic record. It was played at the Saratoga Club House in the summer of 1902. The afternoon of this historic day Gates spent at the race track, and when the last race was run he had lost $375,000. He dined at the Club House restaurant and immediately after dinner began playing Faro, taking the regular house limit of $500 and $1,000. He lost the first few turns, and at his suggestion the game was transferred to a private room upstairs, and the limit was increased to $2,500 and $5,000. Gates continued to lose, and at ten o'clock had dropped $150,000, and was $525,000 loser for the day. He asked for a still higher limit, and was told that only Canfield could grant it, and he went downstairs to Canfield's office and made his request.

"What limit are you playing now?" asked Canfield.

"Twenty-five hundred and five thousand."

"How high do you wish to go?"

"Five thousand and ten thousand."

"You may have it," said Canfield, and as Gates turned to go added dryly:

"Are you sure that's enough?"

447

Betting from five to ten thousand dollars at every turn of the cards, Gates continued to play throughout the night. Two hours after midnight he had won back the $150,000 lost in the early evening, and at dawn when he quit playing, he had won another $150,000, and so had cut the day's losses to the comparatively modest sum of $225,000.

Most of the big Poker games in which Gates participated were played on trains between New York and Chicago, and in private rooms at the old Waldorf-Astoria Hotel, where he was so influential that the management installed a bar for no other reason than that Gates didn't like to drink sitting down. His companions were usually a group of Chicago multimillionaires who spent half their time in New York, and who were described by the New York *Herald* in 1900 as setting "so hot a pace in the metropolis that few can be found able and willing to follow them." They included John A. Drake; Joseph Leiter, a famous manipulator of the wheat market; Loyall L. Smith; Herman C. Frasch, the sulphur king; Herman Seilcken, who had made a great fortune in coffee; Colonel John Lambert; Isaac Ellwood, one of Gates' early partners; and Henry C. Frick. Occasionally Elbert H. Gary, then a judge but later president of the United States Steel Corporation and one of America's foremost industrialists, sat in the game; but he was not as wealthy in those days as the others, and when the stakes were really large he was barred. Once when Gary appeared at the Waldorf-Astoria and sent word to Gates that he would like to play, Gates said:

"Tell Judge Gary the game is going to be so high it would be over his head."

The games played by Gates and his friends were probably higher than any others in the history of Poker, with the exception of the tremendous battles waged in San Francisco by Ralston, Sharon and other Pacific Coast plutocrats. As in the West, a pot in one of Gates' sessions might amount to from $50,000 to $200,-

ooo, and on many occasions there were a million dollars' worth of chips in the game. Perhaps the most memorable of these games were staged during a series of contests, with Gates and Joseph Leiter as the principal antagonists, which began in 1899 and continued for about a year. In that time Gates lost about $1,000,000, of which Loyall Smith won $190,000, John A. Drake and others a total of $75,000, and Leiter the balance. The climax of the Poker warfare between Gates and Leiter occurred in a game at the Waldorf-Astoria in February, 1900. There were six players, including, besides Leiter and Gates, John A. Drake and Loyall Smith. The game was a seesaw affair for several hours, with comparatively little action, but finally Leiter proposed a jackpot with every man anteing $1,000. The cards were dealt twice before openers appeared, and each time the pot was sweetened with $600. There was $7,200 on the table when Gates, with three fours, opened for $5,000. Drake and two others dropped out, but Smith came in, and Leiter bet $15,000. Both Gates and Smith called, and there was $52,500 in the pot. Gates and Smith each drew a card, but Leiter was pat. Gates checked the bet, Smith folded, and Leiter said:

"John, when a man has reached your age he should quit his bad habits. There is only one way to break a man of playing Poker, and that is to make it too expensive for him. It will cost you just $30,000 to see my cards."

Having drawn a nine, Gates had not helped his hand. He studied the cards carefully for several minutes, but still couldn't find anything better than three fours.

"Joe," he said, finally, "I quit. I guess you've got 'em."

He showed his openers and flung his cards away, and with a chuckle Leiter spread his hand. It contained a pair of sevens, an ace, a trey and a king.

When Gates was in New York he made his headquarters during stock market hours in the brokerage offices of his son Charley,

449

whom he had set up in business at the Waldorf-Astoria, under the firm name of Harris, Gates & Company, at a cost of $500,000. There Gates bought and sold stocks, and when he was not too busy would call in his cronies and match pennies with them, or bet on how much a certain stock would go up or down in a given number of hours or minutes. Poker was often played in young Gates' private office after the Stock Exchange had closed, and almost every Saturday afternoon Gates, Drake, Ellwood and others sat down to a bridge game. On one occasion, only three of the regular players were present, and a young businessman, in comfortable circumstances but by no means wealthy, was asked to make a fourth. As they began to play he bethought him to ask what they were playing for.

"Oh, just a little game," Gates said. "One a point."

A dollar a point was pretty high for the young man, but he was a good player, and thought he could manage to hold his own. He played carefully, and when the game ended was 330 points ahead. On the following day he received a check for his winnings, and was amazed to find that it called for $33,000. Then he realized that the game had been for one hundred dollars a point! He tried to return the check, explaining that he could not have paid such a sum had he lost, but Gates told him not to be a fool.

"You won, didn't you?" asked the plunger. "What're you kicking about?"

Gates quit the Stock Market after he had sustained very heavy losses in the panic of 1907, and from that time until his death at the age of fifty-six, in August of 1911, he devoted himself to solid business enterprises and rebuilt his fortune. He gambled about as heavily as ever in private, but with all of the big houses closed he was less and less in the public eye. One of the last stories told of him described his appearance at the Conference of the Gulf Division of the Southern Methodist Church, in Port

Arthur, Texas, on December 15, 1909, when he gave the preachers this remarkable advice:

Don't gamble.
Don't play cards.
Don't bet on horse races.
Don't speculate in wheat.
Don't speculate on the stock exchange.
Don't throw dice.
Don't shirk honest labor.
Don't be a gambler; once a gambler, always a gambler.

6

The only gambling house of the period that in any way rivaled Canfield's establishment was a resort at No. 33 West Thirty-third Street known as the House with the Bronze Door, which was opened in the fall of 1891 and was operated more or less continuously for almost twenty-six years. During most of that time it was owned by a syndicate of gamblers headed by Frank Farrell; Big Bill Kennedy, who had shares in several Tenderloin places; Billy Burbridge, and Gottfried Walbaum, who in 1890 had bought Albert Spencer's interest in the Saratoga race track. Farrell's only other business until the late 1890's was a saloon on Sixth Avenue. But when his friend Asa Bird Gardiner was elected District Attorney in 1897 on a platform of "to hell with reform!" and another friend, Big Bill Devery, became an Inspector of Police, Farrell opened a string of pool rooms and soon dominated this form of gambling. In 1901 Farrell and Devery established the New York baseball team of the American League, and owned it until 1915, when they sold out to Jacob Ruppert and Tillinghast Huston, who changed the name of the club from the Highlanders to the Yankees and developed it into the best baseball property in the country.

During the first six or eight years of its existence the House with the Bronze Door was just another gambling place, equipped and decorated in the usual gaudy manner. But in the late 1890's the Farrell-Walbaum syndicate engaged Stanford White, one of America's greatest architects, to remodel the establishment. White began by demolishing the interior of the building, and then, with $500,000 at his disposal, went to Europe and Asia to search out furnishings and fixtures which would fit in with his plans. One of his finds, unearthed in Italy, was the massive bronze door which was installed at the rear of the entrance hall, and which gave the place its name. Report had it that White paid about $20,000 for this door, and according to the New York *Sun,* "in 1498 it was swinging from the entrances to the wine cellar of the Doges' palace in Venice." White also brought back to the United States, and set up in the House with the Bronze Door, a stairway, with a banister held up by allegorical figures carved in wood, which cost $60,000, and on which ten Venetian craftsmen had worked for two years. Other details of the resort were thus described by the *Sun:*

"The door at the entrance is of wrought iron weighing several hundred pounds. . . . The large reception room at the back of the street floor is of gold, and the floor is covered with red velvet carpet. Back of this is the foyer hall. . . . On the walls are oil paintings which cost a fortune. On the floors were the finest examples of the art of the great rug-makers of the East. The floors were of hard wood, the work of experts. The ceilings were frescoed as only the homes of the rich could be. On the second floor is the large roulette wheel room. It is arched, with the ceiling covered with paintings. On this floor is a bath with a marble reclining slab and other apparatus which is said to have cost the owners $2,000.

"Fair play and courtesy were the keynotes of the place.

The house had the reputation of integrity and honesty. The word of the player was always accepted without question. With admission to the house went the privilege of indulging in all the good things which the place afforded. A visitor was a guest of the house and was treated accordingly. At midnight a buffet lunch was served for guests. Between times wines, brandies, and cigars which cost a dollar apiece were there for those who wanted them. It has been estimated that at least $25,000 a year was spent in providing refreshments and food for visitors of the house."

As an example of the honesty with which the games were conducted in the House with the Bronze Door, the *Sun* told the improbable story of what happened during a police raid in 1902, when three men had on the Roulette wheel stakes aggregating $125,000. Said the *Sun:*

"One of the players, a member of one of America's wealthiest families, . . . had just bet on the turn of the wheel when the blows on the door sounded. He and his friends scurried to the getaway, but the man at the wheel remained to watch where the marble stopped, before he made his escape with the $125,000. He paid over the money to the young winner when all got to the place of safety. . . . The honesty of the man so surprised the lucky gambler that he handed the game tender $10,000 as a reward. The attendant bought a fine house on Long Island with the money the following week."

According to the *Sun,* the Farrell-Walbaum syndicate also owned the property next door, and had a tunnel leading into it from the cellar of the House with the Bronze Door. Suckers and gamblers alike fled through the tunnel whenever a raid threatened.

For several years around 1900 it was common gossip in New

York that an average of $50,000 changed hands in the resort every night. The largest single winning is said to have been $165,000, made at Roulette in June, 1898, by a rich Englishman who gave the money to a soldiers' relief organization. Another Roulette player, if tradition be correct, won $210,000 in two nights, but within two weeks the bank had it all back and $80,000 besides. Unlike Canfield's resort, where the play was limited to Faro and Roulette, the House with the Bronze Door offered a variety of games. In addition to the tiger and the wheel, there were Baccarat and the Dice game called Klondike, and Poker addicts were encouraged to use the private rooms for their sessions. The biggest pot in any of these Poker games is said to have been $27,000, won on a full house of aces over kings. It was popularly supposed that the House with the Bronze Door imposed no limits, but as a matter of fact, although the limits were elastic, they existed, and averaged considerably less than at the Canfield houses.

The most prosperous period of the House with the Bronze Door was from about 1895 to the latter part of 1902, when it was closed by the District Attorney in one of a series of raids which put all of the big houses out of business. Gottfried Walbaum and others reopened the place at various times during the next fifteen years—Davy Johnson ran it for a few weeks in 1906— but never with any great success. In 1917 Walbaum, seventy-two years old and tired of gambling, sold the furnishings at auction and leased the building to Morris B. Horowitz, wholesale dealer in ribbons and millinery goods.

7

The Nemesis of the gamblers, the man who finally closed the big houses and so killed the goose which had laid so many golden eggs of graft and corruption, was William Travers Jerome, Justice of the Court of Special Sessions and later, in the time of his greatest triumphs, District Attorney of New York County. Jerome first appeared in the forefront of the anti-gambling forces in 1900, when he began to issue search warrants against the gaming places, and to accompany the detectives of the Committee of Fifteen on their raids. In an article in *The Independent* of May 25, 1901, Jerome explained that he had adopted this procedure, which was "somewhat unusual but far from being without precedent," because of the ineffectiveness of the occasional raids made by the police. "The gamblers in almost every instance," he said, "received warning, and were enabled to save themselves and their paraphernalia. . . . I took measures to prevent this 'tipping off,' as it is called, and going with the raiding party held court immediately in the evil resort itself, and got positive evidence of the character of the place, and names and addresses of the patrons who were caught, etc. The usefulness of this lies in the fact that juries are loath to believe the evidence of spies who get into the gambling houses under false pretenses. The raids have been so successful that a great deal of evidence has been secured and many indictments found. . . . The gamblers' books, which we secured from their safes, gave up many secrets. . . . We seem to be on the track of the great men who are or were responsible for the recent disgraceful condition of affairs."

The "great men" whom Jerome was after, but who escaped his wrath while the smaller fry, as usual, took the rap, were the members of a syndicate which, as was shown by the testimony before the Mazet Committee, handled the protection money exacted from the gamblers for the benefit of half a dozen powerful politicians. During the last few years of the 1890's this syndicate consisted of Big Bill Devery, of the Police Department; Frank Farrell, the pool room king and part owner of the House with the Bronze Door; and Big Tim Sullivan, State Senator and an important figure in Tammany Hall, perhaps the most important next to Richard Croker, who went insane in 1912 and was mysteriously killed a year later. He left a fortune of almost $2,-000,000. The syndicate was still in existence at the beginning of the twentieth century, although its membership had undergone a slight change, and it was now known to the sharpers as the "gambling commission." In an exposé of gambling headed "This City's Crying Shame," the New York *Times* of March 9, 1900, said that the gambling commission was composed of "a commissioner, who is at the head of one of the city departments, two State Senators, and the dictator of the pool room syndicate of this city, who was before the Mazet Committee and who is allied to Tammany Hall." The *Times* also said that the Commission annually distributed the huge sum of $3,095,000, collected from well over a thousand gambling houses of various types and several hundred Policy shops and envelope games. The newspapers gave these details of the Commission's methods:

"This so-called commission meets weekly in the apartments of one of its members not far from Forty-seventh Street and Broadway. The money is not only apportioned at these state conferences, but licenses to run houses are virtually issued there.

"Not a gambling house is running in this city today that is not known to this board, and not a place is running that does not pay its tax to this board. Its system is as complete as any branch of the city government. There are no leaks, and no unauthorized place can run for twenty-four hours without either putting up or shutting up. . . .

"The requisite for opening a gambling house, large or small, and this includes pool rooms, is to go to the Captain of the precinct. The request to be allowed to open is accompanied by the 'initiation' or 'introduction' fee of $300, and the Captain tells the applicant that his case will be acted on in time.

"A week later the applicant is notified as to his fate. If he cannot open, and cases of this kind are rare, his 'initiation' fee is returned to him. The matter has, in the meantime, been reported to the Gambling Commission, and the case passed on much as a Board of Governors passes upon the application of a man for club membership.

"If the application is favorably passed upon it is not done without an investigation, but that investigation tends for the most part to finding out the ability of the would-be member to pay his dues promptly and whether he is a person who is to be relied upon. The Captain of the precinct is responsible for that part of the matter. For his work therein he is allowed to retain the 'initiation' fee.

"From that time on little that comes from the gaming crib sticks to the Captain's fingers. There are regularly authorized collectors, among them ward men and inspectors, but there is not much leakage before the money finally lands in the Gambling Commission's hands.

"The amount that lands there is made up as follows:

"Pool Rooms, 400, at $300 per month,
    $120,000 per year $1,440,000
"Crap games, 500, at $150 per month,
    $75,000 per year 900,000
"Gambling houses, 200, at $150 per month,
    $30,000 per year 360,000
"Gambling houses, large, 20, at $1,000 per
    month, $20,000 per year 240,000
"Envelope games, 50, at $50 per month,
    $2,500 per year 30,000
"Policy 125,000
                             ———
    "Total $3,095,000

"There are two hundred gambling houses in the city of what is termed the lower class. They cater to the 'piker' class, but their aggregate winnings are enormous. In nearly every one of these there are layouts for roulette, sweat, Klondike, crap, red and black, and faro. With them the tariff is not absolutely fixed, but averages $150 per month. The collections here, as in the crap games, are made every two weeks. It lessens the chances of loss to the Gambling Commission and enables the latter to get in two extra weeks every year.

"The big gambling houses, where there is heavy play and which are patronized by 'swell' players, are a source of large and sure income. The proprietors of these places, among them Canfield, Daly, Ullman, Pearsall, Appleby, Kelly and Johnson, pay $1,000 a month, and in some of these games an interest in the winnings is held by one of the State Senators and the Commissioner, who are members of the Gambling Commission."

Jerome continued to harass the gamblers throughout 1900, while the newspapers, especially the *Times* and the *Herald,* stirred up public sentiment by publishing accounts of their own investigations, with lists of gambling houses and maps showing their location. Early in 1901 Jerome and the Committee of Fifteen returned to the assault, and on February 27th Jerome led the agents of the Committee in raids upon ten resorts, all within a radius of a third of a mile in the Tenderloin district. "They were all found in full blast," said Jerome, "each occupying a full house. Faro, Roulette, Red and Black, Craps and Klondike were all being played." None of these houses, however, was of the first rank; against such places as Canfield's, Daly's, Maynard's, Johnson's, Ludlum's, the House with the Bronze Door, and No. 8 Barclay Street, the Committee of Fifteen had been unable to obtain enough evidence to justify the issuance of warrants. But in November of 1901 Jerome was elected District Attorney upon his pledge to clean up New York, and in particular to close the gambling houses. At the same election Seth Low was chosen Mayor, and Richard Croker, beaten at last, retired from the leadership of Tammany Hall. Devery was out of the Police Department, and the new Police Commissioner, Colonel John N. Partridge, expressed his intention of co-operating with the new District Attorney. He began by reorganizing the police force and trying to weed out the crooks and grafters.

A month after the election the Parkhurst Society, with the support of Jerome and the police, raided the offices of Al Adams and began the prosecution which ultimately sent the Policy King to prison. Both Jerome and Colonel Partridge announced that the arrest of Adams and several of his henchmen was but the opening gun of a campaign to close every gambling resort in New York and to drive every professional gambler out of the city. Most of the big gamesters professed to find these statements very amusing, but Canfield took Jerome at his word; he was shrewd enough to see that with Tammany Hall defeated and discredited, and with honest and able men in the Police Department and the District Attorney's office, gambling enterprises such as he had built up were doomed. On the night of December 31, 1901, Canfield told his patrons that there would be no more gambling at the house in East Forty-fourth Street. When the last player had gone, Canfield and Bucklin carried the gaming paraphernalia to the fourth floor and stored it in a closet. And never again did Canfield operate a gambling game in New York City. But unfortunately for him, no one but himself and a few of his friends knew that he was through.

Jerome was inducted into his new office on January 1, 1902. Next morning every gambling house in New York was shut up tighter than the proverbial drum, and for almost three months not a wheel was spun or a card turned anywhere in the city. Many of the resorts remained closed. Some, among them No. 8 Barclay Street and Lou Maynard's house in Broadway, reopened and closed again almost immediately. In those where operations were actually resumed the games were run very quietly, and only old and trusted patrons were admitted. Jerome and the police made no moves during this period, but the newspaper agitation was renewed in March when it became known that on December 19, 1901, young Reginald Vanderbilt had celebrated his twenty-first birthday by losing $70,000 at Faro and Roulette. Actually Vanderbilt lost the money to Davy Johnson, but since he was known to have played at Canfield's, everyone, including Jerome, believed that he had been trimmed at the house in Forty-fourth Street. The newspaper reporters asked Jerome why he didn't close Canfield's. The District Attorney replied that he was collecting evidence. Nothing happened, however, during the summer, and Jerome's inactivity so encouraged the gamblers that by the early fall of 1902 many houses were running virtually wide open, and it was common knowledge that half a dozen new places were being fitted up in the area between Fifth Avenue and Broadway and Forty-second Street and Columbus Circle. But late in November one Joe Jacobs, a private detective employed by the Citizen's Union, made an affidavit that he had finally been able to get into Canfield's house, that he had gambled there, and had lost money. As a matter of fact all of Jacobs' statements were untrue from beginning to end; he had never been nearer Canfield's gaming tables than the outer vestibule of the house. Two years later, when Jacobs confessed that he had lied, Jerome prosecuted him with the same vigor that he had shown in his attacks upon the gamblers, and the detective was sent to Sing Sing to serve a year's sentence for perjury.

But when Jacobs swore to his affidavit Jerome acted immediately, believing that at last he was in a position to obtain evidence that would convict Canfield. On the afternoon of December 1, 1902, a Justice of Special Sessions issued search warrants against Canfield's, the House with the Bronze Door, and Lou Ludlum's place in Fortieth Street near Broadway. That night, accompanied by Inspector Nicholas Brooks and a squad of policemen, Jerome raided all three resorts. During the afternoon Joe Jacobs had telephoned Bucklin and warned him of the impending raid, and had asked him to notify Ludlum and Billy Burbridge, manager and part owner of the House with the Bronze Door. It was never known whether Bucklin carried out Jacobs' instructions, but he did get in touch with Canfield, who was visiting his family in Providence, and the gambler immediately took a train to New York. He was on hand when Jerome and his policemen, followed by a horde of newspaper reporters, gained an entrance into the house at No. 5 East Forty-fourth Street by climbing a ladder and smashing a window on the second floor. The house was carefully searched, but no evidence of gambling was found until the raiders reached the fourth floor, when they discovered the closet in which Canfield had stored his gaming equipment almost a year before, and dragged out five Roulette tables, three wheels, a Faro layout and several packs of cards, and a large quantity of ivory chips. All of this paraphernalia, to say nothing of a few small but valuable *objets d'art,* was carried out by the police and the reporters through a crowd which filled the street from curb to curb, and hauled away in a wagon.

Bucklin was immediately arrested and taken into court, where he was released on bail after pleading not guilty to charges of being a common gambler and maintaining a nuisance. But no charge was made against Canfield. Two weeks after the raid Canfield brought suit against Jerome and the police for illegal entry, and also tried to institute criminal proceedings. But these were merely defensive gestures, and none of the actions ever came to trial. As a newspaper pointed out, Jerome had been properly armed with a search warrant, and any indictments which might be found against the raiders would have to pass through the District Attorney's own hands. About the first of the year Canfield went abroad, and didn't return to the United States until May, 1903. On June 1st of that year he was at length arrested, but his lawyer immediately obtained a change of venue to Binghamton, on the ground that Jerome's attacks upon Canfield—he had frequently said that Canfield was a felon and that his Roulette and Faro games were crooked—had made a fair trial impossible in New York. At the same time Bucklin's case was transferred to Cortland, N.Y.

Throughout 1903 Jerome tried desperately to obtain evidence of gambling at Canfield's which would be more conclusive than the testimony of a private detective and the finding of a few Roulette wheels in a closet. Several of Canfield's wealthy patrons, brought before an examining magistrate, flatly refused to admit that they knew the gambler or had ever been in his house. One, Jesse Lewisohn, of the banking house of Lewisohn Brothers, who was much in the public eye as a friend of Lillian Russell, was arrested for contempt of court, but was released on a writ of habeas corpus. He carried the case through higher courts until the Court of Appeals ruled that he could not be compelled to answer questions relating to Canfield. The specific question involved was, "Do you know Richard A. Canfield?" Since the decision applied to all of Jerome's potential witnesses, the District Attorney learned nothing whatever from the men whose gambling losses had piled up Canfield's fortune. In consequence, when the gambler's trial was finally called at Binghamton on January 11, 1904, the charges against him were immediately dismissed. Four months later a similar disposition was made of the case against Bucklin at Cortland.

In the meantime there had been no first-class gambling in New York, so salutary had been the effect of Jerome's spectacular raids upon Canfield's, Ludlum's and the House with the Bronze Door. The New York *Sun* in March, 1903, quoted an unnamed but "prominent" gambler as saying that the city "was never so free from gambling houses, as going concerns, as it is now. There are just about fourteen so-called reputable gambling houses in New York," the gambler continued. "Every one of them is closed, and you may take my word for it that they will be closed for a long and indefinite period. . . . They will not undertake to do business in New York until the atmosphere becomes much more thoroughly cleared than it is at present."

Several gamblers who thought the atmosphere had been cleared sufficiently by Canfield's victory at Binghamton, opened their establishments in February of 1904, but hastily closed them when Jerome acquired a new weapon which put them completely at his mercy—a law, passed at the 1904 session of the state legislature, which amended the Criminal Code to provide a mandatory jail sentence for witnesses who refused to answer questions in a gambling case. New charges were at once made against Canfield and Bucklin, and when Jerome received a certified copy of the new statute in May a subpoena was served upon Jesse Lewisohn, whose prompt appeal held up Jerome's fight until fall. But in November the Court of Appeals upheld the constitutionality of the law, and the gamblers, knowing that their patrons would talk rather than go to jail, immediately surrendered. One by one the men who were known to have operated gambling houses were summoned to Jerome's office, where they found, as Davy Johnson put it to a *Herald* reporter, that "he's got us in the hollow of his hand . . . he has a list of the patrons of each of the houses as long as your arm." Jerome compelled every gambler to tell him all he wished to know about gaming in New York, and then agreed not to prosecute as long as the gamester observed certain conditions—first, he must close his resort and keep it closed; second, he must admit a representative of the District Attorney, without question and at any hour of the day or night, to any premises which he might occupy; and third, pass keys of all known gambling houses must be sent to the District Attorney's office. In the main all of these conditions were scrupulously respected until Jerome retired to private life in 1910, and as might be supposed, during these years New York was singularly free from gambling.

Canfield, under indictment as a common gambler, was one of the first of the big gambling house keepers to notify Jerome that he would fight no longer. The situation was far more serious for him than for any of his fellow-gamesters, for Jerome had unearthed the record of his early imprisonment in Providence, and as a second offender he faced the probability of being sent to Sing Sing for two years. All that kept him out of jail was the fact that the detective, Joe Jacobs, chose this particular time to make his confession of perjury. In view of this development, and convinced at last that Canfield's house had been closed for a year when it was raided in 1902, Jerome agreed to let the gambler off with a fine. On December 7, 1904, both Canfield and Bucklin appeared in court, pleaded guilty, and were each fined $1,000. When Canfield's lawyer handed four $500 bills to the clerk of the court, Jerome's case against the gamester was closed, and the career of America's most celebrated gambling house keeper, as far as New York City was concerned, had come to an end.

But in the Saratoga Club House Canfield still owned the most profitable gambling property in the United States. Even at Saratoga, however, life for the great gambler had not been all beer and skittles. His troubles there, and likewise the troubles of the other Saratoga gamesters, began in the fall of 1894, only a few months after he had bought the Club House from Albert Spencer, and were the result of Caleb Mitchell's stubbornness and the election to the State Senate of Edgar T. Brackett, a

Saratoga lawyer and for many years an important figure in state politics. Brackett recognized the fact that the people of Saratoga, as well as the summer visitors, were overwhelmingly in favor of permitting a few gambling houses to operate during the racing season, but he believed that they should be restricted to the side streets. One of the principal hells in Saratoga at this time was in Broadway, in the heart of the business district, and was run by Mitchell, who was just finishing his second term as Village President. Brackett suggested to Mitchell that he move to a less conspicuous location, but Mitchell only laughed and challenged Brackett to make him move. At the 1895 session of the Legislature Brackett procured the passage of a law providing that the Village President of Saratoga be chosen by the Village Trustees instead of by popular vote. Mitchell's successor, elected in the spring of 1895, immediately announced that no gambling houses would be permitted to open, and throughout the season there was no public gaming of any description.

The lid was lifted in 1896 sufficiently to allow Canfield's and half a dozen other big houses to operate, but Mitchell's place remained closed, and he was told that if he attempted to run his games he would be indicted. Mitchell left Saratoga, and for a few years Canfield's Club House, the Chicago, Manhattan and United States Clubs, and a few other houses, enjoyed great prosperity. But about 1899 Mitchell returned and opened a pool room near the race track in partnership with a Texas sharper named Dan Stuart. No action was taken against this resort for a year or two, although the Saratoga police received many complaints from suckers who said that Mitchell and Stuart had robbed them, but it was closed by the village authorities in 1901 at the request of William C. Whitney, head of the syndicate which had bought the race track from Gottfried Walbaum.

Informed that he would never again be permitted to operate a gambling house in Saratoga, Mitchell blamed his difficulties on Canfield and Senator Brackett. He immediately employed the famous New York lawyers Abe Hummel and Big Bill Howe, and began a desperate campaign to close the Club House. Hummel and Howe procured warrants for Canfield's arrest from magistrates in several small Saratoga County towns, but had great difficulty in finding anyone who would serve them. Finally a constable timidly entered the Club House, told Canfield he had a warrant, and asked the gambler if he would please come into court. Next day Canfield appeared and was held for the Grand Jury, but that body refused to return an indictment. Unable to accomplish anything against Canfield, Mitchell turned his attention to Brackett, and during the winter spent most of his time going from place to place in Saratoga telling everyone who would listen that Brackett had driven him out of business and was trying to starve his family. In January of 1902 Brackett put the finishing touches to Mitchell's misery by introducing into the Legislature a bill, which became law in the spring, under which warrants for civil arrest issued outside of Saratoga were not valid unless endorsed by a Saratoga police judge. When Mitchell heard of this measure his denunciations became more and more violent, and he was frequently heard talking to himself and otherwise betraying evidences of great mental stress. On the morning of January 29th he bought a revolver at a hardware store, and then went to the town hall and killed himself in front of the door to Brackett's office. Apparently he had intended to kill the Senator, but a few minutes before he arrived Brackett left for Albany.

Amply protected by Brackett's new law, and for the time being at least very much in the good graces of the village authorities, Canfield went ahead with the improvements he had planned for the Club House, and in 1902 had one of his best years—his profits for the six weeks or so of operation were about $500,000.

He anticipated even greater prosperity in 1903, but during the winter a very definite anti-gambling sentiment developed in Saratoga, and although the Club House was open in 1903, the doors of the gaming rooms were kept closed, and the atmosphere of uncertainty was not conducive to high play. In 1904, frightened by Jerome's success in New York and his narrow escape from prison, Canfield refused to open the Club House, although asked to do so by Saratoga business men and officials of the racing association. In 1905 all of the big houses were in operation, but they were compelled to close at two A. M., and business was very light—many of their richest suckers were kept away by fear of the law which had been so helpful to Jerome. At the beginning of the 1906 season the gamblers were notified that only three places—Canfield's, the Manhattan Club, and the United States Club—would be permitted to open, and that the doors of the gaming rooms must be closed at all times. Canfield opened the Club House on August 6, the first day of racing, but the next day Governor Frank W. Higgins ordered the Sheriff to close every gaming house in Saratoga County. Canfield immediately removed all gaming apparatus from the building, and except for a few days in 1907, when the restaurant was open and an occasional game was played in a private room upstairs, the whir of the Roulette wheel and the click of the Faro casekeeper were heard no more in the Club House which for forty years had been one of the great gambling establishments of the world. In August, 1907, Canfield offered the property for sale, and in 1910 it was purchased for $150,000 by the village of Saratoga. It is now occupied by the Saratoga Historical Society, which maintains a museum on the upper floors and rents the old restaurant and gambling room, on the first floor, for dances and club meetings.

8

When Canfield put a "For Sale" sign on the Club House in Saratoga, he was through with gambling; he refused several offers to manage European casinos, and during the remainder of his life his interests were confined to his art collections, his books, and the manufacture of a patent bottle-stopper in which he had invested $100,000 in 1904. He continued to make his home in the East Forty-fourth Street house until early in 1906, when he disposed of the property and bought a fine residence at No. 9 East Fifty-fifth Street. After a year or so, however, he sold this place also, and moved into a rented house at No. 506 Madison Avenue. With a manservant and a housekeeper, an old Negro woman who had been in his service for many years, he lived there until December 11, 1914, when he died of a fractured skull, received the previous evening in a fall in the Fourteenth Street subway station. He was fifty-nine years old.

Canfield's fortune at the time he closed the Club House amounted to almost $13,000,000, of which about $5,000,000 represented the profits from his various gambling enterprises. The remainder had been won in the Stock Market, and during the panic and depression of 1907 it returned whence it came. When Canfield reckoned his assets after the collapse of the market he still had his Saratoga property, his art collections, and his bottle-stopper investment, and perhaps a hundred thousand dollars besides. He made money in business during the next seven years, however, and added to his capital by the sale of the Club House and his Whistler paintings. Most of the latter were purchased for $300,000 in the spring of 1914 by M. Knoedler & Son. Three of the finest canvases, *Nocturne, Count Robert* and *Rosa Corder,* were later bought by Henry C. Frick, and are now in the Frick Gallery in New York. Whistler's portrait of Canfield was sold by the gambler's family to the Cincinnati Museum.

After his death the estate of the man who had been the richest professional gambler in all history was appraised by the experts of the State Tax Department at $841,485.

BIBLIOGRAPHY

This is by no means a complete bibliography of gambling in America, nor is it a complete list of the sources and authorities which were consulted in the preparation of this book. Those given here were either especially helpful, or contain additional information about phases of the subject upon which I was able, because of limitations of space, to touch but briefly:

A.A.A.: "Gambling; One Point of View of It. How Public Sentiment Permits a Monte Carlo to be Openly Conducted in the West;" *Anglo-American Magazine,* June, 1901.

Aikman, Duncan; *Calamity Jane and the Lady Wildcats.* New York, 1927.

Annals of Gaming, or, the Fair Players' Sure Guide. By a connoisseur. London, 1775.

Annual Report No. 2 of the New York Association for the Suppression of Gambling. New York, 1852.

Anthony, Irvin: *Paddle Wheels and Pistols.* Philadelphia, 1929.

Ashton, John: *History of Gambling in England.* New York and London, 1899.

Asmodeus in New York. Anonymous. New York, 1868.

Benham, W. Gurney: *Playing Cards, History of the Pack and Explanation of its Many Secrets.* London, 1931.

Blackbridge, John: *The Complete Poker Player.* New York, 1875.

Borthwick, J. D.: *The Gold Hunters.* Edited by Horace Kephart. New York, 1924.

Brooks, Henry M.: *Curiosities of the Old Lottery.* Boston, 1886.

Bross, William; Cleaver, Charles; and Jefferson, Joseph: *Reminiscences of Chicago During the Forties and Fifties.* Introduction by Mabel McIlvaine. Chicago, 1913.

Buel, J. W.: *Metropolitan Life Unveiled; or, the Mysteries and Miseries of America's Greatest Cities.* San Francisco, 1882.

Burke, T. A.: *Polly Peachblossom's Wedding and Other Tales.* Philadelphia, 1851.

Burns, Walter Noble: *Tombstone, An Iliad of the Southwest.* New York, 1929.

Busey, Samuel C., M.D.: *Pictures of the City of Washington in the Past.* Washington, 1898.

Byrnes, Thomas: *Professional Criminals of America.* New York, 1886.

—————: *Professional Criminals of America,* New and Revised Edition. New York, 1895.

Cady, Alice Howard: *Dominoes and Dice, a Brief History of These Games.* New York, 1895.

Campbell, Helen; Knox, Thomas W.; Byrnes, Thomas: *Darkness and Daylight, or Lights and Shadows of New York Life.* Hartford, 1900.

Canfield, Kid: *Gambling and Card-Sharpers' Tricks Exposed.* New York, n.d.

Carrington, Hereward: *Gamblers' Crooked Tricks; a Complete Exposure of Their Methods.* Girard, Kan., 1928.

Cavendish: *Card Essays, Clay's Decisions and Card-Table Talk.* New York and London, 1879.

Charles, Robert Henry: *Gambling and Betting, a Short Study Dealing with Their Origin and Their Relation to Morality and Religion.* Edinburgh, 1924.

Chatto, W. A.: *Facts and Speculation on the Origin and History of Playing Cards.* London, 1848.

Clarke, Donald Henderson: *In the Reign of Rothstein.* New York, 1929.

Coates, Robert M.: *The Outlaw Years; The History of the Land Pirates of the Natchez Trace.* New York, 1930.

Collier, William Ross; and Westrate, Edwin Victor: *The Reign of Soapy Smith, Monarch of Misrule.* New York, 1937.

Comstock, Anthony: *Frauds Exposed.* New York, 1890.

—————: *Traps for the Young.* New York, 1890.

Costello, A. E.: *Our Police Protectors. History of the New York Police.* New York, 1885.

Crapsey, Edward: *The Nether Side of New York; or, the Vice, Crime and Poverty of the Great Metropolis*. New York, 1872.

——————: "Faro-Gambling," in *The Galaxy, an Illustrated Magazine of Entertaining Reading*. July, 1871.

Crimes of the Cranks, Anonymous. New York, 1882.

Crockett, Albert Stevens: *Peacocks on Parade; a Narrative of a Unique Period in American Social History and Its Most Colorful Figures*. New York, 1931.

Cunningham, Eugene: *Triggernometry, a Gallery of Gunfighters*. New York, 1934.

Currie, Barton Wood: "The Transformation of the Southwest through the Legal Abolition of Gambling," in *The Century Magazine,* April, 1908.

Devol, George: *Forty Years a Gambler on the Mississippi*. New York, 1926.

Dick, Harris B., Editor: *Dick's Games of Patience and Solitaire with Cards*. New York, 1908.

Dragoon Campaigns to the Rocky Mountains; Being a History of the Enlistment, Organization, and First Campaigns of the Regiment of the United States Dragoons; Together with Incidents, etc., by a Dragoon (James Hildrith). New York, 1836.

"Dying Tiger, The," in *All the Year Round, a Weekly Journal Conducted by Charles Dickens,* November, 1872.

Edwards, Eugene: *Jack Pots; Stories of the Great American Game*. Chicago, 1900.

Eldridge, Benjamin P., and Watts, William B.: *Our Rival the Rascal*. Boston, 1897.

Ellis, John B., Dr.: *The Sights and Secrets of the National Capital*. Chicago, 1869.

Farley, Phil: *Criminals of America, or Tales of the Lives of Thieves*. New York, 1876.

Fisher, George Henry: *How to Win at Stud Poker*. Los Angeles, 1934.

——————: *Stud Poker Blue Book*. Los Angeles, 1934.

Foster, R. F.: *Foster's Complete Hoyle, an Encyclopedia of Games,* Revised and Enlarged to October, 1914. New York, 1914.

Foster, R. F.: *Dice and Dominoes.* New York, 1897.

Fulkerson, H. S.: *Random Recollections of Early Days in Mississippi.* Vicksburg, 1885.

Fullerton, Hugh S.: "American Gambling and Gamblers," in *American Magazine,* February, March, April, 1914.

"Gambling Houses of New York, The," in *St. James Magazine,* Volume 20, 1867.

Gambling World, The, by Rouge et Noir. New York, 1898.

Gardiner, Alexander: *Canfield, the True Story of the Greatest Gambler.* New York, 1930.

Gardner, Charles W.: *The Doctor and the Devil; a Startling Exposé of Municipal Corruption.* New York, 1894.

Grand Exposé of the Science of Gambling, Containing a Complete Disclosure of the Secrets of the Art, as Practiced by Professional Gamblers. Written by an Adept. New York, 1860.

Green, J. H.: *Gambling Exposed, a Full Exposition of All the Various Arts, Mysteries and Miseries of Gambling.* Philadelphia, 1857.

——————: *Gamblers' Tricks with Cards Exposed and Explained.* New York, n.d.

——————: *The Secret Band of Brothers, or, the American Outlaws.* Philadelphia, 1847.

——————: *Report on Gambling in New York.* New York, 1851.

——————: *An Exposure of the Arts and Miseries of Gambling.* Cincinnati, 1843.

——————: *Gambling in Its Infancy and Progress, or, a Dissuasive to the Young Against Games of Chance.* New York, 1849.

Griffiths, Major Arthur: *Mysteries of Police and Crime, a General Survey of Wrongdoing and Its Pursuit.* Two volumes, New York and London, 1899.

Glasscock, C. B.: *Lucky Baldwin, the Story of an Unconventional Success.* Indianapolis, 1933.

Harcourt, Seymour: *The Gaming Calendar, to Which are Added, Annals of Gaming, and Prefixed a Letter to Sir Robert Baker, Chief Magistrate of the Police.* London, 1820.

Historical Sketch Book and Guide to New Orleans. New York, 1885.

Hone, Philip: *The Diary of Philip Hone, 1828–1851.* Edited by Allan Nevins. New York, 1936.

473

Howe, William F., and Hummel, Abraham: *Danger! A True History of a Great City's Wiles and Temptations.* New York, 1886.

Hoyle's Games, a Complete Guide. New York, 1887.

Hoyle's Games, Autograph Edition. New York, 1914.

Hunt, Fred A.: "Poker, Por Poco Tiempo," in *The Overland Monthly,* March, 1911.

Irwell, Lawrence: "Gambling As it Was and As it Is," in *New Century Review,* July, 1899.

James, H. K.: *The Destruction of Mephisto's Greatest Web, or All Grafts Laid Bare; Being a Complete Exposure of All Gambling, Graft and Confidence Games.* Salt Lake City, 1914.

Kernan, J. Frank, A.M.: *Reminiscences of the Old Fire Laddies and Volunteer Fire Departments of New York and Brooklyn, Together with a Complete History of the Paid Departments of Both Cities.* New York, 1885.

Knox, Thomas W.: *Underground, or Life Below the Surface.* Hartford, 1875.

Landauer, Belle C.: *Some Early American Lottery Items.* New York, 1928.

Learock, J. B.: *Delinquency of the State Constabulary.* Boston, 1867.

Lewis, Alfred Henry: *Nation-Famous New York Murders.* New York, 1914.

Lewis, Lloyd, and Smith, Henry Justin: *Chicago, the History of Its Reputation.* New York, 1929.

Life Staked at Cards, a Sketch of the Life of Henry Meyer, a Converted Gambler. New York, 1895.

Lillard, John F. B., Editor: *Poker Stories . . . Embracing the Most Remarkable Games 1845-95.* New York, 1896.

Long, Mason: *Mason Long, the Converted Gambler, Written by Himself.* Cincinnati, 1884.

Lord, W. B.: "Gambling Aboard Ship," in *The Nautical Magazine.* November, 1901.

Lynch, Denis Tilden: *Boss Tweed, the Story of a Grim Generation.* New York, 1927.

474

BIBLIOGRAPHY

MacLeod, William Christi: "The Truth About Lotteries in American History," in *The South Atlantic Quarterly*, April, 1936.

McWatters, Officer George S.: *Knots Untied, or Ways and By-Ways in the Hidden Life of American Detectives*. Hartford, 1871.

Marks, Harry H.: *Small Change; or, Lights and Shadows of New York*. New York, 1882.

Martin, Edward Winslow: *The Secrets of the Great City, a Work Descriptive of the Virtues and the Vices, the Mysteries, Miseries and Crimes of New York City*. New York, 1868.

——————: *Behind the Scenes in Washington*. New York, 1873.

Maskelyn, John Nevil: *Sharps and Flats, a Complete Revelation of the Secrets of Cheating at Games of Chance and Skill*. London and New York, 1894.

Matsell, George W.: *Vocabulum, or, the Rogue's Lexicon*. New York, 1859.

Mayo, Morrow: *Los Angeles*. New York, 1933.

Mordecai, Samuel: *Virginia, Especially Richmond, in By-Gone Days: Being Reminiscences and Last Words of an Old Citizen*. Richmond, 1860.

Morris, John (pseud. of John O'Connor): "The Truth About Lotteries in American History," in *The South Atlantic Quarterly*, April, 1936.

Moss, Frank, LL.D.: *The American Metropolis from Knickerbocker Days to the Present Time; New York City Life in All its Various Phases*. Three volumes. New York, 1897.

Murray, Hon. Henry A., R.N.: *Lands of the Slave and the Free*. London, 1857.

National Policy Players' Guide and Dream Book. Chicago, 1902.

Nathan, George Jean: "The Old-Time Train Gambler," in *Harper's Weekly*, May 21, 1910.

New York by Gaslight. Anonymous. New York, n.d. (about 1858).

New York in Slices, by an Experienced Carver. New York, 1849.

Official Rules of Card Games, Hoyle Up to Date. Cincinnati. Various editions from 1900 to 1937.

Open Book; Cards, Dice, Punch Boards, Hold-Outs, Schemes and

Devices, Secrets of the Gambler, All Exposed in Words of Fire. Kansas City, 1927.

Phillips, Dare: *Stacked Cards.* London, 1934.
Pierce, Bessie L.: *A History of Chicago.* New York, 1937.
Poore, Ben Perley: *Perley's Reminiscences, or, Sixty Years in the National Metropolis.* Two volumes. Philadelphia, 1886.

Quinn, John Philip: *Gambling and Gambling Devices.* Canton, O., 1912.
————: *Fools of Fortune, or, Gambling and Gamblers.* Chicago, 1892.

Raine, William McLeod: *Famous Sheriffs and Western Outlaws.* New York, 1929.
Report of the Trial of Charles N. Baldwin for Libel, in Publishing, in the Republican Chronicle, Certain Charges of Fraud and Swindling in the Management of Lotteries in the State of New York. New York, 1818.
Richardson, Albert D.: *Beyond the Mississippi; From the Great River to the Great Ocean. Life and Adventure on the Prairies, Mountains and Pacific Coast.* Hartford, 1869.
Rogers, H. O.: *The Lottery in American History.* New York, 1919.
Ross, A. Franklin: "The History of Lotteries in New York," in *Magazine of History with Notes and Queries,* February, March, April, May, June, 1907.
Royal, H. W.: *Gambling and Confidence Games Exposed; Showing How the Proprietors of Gambling Houses and the Players Can be Cheated.* New York, 1896.
Russell, William Howard: *My Diary North and South.* Boston, 1863.

Sanford, Mabel Warren: "Women Gamblers," in *Munsey's Magazine,* October, 1903.
Sergeant, Philip W.: *Gamblers All.* London, 1931.
Slang Dictionary of New York, London and Paris. Collected by a Well Known Detective. New York, 1880.
Smith, Matthew Hale; Williams, Prof. Henry L., and Bayard, Ralph: *Wonders of a Great City, or the Sights, Secrets and Sins of New York.* Hartford, 1888.

476

Smyth, Newman: "Suppression of the Lottery and Other Gambling," in *The Forum,* April, 1895.

Snares of New York, or, Tricks and Traps of the Great Metropolis, Being a Complete, Vivid and Truthful Exposure of the Swindles, Humbugs and Pitfalls of the Great City. New York, 1879.

Soule, Frank; Gihon, John, M.D., and Nisbet, James: *The Annals of San Francisco.* New York, 1855.

Steinmetz, Andrew: *The Gaming Table; Its Votaries and Victims, in all Times and Countries, Especially in England and in France.* Two volumes. London, 1870.

"Strange Hands at Cards," in *All the Year Round, a Weekly Conducted by Charles Dickens,* October 7, 1876.

Sutcliffe, Stephen: "In a New York Gambling House," in *Munsey's Magazine,* September, 1903.

Sutton, Charles: *The New York Tombs; Its Secrets and Its Miseries.* Edited by James B. Mix and Samuel A. McKeever. New York, 1874.

Taylor, Rev. Ed S., B.A., and others: *The History of Playing Cards, with Anecdotes of Their Use in Conjuring, Fortune-Telling and Card-Sharping.* London, 1865.

Thorne, T. B.: "Remembrances of the Mississippi," in *Harper's New Monthly Magazine,* December, 1855.

Tricks and Traps of New York City. Anonymous. Boston, 1857.

Tyson, Job R.: *A Brief Survey of the Great Extent and Evil Tendencies of the Lottery System as Existing in the United States.* Philadelphia, 1833.

——————: *The Lottery System in the United States.* Philadelphia, 1837.

Van Cise, Philip S.: *Fighting the Underworld.* Boston, 1936.

Van Every, Edward: *Sins of New York, as Exposed by the Police Gazette.* New York, 1930.

——————: *Sins of America, as Exposed by the Police Gazette.* New York, 1931.

Van Rensselaer, Mrs. John King: *The Devil's Picture Books, a History of Playing Cards.* New York, 1890.

Walling, George W.: *Recollections of a New York Chief of Police.* New York, 1887.

Warshow, Irving: *Bet-a-Million Gates, the Story of a Plunger.* New York, 1932.

Watts, Irma A.: "Pennsylvania Lotteries of Other Days," in *Pennsylvania History,* January, 1935.

Werner, M. R.: *Tammany Hall,* New York, 1928.

Wig and the Jimmy; or, a Leaf in the Political History of New York, The. New York, 1869.

Williamson, Jefferson: *The American Hotel, an Anecdotal History.* New York, 1930.

Wilson, Rufus Rockwell: *Washington the Capital City.* Two volumes. Philadelphia, 1901.

Wilstach, Frank J.: *Wild Bill Hickok, the Prince of Pistoleers.* New York, 1926.

Wyman, Seth: *The Life and Adventures of Seth Wyman, Embodying the Principal Events of a Life Spent in Robbery, Theft, Gambling, Passing Counterfeit Money, &c., &c.* Written by Himself. Manchester, N.H., 1843.

Young, Harry: *Hard Knocks, a Life Story of the Vanishing West.* Chicago, 1915.

Files of *Harper's Weekly, Leslie's Weekly, The Police Gazette, Under the Gaslight, The Sporting Times and Theatrical News, Niles' Weekly Register,* etc., and of newspapers in New York, San Francisco, Chicago, New Orleans, Baltimore, Boston, Philadelphia, St. Louis and other cities.

INDEX

INDEX

INDEX

INDEX

Pendleton, Edward, 137, 140, 141-6, 158, 161, 168, 172, 297, 333, 337, 397, 420, 443

Pendleton, Jacqueline Mills, 140-1

Perley's Reminiscences, 135-6, 142-4

Perritt, Henry, 119-20, 122, 280

Peter Funks, 182

Pharao, *see* Faro

Philadelphia, 6, 77, 124, 125, 127, 172, 184, 185, 397

Phillips, 55

Pierce, Franklin, 146

Pierce, George F., Bishop, 136-7

Pinchback, Pinckney Benton Stewart, 238

Pinkerton, 298

Piquet, 4, 26

Pitch, 49, 51

Pittsburgh, 184, 185

Planters Hotel, St. Louis, 280-1

Plymouth, Mass., 79

Poker, 3, 6, 15, 20-39, 114, 120, 134, 248-9, 276-7, 321-4, 348-9, 352-3, 427, 428, 448-9, 454

Poker Alice, 355

Poker Stories, 28-9, 30-1, 36-7, 210, 230, 231-3

Poley, *see* White, Napoleon Bonaparte

Police Gazette, 305, 366-7, 369, 370-1

Policy, 88-106, 155, 156, 167, 196, 427, 428

Polignac, 50

Pollock, Thomas W., 328

Poole, Butcher Bill, 180, 363, 364, 365-71, 403

Poore, Perley, 135-6, 142-4, 145, 146

Poole Association, 369

Poole Guards, 369, 370, 371

Poque, 20, 21-2

Porter, Rev. Jeremiah, 285-6

Post, George W., 271

Post and Pair, 20

Potee, Bob, 280, 333

Powell, John, 247-9, 251, 280

Poyas, Peter, 83

Pradat, 115

Prescott, Ariz., 346

Preston, William, 392

Primero, 20

Prince, L. Bradford, 348-9

Providence, R. I., 73-4, 184, 422, 423-4

Pueblo, Col., 350-1

Quinn, Hot Stove Jimmy, 306

Quinn, John Philip, 18-19, 265, 266, 284-5, 289-90, 292, 293, 297, 322, 427-8

Race-track gambling, 306, 307, 396, 446

Ralston, William C., 323-4, 448

Randall, George, 263

Randall, Otis, 293

Randolph, Thomas Mann, 76

Ransom, Charles, 372-3

Rasin, I. Freeman, 405

Recollections of a New York Chief of Police, 377-8

Rector, George, 442

Reed, Charles, 387-9, 390, 431

Reid, Frank H., 332

Reindeer (steamboat), 201

Reisenweber's, New York, 442

Rembrandt, 432

Reminiscences of the Old Fire Laddies, 162, 172

Renaud, Bud, 398

Report on Gambling in New York, A, 95, 164

Republican Chronicle, New York, 81

Reuf, Abe, 321

Rhodes, George, 287

Rice, George, 157, 158

Richardson, Albert D., 324-5, 326, 327, 328-9, 335, 339

Richardson, W. H., 259

Richmond, Va., 9, 80, 99, 125, 127, 184, 397

Ridgely, Kate, 363

Riley, Silver Bill, 299

Riley, Sock, 268

Ringo, John, 345

River boats, gambling on, 47, 202-11, 212-13, 229-62

Roach, Dick, 283

Robbins (of Cincinnati), 272, 274

Robbins, Matt, 282, 292

Robert E. Lee (steamboat), 201

Robert Mills, Architect of the Washington Monument, 140

Robinson, Governor, of Kentucky, 392

Robinson, James F., Jr., 392

Robinson's Circus, 244

Rochambeau, 6

INDEX

ABOUT THE AUTHOR

Born to a devout Methodist family in Farmington, Missouri, Herbert Asbury (1891–1963) grew up under the stiff tutelage of generations of Methodist preachers. Rebelling against his overbearing parents, Asbury left the church at the age of fourteen to pursue a life of drinking, gambling, and womanizing.

It was during these years that Asbury gained an interest in the seedier side of America, a theme that would pervade his writing. Among Asbury's books are a number of exposés of the underworlds of America's major cities including *The Gangs of New York*, *The Gangs of Chicago*, *The French Quarter*, and *The Barbary Coast*, which details the underworld of urban San Francisco. He also wrote a number of books dealing with specific aspects of American crime including *The Great Illusion: An Informal History of Prohibition*.